YOUR MARYLAND: A HISTORY

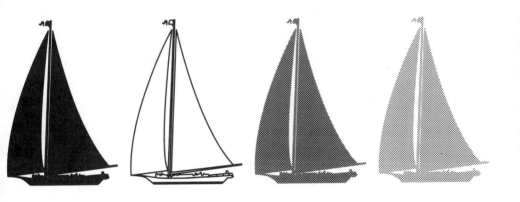

Books by the same author

The Proprietorship of Maryland:
A Documented Account

Maryland's Government

The American Flag

Henry Harford: Last Proprietor of Maryland

A Geography of Maryland

Maryland's Constitution and Government

The Black Experience in Maryland

Maryland Personality Parade

Burt Rutan: Reinventing the Airplane

Aviation Law: An Introduction

Aviation Insurance

Aviation Programs in the United States

YOUR MARYLAND:
A HISTORY

By

Vera Foster Rollo, Ph.D.

1993
Fifth Revised Edition

Cover design by Ray Brown

MARYLAND HISTORICAL PRESS
9205 Tuckerman Street
LANHAM, MARYLAND 20706

Library of Congress Catalog Card No. 92-56701.

ISBN 0-917882-35-0.

Printed in the
United States of America.

TABLE OF CONTENTS

SECTION VII
MODERN MARYLAND

APPENDIX

Cecil Calvert, Second Lord Baltimore, First Proprietor of Maryland

Courtesy Maryland Division of Tourist Development.

ACKNOWLEDGMENTS

My aim in writing *Your Maryland* is to provide in one book the story of Maryland from the time of the first European settlement to the present.

I have called on a great many people to assist me in my researches. Each edition has contained new material and new data gained from still more experts.

Every writer has cause to thank librarians for their help. I would like to thank the librarians and staff of the: Maryland Historical Society, Maryland Room of McKeldin Library University of Maryland, Memorial Library System of Prince George's County Maryland, Maryland State Library in Annapolis, Maryland State Archives in Annapolis and many other librarians across Maryland for their generous and expert assistance.

Appreciation is certainly due Dr. George H. Callcott, Professor of History, University of Maryland who always offered encouragement and expertise. Appreciation is also due Dr. Harold D. Langley, Curator of Naval History, Museum of American History, Smithsonian Institution, Washington, D.C., and Charles Gurney, Desk Officer for Liberia, United States Department of State.

It is not possible for me to adequately thank Dr. Verne E. Chatelain, *emeritus professor* of history, University of Maryland, for sharing his great knowledge with me and for the time and interest he spent in going through the manuscript of this book.

For editing assistance in preparing the fifth edition for publication my thanks to Linda J. Blachly. My appreciation to Sue Isaacs and her staff at Graphica, Inc. for the talent and the tenacity required to typeset over 150 pages revised for the fifth edition and for the new cover design.

The people mentioned here, and many others, including the many experts in offices of the State of Maryland, have been most generous in giving me their time, interest and talent to help me write an interesting and up-to-date history of Maryland. While acknowledging their invaluable assistance, I accept the responsibility for the way I have used information given me.

The reception of *Your Maryland* over the years has been most gratifying. I want to thank the readers of this general history for their letters.

Finally, sincere thanks to my family and friends for their warm support over the years.

Vera Foster Rollo,
Lanham, Maryland
1992

On St. Clements Island today there is a modern cross commemorating the landing of
the English settlers who were members of the Calvert colony.

Just what is "Maryland"?

It is now one of the states of the United States of America and was one of our nation's original thirteen states. You will find that reading about Maryland will be reading about the history of the United States. The history of Maryland often parallels the history of the nation.

Our state was named by King Charles I of England when Maryland was to become a new English colony. He named the colony "Maryland" after his wife, Queen Henrietta Maria (1609 - 1666). How fortunate for us that she was usually known as Queen Mary, for otherwise we might have the long name of "Henriettaland"!

How big is Maryland? It has a total area of 12,186 square miles. The land area is 9,837 square miles. Chesapeake Bay has an area of 1,726 square miles and other water areas make up the other 623 square miles. The Bay is 185 miles long and ranges from three to thirty miles in width.[1] Maryland ranks 42nd among the states in area.

If you measure straight across the map of Maryland from its northwest corner over to the southeast corner on the Atlantic Ocean, you will find that distance is 254.7 miles. The longest distance north to south is 125.5. Maryland is quite irregular in shape and at one point is only 1.9 miles wide. We will explain this shape as we tell the story of our state. As the map shows us, the state extends from the Appalachian mountain chain in the west to Atlantic Ocean beaches in the east.

In fact, Maryland is sometimes called "America in Miniature" because it has such a variety of land shapes: flat plains, marshes, hills, valleys and mountains. Our agriculture and businesses, too, are varied. We can also claim the title of "America in Miniature," because our history mirrors that of the United States of America.

Topographically speaking Maryland has three regions:

The Coastal Plain. The Coastal Plain makes up about half of the land area of Maryland. This area is generally divided into two parts by Marylanders and called the Eastern Shore and the Western Shore. The Chesapeake Bay divides the coastal plain region into these two areas. Much of our state is in the Coastal Plain. This region is also known as the Tidewater region.

On the Eastern Shore, the land is fairly level and the soil is light and sandy. The land, except for the great swamps and marshes used as wildlife areas, is good for farming. The canning industry is active here canning fruits and vegetables by the ton. Poultry production is another important Eastern Shore business. Tourists flock to the Atlantic Ocean beaches during the summer.

Soils of the Western Shore are heavier and often contain clay. The Western Shore is not so flat but has gentle rolling land shapes. Its Southern Maryland section is noted for its production of tobacco and other farm products.

The Piedmont Region. This area is also known as Central Maryland. The Piedmont Region begins in the east at the "fall line" where the land begins to rise over a rock base, and extends westward to the Catoctin mountain range. (The fall line makes a diagonal line from Washington, D.C. to the head of Chesapeake Bay.) Streams in the Piedmont Region flow faster than those of the Coastal Plain due to the greater slope of the land.

The Piedmont Region makes up about one-fourth of our Maryland land area. The land is rolling and, except for some rocky slopes, it is good for raising livestock and crops. There are several quarries in this area which yield much crushed rock and gravel.

The Appalachian Region. This mountainous area is often called Western Maryland. It begins in the east at the Catoctin mountain range and extends westward to the western border of Maryland. It makes up about one-fourth of our Maryland land area and contains roughly 2,000 square miles of land.

This beautiful section of Maryland is divided into four parts by geographers. The *Blue Ridge* portion is made up of a line of mountains which extend north to south across Maryland. To the west of the Blue Ridge is the *Great Valley* portion. West of the Great Valley are tall mountains and deep valleys. This section is called the *Valley and Ridge* area. Ridges of steep mountains cross Maryland here, extending in roughly parallel lines from north to south. Still further west is the *Allegheny Plateau* part of the Appalachian Region. This big, high tableland is the highest part of our state. Most of Garrett County is in the Allegheny Plateau. Though high in elevation, the land here is more level and the slopes less steep than in the Valley and Ridge section.

As one might expect, on the steep slopes of Western Maryland, streams rush briskly along and then, in the valleys, flow more slowly. The steeper slopes are quite rocky and usually covered with trees where they are too steep to be farmed. The valley soils are usually medium to heavy in texture and quite rich. In Western Maryland trees cover the mountains; orchards and grasslands occupy the slopes; and farms and towns occupy the valley floors.

Maryland Climate

The Maryland climate is, as one might guess, quite varied. The climate is affected by Maryland's ocean frontage, by her giant inland sea the Chesapeake Bay; and by her rolling hills and mountains. Naturally then, the Maryland climate differs considerably from place to place.

In the southern and eastern counties the weather is mild in the winter and hot in the summer. Cooler temperatures are normal for the higher parts of the state. The westernmost part of Maryland has the most severe winter weather and the most snow.

Rainfall is generous enough in Maryland for the needs of both farming and industry. Rainfall for most of the state ranges from 25 to 55 inches a year, averaging over 40 inches.

Millions of Years Ago

Long before people lived in our area; far, far back in time, miniature horses, mastodons (giant prehistoric elephants), dinosaurs, saber-tooth tigers and many other strange land animals were here. In the waters were giant sea turtles, crocodiles, whales and other amazing creatures. This was millions of years ago.

How do we know this? By the findings of experts who study fossils, the hardened remains, or the traces of animals, plants and fish left in rock or clay. Several belts of rich fossil deposits run across Maryland. For example, at Halethorpe, Muirkirk, Beltsville and Bladensburg, miners and construction workers have in their digging found bones and teeth of dinosaurs.

The Cliffs of Calvert are also famous for their fossil deposits. These are about one hundred feet tall and stretch for thirty miles along the western side of Chesapeake Bay. Every heavy rain brings new material to the surface. Whale ribs, crocodile teeth, parts of crabs, ancient barnacles and turtle shells have been found at Calvert Cliffs. Many of the species represented by these traces and remains are now extinct.

The climate of the area was different then, millions of years ago. Our section of the Atlantic coastline rose higher above sea level than it does now. In this area water flow cut a deep river valley. When the ocean level rose the valley filled in with water and the Chesapeake Bay was born.

Rivers of Maryland

The Potomac River is a great Maryland waterway. It belongs to our state, for the boundary line of Maryland is the Virginia shoreline of the river. The Potomac begins as a small stream at the south corner of

Garrett County. The river winds down through the mountains, across the Great Valley, through the hills of the Piedmont Region to Washington, D.C. From here it continues on the east and south to empty into Chesapeake Bay. It grows in size and volume with every stream that drains into it along the way.

There is an interesting river in Western Maryland in Garrett County. It is the Youghiogheny River which drains its waters northward! Eventually its waters flow into the Ohio River, then into the Mississippi and finally, into the Gulf of Mexico. Also in Garrett County is the beautiful Savage River which drains the other way into the Potomac River.

As the Potomac flows by Washington and Frederick counties, several creeks and the Monacacy River empty into it. At the District of Columbia the Anacostia drains into the Potomac. Small streams lace the Maryland shore of the Potomac as it flows by the western borders of Prince George's, Charles and St. Mary's counties.

The Patuxent River flows between western Montgomery and Howard counties and winds its way southward and eastward down through the peninsula that is the Western Shore of Maryland. This river supplies much of the drinking water used by nearby Maryland communities. It is a long river and empties into Chesapeake Bay between Drum Point and Cedar Point.

In the Annapolis area the Severn, South and Magothy rivers enter Chesapeake Bay. In the Baltimore area important rivers are the Patapsco, Back and Gunpowder. A little north of Baltimore the Bush River drains into the Bay. At the head of the mighty Chesapeake Bay the giant Susquehanna River empties into the Bay.

The rivers of the Eastern Shore are also both beautiful and useful. We have space here to name only a few principal streams. At the northern end of the Chesapeake Bay is the Elk River. It is this river which leads ships into the Chesapeake and Delaware Canal. Oceangoing vessels may cross from Chesapeake Bay into the Delaware River. Using the canal saves many miles.

South of the Elk is the Sassafras River. This river harbors scores of pleasure craft and has a fine marina as do many Eastern Shore waterways. Farther south are the Chester, Miles, Tred Avon and Choptank rivers, all draining into the Bay.

The Nanticoke and Wicomico rivers flow out into Tangier Sound, still farther south down the Bay. (There is a second Wicomico River in Maryland, over on the Western Shore which drains into the Potomac River.)

On Maryland's Atlantic coastline we find three "bays" separated from the ocean by Assateague Island. (Technically speaking, these bodies of water are really lagoons. A lagoon is a sheltered body of water protected by a barrier beach.) These are Chincoteague, Sinepuxent and Assawoman bays.

The waterways of Maryland add much beauty to the state. About 2,350 of Maryland's 12,186 square miles of total area are made up of water surface. These watery miles are a source of pleasure for Maryland's visitors and residents. As we will see in a later chapter, Chesapeake Bay and the rivers of Maryland are also sources of considerable profit for watermen.

Some Interesting Facts

The population of Maryland in 1990 was nearly 4.8 million people. Great numbers of Maryland people live and work in or near Baltimore City or Washington, D.C. About one-quarter of our Maryland population is located in Baltimore City and another one-quarter is located near the city in Baltimore and Anne Arundel counties. Another one-quarter of Maryland people live in the counties of Prince George's and Montgomery, which border Washington, D.C. You can see that three-quarters of our people live near the center of Maryland.

The incorporated cities of over 10,000 people in 1990 were: Aberdeen, Annapolis, Baltimore, Bowie, Cambridge, College Park, Cumberland, Frederick, Gaithersburg, Greenbelt, Hagerstown, Hyattsville, Laurel, New Carrollton, Rockville, Salisbury, Takoma Park and Westminster.

There are also many communities of over 20,000 persons in Maryland known as "unincorporated places." Of these, Bethesda, Silver Spring and Wheaton all have well over 50,000 residents. Catonsville and Essex, too, are large unincorporated communities with over 35,000 persons in residence. Among the unincorporated places with an over-20,000 population are: Aspen Hill, Arbutus, Dundalk, Carney, Columbia, Ellicott City, Glen Burnie, Lockhearn, Middle River, Milford Mill, Oxon Hill, Parkville, Pikesville, Potomac, Randallstown, Security, Severna Park, South Gate, Suitland-Silver Hill and Towson.[2]

With Maryland's population near five million persons, it is not surprising to find that the state budget each year is now nearing nine billion dollars. Over two-and-a-half billion dollars of the budget is spent for public education.

We end our brief discussion of Maryland's geography with comments on Maryland's Port of Baltimore. This great port is unique in being the most inland of Atlantic ports in the United States. It generates billions of dollars worth of business each year. It ranks among the largest of the nation's seaports in both domestic and foreign tonnage.

The scene is set. The story of your Maryland awaits you in the following pages.

---

1 The Bay widens to 30 miles across in Virginia territory below Smith Island, Maryland.
2 Sources: *Statistical Abstract of the United States: 1991*, Washington: U.S. Department of Commerce, Bureau of the Census; Public Information Office, Port of Baltimore Authority.

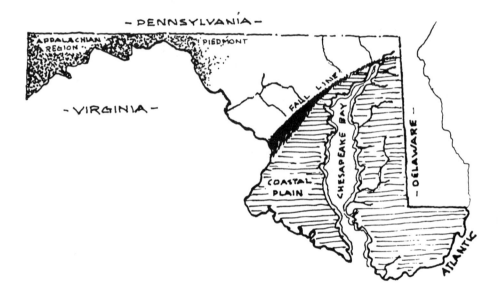

YOUR MARYLAND

SECTION I

COLONIAL MARYLAND

The Ark and The Dove
— by Mall

CHAPTER I

EUROPEANS REACH MARYLAND

THE first people to live in Maryland were "Indians." The people native to the Americas were called this because when Christopher Columbus reached the Americas, he believed that he had found a short route to India and that the dark-skinned tribes of people he met were "Indians." Now, to keep the two peoples distinct, we call the people native to the Americas, American Indians.

By studying weapons, pottery, tools and shell mounds found in our state, scientists find that American Indians have lived in Maryland for 12,000 years.

The Paleo-Indians (ancient Indians) were hunters and gatherers. They are believed to have arrived in what is now Maryland around 10,000 B.C.

In the Archaic period (8,000 B.C. to 1,000 B.C.) Indians survived with different tools and weapons. They lived on fish, shellfish and by hunting. They also gathered berries, fruit, nuts, seeds and plants. The Indians made bowls of stone. They cooked their food and learned to make houses of saplings covered with bark or animal skins.

The Woodland period extended from 1,000 B.C. to 1,600 A.D. This period is divided by archaeologists into three time periods, Early, Middle and Late.

By the Late Woodland period (1,000 A.D. to 1,600 A.D.) Indians had learned to grow much of their food. They did not have to move around as frequently as Indians had done before this time in order to live off the land. The Woodland Indians were expert hunters. They used the bow and arrow. Also, they trapped fish and gathered shellfish in season. The Woodland Indians made clay pots and bowls and lived in houses made of saplings covered with skins and bark. They used leather and fur for clothing.

These Late Woodland Indians met the Europeans who came to the Chesapeake Bay area.

Explorers

Columbus may not have been the first European to see the New

World of the Americas. As long ago as the year 865, according to old legends, Irish traders crossed parts of the North Atlantic. And, in the year 874, Norsemen came to Iceland with their families and slaves. The Norse settlers set up a republic, although they later became subjects of the King of Norway.

Later, from Iceland, Norse ships reached Greenland in 982. Eric the Red was one of these master seamen. He settled in Greenland. Bjarni Herjulfsson sighted Labrador in 986 but did not land there. In the year 999, one of Eric the Red's two sons, Leif, sailed to Norway. He planned his return trip by a most daring route, by going straight westward into the Atlantic. He missed Greenland, however, and landed in a strange land. Most scholars now agree that the lands he later described were on Baffin Island and Labrador. They believe that his "Vinland" might have been the Island of Newfoundland.

Young Leif saw in this new land grasses and grapes growing wild. He named the land Vinland (Wineland) and stopped long enough to cut timber. Such tall timbers were very valuable and very hard to get in his homeland. So, in addition to fresh water and food, he took aboard his ships timbers "big enough for house building." Setting sail to the northeast he went home to Greenland where he was known, after this, as "Leif the Lucky."

Now, another Norwegian, called Thorfinn Karlsefni, heard of Vinland while trading in Iceland. He raised an expedition of people and set out to see for himself. The families took cattle, food, clothing, and the tools they would need to make a settlement. First they sailed westward and then, following the coast of Labrador, southward, where they finally came to a place where "even in winter no snow fell." (Winds from the south temper the climate of the northern tip of Newfoundland.) The winters were rather short and mild. (In 1962 a Norwegian scholar, Helge Ingstad, discovered a Viking settlement near the northern tip of Newfoundland. Carbon-14 testing dates the site at about A.D. 1000.)

Though the new lands were certainly as rich in game, grapes, and fish as the Norwegians had been told, they found it most uncomfortable for settlement. Swarms of natives attacked them several times. (Not until later were colonists from Europe able to resist the natives with guns and cannon.) After about two years, around the year 1006, the party returned to Greenland. For five hundred years thereafter no other Europeans are known to have set foot on North American land.

Following the first great voyage by Christopher Columbus in 1492, exploration of the New World began in earnest. The Spanish,

Portuguese, Dutch, English, and French ships made many voyages. The captains of the ships claimed the lands they saw for their kings. The Spanish, for example, claimed the Caribbean Islands, parts of South America, Mexico, and Florida for the Spanish crown. Stories of Spanish discoveries of vast treasures of gold and silver soon whetted the appetites of British monarchs.

In 1498 King Henry VII of England financed a voyage by John Cabot, an Italian, who sailed down the east coast of North America perhaps as far as Maryland. The shores he saw he claimed for the English crown. In 1524, Giovanni da Verrazano landed briefly (it is now believed) somewhere on the Atlantic coast of the Delmarva Peninsula. He was exploring for the King of France. The English claim on Maryland was later disputed by Spain on the grounds that their explorer, Pedro Menendez Marques, saw the Chesapeake Bay region in 1573, a land with "many rivers and harbors," and Maryland was thus Spanish territory. The Spanish were very active in attempting to colonize the New World. They claimed almost all of South America with the exception of Brazil, and there were Spanish missions established in North America north of Florida, through Mexico and into the south and west of the North American continent.

The English at first were slow to colonize the lands they had claimed in North America. England, while under the rule of Queen Elizabeth I, was involved in conflicts of interest with some of her European neighbor countries. Then too, without the expense of colonization, English privateers seemed to get a plentiful share of New World gold for England by capturing Spanish ships!

Eventually, English settlers were left in 1580-1590 on Roanoke Island, Virginia[1] and seemed to be doing well. However, English ships which were to return with supplies were delayed by the war with Spain. Several years later English ships that finally arrived in Virginia found that the colony of one hundred men, seventeen women, and several children, was gone! After this mysterious and tragic failure, more years passed until, in 1607, the first successful English colony in North America was established at Jamestown, Virginia.

The colony had a very difficult time. Many people starved; many died of disease; and many were killed by the Indians. A leader emerged, Captain John Smith. He had learned to deal with the Indians. This talent, and his ability to organize the colonists, led to his being appointed their leader. He was an exceptionally energetic and interesting man. He brought the Jamestown colony through the first terrible winter in Virginia. Barely enough of these first settlers survived to plant crops and to build a town during the following spring and summer.

Early explorers had thought that Chesapeake Bay might extend all the way to the Pacific. (Vasco de Balboa, a Spanish adventurer had been the first to view the Pacific from American soil when he crossed the Isthmus of Panama in 1513.) John Smith, full of enthusiasm and curiosity, set out to see if Chesapeake Bay did extend through to the Pacific Ocean. In a small boat with a complaining crew, he explored and mapped the Bay. His map was a good one and was used for many years.

When Smith returned to Virginia, he told of a beautiful country to the northwest, full of giant trees, open glades, plentiful game, and waters crowded with fish and duck. It was a wonderful land, he reported, though one had to be careful not to be lured up narrow waterways into an Indian ambush.

William Claiborne

Back in England, John Smith's stories of Virginia and the area that was to become Maryland, came to the ears of a young man not long out of Cambridge University, William Claiborne. What an opportunity for adventure and riches, Claiborne thought!

Claiborne went to Virginia and was made surveyor of that colony. In two years he completed a map of Virginia and was given 17,500 acres of land for his work. He became a respected and wealthy man. He was a member of the Virginia Council and then became Virginia's Secretary of State.

Often Claiborne plunged into the virgin forests of Virginia and Maryland. He crossed new waterways. He found that he had a talent for getting along with the Indian tribes. He could talk with them and trade with them. He learned how to keep the Indians from confusing or "bluffing" his traders. However, his teams of traders found it a good idea to travel in parties of from six to eight men in a boat. They carried guns, as well as trade goods, and were careful not to enter into traps.

Since Claiborne liked to explore and was not afraid of the Indians, the governor of Virginia asked him to explore more of Chesapeake Bay. This was in March of 1628. On this trip Claiborne found Palmer's Island[2] at the head of the Bay, where the Susquehanna Rivers enters. He explored another island (Kent Island) and liked it so well that he bought it from the Indians there. On both of the islands he set up trading posts. The furs that the Indians brought in were worth a great deal of money.

Each year seemed to bring Claiborne more and more success. By May of 1632 he had a license from King Charles I to keep up his trade in "all parts of America not given to other traders"! He was also authorized to govern, direct, correct, and punish persons in those lands as necessary. Nothing, it seemed, would stop William Claiborne from becoming almost a king in this beautiful, this enormous, new land.

---

1 This area was then named Virginia, but it is now a part of North Carolina.
2 It is now called Garrett Island.

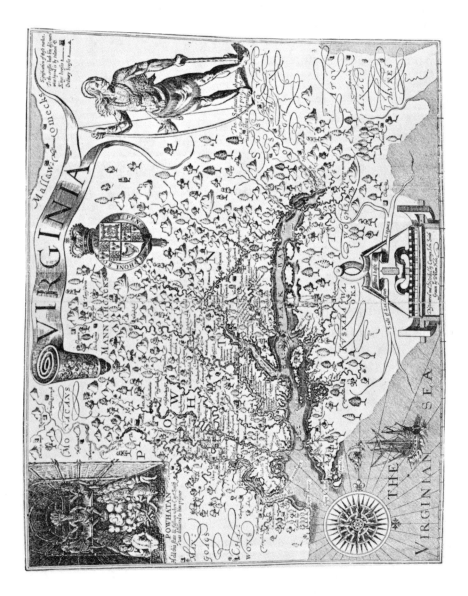

John Smith's Map of Maryland.

5

CHAPTER II

ENGLISH KINGS AND QUEENS

THIS listing of English kings and queens is included because the rulers of England had a lot to do with the way in which Maryland began and had a great influence on its colonial history. Needless to say, the British royalty had a great deal to do with the history of the American Revolution and the War of 1812, as well. So, to help you to keep dates and English rulers straight, here is the list:

	Ruled	
HENRY VII	1485-1509	
HENRY VIII	1509-1547	
EDWARD VI	1547-1553	(He was nine years old in 1547 and was an invalid.)
MARY I	1553-1558	(She married Philip of Spain.)
ELIZABETH I	1558-1603	(She became Queen of England when she was 25 years of age. She never married.)
JAMES I	1603-1625	
CHARLES I	1625-1649	(His wife was Queen Henrietta Maria for whom Maryland was named.)

From 1642-1646 a great civil war raged in England. Then a second civil war. In 1653 Oliver Cromwell was made ruler of England as head of the Puritan forces. He was given the title "Protector." Cromwell died in 1658 and his son, Richard Cromwell, was made Lord Protector of England (1658-1659).

CHARLES II		In 1660 he was restored to the throne and ruled to 1685.
JAMES II	1685-1688	
MARY II and WILLIAM III		Queen Mary II ascended to the throne jointly with her husband. The executive power was given to the husband. They ruled together from 1689 to 1694. When Mary died in 1694, her husband William III ruled alone until his death in 1702.
QUEEN ANNE	1702-1714	
GEORGE I	1714-1727	
GEORGE II	1727-1760	

GEORGE III   1760-1820

The English monarchs from King Henry VII through Elizabeth I were known as the Tudor line of rulers. The English monarchs, from James I through James II, were called the Stuart line. And from 1689 and into the reign of George III the English rulers were known as the Post-Revolutionary Monarchs. The three Georges were also called England's Hanoverian line because of their descent from the German house of Hanover.

Maryland Historical Society.

Drawing of a Plantation.

CHAPTER III

THE FOUNDING OF MARYLAND
AND ITS ENGLISH BACKGROUND

BEFORE we learn how Maryland was founded, we should understand some of the conditions in England in that period for those conditions form an important part of the background of Maryland's settlement. Events in England had a considerable, and direct, influence on events in Maryland throughout its early history.

About 1600, England was racked by severe religious and political strife. Why was this? Well, for centuries, England, like most of Europe, had one recognized church, the Roman Catholic Church, with the Pope in Rome at its head. According to the belief of the times, kings were given their power "by divine right" from God. This alone would give the Pope and the Church tremendous influence on kings, the nobility, the people, and on every part of the fabric of the society. The Church was immensely rich, unfortunately it was also somewhat corrupt at that time. The Church, to a great extent, controlled the culture of its members, and controlled the administration of justice, education, and the emerging press. The Church then, could wield immense political power. It was an important part in the lives of most people.

In 1534, Henry VIII, King of England, rebelled against the Roman Catholic Church. The Pope had refused to allow Henry VIII the right to divorce his Spanish Queen, Catherine of Aragon. Angry, Henry VIII created a new church with himself at its head. This was the Church of England. Not only did Henry VIII create a new church, but he began to take the land and wealth of the Catholic Church in England. He assumed the right to appoint bishops and priests, and prescribed articles of faith!

Henry VIII was not alone in throwing off the control of the Roman Catholic Church. At about that same time Martin Luther was buffeting the Catholic Church in Germany.[1] John Calvin was doing the same in Switzerland; the Presbyterians were active in Scotland; the Huguenots were busy in France. In other words, the Reformation was on in earnest. Only in Spain did the Inquisition effectively crush any outbreak of the new "heresies."

Mere words hardly tell the effect these actions had on the English people. A people's religion, ingrained for hundreds of years, is not easily cast off. But, Henry VIII was an extremely forceful person. The people he did not convert by reason, he converted by threat. Those who protested openly, he had beheaded or burnt at the stake.

When Edward VII, only a boy of nine, succeeded Henry VIII in 1547, the Church of England became stronger. Confiscation of Catholic property and the persecution of Catholics continued. But Edward, ever ailing and an invalid, did not "rule" long. He died in 1553.

Mary I, the daughter of Henry VIII and the Catholic Catherine of Aragon, became Queen of England. A confirmed Catholic like her mother, Mary at once set about restoring England to the Roman Catholic Church. She began a relentless extermination of all proponents of the Church of England. During her five-year reign, from 1553 to 1558, some 300 persons were burned at the stake for "heresy." She showed such energy in killing off non-Catholics that she earned the name "Bloody Mary."

After Mary's death, Elizabeth I, a Protestant, succeeded to the throne. Once again the wheel of religious struggle made a complete turn. The English people now had to belong to the Church of England or be hounded by the Queen. Elizabeth ruled almost forty-five years, and during this time the Church of England was firmly established. Elizabeth had Mary, Queen of Scots, a Catholic, beheaded for "treason."

When Elizabeth died in 1603 she was succeeded by James I, and the Protestants remained in control. In fact, an especially militant group of Protestants, known as Puritans, began to gather strength. They were impatient with the slowness with which the remaining traces of Catholicism were being done away with. They kept a watchful eye on the King, whom they suspected of favoring certain Catholics. The Puritans were especially angry when King James tried to marry his son to a Spanish princess. The princess was, of course, Catholic. Somewhat later, the Puritans beheaded a King of England, Charles I.

Imagine trying to worship God according to your conscience in the England of the 1500's and 1600's! Conditions continued to worsen, and a terrible civil war lasting four years was fought over essentially religious matters.

Land

England had, at the time we have been discussing, almost entirely an agricultural economy. Agriculture requires land. The King of England or the Queen, the nobility, and the churches owned most of the land, possibly 95% of it. The mass of the people worked the land for the owners and were really little more than slaves. They had practically no hope of ever owning land themselves.

Even in wealthy families, land was a problem, for according to the prevalent laws of primogeniture[2], the eldest son inherited all of the land when the father of the family died. The younger sons usually joined the army or the navy or went into the church. If they did not choose these, opportunities were limited. The merchant and tradesman class was beginning to gain prestige, but even this rewarding work was considered beneath the dignity of the nobility and the gentry. So, from near the top to the bottom of English society, more and more people yearned for land.

Taxes

England had been involved in wars for hundreds of years. Sometimes she fought the French, sometimes the Spanish, sometimes with one of these nations as an ally, and at other times fighting her former ally! These wars were sometimes fought for a good reason but mostly they were fought for petty, ridiculous reasons. But, whatever the reason, all of these wars were costly. The English people—nobles, merchants, tradesmen, and workmen—groaned under the continuous heavy load of taxes.

Imagine then, how the stories of a new, limitless, abundant land, thousands of miles away from a brawling, stifling Europe sounded to many Englishmen. In the New World there was beautiful land, enough for everyone. There might be gold to be found. Perhaps in America one could worship as one wished. There was both opportunity and adventure beckoning across the ocean.

---

1 In 1517 Martin Luther nailed his theses on the door of the church at Wittenberg (Germany). In 1534 the Act of Supremacy proclaimed Henry VIII supreme head of the Church of England.

2 Primogeniture is a term meaning the right of the eldest son to inherit the family land. This excludes younger sons and female family members.

CHAPTER IV

THE REMARKABLE GEORGE CALVERT

ONE man can often begin a chain of events. One person can start a group of people moving. Such a person was George Calvert, an Englishman who lived from about 1580 to 1632. The effects of his thinking and his actions are with us today in Maryland. To understand this, let us look at his family background, his education, and his life.

George Calvert was born the son of a wealthy family, though not a member of the English nobility. He was educated at the famous Trinity College, Oxford—England's oldest and finest university.

His studies in Greek and Roman government and in English history and government shaped his later thinking. He learned that a most important charter had been signed, though reluctantly, by King John of England at the demand of powerful English barons. This charter, called the Magna Carta had been signed at Runnymede, on June 15, 1215. It guaranteed personal and political liberties to some of the people of England.

The upper classes in England were the only ones who had many rights. The idea of common folk of England having a say in the government was still practically unheard of, even in the time of George Calvert in the late 1500's. Yet the Magna Carta, granting the nobles of England certain rights "paved the way" for this idea.

Young men of wealthy families who were inclined to study could learn all of this and much more. They could learn the sciences of the day, architecture, religion, and languages. They were expected to ride well, to fence, and to have certain social refinements.

Those students not inclined to study found the wealth and position of their families protection enough for whatever roughhousing, drinking, gambling, and carousing they chose to do. Some, away from their families in their college days, learned nothing at all. George Calvert, however, took advantage of his college years and won his degree. He finished off his education with a tour of Europe.

George Calvert married Anne Mynn[1], who bore him eleven children before she died, in childbirth, in 1622. He later married again, but the maiden name of his second wife, Joan, is not known. Joan, too, bore him several children.

11

George Calvert
First Lord Baltimore

In the years following his college days, it was not only George Calvert's education but his steadfast personality and good mind that won him honors in the government of King James I. Calvert became England's Secretary of State. By 1624, few men in England had more influence than he. He had been granted the island of Avalon in Newfoundland in 1621. Then, in the year 1624, he decided to leave the Church of England and become a Catholic. Due to his change in religion and for political reasons, too, he resigned his post as Secretary of State.

King James I, in spite of this, remained his friend and kept him as a member of the Privy Council. The king gave him not only great estates in Ireland, but raised him to membership in the Irish peerage in 1625, with the title of Baron of Baltimore, First Lord Baltimore.

After the death of King James, on March 27, 1625, King Charles I wanted George Calvert to remain a member of the Privy Council. At Calvert's request, however, King Charles agreed to Calvert's retirement from the royal court.

In spite of the friendship of King Charles I, George Calvert knew that being a Catholic was not popular or safe in England at that time. He decided to develop his island grant of Avalon. He was now in his middle forties. He sent out both Catholic church members and non-Catholics to colonize the island. He went out himself when he saw that the colony was not doing well. When he arrived in July, 1627, he found a fine house built for him, thirty other homes, a fort with cannon to protect the harbor, a church, wharves, and warehouses. Abundant fish became a large source of food and money for the colony. Game was fairly plentiful and some copper mining was done. Crops were hopefully planted.

Calvert found himself not only supervising all this, but fighting off French warships and setting out to sea himself. He sailed out, battled French raiders, and captured several ships. These same ships later helped him to throw back attacks of pirates.

But now, other enemies were closing in. Cold and disease struck in the unusually bad winter of 1628. Food became scarce. In his great house Lord Baltimore and his servants tended the sick. George Calvert realized that he needed a warmer climate to have a really prosperous colony. He had hoped that Avalon, being about the same latitude as England, would have the same climate. However, the ocean currents that warm the climate of England, do not reach the island Calvert hoped to colonize.

Calvert sailed to Virginia. He arrived there in October, 1629. He was, remember, still very popular with the King of England and so was a very powerful man. Authorities in Virginia were afraid that he would be granted lands that they wanted, yet they had to be polite to him for fear of the King's displeasure if they were not. They decided to find a way to keep him from settling in Virginia. They insisted, when Calvert arrived, that he swear an oath of loyalty to the Crown and to the Church of England. Calvert gladly agreed to swear loyalty to the Crown (the King) but refused to swear loyalty to the church in which he no longer believed. So, he was refused permission to stay in Virginia.

Now Calvert, on his way to Virginia and after leaving there, heard much of the good lands to the south of Virginia, and of lands also, to the north of that colony. He saw for himself the beauty of the Potomac River, the mouth of the great Chesapeake Bay, and the fertile forests and fields beside the waters in the area. After the bleak winter he had just spent in Avalon, the climate appealed to him. Thoughtfully, George Calvert returned to England. Lady Baltimore and some of their children remained behind in Virginia.

In December of 1629, Lord Baltimore asked the King to allow him to send for his wife and children who had been left in Virginia. The King agreed to this request. While awaiting the return of Lady Baltimore, George Calvert asked King Charles I to give him a grant of land to the south of Virginia. The King did not object to this idea but other persons wanted the land and the Virginia people, too, objected to Calvert's getting the land south of Virginia. So, after some delay, it was decided that Calvert was to be granted lands north of the Potomac River, instead. These lands, you remember, were also lands that the Virginia people would like to have. But the King set people to work preparing the official papers.

In the meantime, after the King agreed to let Calvert send for his wife (December, 1629), many weeks passed before Lady Baltimore received word that she was to return to England. She and the children, together with "a great deal of plate (items made of valuable metals such as gold and silver) and other goods of great value," boarded a ship for England. Just short of safety the ship was blown upon some rocks and sank. The people were saved, so far as we know, but the great fortune in gold and silver was lost.[2]

Before the charter of Maryland was ready, on April 15, 1632, George Calvert, First Lord Baltimore, died. The official charter was to be signed by his son Cecil, who now inherited from George Calvert lands, wealth, and the title. Cecil Calvert was now the Second Lord Baltimore, and he set about carrying on his father's work. He had, by that time, married the beautiful Anne Arundel, daughter of "Thomas

14

Arundell, of Wardour Castle, a Catholic peer."[3]

When King Charles I met with Cecil Calvert on June 20, 1632, to sign the Maryland charter, the king noticed that the name of the province had been left blank. The king asked Cecil what he should call the province. Cecil answered that he had wanted it named in honor of the King, but that the name Carolina had already been used.

"Let us, therefore," said the King, "give it a name in honor of the Queen. What think you of Mariana?" But Cecil Calvert remembered that a Jesuit by that name had written against the monarchy. Then the King suggested the name, "Terra Mariae," which means Mary Land. The two men agreed, and the name was written into the charter.

---

1 Some histories show this name as Wynne, but Anne's father signed his will, "George Mynn," and on his epitaph the name is also "Mynn."

2 This event probably happened in 1630, for according to the Old Style calendar, the new year began March 25th, which would allow over a year after the king agreed to Lady Baltimore's return. Events did sometimes move very slowly, however, in that day of sailing ships, so it could have occurred early in 1631, though this seems doubtful. By October 11, 1631, Lord Baltimore refers to her death in a letter to his friend Wentworth, Earl of Stafford.

3 The marriage took place in 1628.

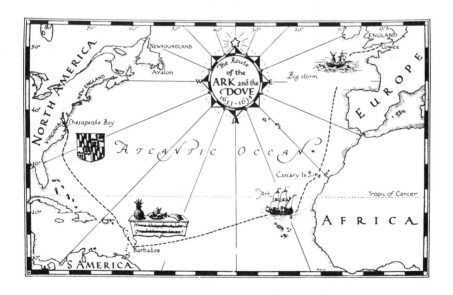

CHAPTER V

THE VOYAGE — PART I

By the time two small, wooden sailing ships lifted anchor, on the 22nd day of November, 1633, and set sail from Cowes, Isle of Wight, England, much planning had been done. The Second Lord Baltimore, Cecil Calvert, was sending colonists to set up the English colony of Maryland on the North American coast. The Calvert family had learned a great deal from the attempts of other groups to colonize that coast and had learned, too, from their own experiences in the colonization of Avalon.

Cecil Calvert was staying in England to watch over the family estates and to maintain friendly relations with the King of England. Cecil sent his brother, Leonard Calvert, to lead the expedition, with the help of another brother, George.

People

How many people came to Maryland? The exact number is not known. Lord Baltimore wrote in a letter to a family friend[1] about the difficulties in getting the ships away from England. Powerful men, Lords of the Council, had sent "examiners" to get loyalty oaths from the people aboard the ships. Catholics did not like to take these oaths since it involved promising loyalty to the Church of England. So, the examiners found only 128 people on the ships to take the oath. The rest of the people, including two Jesuit priests, rejoined the ships at the Isle of Wight later.

In this same letter Lord Baltimore says, "There are two of my brothers gone, with very near twenty other gentlemen of very good fashion, and three hundred laboring men well provided in all things."

Historians seem to agree that there were at least 220 people in the first colony and that, perhaps, 128 of them may have been Protestants. In a report, however, one of the Jesuit priests commented that "three-quarters (of the people) are heretics." The families of rank may have been made up of quite a few Catholics for in another report about the voyage of the ships the writer says there were "gentlemen of fortune . . . nearly all Catholics."

The ships were the *Ark*, of about three hundred tons, and the *Dove*, of about fifty tons. With the ships went two Jesuit priests, the

Fathers Andrew White and John Altham, plus many people chosen for their skills at farming, carpentry, brick making, and other trades useful to a new colonial venture. Father White was, fortunately for historians, a writer of many reports and letters. Since so many other records of the first Maryland colony have been lost, his writings are mainly relied upon to tell us about the voyage to America and about the early years in Maryland.

Equipment

Not only were the right people important to the success of the venture, but the right supplies as well. Planning such an expedition is similar in many ways to our present-day planning for voyages into outer space. In both cases it is important that foods take as little space as possible and that they be stored in such a way that they will not spoil.

Food for the voyage, and enough to keep the settlement alive in case no other food were found, had to be provided. Water was stored aboard in great casks; and as much, if not more, beer was aboard!

Clothing for all had to be carried along. Both summer and winter clothing would be needed. The ships were armed with cannon. The colonists were armed with long, muzzle-loading guns, swords, pikes, and various types of knives. The guns could belch quantities of noise and smoke but were not very accurate except at very short range.

Stored carefully away were seeds, roots, and all sorts of plant cuttings to be used to plant fields and gardens. The colonists and their leaders had tried to think of every sort of tool that might be needed for farming, for building homes, fortifications, and the small boats they would need. They carried many "trade goods" which would be useful in dealing with the Indians. Farm animals they hoped to be able to buy in America.

Timing

One lesson the Calverts had learned very well indeed was that of correctly timing such a venture. The voyage left England in the fall so that the band of colonists would arrive in America in the spring. They would then have time to grow food for the following winter and would not need warm houses for several months. By planning ahead the Calverts hoped to prevent their people from suffering from starvation and cold as had so many early settlers of North America.

Why They Went

To start off on such a dangerous and uncertain voyage, to plan a new home in an undeveloped land, to begin a whole new life for oneself, there must be very important reasons. Did the colonists seek freedom of religion? True, for many who came this was one of the main objectives. Yet English conditions in this period had been disappointing to large numbers for other reasons. Many found it impossible there to earn a decent living, to have personal independence, or to satisfy ambitions to work their way up in the world. Then, too, there was a general hunger for land and other forms of property. So, many came in order to be able to earn more money and to have more property. This may be called the "economic" reason.

Some people, moreover, came for the sheer adventure of it—such as soldiers, adventurers, as well as younger members of wealthy English families, and other daring individuals.

The Calverts shared, perhaps, in all three of these desires. They hoped to make a success of this colony in order to provide a place where their settlers could worship without danger. They hoped, too, for wealth and continuing family security. Yet, they were an intelligent, venturesome clan and were not afraid of the considerable risks involved.

The Voyage

It seemed at first that the two ships would never leave English waters in safety, much less cross the hundreds of miles of ocean ahead. The *Ark* and the *Dove* had difficulty getting through the "Needles," a mass of rocks and breaking waves at the end of the Isle of Wight. No sooner had they gotten by this first peril, than they had to worry about the next.

There were pirates and Turkish raiders infesting the waters through which they must sail. The two ships were not to sail directly westward to Maryland. Instead a southwesterly course was planned (see map). The leaders of the expedition intended to use the Canary Islands, Cape Verde Islands, and the Barbados as "stepping stones" across the vast Atlantic and hoped that this route would give them favorable winds. Once across the Atlantic, the ships could sail northward up the coast of North America to Maryland.

The *Ark* was not only the larger of the two ships, but was also better armed, carried heavier cannon, and had more soldiers aboard to repel pirates. Besides being smaller, the *Dove* was not quite such a trim, good ship as the *Ark*, or, in the words of that time, she was not "so good a sailor."

It is not surprising, then, that trouble was ahead for the *Dove*. Good fortune favored the two ships, however, as a strong merchant ship, the *Dragon*, hove into view—big, well-armed, and going their way! Joining the *Dragon*, the *Ark* and the *Dove* sailed along, and the colonists felt happier with the merchant ship near. The *Dragon* seemed to be a good omen, indeed.

But, five days out, a great storm began. Winds howled and skies grew dark, nearly black, on that November day. Winds grew stronger. Great waves lifted and then dropped the creaking wooden ships and gales tore at their riggings.

The storm grew so fierce that the big *Dragon* turned back for England. The captain of the *Ark* decided to keep on. The captain of the *Dove* also, despite the smaller ship and less able crew, decided to keep on. The storm was growing more intense now.

"We'll hang a light on the top of the mast," a seaman bellowed across the water to the *Ark*. This light would help the *Ark* to keep the other ship in sight during the night ahead. "If you see two lights," the seaman called from the *Dove*, "you'll know we need help."

Below decks, frightened men, women, and children huddled together. They dared not cook food lest their fires set the wooden sides of the ships afire. They had to guard the lanterns carefully, too. The noise was fearful in the dark interior, as the ships rolled and pitched, creaking in every timber. The plunging of the ships made many of the passengers seasick. None were comfortable, and none could help but wonder if the voyage might not soon end with the ships, and all aboard them, at the bottom of the sea.

In the middle of that dreadful night, the storm grew much worse. Through the driving spray and wind the officers of the *Ark* were dismayed to see *two* lights at the masthead of the *Dove*. They could not help her. It was all they could do to keep their own vessel afloat, and in any event, there was not time, for in a moment the lights of the *Dove* had vanished.

All night, look and search the darkness as they might, the people on the *Ark* could not see the *Dove*. When morning came, they hoped they would see her; but at daylight there was not a trace of the little pinnace.

---

1 Lord Wentworth, Earl of Stafford, Stafford's Letters; Scharf, History of Maryland, Vol. I, p. 68.

CHAPTER VI

THE VOYAGE — PART II

AFTER the storm the weather grew bright and mild. The *Ark* sailed on, past the Canary Islands off the west coast of Africa, then westward toward America. Crossing the ocean by sailing ship in those days was a slow process. They had left England in late November, celebrated Christmas at sea, and on January 5, 1634, they arrived at Barbados Island in the Caribbean. They were very short of provisions.

There, the people rested, mended rigging, and bought stores. They looked up one day and could scarcely believe their eyes—the *Dove* was sailing into the harbor! You can imagine the joy aboard the *Ark* as the people greeted the sister boat. "What happened?" they wanted to know. The people on the *Dove* told them that the storm had been too strong, and that they had turned back to the shelter of an English port. When the weather had cleared, the *Dove* had set out again, crossed the ocean, and arrived in the Barbados harbor in time to meet the *Ark*.

As they rested in Barbados, the settlers took on fresh supplies of water and food and other things, though not without difficulties, as Father White wrote, ". . . we arrived hopeinge for some refreshinge by convenient good dyet some few dayes, but in part we were deceived for everything bore so high a price, that nothing could be had, but it cost our eies!"

Finally, refreshed, the settlers set sail again, this time bound for Virginia. Sailing away they marveled at the things they had seen on the Caribbean Islands . . . Indians, hammocks used for sleeping, new fruits, strange vegetables, trees and vines. They had very much noticed the heat, too. Faithfully, in great detail, Father White set these items down.

The leaders of the colonists wondered as they went, if the governor of Virginia would welcome them, for the Virginia company had never relished the idea of the powerful Calvert family obtaining land so near Virginia. Fortunately, letters from the King of England caused the Virginia governor to treat them kindly enough when they landed at Jamestown late in February. In Virginia they bought pigs, cows, and other things. Soon they set sail up Chesapeake Bay, bound for the Potomac River and Maryland.

Everyone aboard the ship was delighted with the balmy weather so early in the year and with the "wide expanse of the noble bay," the mighty forests they saw. "They gave thanks to God for the beautiful land which He had given them."

On the land, as the ships approached, Indians peered out. All night long council fires had burned. The native Americans had no way of knowing if the settlers were fierce and warlike or peaceful. As the colonists sailed toward shore they saw on the beaches groups of natives armed with bows and arrows, clubs and spears. The next night alarm fires burned throughout the countryside. Indian messengers raced from tribe to tribe. "Canoes as big as an island have brought as many men as there are trees in the forest," the messengers reported.

Inside the Potomac the ships approached St. Clements Island[1]. It was just a small island and not suitable for farming or a settlement, but, if necessary, it could be used as a fort until they knew whether or not the Indians would attack.

The day of the landing was March 4, 1634 (according to the old style, Julian, calendar).[2] Later, on March 25 (old style calendar), Father White led the colonists in a religious service, thanking God for their safe arrival in Maryland. A large cross was set up at this time. According to the old style, Julian, calendar, March 25th was the first day of the new year. We celebrate March 25 today as Maryland Day.

Governor Leonard Calvert first saw to it that his settlers were comfortable enough and safe for the time being. He then picked a band of men to man small boats. His plan was to meet local Indian rulers and to search for a permanent site for a settlement. As Governor Calvert and his men moved away, the colonists left behind waved, wondering if they would see them safely returned again.

1 The island was first known as St. Clements Island, later it was called Blakistone Island, but still later, the original name was restored.

2 Why was it an "old-style" calendar? Because today we use a different one and no longer use the Julian calendar. The Julian calendar was widely used and was put into official usage by Julius Caesar, ruler of the Roman Empire, in 46 B. C. It was in error by several days in the year 1582. In this year Pope Gregory XIII authorized a new system, invented by the astronomer, Luigi Ghiraldi, of Naples. This was to be called the Gregorian calendar.

Use of this new calendar spread because it was more accurate than the Julian calendar. In 1752 Great Britain adopted the Gregorian calendar. This meant that the British colonies, too, all began to use the new calendar. To do this they had to drop eleven days. An English royal decree went out saying that the day after the second of September, 1752, was to be called the fourteenth of September! Also, in 1752, the official New Year's day was made January first instead of March 25th.

To figure dates according to the Gregorian calendar, which is still in use today, we must add several days from all dates before the year 1752. To change dates from Julian, or old-style, calendar dates to our present Gregorian system we must: for the years 1582 to 1700, add ten days; for the years 1700 to 1800, add eleven days; for the years 1800 to 1900, add twelve days; and for dates after 1900, add thirteen days.

CHAPTER VII

THE UNEXPECTED

THE colonists staying behind on St. Clements Island watched Leonard Calvert and his small band of men go. They were worried, for in Virginia, a wealthy and experienced trader, Captain William Claiborne, had told them that he had just come from Maryland, and that the Indians were preparing for war. Actually it would seem that Claiborne or some of his men had been busy alarming the Indians. The Indians had been told that the white men were coming to drive them from their homes.

Captain Claiborne hoped that the Calvert family colony would fail so that he could continue his very rich fur trade with the Maryland Indians. Other Virginians encouraged him to make trouble, too, because they felt that the land now chartered to Lord Baltimore should belong to Virginia. Claiborne had even grander ideas. He hoped to expand his influence and govern not only Kent Island but get much of Maryland for himself. So, as Governor Calvert and his little party sailed up the Potomac River, they expected trouble. This, however, did not stop them as they were determined to seek out the chief Indian leaders.

At length they landed at the Indian town of Piscataway, on the Piscataway Creek, at a point across the Potomac River from the present site of Mount Vernon. There they met the Emperor of the Piscataway tribes. Over five hundred warriors had joined the Indian ruler to greet the white visitors. Governor Calvert used Captain Henry Fleet, a Virginia trader who knew the language and customs of the Indians, as his interpreter. Governor Leonard Calvert and the Emperor had a friendly visit. The Indians provided refreshments and offered the Governor land on which to build a town. This was too far up the river, too deep in Indian country, Calvert felt, so he thanked the Emperor but did not accept the land.

Now, guided by Fleet they went back down the Potomac. Fleet recommended a place downriver from St. Clements Island for a permanent town. He led them to a river branching from the Potomac, which they first called St. George's, but which later became known as the St. Mary's River. This smaller stream with deep water afforded a good harbor for many ships. Fleet who knew the region well, recommended a site well inside the St. Mary's River for a first settlement. When they arrived at the place, Governor Calvert agreed with Fleet, that it was a most suitable and beautiful location. There was water enough for a deep harbor for the *Ark* and the *Dove*. There was a good site for a fort on the high bluff by the harbor. Fresh water was obtainable from nearby creeks and springs.

An Indian village stood on the spot. Encouraged, as he had been by the peaceful reception given by the Piscataway Indians, Calvert now decided to negotiate with the King of the local Yaocamicoes. With Fleet translating his words, Governor Calvert told the Indians that the white men had come in peace. He gave the local village king presents and said that he would like to buy land from the Indians with other gifts. The Indians liked the bright blankets, the axes, knives and trinkets that Calvert offered. The Indians and Europeans admired each other's weapons and dress.

After making polite speeches and presenting gifts, the Europeans listened with pleasure as the Indians offered them half of their village at once. The other half would be given them when the crops of the Indians were harvested. The Indian king explained that the Indians planned to move to a new village site.

The idea of having immediate shelter from weather, animals and insects was most welcome to the newcomers. As you can see from our picture of an Indian village, the houses were simple but skillfully made. The Indians used well things at hand to build the houses—saplings, thatch, sticks, bark and grasses.

It was fortunate for the Calvert's colonists that the Indians of this area were farming Indians. They were less warlike than the Susquehannocks who lived farther north. The Susquehannocks depended almost entirely on hunting for food.

Governor Calvert paid the Yaocomicoes for the land by giving them more gifts: hoes, yards of cloth and other things that were new to the Indians. This was on March 27, 1634, old style calendar.

Leonard Calvert now sent for the *Ark* and the settlers. The people had been living for the most part aboard the *Ark* while awaiting word from the Governor's exploring party. Their only mishap in the meanwhile had been the upsetting of a boat containing laundry and laundry maids. The servants were rescued, but much linen was lost. This small misfortune was soon forgotten, however, when the arriving messengers told the colonists that a wonderful place for a town was to be theirs.

As the settlers moved and took possession of their new land, flags flew, cannon boomed, and a procession was formed. All came ashore dressed in their finest clothes for the occasion. The name of the village was changed from Yaocomico to St. Mary's City[1] in honor of the Virgin

23

Mary. So it was that, within a short time after first landing in Maryland, Governor Calvert and his colonists had negotiated for land for their first settlement. The selection of this site was to have much to do with the way things went. It was not located, as was Jamestown, in an unhealthy, low-lying swampy area. Fresh breezes swept across the water and kept some of the insects away. Fresh water was available.

One can imagine how happy the colonists felt. The land was beautiful and plentiful; it looked rich for farming; and the weather was mild and bright. The feared Indians were proving cordial and helpful. Each day the settlers prayed to give thanks for the end of their long, dangerous voyage. They prayed, too, for help in the days ahead. They began to unpack the chests packed with their belongings. They began, too, to learn many things from the Indians, and happily set about providing food and shelter for the months ahead. They did not then know that Europeans, not Indians, were to bring the next stern test of this young colony.

---

1 This was spelled St. Marie's for a long time.

E. Leutze painting   **Landing on Blakistone Island**   (Maryland Historical Society)

CHAPTER VIII

MARYLAND'S FIRST TOWN

NOTHING could have been more unexpected than the peaceful, happy days that followed the landing of the English colonists in Maryland. Both European and Indian leaders had wondered if the coming of the colonists would mean a time of war and death. As it was, the Indians withdrew as they had promised, leaving half their town. They now located their new village so that the English town was between them and their enemies, the Susquehannocks. Now the Susquehannocks could no longer pounce upon the Yaocomicoes to kill warriers, take food, fur robes, and women.

The death of either a warrior or woman was a serious loss to a tribe. In the case of the mother, the house had no one to care for the children, to prepare the meals, to sew, and to keep the man of the house and the children together. Sad, too, when the man is killed and no longer can go out to hunt and fish for food, help build shelters and bring in furs for clothing and other uses. Just as fathers today earn a living for their families, so the Indian men provided for their wives and children. They were ready, too, to fight the raiders and protect their lands and people.

The Yaocomicoes were glad to have the guns of the English blocking the warpath of the Susquehannock Indians. The first English to settle in Jamestown, Virginia, had suffered terribly from Indian attacks. The members of the Maryland colony knew of this. Since the settlers could not be sure that the Indians would all be as friendly as the first tribes they met, one of the first construction projects was the building of a stockade and fort. The Indians themselves, in some parts of Maryland and Virginia, used stockades of tall, pointed logs to protect their towns. When the English had finished the stockade, the women, children and farm animals, in case of attack, could come inside while the men fired from the stockade at the attackers. This same kind of fortification was likely to be used whenever new settlements were made in Indian lands.

The English settlers brought many new ways to the Indians. Now, instead of burning trees to clear the land, Indians could use iron and steel axes to cut the trees down. The new steel knives also helped the Indians a great deal in their work, as did the white man's hoes. New bright beads and gay, colored cloth, too, began to be worn by the Indians.

In fact, the Indians and the English found that they liked one another. The settlers found the Yaocomicoes brave, strong, gentle, grave, and courteous. Since the colonists were strongly interested in religion, it impressed them that the Indians worshipped one supreme God and several lesser spirits. The English learned that on occasion, several Indian villages would send people to a central village for religious ceremonies.

All was quiet and peaceful until the settlers had been in Maryland almost one month. Then, without warning, the colonists noticed a change in the way the Indians acted. Overnight the Indians became cool instead of friendly.

The work of building the little town had been going along very fast. New crops had been planted beside the native crops already growing. Colonists were in the vacated Indian huts and had been enjoying the work, the weather, and the good will of the Indians. Now, fear dwelt in the settlement. Uneasily the people left their planting and homebuilding for the time being. They turned more energy to completing their fort. In six weeks the block house was finished. As they worked on the block house, however, they were careful to maintain good relations with the Indians as always. This seemed to give the Indians new faith in the settlers, and once again they became friendly.

The English learned later that Captain William Claiborne, the Virginian, (and possibly Captain Henry Fleet) had told the Indians that the settlers were really Spaniards and secret enemies of all Indians. Captain Fleet's part in this matter was not clear. He was given lands by Governor Calvert in payment for his help in establishing the colony, yet the record shows that he was sometimes slow to pay his debts and seems to have favored the Maryland settlers on occasion and then, at other times, to have sided with Claiborne and the Virginia interests. It does seem that the person in whom Fleet was most interested was Captain Henry Fleet!

At any rate, the settlers' restraint and care, where the Indians were concerned, gradually quieted the rumors and fears. And so, the Indians became again friendly and content, and the settlers returned to the work of building their town. St. Mary's City, the first capital of Maryland, soon took form on a bluff forty feet above the waters of the St. Mary's River.

It is not true that the first homes of the Maryland settlers were made of logs. The first dwellings were Indian houses; then English-style dwellings were built. During the first summer, the colonists built homes made of wooden slabs with roofs made of shingles. Brick dwellings were soon to follow.

By 1664, the Assembly at St. Mary's City passed a law that could be called our first Maryland building code. This law ordered that all houses built in the town should now be at least twenty feet square, two and a half stories high, and were to be built with chimneys made of brick. In Maryland the first chimneys had been made of green logs, lined with clay. As these aged, they became fire hazards.

Fireplaces were the heart of the home. They were used to heat the houses, for much of the light after dark, and for cooking. With mile after mile of forest near, there was no lack of fireplace fuel!

Cooking and baking in a fireplace took skill. A long metal rod crossed the inside of the fireplace. Pots were hung from this. Covered pots, placed not too near or too far from glowing coals, served as ovens for baking. Iron kettles and other cooking utensils were, for a long time, very rare in the colonies. They were hard to get and hard to replace, so it is not surprising that they were treasured, handed down, and frequently mentioned in wills.

Some of the platters, plates, and spoons were made of wood. China and pottery-ware had to come from England and could easily be broken. Also, the wooden plates did not dull the edges of the knives used to cut up the food. The wealthy families prided themselves on eating from dishes made of silver or china. Cups, mugs, and other dishes were often made of pewter, an alloy of tin with lead.

Only the rich could afford furniture from England; others had handmade wooden chairs, tables, and benches. Wooden pegs were often used, instead of nails, and served very well. Houses survive today that were built with the help of wooden pegs to join the planks and beams, back in the early 1700's.

Anything made of metal had to come from England. Nails could be made in Maryland, one at a time, by a blacksmith. He shaped and cut each one from a long metal rod imported from England. In later days when a farmer found his land too poor to suit him, he would pack up his family and move westward. Often he would pause to burn his cabin down so that he could recover the nails he might have used in its construction.

St. Mary's City became larger than the older English settlement at Jamestown, Virginia. The Maryland capital, by 1678, had buildings

27

of considerable quality and number, though scattered for some distance along the shore of the river.

Plenty of Land!

The charter of Maryland granted Lord Baltimore a giant tract of land. It extended from the Potomac River on the south, to the fortieth parallel on the north.[1] Its western limits were but vaguely described. At that time no one had been across the Appalachian Mountains to the sources of the Potomac River and so the westward border was most indefinite. The charter said only that the meridian line north and south, crossing the source of the Potomac River, was to be the westward boundary line.

Originally, Maryland covered all of what is today Maryland, all of Delaware, Pennsylvania as far north as Philadelphia, parts of what is now Virginia, and a part of what is today West Virginia. Thus, there was no lack of land.

Land was given to settlers in certain ways. This was by following a set of rules called "conditions of plantation." In the first years, if a settler brought over with him as many as five persons, he was entitled to 2,000 acres of land. If he brought less than five people, he could still have 100 acres for himself and for each man he brought; 100 acres for his wife and every servant; and 50 acres for each child under sixteen years of age.

The local system of administration was to divide the area into "hundreds." The hundred was an old division of an English county dating from Anglo-Saxon times. The origin of the term is lost, but it probably received its name from the organization around royal estates of districts rated at a hundred taxable units.[2] The county, as it became established, was made to include a number of the hundreds. St. Mary's County which was set up in 1637, was the first county to be established in Maryland.

In the Maryland charter, the King of England agreed that "the people, and their lands, and goods are forever exempted from taxation by the King." Remember this promise, for it will explain why Maryland people felt so strongly in later years, about English attempts at taxation.

Serenity at St. Mary's City

But we are getting ahead of our story. The first settlers worked through the first summer, harvested their crops, and traded for more corn with the Indians. They found, by the end of the summer, that they not only had plenty of food for the winter, but enough corn left over to send two shiploads back to England. The money that this crop brought in was used to buy more metal tools, salt, and other items the colonists needed.

Out in the fields, the cattle, chickens, and pigs bought from the Virginians were growing fat. Nearby waters offered many kinds of fish and other seafood. The forest teemed with deer, bear, turkey, and other game.

The Maryland colonists had a completed stockade and fort. The cabins and huts were ready for the cold winter. Life looked very good. Freedom of worship, a just government, and even a little self-government was theirs. The future held no problems, or so they may have thought that first peaceful fall.

---

1 The 40th parallel runs east to west. This line runs just north of the city of Philadelphia.
2 **Maryland Historical Magazine,** article by Louise Joyner Hienton. Vol. 65, No. 1, 1970.

Colonial children often had to help with work.

Colonial Days

30

CHAPTER IX

CAPTAIN CLAIBORNE'S STORY

J UST when the Maryland colonists had established themselves and could expect a breathing spell, a serious danger came, but not, as one might expect, from the Indians. It came from Captain William Claiborne, the Virginia trader on Kent Island.

To understand Virginia's, and Captain Claiborne's, interest in Maryland we have to go back a little. The land grant made in London in 1606 to the London Company *included* that land that later became Maryland! Other charters, in 1609 and in 1612, changed this grant, and changed the name to the "Virginia Company." Great new tracts of land were granted. The Virginia Company, of course, was the one that had founded the first successful English colony, Jamestown, in 1607.

But the Crown became dissatisfied with the way that the Virginia Company was operating, so, in 1624, the King of England took back its charter. He changed the government of Virginia to a royal government, with a council in Virginia to direct the affairs of the colony. What happened to the land? The land originally given to the London and Virginia companies reverted to the ownership of the Crown. This left the King free to make new grants of land to more promising colonial plans in America.

One of the new grants was that of Maryland to Lord Baltimore. But what has all this to do with Claiborne? Quite a lot, for before the Maryland settlers arrived, Claiborne had been given a license to trade with the Indians in the Chesapeake Bay area. He was a wealthy and respected man in Virginia and had been secretary of that colony. Financed by Cloberry and Company of London, he had built a trading post on Kent Island in the year 1628 and was enjoying a profitable trading business, especially in furs, with the Indians. Then too, Claiborne dreamed of expanding his power and wealth and, with a grant of land, ruling much territory.

Since Claiborne had gotten to Kent Island first, the King of England instructed Lord Baltimore to allow him to continue to trade there, but under the Maryland, rather than the Virginia government. Encouraged by Virginia interests, however, Claiborne refused to acknowledge Lord Baltimore's offer to trade under the new arrangement.

A sea captain, Thomas Young, in a letter[1] to England, told of meeting Claiborne after Lord Baltimore's colony was founded at St. Mary's City in 1634. In their talk aboard Young's ship, the sea captain was told "of the many wrongs done him by the colonists." The two men talked until late into the night. The following morning Claiborne left, promising to meet with Young at Point Comfort. However, Captain Young notes in his letter, "I perceaved afterwards he ment it not."

Later that day Captain Young met Governor Leonard Calvert and was received with much courtesy. Captain Thomas Cornwallis told Captain Young that Claiborne had broken agreements with the Maryland government. Since Claiborne had refused "as free liberty to trade as themselves," Governor Calvert had ordered that Claiborne not be allowed to trade at all without permission from the Maryland government.

Early in 1635 Claiborne was angered by the colonists when they captured one of his trading boats. He armed a boat with fourteen men and an officer and sent it out to capture any boats belonging to Governor Calvert's colony, it met on Chesapeake Bay.

Governor Calvert heard of this and sent out two boats under the command of Captain Cornwallis to meet Claiborne's boat. The boats met in April in the Pocomoke River on the Eastern Shore of Maryland. Claiborne's crew opened fire. The colonists returned shot for shot. The battle ended with one colonist killed; the commander and three crewmen in Claiborne's crew were also killed. The rest of Claiborne's men were captured and taken back to St. Mary's City as prisoners. Another fight in May, also near the Pocomoke River, resulted in bloodshed, but few details are available about this encounter.

When Claiborne heard of the results of the encounters, he returned to Virginia. Governor Calvert asked the Virginia government to give Claiborne to him, but the Virginians instead sent Claiborne to England for trial. In England Claiborne was not tried; rather he asked the King for a charter to Kent Island. King Charles I finally handed down his decision. William Claiborne, said the King's order, had no rights to Kent Island; also he was denied trading rights, and henceforth must obey Governor Calvert.

Now the trading company in England which had been financing the trading post venture on Kent Island sent out a new trader, George Evelin. Evelin was to operate the post on Kent Island and to obey the laws of Governor Calvert.

Claiborne returned to Virginia and, to repay him for the loss of his trading post, was made Treasurer of Virginia for life. All of Claiborne's requests, however, for the return of his island were denied.

Claiborne stayed in Virginia, angry that he had not been able to extend Virginia's territories and power, and feeling that he had not been treated fairly in the whole affair.

1 **Narratives of Early Maryland,** letter from Captain Thomas "Yong" to Sir Toby Matthew, 1634.

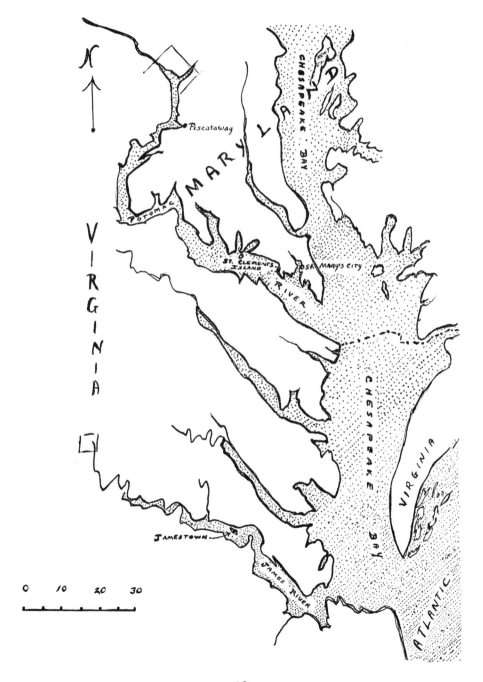

CHAPTER X

PRIESTS, HEALERS, AND EXPLORERS

THE early settlers in Maryland had with them two dedicated men of religion, whom we have mentioned before, the priests, Father Andrew White and Father John Altham.

The moment the settlers unloaded the *Ark* and the *Dove*, the two Jesuits set to work to make an Indian house into Maryland's first chapel. But the Jesuits did more than meet the religious needs of the Catholics of the colony; they also began to work among the Indians— teaching and healing.

The priests had come to Maryland, longing to teach Christianity to the Indians. Soon they plunged into the wilderness by boat and on foot. Visiting with the Indians, the priests won many friends for the settlers. By 1639 they had converted to Christianity the King of the Patuxent Indians and were given a plantation called Metapannayen. They traveled far and wide. Father Altham, for example, traveled sixty miles up Chesapeake Bay to Kent Island. (Father John Altham died on November 5, 1640.)

While Father White was staying with the Piscataway Indians, the Tayac (which means the "chief chief" or Emperor) became very ill. Forty Indian medicine men tried every remedy they knew to drive the illness from their chief. The chieftain got no better. In desperation the Indians turned to Father White, who was by this time becoming known for his knowledge of medicines and his care of the sick.

Father White did not hesitate. Surely, he thought, God would help him heal this savage chieftain so that the knowledge of Christianity might spread. Father White dosed the chief with "a powder of known efficacy" mixed with holy water. Then the following day Father White opened one of his patient's veins "for bloodletting." After this the sick man grew better and Father White carefully nursed him back to health.

This treatment of a disease perhaps would hardly be very popular today. Yet, in 1640, this was the usual way of handling the patient. Physicians of that time saw a sick person with a fever, his heart beating fast, and thought that the problem was that the patient had too much blood! The simplest thing, then, the doctors thought was to let some out by bleeding the patient.

Grateful to be alive through the efforts of the priest, the Piscataway emperor and his family agreed to become Christians, and the emperor caused a bark chapel to be built in his town.

Each year brought a few more priests to Maryland to work. They traveled the great forests and rivers in pairs, or alone, to meet new tribes of Indians, often protected only by their faith. Gradually they learned how to speak the Indian language, but still depended upon an interpreter. They also prepared a grammar of the Indian language which most unfortunately appears to have been lost. They usually traveled in a galley, a boat with a sail, which was also equipped with oars. In a little chest the priests carried their food, holy water, and wine for religious ceremony, as well as vessels and an altar for services. In a casket were little gifts, bells, combs, knives, fish hooks, needles, and thread.

At night they often set up a small tent ashore. To add to the corn and dried meat they carried, they hunted at the end of the day. Though danger was all around them, the hardy, devoted priests enjoyed their life and work.

The winter of 1640 was a hard one for the Indians. The summer had been very hot and dry. The crops had not done well at all. The priests then had a chance to return the generosity of the Indians by furnishing them with corn. This the priests did, purchasing the grain when necessary, at quite a high price.

Early in 1641 the Emperor of the Piscataway Indians brought his seven-year-old daughter to be educated in St. Mary's City. Governor Leonard Calvert and Mistress Margaret Brent agreed to care for the little Indian princess and to see to her education. (The historian Scharf mentions that the Emperor's two sons were also "receiving a Christian education at St. Mary's.") The little princess was given the name Mary. She lived in the Brent home, "Sister's Freehold." When Mary grew up, she married Mistress Brent's brother, Giles Brent.

Unlike some other colonies, the early settlers of Maryland were spared from attack by hostile Indians in those early days. The way in which Governor Leonard Calvert dealt with the Indians and the work of the priests, too, helped bring about this peaceful state of affairs.

Though other priests came to Maryland to help the first two Jesuits there were less than two dozen present at any one time in Maryland during the 17th century.

CHAPTER XI

THE MARYLAND INDIANS

ONE of the first things about which Father White wrote in his reports and letters to England and to Rome, was the amazingly good health of the Indians he saw in Maryland. Why was he so impressed? It was because the priest was accustomed to seeing so much disease and so many handicapped people in Europe. To see so many tall men and women in perfect physical condition was a complete surprise. He had not dreamed that people could be so well, so physically perfect.

Others in Maryland often mentioned, too, in their letters home that the Indians were fine, well-muscled, coppery-skinned people with good teeth and dark, strong hair. The English marveled that, even to quite an advanced age, the Indians remained active, and continued to have keen eyesight and strong, lithe bodies. The Europeans noticed that the Indians trained themselves to ignore heat and cold.

The Indians took great pride in their physical endurance. They liked to be able to withstand pain without flinching. Torture was practiced on important captives by some of the Indian tribes. It was a point of pride that the one being tortured should entirely disregard his pain and horror! The torturers cut, burned, and tore at his body trying to bring forth a groan or a grimace. But between bouts of torture, the captive might even manage to talk with his captors, ignoring his pain and showing no fear. This cruel and strange custom of torture was most prevalent among the hunting Indians. The Indians who devoted more time to farming seemed to be a more peaceable people. Indians deliberately toughened their bodies to withstand all sorts of strain and weather. They were proud of their ability to hunt without rest and to run for long distances.

Since much of their clothing, robes, and food depended on hunting skills, the Maryland Indians, while unusually good at farming, were also skilled huntsmen. They could move through the trees and undergrowth silently, frequently camouflaging themselves in the hides of the deer. They would sometimes mingle with the wild herds in order to get close enough to bring down a deer. They were expert, too, in trapping small animals and fish.

The new settlers learned gradually that the Indians were able to travel great distances, and quite rapidly, when they wished. Trails led back into the western mountain country, and trails extended north and south along the mountain ridges. The hardy Indians were completely at home in the vast wilderness that was America. They could go back and forth from what is now Canada to the Potomac River and southward. Each tribe held a particular territory, and thus the movement of Indians depended on either getting the permission of these tribes to travel through their territory, or perhaps in eluding them.

The newcomers noted also that while the Indian men and boys did most of the hunting and fishing, it was their women who tended the fields of corn, squash, pumpkins, sunflowers, beans, and tobacco. The Indian women also cared for the children, made clothing, and cooked for the family.

Tobacco, corn, and potatoes are plants native to the Americas. Until found in the New World, these plants were not known to Europeans. The Europeans who came to Maryland learned much from the Indians. They learned new ways of hunting, fishing, farming, and even new ways of preparing food.

The settlers watched the Indian men bring home deer and bear. The meat was eaten. The skins were scraped and worked by the women to make supple, soft winter robes and to make clothing. The Indian women showed the settlers how this was done.

The colonists learned from the Indians how to prepare hominy from corn; to prepare fish; to cook new stews in big, clay pots; to smoke fish for later use; and how to dry meat so that it would not spoil.

Some Indian Customs

Early reporters of the Indian way of life found that though the Indians did not understand the English ideas about property ownership, still the Indians were quite a moral people and had their own high code of behavior. It was not wrong, the native Americans felt, to lure an enemy up a narrow creek and then fall upon him in great numbers. This was called an ambush by the English. Today we might also label it guerrilla warfare.

Indians had a concept of property that differed from that of the European. Individuals and families might be assigned a certain plot on which to build a home and plant a garden, in an Indian village. But the idea of individual property ownership and land ownership was strange to the Indians. True, as has been mentioned, tribes often claimed the right to hunt in certain areas; and there were sometimes wars waged between tribes over disputed hunting grounds, the winner then having the right to hunt in the contested area.

The tribes in Maryland were associated loosely in what may be called a confederation but this did not produce a powerful central government. Villages belonged to loosely organized kinship groups headed by a *tayac*, or "chief chief." The Europeans generally referred to the *tayac* as an Indian emperor.

Living so close to nature, the individual Indians that survived were usually the strongest and most able; and the weak and the crippled were likely to die at a younger age, leaving the survivors to rear the greater number of children. This process of "natural selection," helps to account for the good health of the Indians that the English first met. The people best adapted to life in the wilderness survived and passed on to their children traits that would help them in turn survive.

The very way of life of the Indian also tended to produce health among those strong enough to endure. The active, outdoor life, the fresh air, good water, good diet, and the way in which they clothed and sheltered themselves, all helped to make them strong and well.

Each village had its local chieftain. These were apt to be selected through the mother of the "royal line." The chiefs themselves being of course, sons of the "royal mother." The chief normally consulted his council and warriors before making his decisions. The men of the village occupied themselves with fashioning weapons, pipes and many other things. They made fire-making drills so that a fire might be started should the coals of the fire not be saved for some reason. The Indians liked, too, to make strings of shells by drilling holes in each shell so that the shells could be strung on a leather thong after being carefully polished. These strings of shells were used as a kind of money, or *wampum*. The most valuable kind of "shell money" was called *peak* or *wampum-peak*. It was made from clam shells; some of which were purple and others white. A less valuable kind of sea shell, or cockle, was made into Indian money called *roanoke*. These shells, too, were strung on sinews or thongs, but were not so polished and shaped, like *peak*. *Peak* and *roanoke* were used by the Indians in trade with other Indians. Traders from Europe learned to use the Indian form of money, too.

Indians generally took only one wife, but the chief might have several. If a tribe lacked women, the warriors might swoop down upon, and raid, another tribe in order to obtain wives. The women did many useful things. They cured, for example, the skins used for clothing, footwear, and robes, and they did a great deal of the hard work of performing household duties and in raising crops. And so they were very useful and were prized by all of the tribes.

Indian men directed the planting of the gardens and the girdling of trees. Trees, incidentally, were "girdled" by cutting the bark away all the way around the trunk, so that the tree would die and the field would be open to sunlight. And, of course, the men did the fighting when there were wars to be waged.

Indian Clothing and Decoration

The clothing of the Indian women was just as scanty as the men's in the summer. They wore a sort of apron made of supple leather. Their clothing was also apt to be fringed and decorated with beads, like that of the men. Women, too, wore beads of copper, colored stone, and shell. Bracelets and necklaces also were very popular. Teeth of animals, rattles from snakes, bird claws—all of these contributed to the Indian dress. The women liked hair ornaments, though they did not wear feathers as much in their hair, as did the men.

Men in the summer were likely to wear a sort of kilt made of animal skins. Certain ornaments were worn by chieftains to indicate their rank. An example was a flat piece of copper hanging from a beaded necklace which might have this meaning. Men, also, liked to decorate their skin clothing with beads and fringes. In fact their dress was much brighter than that of the women.

The Indians not only decorated the skins of animals that they wore, but they decorated their own, too! Tattoos made colorful designs on their coppery skins. A tattoo might mean that a woman was unmarried. Another might suggest that the Indian brave was a good hunter.

Paint on their bodies made the Indians often seem very fierce to the settlers. But the Indians that the settlers first met, though they wore intricate designs of red, blue and black, and sometimes green, yellow and white, were in general a peaceful people. These Indians were called the Yaocomicoes, Piscataways, and Patuxents.

Some Maryland Indians, however, could be cruel. The Susquehannocks and Nanticokes sometimes tortured their captives. The Iroquois Indians, who on occasion conducted raids into Maryland, were hunters and were also very fierce and warlike.

Sometimes, to protect themselves from insects, tribesmen smeared clay or grease over their faces. The Europeans admired the way the Indians coped with such discomforts.

The men wore more elaborate hair styles than did the Indian women. A brave might shave half of his head. Another might tie up his straight, black hair into "locks," separating it into bunches and tying it with strings of shells. Most of the Indians customarily wore their hair quite long.

Summer clothing consisted of hide from which the hair had been scraped. Most Indian footwear was made from skins, but sometimes bark from trees was used.

Winter clothing used by the Indians was made from skins with the fur left on. To protect themselves from the cold, they wore long cloaks of this soft, warm, animal hide. Leggings and heavier moccasins protected their legs and feet. Robes or hides served as covers at night.

The Indians had a complex, rich, religious life. The Indian deity was called "Manito" and was considered by them to be the giver of all good life. They prayed to him and usually made to him a sacrifice of the first of their fishing, hunting, and crop-raising ventures.

Several of the Indian beliefs were similar to those of Christians. The Indians believed that if one lived a good life, after death he would go to a happy land; but that if one had lived a bad life, then one would go to a place of eternal suffering. Another similarity in their religion was the story of the Flood and the Ark, a story very much like the one told in the Old Testament of the Bible.

Remember, many centuries before, some colonists from Norway had arrived in the northern part of North America and had tried to settle the northeastern lands. It is an interesting question as to whether the similarities in the Indian and Christian religions were just coincidence, or whether they came from stories some ancient settlers might have told Indians.

Houses of worship in an Indian village had peaked roofs. As you may have noticed, this is true of almost every country in the world . . . places of worship are often peaked, spired, or towered.

In their worship the Indians danced, using gourd rattles, singing and praying together. They sometimes smoked their pipes as a part of the ceremonies to bless and purify themselves. Religion took up considerable time for the Maryland Indians. There was a ritual for every season and occasion, it seemed. The Indians were afraid of an evil spirit called "Okee" and sacrificed food and tobacco to him so that he would not cause them trouble. The "medicine men" of the tribe were respected and sometimes feared for their powerful magic.

To the Indians, many things were thought to have a spirit. They especially respected the spirits that they believed lived in stones. There were other spirits, too, they felt, in animals, thunder, lightning, water, and the sun. They believed in these and many other spirits. All of these required respect and sacrifices to the gods so that the hunt, the harvest, the battle, or the fishing might be successful.

Maryland Indians divided the year into five seasons. Winter they called *cohunk*. Next came the "budding of spring;" then the season for the "earing of the corn;" then, "highest sun" season (summer);

and finally, the "fall of the leaf," or "corn-gathering," season.

Settlers' Relations With Indians

The fate of the first colonists depended to a great extent on the Indians. Had the tribes they first met been warlike and unfriendly, the few Europeans, even with their guns and cannon, would not have been able to resist the numerous Indians for very long. Had the tribes united to drive the English out, the colonists would have had to withdraw or die. The emigrants were fortunate. They were able to bargain with the Indian chieftains.

The Maryland Indians first met by Lord Baltimore's settlers hoped for peace and trade. They reasoned that it would be good to get European hoes, sharp knives, hatchets, shining beads, trinkets, and those wonderfully bright lengths of cloth that the Europeans were known to trade for furs.

Though Governor Leonard Calvert bargained with the Indians for land he believed that legal ownership of the North American coast belonged to his English king. Governor Calvert believed that the king was legally correct in granting Maryland to the Second Lord Baltimore. The Indians feared that newcomers might kill them off and had, apparently, only a lesser concern that the English were after their lands. Land was so plentiful and the English seemed to need so little. It was not long before the Indians, too, began to believe in the power and rule of the English king and in the right of these Europeans to rule the lands they took. The Europeans justified their taking land from the Indians by saying that the Indians would be better off with modern tools, European law and the Christian religion.

It was very lucky for the Maryland colonists that they happened along just when the Yaocomico tribe was planning to leave the St. Mary's River area in order to move away from hostile Indians. The Yaocomicoes welcomed the settlers because the Europeans would serve as a barrier between themselves and their enemies. So it was that the English learned much from the friendly Indians, and were able to establish peaceful trade relationships at an early date.

The colonists added to their medicine chests many Indian herbs, salves, and oils. Indians treated the sick by giving them medicines made of barks, leaves, and plant roots. They used certain ceremonies and prayers too. Sometimes the Indians would place a sick person in a small cave dug into a bank, or in a small mat-covered building where they could be "sweated" in steam from water poured over hot stones. Does this remind you of the *sauna* bath so popular today?

Though the colonists planned to build English-style homes as soon as they could, they learned the Indian style of building dwellings. This knowledge served them well during the summer and again whenever they needed to make a shelter quickly on a new farm or for a new family.

Another lesson learned from the Indians was their way of making canoes from logs. The settlers admired the way the natives navigated these small craft across the vast Chesapeake Bay and up the big rivers nearby.

Indian Houses

Indians located their homes near a good water supply. They built them by driving long limbs into the ground; then, pulling those limbs together at the top, they tied them tightly together. This gave the roof an arched shape which shed the rain and snow quite well. The roof and the sides were covered with sheets of bark or woven mats.

In the summer these sides could be lifted to admit cool breezes. This also admitted insects, but the Indians protected their skins with clay and grease. The English must have suffered a great deal from the hordes of mosquitoes and other biting insects. In the winter the Indian houses were heated by fires on the floor. They were quite warm and rather smoky! Yet even the cold winters must have been happy times when there was enough corn stored away and game was plentiful. There were tales to be told by firelight; the family was gathered together; fur robes were snug around them, and a savory stew was cooking in the big clay pot by the fire.

The Fate of the Indians

Since this chapter tells the story of the Indians of Maryland it is necessary to say that the coming of Europeans was very bad for the native Americans. Some became addicted to alcoholic drinks. European tools, weapons, utensils and clothing were adopted. The Indians forgot their own wonderful skills. Fifty years after the arrival of the English, the Indians had almost forgotten how to make bows and arrows.

Tribes shrank. In the early 1600s there were an estimated five to seven thousand Indians in Maryland. By 1700 there were just a few hundred Indians left. More and more land was taken by settlers. Laws were made which the Indians could not understand. The Indians' weapons were no match for those of the white men. So the Indians retreated, only to find that tribes to their rear felt imposed upon and attacked the retreating Indians. In those first years of colonization, since the Indians had so many more men to fight with, had they banded together, they could have driven the colonists away; but their technology was not advanced enough to enable them to combine forces. True, tribes were loosely leagued together and could communicate with

Indian runners. The runners remembered or carried picture-written messages. This organization, however, was not enough.

The worst enemy of the Indians were the diseases which came with Europeans. Thousands of American Indians died from smallpox, measles and tuberculosis. Whole villages were wiped out by disease.

The fierce, brave Susquehannocks withdrew into western Virginia. They were attacked by the Virginia militia. Worried and angry, the Indians kept trying to find hunting grounds and to resume the life they used to live. When they came upon lonely farms or homes, they sometimes attacked, killing settlers and taking food and equipment of all kinds. Fear of Indian attack caused some early frontiersmen to build into their cabins or houses a small hidden room where they could hide until the Indians left. The fierceness of the Indians and the violence of their attacks created much fear.

Finally the surviving Susquehannocks, only a small band now, after the attack by the Virginia militia, turned sadly northward, homeward. They agreed to submit to their Indian enemies if they were permitted to stay on Maryland and Pennsylvania hunting grounds. But, even this did not give them back their old way of life. In the end the last Susquehannocks were massacred by Pennsylvania colonists.

Indians in Maryland Today

Some Indians finally asked the colonists in Maryland for a reservation. Land was set aside for them near what is today the town of La Plata in Charles County. Two other reservations were located near Piscataway Creek and near Nanjemoy Creek, in Prince George's and Charles counties.

On the Eastern Shore the Nanticokes were able to withdraw to a reserved space on the Nanticoke River. This is near the town of Vienna, in Dorchester County. Two other reservations were located on the Pocomoke and the Wicomico rivers on the Eastern Shore. But, the reserved land was not enough to give the Indians back their old healthful life. Most of those who did not die left Maryland. The reservations were eventually abandoned. The reason that the Indians moved away from the reservations was that there was no way for them to make a living. Many continued to die from diseases. Some Indians owned property here and there in Maryland. Before the American Revolution began the Proprietor of Maryland managed to sell all remaining reservation land.

The United States census in 1990, however, has reported that

13,000 citizens of Maryland regard themselves as American Indians.[1] In Charles County and in other counties of southern Maryland there are descendants of the Piscataways. In Charles and Prince George's counties there are fairly large groups of people called the Wesorts who are partly of Indian descent. In the Appalachian Mountains of Maryland there are groups of Indians in Frederick and Washington counties.

Many Maryland waterways are known by their Indian names: the Potomac River, Chesapeake Bay, Patuxent River, the two Wicomico rivers and scores of others. Many Maryland place names are also derived from Indian names and words.

---

[1] *Statistical Abstract of the United States: 1991,* p. xiii.

Indian Village

Maryland Historical Society

44

CHAPTER XII

OLD WAYS AND NEW WAYS

AT first most of the Maryland colonists stayed in the vicinity of St. Mary's City. They lived in the Indian huts until they could build permanent homes. So, as soon as the gardens were planted and the fort was completed, small homes of wood were constructed. Streets were laid out and a chapel was built.

Both Catholics and non-Catholics seemed to get along well together. Lord Baltimore had cautioned his brother to make sure that there was no quarreling over religion. Such peace between religious faiths was most unusual in that day; however, freedom of religion was one of Lord Baltimore's reasons for founding the colony. He did not want to anger the strong Protestant groups in England, and yet he wanted Maryland to be a place in which Catholics as well as others would be able to worship peacefully.

A Taste of Self-Government

One other development appeared in Maryland, even before crops were planted. The settlers began to work out a system of self-government. This was not altogether planned and it came about rather naturally. It must be remembered that each man was free to voice his opinions and had a vote. During the first winter of the colony, in 1635, the colonists gathered for a meeting which in due time came to be known as the Assembly. (Indentured servants of course, did not have a vote; neither did slaves nor women.) Both the ordinary free man of property and the "gentry" had a voice in making rules to govern Maryland.

After the Assembly in 1635, the colonists sent to the Second Lord Baltimore in England some suggested laws for his approval. Lord Baltimore probably had meant for the system to work the other way around. He felt that *he* should be the one to write the laws of his colony, so he refused to accept these first enactments of the Assembly. Instead, he wrote a new set of regulations and sent them back with an order to gather the free men together again in another Assembly.

It was early in 1638 when the Assembly met again at the little capital city. By now, some farms and plantations were located up waterways some distance from the town; and so not all of the freeholders could afford the time to attend the Assembly. Many, perhaps did not want to leave their homes unprotected. Some of the men who had to stay home, therefore, sent their votes by others who could go, making them their delegates. It should be noted, however, that the governor had the power to summon particular individuals to attend if he so decided.

In the Assembly meeting of 1638, Lord Baltimore's plan of government and his laws were read. Now it was the colonists' turn to say, "No!" They would not vote to accept the Proprietor's laws and set about making changes.

Forty-one laws in all were voted on and sent to Lord Baltimore. At first he almost decided that he would veto them all. Then he thought better of it. Such an act might result in a period of confusion in the growing colony and he might alienate his colonists to his great harm. He had to consider also, that it took months for letters to travel back and forth. So he decided to let the people make their laws, but he reserved the power to veto laws he did not like. This he undoubtably could do under the power granted him by the Maryland Charter.

In a similar way this sort of development was happening in all of the English colonies along the east coast of North America. In New England the town meeting had come to be almost a lawmaking body. In Virginia, for instance, the House of Burgesses had become the voice of the colonists in that colony's government.

Changes were occurring in England, too, especially with the rise of Parliament. Its leaders had become very powerful and very good at politics. It was no longer enough to be born a king, or of noble blood, to rule England. The group of men who made up the English Parliament had to be considered now. Lord Baltimore thus had to be very skillful in his dealings not only with the king but with Parliament and with his colonists, too. He hoped that including Protestant colonists in his plans for Maryland would make the venture acceptable to the powerful Puritans now in the English Parliament. The Puritans were leaders in the established church who hated the Roman Catholic Church.

The first years in Maryland passed rather peaceably by. The little town of St. Mary's City appeared to be secure with its sturdy fort and its homes both great and small. But, the most important thing built there was the establishment of two basic ideas: first, that every free man was entitled to a voice in his own affairs; and secondly, that different religious faiths could exist side by side without the creation of one established church. Even so, after 1649, religious freedom was somewhat narrowed by laws that allowed religious freedom only to those persons who professed some form of Christianity.

CHAPTER XIII

MARYLAND INHERITS ENGLAND'S CLASS SYSTEM

THOSE studying Maryland history will have noticed that there were distinct classes of people in the colony. While today we strive toward the ideal that every citizen is equal to every other and should have equal rights, yet, in Maryland's colonial period a definite system of rank was recognized and accepted.

On the Plantation

The master of a plantation directed the planting of crops, as well as their processing, transport, and sale. He also decided the kind of a home he wished, what buildings were to be erected, and what equipment was to be secured. His wife supervised the running of the household, but she, too, was under his direction. In England a landowner would often give the direction of farm work to an overseer. This was sometimes done in America, but since good employees were scarce, more often than not the landowner planned the work of the plantation himself and saw to it that it was done. Colonists who would have been overseers in the old country, in America were likely to ask for land for themselves.

There was usually an important lady on the plantation to guide household affairs and to act as the hostess when the owner entertained. She might be his wife if he were fortunate enough to have one; his daughter, if she still lived at home; or perhaps a competent female relative. There were meals to plan, and this was not as simple as it sounds. Foods for the household were largely produced on the plantation—meat, poultry, grains, fruits, and vegetables. Game, fish, and other seafood might be secured nearby. The plantation owner or his workers were often skilled hunters. The wife of the plantation owner served as his hostess, managed the care of the house, selection, storage and preparation of food and beverages. Hospitality was an important feature of Maryland life.

The lady of the plantation had many duties. She trained the servants. She also ordered cloth and clothing so that the family and all of the people on the plantation might be clothed. She saw to it that the house and its gardens were kept in order. She put by supplies of blankets and linens. She kept on hand a chest of medicinal herbs, salves, mixtures, and lengths of clean, old cloth to be used for bandages.

The landowner was likely to ride in his fields daily to see that the work he had planned was being done. He kept records of which crops did best and which farming methods proved most successful. A plantation owner had to be sure that labor was available to work the fields, tend the gardens, orchards, horses, and other farm animals. The plantation was, for practical purposes, a self-sufficient little feudal community under his direction. He spent time training men to do various kinds of work and sought out skilled men to come to the plantation—such as carpenters, blacksmiths, boatmen, herdsmen, field hands, house servants, and even tutors for his children.

The landowner and his lady accepted their place in life. The people on the plantation accepted the fact that the owner must be obeyed. They expected the owner to treat them fairly and to help them when they were sick. The owner wanted servants who were loyal, obedient, and respectful. Workers were admired for their special skills. A certain cook might be known throughout the area for her delectable dishes. Almost every young lady on the plantation had a servant with her for many years upon whom she depended and in whom she might confide her innermost thoughts. There was pride in a job well done when the servants worked well together and when they were treated fairly.

There were many things that a plantation owner had to know in order to succeed. Once he obtained his land he sometimes surveyed it himself. He often chose a hilltop for his home in order to take advantage of cool summer breezes. If the home could be located beside a navigable waterway where he could easily travel by water and ship his plantation products by water, then conditions were very nearly ideal. He also had to plan and have built outbuildings for cooking, as well as for soap making and laundry. A blacksmith shop, smokehouses for curing meats, and cabins for the servants and slaves also had to be built. If the workers had special work to do, such as harness mending, shoemaking, or carpentry, then places for them to work had to be provided.

Differences Between Manors and Plantations

When seeing any large old home out in the country, many of us may say, "What a beautiful old manor house!" But, what is a manor? It was a large grant of land given to a person. On the manor the owner had the right to hold regular courts of law with himself as its judge. At these courts he heard complaints and cases and decided them himself. He was a very powerful man on his manor. When such powers were given with the land, then the owner's house quite properly could be called a "manor house."

Such grants were comparatively few. Most of the land was given in smaller lots of several hundred acres. The owners of these did not have the power to hold court and judge cases that the manor owner did, so these grants could more accurately be known as "plantations."

The Class System of Europe

Back in England, for hundreds of years, people had been divided into definite classes. In England, in the 16th and 17th centuries, servants were expected to speak meekly and to work as long and as hard as the master desired. They did not expect to be more than servants, ever. Tradesmen had a bit more freedom, a bit more comfort; yet they, too, dared not hope to become a part of the gentry or the nobility. Women of all classes had few rights indeed, though wealthy women were much better treated, as a rule. Women were governed by the man who headed the family. They could not vote, and even their right to own property was limited.

At the top of the class structure were the gentlemen of property and rank. They had a great deal of power, most of the money, and most of the land. They were often descended from families related to the kings of England or noble families from France or other European countries. They were born into wealth and titles and were often given even more. Some lands and rank were given for bravery upon the battlefield. The army and the navy offered some hope of advancement for middle-class men, as did the church, but, in both the military and the church, the better posts usually went to the gentry.

The Class System in Maryland

In Maryland, as in most English colonies, there was a great deal of difference between the lives of the wealthy and those of the poor! Today, we visit the old, well-built homes of the well-to-do and think that life back in the 1600's and 1700's was a pretty comfortable affair. This may not be altogether true. Most of Maryland's people lived in small houses and had few comforts. These small farm homes and modest town houses, being less well-built and less valuable and attractive, have not always survived. Many have decayed, burned, or have been torn down.

Thus, there were several classes of people in colonial Maryland; the gentry, the small farmers, tradesmen, bondsmen and bondswomen, servants and slaves. Let us see how their place in life affected them.

The Wealthy

Wealthy families had servants and slaves to do the housework and the farming. The work of the wealthy involved the keeping of records and the planning and supervision of the development of the land and other properties. They were responsible for many people.

The rich lived in beautiful homes and entertained a great deal. They liked to visit one another for long periods. They enjoyed parties, balls, music, racing, cards, and other amusements. The rich wore satins, silks, fine linen, laces, brocades, and wigs.

Food was served with care, style, and in great variety to the wealthy. Wines were popular, as were rums and brandies. These were consumed in considerable quantity. So much rich food and drink was used that gout, sometimes called "the rich man's disease," was not uncommon. The family ate in luxurious dining or breakfast rooms.

Wealthy people had the most comfortable rooms in the house. The servants were given lower rooms or attic rooms which were not so large or convenient. Warm water for bathing was carried up to the members of the wealthy family and chamber pots were carried down.

Tradesmen

Since there was no mass manufacturing of goods, the small tradesman was needed. There was the barber, the hatmaker, the milliner, the tailor, the bootmaker, the silversmith, the saddler who made saddles, bridles and harnesses, the carriage maker, and scores of other tradesmen. There were small taverns in almost every town and many "ordinaries" or places where one could eat and drink.

As in England, the tradesman was often abused by the wealthy customer who did not pay his bills. The tradesman could, of course, legally try to collect. The tradesman could hope to better his condition and one day attain a modest little home, fairly good clothing, and a certain amount of respect from the town.

Servants

Some servants were free men who worked for food, clothing, and shelter and were given a small wage.

Another kind of servant was a bondsman or bondswoman. These were people who had agreed, before leaving England, to work a cer-

(Joseph H. Cromwell, C & P Telephone Company of Maryland)

Doughoregan Manor, the home of the prominent Carroll family of Maryland, still stands near Ellicott City, as this recent photograph shows.

tain number of years to pay their passage to Maryland. Sometimes, before this time was up, a master might not need the bondsman and would sell his services for the unused time. The bondsman then went to the new master and served him. Men of education sometimes bonded themselves in this way, serving as tutors, bookkeepers, secretaries, or store keepers for a master until their debt was repaid. Often this was the only way a man or woman might escape a most uncomfortable way of life in England and the only hope he might have of improving his life and status.

Bondsmen or bondswomen might also be people who were convicted of crimes in England. These people were sometimes offered the choice of staying in prison (and prisons were horrible in those days) or of going out to the colonies as bonded servants. In this way labor to work in the colonies was obtained. Prisoners released in this way, for the most part, gave no trouble. They were glad to work out their sentences and made good free men and women later. Some convicts, however, who had committed the more serious crimes and then were sent out to the colonies did make trouble. Colonial officials often protested the practice of sending such people to Maryland.

Some servants and bondsmen were treated kindly and fairly. Others were overworked, underpaid, and treated very badly.

Small Farmers

Not all settlers who came to Maryland were given large grants of land. Some brought with them few people and little money and so could afford only modest farms. They, however, were frequently dependable colonists determined to succeed. They worked hard, hunted the forests for food, grew crops, and raised animals and poultry. On these small farms, the housewife did her own work if she did not have a servant, as she probably did not. She had to concern herself with many tasks—laundry, dishwashing, food preparation, and sewing. All of these tasks required good and skillful hands.

The children, too, helped with the work, and schooling for them was limited. Indeed, there were few free schools in Maryland, and parents could not usually afford to send children away to school; nor could they afford a tutor. Besides, there were the many tasks at home, demanding their help.

By the time he was eleven or twelve, a farm boy almost always could drive a team of horses, help hitch a span of oxen to a sledge, row a boat, hoe, chop wood, and manage farm animals. Often he was proficient with a gun in the forest or in fishing in streams nearby. Thus, children helped feed the family by bringing home part of the food supply.

Girls learned early to sew, cook, scrub the house, make a good fire, bake bread, and do the laundry. They picked wild berries and made pies with them. They gathered nuts and saved some for the winter. Some fruits and herbs were dried in the sun; some were strung on threads and then hung inside to dry. The older girls helped the mother tend the younger children and helped with many other tasks.

A girl might have a doll, usually a homemade one and not very beautiful, but much loved. To surprise a girl at Christmas, mothers and aunties sewed tiny dresses and bonnets for the doll or made new dolls of wood and cloth. But, by the time a girl was ten or eleven years of age, she was too busy with numerous household tasks to have much time left for her doll.

In this kind of life, children might watch with fascination as a father poured melted lead into molds to make bullets for his gun and as mother poured hot wax into molds to make candles to light the long winter evenings. The children helped, too, with soapmaking, but, like making bullets and candles, it involved fires and melted liquids, which were quite dangerous.

The Bible was the book most likely to be found in a home in early Maryland. Parents who could read, read this and books on religion. If children were taught to read, and many were not, it was usually from the Bible. There were family prayers at mealtimes and often again in the evening. Religion was very much a part of family life.

Education and Training of Children

The children of wealthy families led a quite different life from those who were not rich. The rich usually dressed their children in fashionable clothing and educated them well.

The son of the master of a plantation was taken by his father about the land to learn how to raise tobacco, to direct workers, and to supervise all kinds of farm work. The lad absorbed from his father a love of growing things, an interest in new trees, and good horses, and a skill with firearms.

An educated gentleman was expected to understand more than farming. He must have refined manners, speak good English, know about horses, and perhaps be able to fence (duel with long, slim rapiers). He was expected to know some Latin, have at least a smattering of foreign languages, a background in history, some notions of classical Greek philosophy, and perhaps some idea of the law. The gentleman, also, might have a knowledge of wines and an interest in architecture and the sciences of the day. When he grew up, he would be expected to cast his vote for his representative in the Assembly and perhaps personally serve in the government.

When the son of a rich man was about twelve years of age, if there were no local school good enough or tutor advanced enough, and there generally was not, he would be sent off to school in England or in France. Many of the sons of wealthy Catholic families attended Jesuit schools in Belgium, France, or Italy.

Girls, in contrast, were given quite a different education. They were not sent abroad for their education. They learned at home the proper way to run an elegant house. They learned to read and how to write graceful letters. There were complicated manners to understand and exact forms to use in writing invitations and formal letters.

Girls followed their mothers about and learned how to train servants, how a table should be set for a dinner party, how to prepare bedrooms for guests, and scores of other details. Recipes were handed down from mother to daughter, carefully written out by hand.

Young ladies were expected to be able to dance, recite poetry, sing, make polite conversation, play a musical instrument with grace, and to do fine sewing and embroidering.

Since it was considered unladylike to sit a horse astride, girls and ladies rode sidesaddle. Special saddles were required. This way of riding a horse is not easy and demands wonderful balance and horsemanship. The ladies often became quite skillful and sometimes joined the men in racing on fox hunts, full tilt across pasture, field, and fence.

Pastors, priests, or educated but not wealthy gentlemen often opened private schools. They earned money by teaching the sons from well-to-do families. But, most of these schools were not as satisfactory as most parents would have liked; and, moreover, there were actually few schools in Maryland of any sort in the 1600's and early 1700's. Frequently the best solution seemed to be to hire tutors to live in the home and to teach boys and girls to read and to write. The girls might learn enough arithmetic to help them with their household duties. Boys were taught higher mathematics, Latin, history, and philosophy.

The children born to servants had small chance of learning to read and to write. They were happy, indeed, if by some miracle they did get the opportunity to do so. Perhaps it was the pastor or the priest who found ways to teach a few of these children. Tradesmen in the towns might, in some cases, find a school they could afford for their children. A few months or years of schooling were considered adequate for the sons of these middle-class families. Girls usually received less education if any at all. Children of servants and tradesmen learned a great many practical skills which fitted them to earn a living later on.

Free men were among the first persons of African descent to come to Maryland. Among the first settlers of Maryland were John Price, Mathias Tousa and another man. These were described as servants by historian J. Thomas Scharf as he wrote of the settlement of St. Mary's City in his *History of Maryland*. Also, Father Andrew White, a Jesuit priest, in his narrative of the earliest days of the colony mentions that one of the four servants he brought into Maryland from Virginia in the year 1635 was Francisco, a "molato." We have the names, then, of at least three very early African immigrants to Maryland.

Africans were brought to Virginia as early as 1619 as servants. In Maryland, as in most of the early English colonies, Africans came as servants and slaves. Also, many Europeans came to the colonies as servants and as indentured servants.

Due to the class system that existed in England and to a great extent in the English colonies, neither white nor black servants expected to rise very far in the social order. A servant in those days was expected to remain a servant. Gradually, over the years, the free white man gained more social mobility but the black servant could only hope to be able, sometimes, to earn his way out of bondage and to obtain a little land of his own.

To do all of the hundreds of tasks of the farms, plantations, towns and homes, many workers were needed. Men, both black and white, who were free wanted land for themselves and wanted to work for themselves; so labor was hard to get. Maryland landowners to obtain workers bought them from traders. Captains of ships sent out to buy people in Africa or in the Caribbean were called "slavers." From these men enslaved workers were purchased at Maryland and other colonial ports.

In England in the 1600s, if a person was a slave and was baptized as a Christian, then that person was considered free. To keep black Christians from obtaining their freedom under this law, and yet to be able to give them religious education, the Maryland Assembly passed a number of laws concerning people of African descent in 1664.

These laws made slavery legal in the colony of Maryland. The laws said that black servants could no longer work out their terms of indenture; and, if they had the status of slaves, then they had to remain slaves for life. Another law was directed at marriages and children. Free English women sometimes married black men and these marriages had been recognized under the laws of England. The new rule in Maryland after 1664 declared that if a freeborn English woman married a slave, she herself must serve that man's owner and the children of the marriage would also be slaves . For those women who were presently married to black men, the rule now was that the children must work for the master of the woman's husband until they reached the age of thirty years! Clearly, these laws were made to discourage interracial marriages and also to prevent persons of African descent from working out their terms of service on the same terms as indentured European servants.

In August of 1681, however, the Act of 1663-1664 was repealed. A new Maryland law declared that, thereafter, children born of white mothers and children born of free black mothers were to be free. Before 1692 more laws were enacted in Maryland to try to prevent and punish interracial marriages.

In Maryland other laws were later passed to prohibit English women from marrying black men who were slaves, as well as to prohibit English men from marrying black women. It seems strange to us today, but as recently as 1966 and 1967 these colonial laws against interracial marriage were enforced in Maryland. Finally the General Assembly repealed the old law. As of July 1, 1970, marriage license office personnel in Maryland were no longer required to ask applicants for their racial background.

How They Came

The Royal African Company, formed by English businessmen and chartered by the King of England, had a virtual monopoly on the legal slave trade to North America from 1672 to 1698. By the beginning of the eighteenth century (the 1700s) the import of Africans was increasing and independent traders began to share in the trade. Captured people often had experience in farming in their homelands. They knew how to grow crops and tend livestock. Some also had skills as artisans learned in Africa.

Once in the Americas, workers learned carpentry, metal working, shipbuilding, brickmaking and other trades. African women learned to weave, bake, sew and to nurse children, increasing their original skills. They were valuable workers. Most workers, however, brought to the Maryland colony, both men and women were employed on the thousands of acres of land. To furnish this desired labor, slave trading became one of the world's largest businesses and many fortunes were made in this cruel trade. In one year alone, 1698 , Governor Francis Nicholson reported that 470 more Africans had been imported in the Maryland colony.

The traders sought Africans to fill their ships. Black people were often seized far inland and brought to the African coast by Arab traders, or by black chieftains who had captured them in tribal warfare. Later on, traders themselves headed expeditions to buy more people from villages many miles inland. The villages were normally visited in broad daylight and people for sale purchased on the spot. At times, however, traders would return at night to seize and carry off still more people to fill the ships.

The scenes on these sailing ships were apt to be terrible indeed. The captains were interested in getting as many people onto the ship as possible to make the trip and live through the experience. Even under the most favorable conditions the long trip across the Atlantic was difficult. For the Africans it ranged from miserable to unbearable. There were many deaths due to crowding, disease, shock and ill treatment. The captives were pushed into the dark holds of the ships, chained and taken from all that was familiar and dear to them. It is little wonder then that there were many deaths from despair and suicide. Records reveal as many as 300 to 500 persons were packed aboard some of these sailing ships.

Thousands of Africans came to the Americas from a portion of the western coast of Africa known as the Gold Coast. This area is on the southern side of the great bulge of the African continent which projects out into the Atlantic Ocean. Traders from the northern colonies in North America, who were called Yankees, found the Gold Coast trade pretty well monopolized. The Yankee trader was likely then to round the southern tip of Africa and set up bases on the island of Madagascar, just off the southeastern coast of Africa. There they found African traders waiting with many captives to sell.

Black Immigrants Enrich Their New Land

The unfortunate African, captured and sold into bondage, was able to bring nothing with him (or her) to America in the way of worldly possessions. Yet the African did bring, if an adult, a certain amount of "cultural baggage." If only a young person, the African was uprooted and separated from his tribe, and so lost much knowledge of African ways. Yet, considerable knowledge of farming, herding, irrigation and other agricultural skills was carried to the Americas in the minds of these Africans.

Some remembered, too, a good deal of their rich unwritten African literature—stories, legends, proverbs, riddles and ideas that had been passed down by word of mouth for generations. The uprooted African did not always forget his old religious beliefs and his old customs. For

57

that matter, African songs, dancing, new rhythms and ways of singing were to greatly influence the development of a uniquely American music. The folklore of the people from Africa became a part of American folklore. Later, the influence of African art was to be felt in both Europe and the Americas.

Black Pioneers

As the African boys grew up in Maryland, some took care of the farm or plantation buildings. Some cared for livestock and poultry. Others worked in the fields tending food, forage and tobacco crops. A few of the young men were brought to the great house of the plantation owner. There they learned to be butlers, valets, waiters and gardeners. Some learned to work with metal, wood and stone as skilled artisans.

Some of the African girls were trained to do household work. They were taught customs to observe and learned about cooking, keeping a home bright and clean. They might act as kitchen workers, or serve in the dining room. Some acted as ladies maids. They helped keep linens and clothing clean and pressed. Some made clothing for the owner's family and for workers and became expert seamstresses.

Many of the African women were sent to work in the fields. Some worked in the kitchens where food for the workers was prepared. Women were adept in processing the tobacco crops.

If an African worker lived in a town they were apt to work in a shop or in a home.

There was a sort of class system among the African workers. House servants felt a bit above the artisan; but the artisan believed that he was a bit above the coachman or herdsman; and the field worker ranked lowest of all. Their clothing reflected this rank with the house servant quite nicely dressed and the field worker having only very rough, plain clothing to wear.

Much depended on the man who owned the African workers. He might be very kind, or he might be very cruel. In America the black people learned and watched. Some appeared content but most wished that there were some way that they could be free.

Servants in Maryland

In colonial days in America, servants were paid very little. They were often glad to get any sort of employment, however, for the alternative was hunger and want. All across Europe and the Americas, servants were often treated very badly. In Maryland, it seems, they did have some privileges.

Father Andrew White in his *Narratives of Early Maryland* tells us that in 1655, "Servant's complaints are freely harkened to and their masters compelled to amend or set slave free." It would appear that servants fared better in Maryland than in England. About five years of service was generally needed to repay an indentured servant's passage money. Some indentures were longer. Many masters would allot to their indentured servants a plot of ground on which to grow tobacco, to raise vegetables or to raise cattle, pigs or chickens. If the servant worked hard, he could earn and save quite a nice sum of money by the time he was set free. Harsh masters, on the other hand, would free servants at the end of their terms with the least possible equipment and clothing.

In general, in Maryland the labor of both men and women servants, though very hard by today's standards, was not as hard as in England. There servants often worked from before daylight until after dark. In Maryland, Saturday afternoon was often a servant's time off, as were Sundays and some holidays.

Letters written back to England from Maryland commented on the fact that servants were treated fairly well. The people from England also wrote back there to remark on the bright, mild Maryland weather. They were impressed, too, by the abundance of every kind of animal, fish and fowl. They marveled at the vast stretches of land in America.

In the American colonies a subtle change was taking place. There was still a rigid class structure but there were ways of working one's way up in the system. Sharing the work and hardships of the new land earned the common man or woman respect and more rights in the New World.

CHAPTER XIV

FIRST HOMES

IN St. Mary's City the first homes were quite small. The only tools were axes, hand saws, adzes, wedges, and hammers. Building even a small house was quite a time-consuming process. Since nails were handmade and not plentiful, wooden pegs were often used instead. Each end of the peg was heated and then it was inserted into the hole. When the peg later absorbed water, it would fit tightly.

Many of the small cottages had earthen floors. Rough tables and benches could be made by driving stout stakes into the floor and fastening rough planks across them. Walls were built of planks or bricks. (Log cabins came into use in later years, mostly for frontier homes or outbuildings.) Beds, too, could be made with two stakes supporting one side of the bed and the other side fastened to the wall.

Every home had to have a fireplace for heating and cooking. Often these gave most of the winter and evening light as well. Pine knots, candles, and later, lanterns were used for light.

The first windows often were covered with oiled paper or thin, scraped animal skins. These let in a little light. Settlers kept their windows small at first in order to defend their homes more easily.

Shingles to cover roofs were made by splitting off pieces of wood from short logs. There was stone to construct fireproof chimneys, and clay suitable for brick making was found.

Since wood was so abundant and easy to get, even the larger homes were not always made entirely of brick. Great chimneys and the end walls were most frequently made of brick, while the longer walls were often made of wood.

After the first few years the wealthy settlers were able to build homes more like the comfortable ones they had left in England. The number and size of the chimneys was a sign of substance, wealth, and prestige. So, though at first the homes were all built with only one or two rooms, plus perhaps, a loft above, soon larger houses came to be built.

A look at surviving colonial homes shows that kitchens were not very convenient. Kitchens of the larger homes were set apart from the main building; sometimes they were in an entirely separate structure. They might be connected to the main house by just a roof. This separation was to prevent loss by fire. In some homes, the kitchens were located down a winding stair, frequently quite a long way from the dining room.

Each home must have some kind of water supply. A good spring or a clear stream would serve. If these were not available, a well had to be dug and the water hauled up by a bucket tied to the end of a rope or chain. Water had to be heated over open fires outside, or in a fireplace pot.

To keep milk, butter, cheeses and other things cool, many households had a "spring-house," which had a cool stream of water flowing through its foundation. Milk and other foods were set down into this water in clean containers or trays and, thus, did not spoil so quickly. Many larger homes sported strange little structures on the lawn, half-buried in the ground. If you looked inside you would see that the floor was well below the surface of the ground. These were designed to keep ice. Ice was cut in the winter and stored in these little houses, insulated with straw.

Inside the homes, furniture was a problem. The gentry had fine furniture shipped over from England. Other people had to build much of their own furniture. As the colony grew, cabinet-makers came to Maryland and gradually the furniture in the homes improved.

Even the fine homes sometimes lacked a windowpane or an essential bit of china, for almost everything manufactured had to be imported across the hundreds of miles of ocean from Europe.

It was not long before housewives planted near their homes the seeds and roots brought so carefully from England. Flowers and shrubs grew well in the mild climate and rewarded the women with their gay, familiar colors all summer. Owners of large estates laid out quite formal gardens.

Terraces, called "falls," led down in easy stages to the owner's wharf, which was called the "landing." Through the gardens ran straight walks called "forthrights" which led down to the landings or to summerhouses or to little "necessaries," or to circles of box-wood and imported trees.

Boxwood was used to edge flower beds. Imagine the beauty of a clipped, grassy walk, a dark green boxwood border, and overflowing the flower beds—flowers grown from English seeds. Remembering their English homes, the colonists planted English trees, hedges, ivy, and yew.

The Governor's Castle (St. Peter's) at St. Mary's City

The largest house of its time in the colonies was the "Governor's

Castle," built in St. Mary's City. The brick house was begun late in 1638 and was completed in the first months of 1640. The building has disappeared, but stories were passed down of the building and its location. Its fifty-five-year life was an active one and the end of the mansion, a dramatic one!

"Governor's Castle" was built by Thomas Cornwallis. In 1659, however, he sailed to England and did not return. His mansion stood waiting in St. Peter's field until, five years later, a new owner was named. This was Chancellor Philip Calvert, an uncle of Charles, the second Lord Proprietor. For the next twenty years the house was called "The Chancellor's House at St. Peters."

We get a little ahead of our story here, but we want to tell you what happened to this interesting place. When the Chancellor died in 1682, the house was left to his nephew Charles Calvert, who was now the colorful Third Baron of Baltimore and the second Lord Proprietor. Charles Calvert lived in Maryland in a kingly fashion, surrounded by courtiers and every luxury. After he returned to England, it is believed that Sir Lionel Copley lived at the Castle while he served as Maryland's first royal governor from 1691 to 1693.

Copley's governorship was a strange one. He was blamed for wrongly taking Maryland funds and for dishonesty in his dealings with the Indians. In fact, legend has it that one of the Indian chiefs was so despairing of justice that he cut his throat in the kitchen of the "Governor's Castle" in 1693! But now the house was near the end of its life.

Royal Governor Sir Francis Nicholson (1694-1698) in October 1694, had forced through the Assembly a bill to make Annapolis the capital of Maryland. Some believe that this was the reason that "The Castle" was destroyed by seventeen kegs of gunpowder stored beneath it. At any rate the building was "blown sky-high." As the years passed, its bricks were taken for other buildings or crumbled into the ground.

It was not until September of 1940 that the existence of this very early American building was proved. Dr. Henry Chandlee Forman, architect, historian and author, began to supervise digging to try to find the historic mansion, rumored to have been built back from the river bluff at St. Mary's City. Nothing could be seen above ground, but by exploratory trenches Dr. Forman discovered the brick foundation in the middle of a tobacco field. He found that it had been a large square building, fifty-four feet to a side. It had been two stories tall. Its narrow casement windows had had diamond-shaped window panes. Tall chimneys were constructed from the front to the back of the great house. A small spiral stairway gave access to upper rooms. It was a style of building called "Jacobean." Outside was a grassy sweep of walled courtyard. It must have been a most impressive building.

Surviving Colonial Buildings

Maryland has a really amazing number of colonial homes which are still in good condition. In Annapolis there are streets lined with colonial homes and buildings. As we mentioned before, few houses of the poor remain.

Several homes in Maryland are open to the public and are well worth viewing. One can see the fine workmanship and carving of the great rooms and dining halls, and the complicated brickwork of outside walls, as well as the great chimneys. It is probably true that Maryland gentlemen liked to make impressions on their friends; and they wanted to live in a gracious, luxurious style.

It is a tribute to their determination and optimism that these people, thousands of miles from their English homeland, with thousands of miles of wild forest and mountains to the west, were able to build for themselves an English style of living in a new land.

Puritans Find Refuge

Getting back to our story of the settlement of Maryland, we notice that, in 1642, a group of people known as Puritans were living in Virginia. They had been doing well there. Now, however, they were asked to take religious oaths to which they seriously objected. Lord Baltimore already had made it clear that these people were welcome to come to Maryland, with equal civil rights under the Proprietor's protection. Very few at first accepted.

But, after more difficulties both political and religious in Virginia, in the spring and summer of 1649, and during the following year, about three hundred people came to Maryland. They settled at a place on the Severn River, near the present site of Annapolis, which they called "Providence."[1]

The Puritans were granted large tracts of land. They were given the right of local self-government, religious freedom, and equal civil rights. Had not government forces from England interfered later, Maryland might have continued to enjoy religious peace and freedom with Anglicans, Puritans, Catholics, and others living and working together.[2]

---

1 Old Providence Town is no longer in existence.
2 Matthew Page Andrews, **History of Maryland, Province and State.**

CHAPTER XV

THE CLOAK-AND-DAGGER YEARS
(1643-1657)

THE sweeping changes that occurred in Maryland from 1643 to 1657 may seem to read more like fiction than fact! Even today students find it difficult to keep track of all of the dramatic events that took place in those years.

More and more people had come to Maryland to enjoy the freedoms here and the wonderful chance to own their own land and to escape many of the hardships of England. In England, too, in this period the country was boiling with unrest. So uneasy was the atmosphere in England, in fact, that Governor Leonard Calvert sailed for home in 1643, because of his fear of what these changes might mean for the Maryland colony. Governor Calvert soon learned that Puritan forces, led by Oliver Cromwell, were about to take over the government of England from King Charles I. The unfortunate King Charles I had been imprisoned in 1641.

And now, in Maryland, in 1643, William Claiborne thought he saw his chance to take advantage of the unrest in England to re-establish himself in force at Kent Island. He had always regarded the island as his property and had felt that it had been taken from him unfairly. At the same time a trader, Richard Ingle, swooped down on St. Mary's City with an armed ship. He captured the little city. The crew of his ship, "like pirates" the residents claimed, robbed homes and burned some houses. They broke into the house where the Assembly met and stole the great silver Seal of Maryland. To this day, the Seal has not been found. Even worse, the records of the first ten years of the colony were burned, or scattered and lost.

Father White was seized. With chains on his arms and legs he was sent back to England. As a Catholic priest he was to stand trial before Cromwell's Puritan government, for Catholicism was forbidden by that government.

In England, Father White eventually was declared not guilty of wrongdoing, but he was sent out of the country (exiled) and forbidden to preach there again. This, nevertheless, did not stop this strong Maryland colonizer. He managed, later, to come back to England, much to the embarrassment of certain members of the Puritan government, and true to his faith, Father White preached and worked to a ripe old age in spite of more opposition. His reports and writings are still one of our best sources of information about Maryland's early days.

In Maryland, in the 1640's, the peaceful days were at an end! Not only was the government in danger but warriors of the Susquehannock Indians began to go on the warpath. Hourly, homes and farms were threatened by bands of Indians, armed not only with clubs, spears, bows and arrows, but with European guns and knives as well. Fear of death, of homes burned, of families murdered, and of Indian torture swept the small foothold the English held in Maryland.

In 1644, the colonists felt more hopeful as Governor Calvert came back from England with fresh instructions from his brother Cecil Calvert, the Proprietor. Governor Calvert tried to recapture the government of his Maryland colony, but Ingle and his followers were too strong. Governor Calvert was forced to flee to Virginia where he awaited a chance to take back his government again.

The next two years were hard for him. Every day, it seemed, news filtered into Virginia of disorder in Maryland, Indians raiding, and robbery and injustice from "that pirate Ingle," as he was sometimes called. It was a time of harsh government for Maryland settlers.

In 1646 the time was ripe, Governor Calvert felt, to regain the colony. And so it was, for Leonard Calvert was able to come back to St. Mary's City with little trouble. Soon, too, he was able to drive the men working for Claiborne off Kent Island. The island for a long time had been a breeding ground of trouble for the Calvert government.

Governor Calvert set to work, putting down the Indian raiders, calming the people, and working to bring order and justice back to Maryland. Trade began to pick up, and farms began to yield profits again. But Governor Calvert did not have long to enjoy his Maryland home. In June of 1647, he died in St. Mary's City, surrounded by his family and his friends.

Mistress Margaret Brent

Before he died, Leonard Calvert did a most unusual thing for that day and age. He made his female relative, Mistress Margaret Brent, his sole executor, telling her to "Take all and pay all." An executor is one who carries out the provisions of a will.

The soldiers, hired by the Governor to regain control of Maryland, were beginning to mutter and talk of taking over the colony because they had not been paid. Mistress Brent calmed them. She quickly sold some cattle belonging to the Calvert family and paid the soldiers. Her manner and leadership must have been unusual for it earned the respect of the soldiers, and old records state that but for her action "the colony would have been ruined."

This was not Mistress Brent's first executive job. She and her sister, Mary, had come to Maryland in 1638. They brought nine colonists with them and were given considerable land. To get more workers and more land, they sent back to England for more colonists. They called their home "Sister's Freehold." A brother, Giles, often stayed with them. It was to "Sister's Freehold," that the little Indian princess, whom they named Mary, had been brought for her education in 1641. Mistress Margaret Brent was one of America's first women to own land in her own name. She managed her plantation very well.

She must have been a charming woman for one suitor thought so much of her that he left her some property in his will. But, at that moment, Mistress Margaret Brent was busy acting virtually as Treasurer of the colony, as well as the legal representative of Lord Baltimore and his dead brother, the Governor.

When the Assembly met in the year 1648 in St. Mary's City, Mistress Brent appeared before the men gathered there and asked for the right to vote. Because of this she is often called America's first suffragist; and indeed this was a new idea—namely, the vote for a woman! Despite her unquestioned ability and the respect for her among her friends, this request was too much for the men of that day. They were shocked and refused to allow this to happen. Women vote? It was unthinkable!

Yet, had not Nicholas Causine, in the Assembly of 1641, risen to present a strong plea for the justice of permitting a woman to own property after marriage and to own in her own name, property she had owned before marriage?[1] It must be remembered that a husband at that time had complete control, not only of his wife, but of her property, too.

Though the Assembly turned down Margaret Brent's request for the right to vote, it was necessary for her to come before the Assembly several times with respect to the business of the colony and other legal matters. In doing this she may be thought of as being America's first woman attorney.

The little Indian princess, Mary, when grown to young womanhood, agreed to marry Giles Brent. It was thought possible that the princess might become Queen of the Piscataway Indians, as her father, the Indian Emperor, had hoped. She was not destined, however, to become an Indian queen and perhaps the richest landowner in America; but rather, she lived out her life as the wife of Giles

Brent and the mother of his children.

Eventually, Mistress Brent, her sister Mary, her brother Giles, and his wife, the princess Mary, moved to Virginia to live. There, on a plantation called "Peace," Mistress Brent made her will in 1663. She died about ten years after this.

New Governors

Thomas Greene, a Royalist (one partial to the King), a plantation owner, and a Catholic, was to serve as Maryland's governor for about a year after the death of Leonard Calvert. Then Lord Baltimore replaced him with William Stone, a Protestant and probably a Puritan, so gaining a representative who was friendly with the ever more powerful Parliament in England. This concession, it was hoped, would help to protect Lord Baltimore's control of Maryland. Again, politics in England affected events in Maryland. In 1649 William Stone took up his duties as Governor in St. Mary's City.[2]

The Toleration Act

One of the last important documents that Cecil Calvert was to write for his Maryland colony was the final part of the "Toleration Act," which was to be passed by the Maryland Assembly of 1649. As one reads both parts of the Act, one finds that the first part sounds more like the work of George Calvert, First Lord Baltimore, so Cecil Calvert may have used some of his father's ideas for this part.

In Maryland, in April, 1649, the men were called to the Assembly. Most arrived at St. Mary's City by boat. Some walked or rode in, splashing through muddy trails from plantations and farms. Among the laws they worked on that session was "An Act Concerning Religion."

This Act is unique to Maryland, for as we have mentioned before, the English colonists in the other North American colonies of the English, were inclined to be very intolerant indeed. In a way the Act may seem intolerant to us today, for it does not advise tolerance of those persons who are not of the Christian religion.[3] Still, for its day and for a long time afterward, the Toleration Act, as it came to be called, was very liberal.

The first part of the Act said that persons denying the divinity of Jesus Christ should suffer death. It said, too, that people taunting others on account of their religion should be fined or whipped; and that persons not keeping Sunday as a day of rest and worship should be fined or put into prison.

The second part of the Act directed that no person in Maryland should be in any way troubled or interfered with on account of his or her religion. Further, said the second part of the Act, freedom of worship is not to be denied anyone believing in Jesus Christ.

Maryland became known as a haven for persons of the Christian faith, who wanted religious freedom. So it can be understood why Maryland came to be called the "land of sanctuary."

Governor Stone's Troubled Years

Oliver Cromwell was growing more and more powerful in England. In the year 1649, King Charles I was led from his prison cell to die. His head was chopped off by the executioner's axe.

Cromwell sent to Maryland four Commissioners, in 1652, to see that the colony obeyed the new Parliamentary (Puritan-controlled) government; and one of these Commissioners, as it turned out, was William Claiborne! When the Commissioners tried to take over the government of Maryland from Governor Stone, however, the people were so obviously angry that Governor Stone was allowed to continue to govern from 1652 to 1654.

Governor Stone was a patient man, and cooperated with the Commissioners while waiting for instructions from Lord Baltimore. When the letter came to "take charge of Maryland in the name of Lord Baltimore," Stone took immediate action. Messengers were sent to ride out to gather colonists loyal to Lord Baltimore.

Now it was one thing for the Commissioners to let Governor Stone work for them, and quite another thing to let him take his orders from Lord Baltimore. Claiborne and his friend, Richard Bennett, were shocked to hear of this new turn of events. Claiborne was an extremely able person, and though he had been quick to regain control of his Maryland lands on Kent Island, he had not been as harsh toward the Maryland colonists who had fought him as might have been expected. Now, however, Claiborne and Bennett hurried to Providence, the Puritan's town on the Severn River. They returned to St. Mary's City with a large body of Puritans and succeeded in driving Governor Stone from Maryland. The Puritans with Claiborne, now ruled in reality. They proved to be cruel and harsh in their government. Catholic families were forbidden to worship openly in the Roman Catholic churches. Many Catholics built into their homes small family chapels. Also, in some homes, by chimneys, in attics, and inside walls, were small hiding places in which priests could take refuge, if necessary.

Governor Stone did not rest. He soon prepared twelve small boats; and, in March, 1655, he set out to attack the Puritan town of Providence. Stone did not forsee the fact that, as he went up the Severn River, a sea captain, Captain Roger Heamans, of London, would be able to swing his big ship, the *Golden Lion*, across the channel. This big ship and a smaller trading vessel from New England so blocked the river that Stone and his men were forced to make a land attack. Their retreat route back to Chesapeake Bay also had been closed.

But once ashore Stone's determined men charged the Puritans, shouting, "Hail for St. Mary's!" From Providence 120 Puritan soldiers pushed forward calling out, "In the name of God fall on! God is our strength!" You can see that the fate of Maryland in those days often depended on only a few dozen men. Though faced with trained soldiers, at first Governor Stone's men did well. Then the Governor was wounded and captured, and his men were defeated.

Following the Battle of the Severn, as the engagement at Providence came to be known, the Parliamentary Commissioners appointed William Fuller and the Council to govern Maryland from 1654 to 1657. Maryland was truly ruled now by the Puritans, and the people of other faiths must now practice their religion secretly.

1 Katherine Scarborough, **Homes of the Cavaliers.**
2 Governors of Maryland at this time may be listed as follows: Thomas Greene, 1647-1649; William Stone, 1649-1652; Parliamentary Commissioners, 1652; William Stone, 1652-1654.
3 In his lectures at the University of Maryland, Dr. Verne E. Chatelain, emeritus professor of History, points out the fact that the first days of the settlement of St. Mary's City were marked by a more complete religious toleration than is granted in the famed "Toleration Act."

Letters were written with a quill pen. Ink was blotted by shaking sand from a shaker. There were no envelopes. Letters were folded and sealed with melted wax into which the writer pressed a seal, insignia or his signet ring.

CHAPTER XVI

STRUGGLE FOR POWER 1657-1676

I T seemed to many, after Governor Stone's defeat, that the Puritan government of Maryland would never end. For six long years (1652-1658) these bitter enemies of Lord Baltimore ruled the colony. Everyone in Maryland was supposed to support the Puritan beliefs. It seems strange to us today to think that Christians could so oppress one another — that a religion of brotherly love could be so misunderstood. Still, the people had to wait for better days.

In England, Oliver Cromwell, now Lord Protector and head of the Parliamentary government, heard two things at about the same time. He had before him a growing pile of reports on the injustices being inflicted on the people of Maryland by the Puritan-led government there. He was listening, too, to Lord Baltimore's requests that the government of Maryland be returned to the Calvert family, and so after carefully considering the matter, Cromwell decided to act. He notified Lord Baltimore that Maryland was once again to be under Lord Baltimore's control.

News of this soon reached Maryland. Yet it was six months before the Puritans could be subdued and the government of Maryland returned to Lord Baltimore, in the year 1658. Now it was hoped that peace and religious freedom would return to the Chesapeake Bay colony.

Times were still unsettled, for men were questioning whether to be loyal to the English Parliament or to the exiled English heir to the throne, Charles. Oliver Cromwell died in September 1658 and his son, Richard Cromwell, became Protector. Richard held the office for less than a year. It was a time of unrest when men wondered where their loyalties might lay and whether it might not just be best to get for themselves all the power and wealth possible.

This was the situation when Josias Fendall, appointed as Lord Baltimore's representative, began to govern the colony. In the next two years he began to scheme and plot. He was not loyal to the Baltimores. Whether he wanted power for himself or whether he wanted to make Maryland independent of England, we do not know. We do know that he tried to make laws as he pleased. Thanks to the men of the Assembly, he did not succeed for long. When Lord Baltimore learned of this scheming, Fendall was dismissed.

Again, Lord Baltimore selected a brother to govern Maryland, Philip Calvert. Philip governed from 1660 to 1661 and then turned the colony over to his nephew — another member of the family, the next governor, Charles Calvert. Charles was a son of Cecil Calvert, the Lord Proprietor of Maryland and Second Lord Baltimore.

Charles Calvert arrived with a kingly court of high ranking gentlemen and ladies and with scores of servants. To the colonists his royal manner of living was most glamorous. He lived in the best of houses, among them the "Castle" at St. Mary's City mentioned earlier. He built hunting lodges with hundreds, even thousands, of acres of land about them. Blooded horses, fine wines, satins, brocades, and laces were shipped in great quantity to the various Calvert households. In Maryland, as in England where King Charles II had been restored to the throne in 1660, this luxurious way of living was colorful, interesting, and welcome after the hard rule of the stern Puritans.

During the governorship of Charles Calvert, from 1661 to 1676, trade prospered, people came to Maryland; the number of plantations and farms grew. He governed well though the Puritans continued to plot for power, and many complaints were heard about his putting so many of his relatives into office. Still, his government of Maryland seems to have been one that made most of the colonists happy. At least under his rule there seems to have been steady and orderly governing of the colony.

An essential requirement for prosperity, it should be remembered, is a stable, dependable government.

Under this new governor, Charles Calvert, there was a continuation of the Calvert family policy of granting religious toleration.

The Death of Maryland's Friend

Cecil Calvert, Second Lord Baltimore, died in 1675. Governor Charles Calvert, his son, then had to return to England. Travel by sailing ship was so slow that it was 1676 before he could get to England and assume his duties as the Third Lord Baltimore.

For forty-one years Cecil Calvert had worked to make the Maryland colony a successful one. In spite of the rise and fall of English kings, and in spite of many who tried to influence the English government against the Calvert family, Cecil Calvert had given the colony for the most part, a stable government which enabled it to grow and prosper.

Cecil Calvert had studied many reports and letters from Maryland. Cecil wanted to visit his American colony but never saw it himself. All his life it had been important that he keep an eye on political events in England.

It was Cecil Calvert who had planned to send the right supplies at the right times, who had recruited people of wealth, and who had gotten trained workmen to go to Maryland. From the Calvert family estates elsewhere had come much money to help Maryland through its first years. You will remember that the colony of Avalon continued to exist until just two years before Cecil Calvert died. The Avalon colony was burned by the Dutch in 1673.[1] Cecil Calvert had had to manage the affairs of that colony, as well as those of Maryland and of the Baltimore estates in Ireland.

At Cecil Calvert's direction, all kinds of birds, animals, and plants had been sent to him in England. In turn, he had encouraged settlers to bring to Maryland favorite English trees, shrubs, and crops to see how they would grow in America.

Though Cecil Calvert had objected at first to self-government in Maryland he had let it develop there. The right of self-government had made considerable gains under the Calvert family rule, though really the Calverts would have preferred a more "status quo," that is, leaving the power in the hands of the Proprietor as it earlier had been under the Charter.

The Calvert family sought freedom to worship as Catholics in Maryland. This was one of the main reasons for seeking an American colony. Unlike other founding families, however, they did not try to impose their own religion on others.

---

1 The colony of Avalon was neglected and disappeared after the 1673 fire. In 1754, Frederick Calvert, the Sixth Lord Baltimore, tried to revive the claim, but it was denied.

Leonard Calvert Monument in St. Mary's County where colonists first assembled.

CHAPTER XVII

CRIME AND PUNISHMENT IN COLONIAL DAYS

T HE "good old days" were not so good for criminals in colonial Maryland! To understand those days one must not study just the pleasant customs, but rather recognize some of the cruel practices that existed. Not only do technology, transportation, and agricultural techniques improve, but so may government techniques change for the better.

In England, the mother country, punishments were cruel in colonial days. A servant, a slave, or a poor man faced severe penalties for even small crimes. Men of rank and wealth usually fared better! Let us take a look now at a part of Maryland history that was not pretty or quaint, but that nonetheless did exist.

Jails and Punishments

At first there was no need for a jail; but, as soon as Maryland became more settled it became the custom to provide one for each town of any size. The jail was likely to be the first of the public buildings built. Sometimes these had rooms made of thick planks, equipped with iron rings to hold chains. Prisoners were chained partly to prevent their escape and partly as a part of their punishment. A sheriff when it was thought necessary, might keep prisoners in his house or in one of his outbuildings.

On plantations, too, there was almost always some place to confine unruly slaves or servants. In a house in Bladensburg, Prince George's County, once a busy, inland port, one can see the iron rings set into a basement wall for this purpose. Cells for prisoners or slaves were often dark, damp, and almost airless, and were often infested with lice and rats.

Near the local jail and courthouse was the grim whipping post. Colonial judges felt that men in jail were an expense to the public (as they certainly were), and so the authorities often ordered whippings rather than jail sentences. Indeed, when the judge sat in his court, he frequently ordered the emptying of the jail, giving death sentences for serious crimes and whippings for others until the jails were cleared out.

Some settlements had a pillory, or stocks. The person to be punished was held by his head and hands, and sometimes by his feet, too, in a wooden device and left in public view for a stated time. This does not sound too bad until you think about it. The prisoner in the pillory couldn't brush away the swarms of mosquitoes and flies from his face and hands. Any passerby could throw mud, stones or rotten vegetables at him. Anyone could stop to jeer and taunt him. Cages were sometimes used instead of pillories.

Slave blocks, made of stone or big chunks of wood, were placed near the jail. Here slaves were offered for sale. While they awaited sale day, they also were likely to be kept in the jail, or perhaps in "slave pens." Newspapers and handbills in the 1700's and early 1800's advertised the wares of the slave dealer and the time and date of the sales.

Branding, too, was a punishment used in colonial days. There was searing pain as the branding iron burned the skin of the criminal's hand, forehead, or cheek. There was the more lasting pain and humiliation of bearing the brand for life. The letter "T" meant that the man had been convicted of being a thief. The letter "P" was used for liars or perjurers.

Convicts, as we mentioned before, were sent from England to Maryland and other colonies, though the colonial governments often protested the practice. In England, a man or woman could be sentenced to hang for quite a small theft or other wrongdoing. Judges, reluctant to hang these people, were apt to give them a choice of either hanging in England or working out a sentence in America. This was an easy choice for the prisoner! When the crime was that of murder, or one of great violence, the convict was more apt to be dealt with in England and not deported to America. Many of the convicts who came to the colonies became valuable citizens and happy ones; though some, of course, did not.

Witchcraft

In Maryland the people may have been superstitious, but the colony escaped the rash of witchcraft trials that broke out in New England. Perhaps there was less superstition in Maryland. So, in spite of the unfortunate end of an old woman, Elizabeth Richardson, accused of witchcraft and executed aboard the ship *Charity* on its way to Maryland, it is a fact that trials for witchcraft were rare in Maryland. In 1685 there was one such trial, which indicates that some probably shared a belief in witchcraft.

A woman called Rebecca Fowler was indicted (formally charged) by a grand jury on September 29, 1685. She was accused of causing through exercising supernatural powers, bodily harm to many people. Her victims were said to "waste away" and die as a result of her sorceries, so said the grand jury. At her trial she rose and pleaded "not guilty." She denied using charms, witchcraft, or sorcery of any kind. Then evidence was heard of the strange deaths of her victims. It seemed to some that she had had a part in bringing certain people to unnatural and untimely ends. Yet, after hearing her accusers and the witnesses, the jury had difficulty in saying that she was a witch. In the end, the jury spoke, saying they believed that Rebecca Fowler was guilty of the facts of the case, but whether or not this was witchcraft, they did not know.

This placed the decision in the hands of the judges. These men, well educated for their day, thought the matter over, and then agreed that she should be sentenced to be hanged. This grim sentence was carried out on October 9, 1685. It won for Rebecca Fowler the doubtful distinction of being the only person in Maryland ever to be executed for witchcraft. In Maryland, there were laws against witchcraft or the practice of sorcery, and one might be given, if convicted, a sentence of death, life imprisonment, or exile.

The Drinking Problem

Drunkenness also was a problem in the colony. Too much wine, rums, and other alcoholic beverages caused much "disturbance of the peace" in the settlements. All too often, too, it led to other crimes, just as it still does today.

In England wine or ale was served at mealtimes as a beverage. Considering the fact that the water supplies were so often contaminated, perhaps this was not such a bad idea. But men usually drank freely of many strong liquors. Casks of "spirits" were carried on trips and were carefully guarded.

In the colonies there did seem to be a bit of a trend toward temperance. The religious feelings of the colonists perhaps had an influence. Or perhaps it was just a matter of pride for a strong man to refuse to drink too much. A visitor to Maryland wrote that it was "no longer the custom of the host to force his guests to drink until they could scarcely stand. Nor was it a point of honor to send them home reeling in the saddle."

Still, courts of law in the 1600's and 1700's often had to punish men for acts of violence or cruelty committed while under the influence of alcohol. With the passing of the years, Maryland people came to respect the temperate man more and more. Practices and customs in America could change and were changing.

Crimes Against Workers

Though servants fared better in Maryland than in England, as we have mentioned, still many cruelties occurred. The court records show that Maryland masters were frequently brought to trial for neglecting workers when they were sick, for "beatings without cause", and for other mistreatment.

When a man or woman servant died as a result of a beating, the master was apt to be rebuked and fined. Today, of course, he would be tried for murder. Sadly, such violence against servants and slaves did happen all too often. The fact that the Maryland laws took a stand against such deeds was at least a step in the right direction and gave the workers some protection. Justice possibly was on its way, even though many crimes against workers still went unpunished on lonely plantations and farms.

Judges and manor owners sentenced men to be punished by whipping.

Stocks near the town jail.

CHAPTER XVIII

MEDICINE IN COLONIAL TIMES

A look at a list of illnesses common in America about 1638, makes us realize how miserable and uncertain life could be in colonial times. Diseases to be treated or endured were: ague, fevers, dropsy, scurvy, toothache, abcesses, ulcers, cankers, boils, sores, apoplexy, dysentery, insanity, scaly heads, and itches! The persons who treated the ill were poorly trained for the work, being mostly members of the barbering profession! The very few colonial physicians were known as chirurgeons. They had not only disease to treat, but cuts, gunshot wounds, and bruises suffered in fights and accidents.

Children suffered from rickets and scurvy because they lacked sunshine in the winter months or because they did not drink citrus juices or get enough milk. Smallpox and influenza all too frequently swept through the colonies. Mosquitoes carried malaria and other fevers, though the doctors of that time did not know this. Rather, the doctors suspected bad air from swamps as the cause of these fevers. Epidemics of various sorts carried off hundreds of people in the first two hundred years of the American colonial era.

Indians, too, died off by the thousands of measles, tuberculosis, and other diseases brought to America by the Europeans. In turn, new settlers were thought to be sick with mysterious illnesses from which they either died or came to adjust to in the new land!

If one had a toothache, about the only treatment was to have it pulled out. Unfortunately there was no painkiller save whiskey and opium. Only a few of the rich had dental plates. These fitted poorly and were made of wood, ivory, and metals. Many men and women had badly decayed teeth. A toothless old age was not uncommon.

Since there was no anesthetic save opium and whiskey, all surgery was a very frightening and serious matter. It was not painless as it is today with our modern anesthetics. Indeed, surgery was so extremely crude that patients often died of shock and infection, following even "successful" operations. Yet, some survived, for seamen with wooden "peg legs" or arms that ended in a hook to substitute for a missing hand were often seen on the waterfronts of Annapolis, and later, Baltimore.

In the early days in Maryland priests, with herbs, did their best to heal the sick. In each family, too, housewives had their favorite home remedies to treat illnesses. It is hard to say which, if one had a choice, one would choose — the mysterious and deadly illnesses, or the frightening medical treatments at hand.

When a colonist was ill, he was nursed at home by the family and the servants. Only when one was terribly sick did the family try to get a doctor to come to see the patient. In 1640, chirurgeons were often barbers combining surgical and medical work with their haircuts and shaves! Yet, even these crude physicians were in demand. Any help is better than none when one is dying. In return for his services, the chirurgeon was often paid in tobacco.

Treatment included bloodletting, purges, emetics, sweat-producing drugs, and the application of live leeches. In fact the widespread use of this obnoxious treatment caused physicians to be called "leeches." Wounds were sometimes sealed by burning them with a red hot iron. Many men died as much from shock at this treatment as from the wound.

Perhaps a little more helpful, or at least less harmful, were sleeping drugs called dormatives, usually opium. There were herbal salves, plasters, ointments, oils, and herb baths, too, that were considered useful.

It is hard to say where medical treatment left off and superstition took over in those days. Necklaces were worn to prevent diseases. Pills of every description were sold to prevent colds, coughs, and "consumption" (tuberculosis). Salves which claimed the power to heal rheumatism, sprains, and bruises were sold! Now all of these remedies would have been fine if they had worked, but few were helpful. Perhaps, however, they did serve to comfort people. With a little bag of herbs against one's chest to ward off disease, and a rabbit's foot in one's pocket to ward off bad luck, one could go about the day's work with an easy mind!

Most helpful to good health, though the colonists did not realize it, was the pure water, fresh air, uncrowded living space, the bountiful meat, fish and vegetable foods available, plus the considerable exercise involved in daily living.

Most successful in treating the sick were those physicians and practical nurses who, though ignorant of germs and bacteria, kept their patients clean and comfortable and gave them no harsh remedies or treatment. Devoted and gentle nursing was often then, as it still is, a most important part of the patient's recovery. Every colonial wife was expected to nurse her family through illnesses. This, too, has not changed today. But today we can call in a trained doctor and order drugs, and we know many things about disease and nursing that were not dreamed of in early Maryland. So, in this regard times have changed for the better.

There were women who were experienced in helping at childbirth and these were called midwives. Some of these women were gifted with the knack of instinctively doing the right thing for their patients. Midwives delivered almost all babies until late in the 19th century when doctors began to be called in. All babies were born at home in colonial days. Even much later, when hospitals were built, home births were preferred, for deadly fevers and infections often swept hospitals until the medical profession learned more about how germs were spread. Midwives had little medical training, and nurses even less. Yet, some of these women are reported to have had quite wonderful records in helping patients. Of course, it should be emphasized that women in colonial times were never trained to be doctors.

The average life span was not great in colonial times. If diseases failed to kill one, there was the danger from the daily use of axes, knives, guns, lamps, and fires, and from the hooved and horned farm animals. Little wonder then that every home had its chest of bandages, herbs, and salves ready. Children often died in their first year.

Yet, in even these early days of medicine, not everything was bad. From experience and concern there slowly grew more and more real knowledge of medicine.

Amputation in the 1700's was a dreaded operation. The patient often died as much from shock as from his original injury or infection.

CHAPTER XIX

ANNAPOLIS

ANNAPOLIS has always been a "water town." It is located on Chesapeake Bay at the mouth of the Severn River. Beautiful creeks extend into the city, and sea gulls soar overhead. The very beginnings of the city are linked with the Severn River. It was beside the sheltered Severn that the first settlers of the area, in 1648, built a small town called Providence. They were, as has been noted, Puritan emigrants from Virginia. Puritans had lived in Virginia since 1619, if not before that date, but later restrictions brought them to accept Cecil Calvert's invitation to live in Maryland. Maryland has been called the "Land of Sanctuary" because different religious groups found freedom here.

Indians proved to be troublesome and numerous around the wooden dwellings of the little town of Providence, which was located near the present Greenberry Point light. Governor Stone sent a commission of five men to sign a treaty with the Susquehannock Indians. This treaty of 1652 is said to have been signed beneath a huge tulip poplar tree, which is still standing on the campus of St. John's College in Annapolis. After the signing of this treaty, serious troubles with these Indians seemed to be at an end.

Providence did not grow, however, for settlers found that town life did not appear to offer as much as life on a farm or plantation. This first settlement at Providence finally disappeared altogether.

Yet, soon the town of Annapolis was to replace St. Mary's City as capital of Maryland. To understand this the reader must see what political events were taking place. Changes in the English government and in Maryland's government were going on.

As you remember, in England, Oliver Cromwell and his Puritans took over the government of England from King Charles I. Cromwell, as Lord Protector, with Parliament, ruled England from 1653 until Cromwell's death in 1658. Cromwell's son took over for less than a year. Then King Charles II was restored to the English throne in 1660.

Mirroring these English events, Maryland saw a Parliamentary commission, in 1652, made up of Richard Bennett, a Puritan, William Claiborne, and two others. The commission was to see that Maryland recognized the authority of England's Parliamentary (Puritan) government. Claiborne quickly reoccupied Kent Island but did not attempt to take over the government of Maryland for himself. As has been said, Governor William Stone submitted to these commissioners who represented the current government of England, from 1652 to 1654.

After 1654, it has been noted that Governor Stone began to follow the instructions of Lord Baltimore, but, then, he was forced out of Maryland by Bennett and Claiborne. But the Governor returned in 1655 with about one hundred and thirty men to attack Providence. The Battle of the Severn, described earlier, resulted; and Governor Stone was defeated. The Parliamentary Commission then appointed Captain William Fuller and the Council to govern Maryland. From 1654 until 1657 Maryland was completely under Puritan government.

In 1656 Josias Fendall was appointed Governor of Maryland by Lord Baltimore. In 1657 Fendall met with Puritan leaders in Maryland and, following Lord Baltimore's orders, offered terms of peace. Both sides agreed to a peaceful settlement of their troubles, and Governor Fendall took over. Had Fendall been a more reliable man, all would have been well in Lord Baltimore's colony. But, in 1659, perhaps hoping to seize power for himself, Fendall proved to be a poor governor for Lord Baltimore. At any rate, by 1660, with King Charles II on the English throne, and Philip Calvert in Maryland as governor, Maryland settled down to being the "the land of pleasant living." The rebellious groups were pardoned. Even Fendall and a man called John Hatch were held only a short time before being released.

Now what has all this to do with Annapolis becoming the capital of Maryland? These events have been given to explain why the change of location was to come about later on.

In 1661 Charles Calvert, the eldest son and heir of Cecil, Second Lord Baltimore, came to Maryland to govern the province. His was a happy governorship, though he did seem to employ a great number of relatives as officials. Still, the colony prospered. St. Mary's City grew and several fine houses were built in the area. In 1675 Cecil Calvert died, and Charles Calvert returned to England to become the Third Lord Baltimore. Now Josias Fendall turned up, bent on more trouble. This time he was in the company of a man from St. Mary's County called John Coode. In 1681, finally, Fendall was convicted of conspiring against the Maryland government and was banished from the colony. Coode escaped punishment.

Events in England were now to affect Maryland again. In the English Revolution of 1688, King James II of England was deposed. The reign of William and Mary began. Queen Mary (Stuart) was a

Protestant. So, again trouble was ahead for the Maryland province of Lord Baltimore. Quickly a message was sent from England by the Third Lord Baltimore to Maryland, instructing the Maryland government to send word that they would obey William and Mary. Unfortunately, the messenger died on the voyage, so Maryland was silent and did not acknowledge the authority of William and Mary. A second messenger was sent out, but too late to keep ugly rumors from spreading about unusual occurrences in Maryland.

Rumors in Maryland suggested that the Catholics were planning to join with the Indians, to kill off all the Protestant people in the province! John Coode (remember him?) seems to have been especially active in spreading these tales and other stories equally untrue. Coode with Nehemiah Blackistone got about 800 men together and marched on St. Mary's City. These men took over the little capital and then chased the Council to Mattapany where the Council members were forced to surrender. For the time being, however, most of the people of Maryland did not really know what was happening. But John Coode was now the head of the Maryland government.

King William asked the Lords of Trade and Plantations to suggest a solution. In 1690 that group suggested that the King send a Royal Governor to Maryland, though Lord Baltimore should still be given the profits from Maryland. The first Royal Governor was Sir Lionel Copley, who came to Maryland in 1692 and died in 1693. Other Royal Governors followed, but to shorten our story, we jump ahead to the year 1694 when Royal Governor Sir Francis Nicholson arrived.

For the first ninety years of colonization, Maryland had had only two community settlements, St. Mary's City and Anne Arundel Town—a small place that had grown up at the mouth of the Severn River in the last half of the seventeenth century. The chief business of Anne Arundel (later named Annapolis) was trade with the Indians, and its chief exports were tobacco and furs. It was named for the wife of Cecil Calvert, Second Lord Baltimore. A county, called Anne Arundel, had been set up in 1650.

As farms and plantations spread up waterways and ever farther inland, Maryland people found it more and more difficult to reach St. Mary's City. Members of the Assembly complained of the time needed to travel to the capital at St. Mary's City. And, indeed, St. Mary's had not grown very much. It never had more than about sixty houses, and these were scattered over about a five-square-mile area.

Not long after Sir Francis Nicholson arrived in Maryland, he ordered that the Assembly meet in Anne Arundel in February, 1695. The Assembly met in this place near the Severn, in the home of

Major Edward Dorsey. This brick mansion still stands in Annapolis on Prince George's Street. Soon Nicholson decided to move the seat of government from St. Mary's City to Anne Arundel Town.

The residents of St. Mary's City were very upset. They would lose trade and prestige, and the value of their land would be lower. Despite serious threats of rebellion, Governor Nicholson nevertheless told the sheriff that he wanted the government equipment and records moved before winter to Anne Arundel Town on the Severn River. (It was at this point that the "Governor's Castle" at St. Mary's City was blown up) Briskly, Governor Nicholson proceeded with the move.

Not long after the change, the name of the new capital became Annapolis in honor of Princess Anne. Princess Anne was later to become the Queen of England. This practice of naming towns and counties for royalty accounts for quite a number of place names in Maryland.

Sir Francis Nicholson

Sir Francis Nicholson won the admiration of many for his energy, his forceful political leadership, his ability to plan and to govern. He annoyed both his enemies and sometimes his friends, however, with his "fiery tempers." He did not like Catholics and enforced English laws that restricted them. He was a passionate man, high-handed and fond of all the fashionable vices of the day — wine, women, and gambling!

On the other hand Nicholson had a strong sense of duty and was not above reaching into his own pocket to help causes he thought should be encouraged. The colonies north of Maryland, beset by French raiders, received aid directly from Sir Francis. He also gave money to the "King William's School" in Annapolis. It is now St. John's College.

He liked city planning, too. After he left Maryland to become Governor of Virginia in 1698, he uprooted the Virginia capital from Jamestown and set it down at Williamsburg, planning city streets and zoning in a most energetic way. (To get ahead of our story a little, Nicholson went on to Nova Scotia and to South Carolina as royal governor of those English colonies, after leaving Virginia.)

While in Maryland, Governor Nicholson planned Annapolis around two big circles. From Church Circle and State Circle, the streets radiate out like spokes from the centers of wagon wheels. Annapolis in the 1690's had only a few dozen houses. Nicholson hoped to make it grow faster. When he laid out the town plan, Sir Francis lined up its streets with the points of the compass. Five streets in modern Annapolis still have their original names, taken from the points of the compass as befits such a water town. The streets are North, South, East, West and Northwest streets.

Zoning Firsts

If one visits Annapolis today, he will find many colonial buildings still in use. Most of them are built right up to the sidewalk in the English fashion, with gardens behind them. Annapolis was zoned by Nicholson for the quiet enjoyment of life for the wealthy classes who were given spacious lots. There were more modest lots for the homes of the workmen. Workmen engaged in noisy or pungent work such as blacksmithing or hide tanning were given lots well away from the residential sections.

Tradesmen, such as bakers, brewers, tailors, dyers, and others, were allotted land in the "present town pasture" not to exceed one lot, or acre of land, to any one tradesman. Bankers and attorneys had offices within sight of the two town circles. This is still the case in Annapolis to a considerable extent today.

Plans were also made to provide docks for ships, fishing vessels, and pleasure boats, along the waterfront.

How Annapolis Grew

Among other buildings credited to Sir Francis Nicholson's encouragement is the Old Treasury Building which was built in his time and was at first used for the Governor's Council meetings. It still stands on the grounds of the State House.

In the years that followed its becoming the capital city, Annapolis grew into Maryland's largest city, while St. Mary's City as a community, steadily declined. Annapolis had one of the earliest newspapers printed in the colonies, *The Maryland Gazette*, established in 1727. For a long time this was the only newspaper in all of the English colonies in North America.

One of the earliest theaters in America was also built in Annapolis. Since Annapolis was the capital city, naturally the Governor and other officials now lived there. It also attracted attorneys, wealthy planters, shop keepers, boat builders, fishermen, and tradesmen. Though it grew somewhat slowly in size, it came to be called often the "Athens of America" and the "Paris of America," thanks to its fine balls, its theater, its horse racing and musical events, and its parties.

Chesapeake Bay and the nearby rivers provided the citizens of

Annapolis with a convenient means of travel by boat. They could visit other colonial ports and towns in this way; also, they could order goods and send their letters by sea. The Bay, too, was a broad highway over to the Eastern Shore, and people could easily visit many places in the Bay area. As early as 1608, Captain John Smith had noticed the good harbors at the Severn and in other nearby rivers flowing into the Bay. The good harbor of the new capital city attracted ship's captains, and this, too, helped Annapolis to grow.

A ferry service was begun on the Severn River to serve "the publique," and its ferry keeper was paid 9,000 pounds of tobacco a year to operate it. In fact, the ferry was kept in operation until it was replaced by a bridge in 1887.

Taverns of the day were popular, and we note from old records that one very warm, dry day during the first session of the Assembly, the entire body adjourned to an ale-house, much to the indignation of Governor Nicholson!

St. Anne's Parish

Sir Lionel Copley, the first royal governor of Maryland (1692-1693) had the Maryland Assembly declare the Church of England as Maryland's official church. Thirty parishes were set up in ten Maryland counties. St. Anne's Parish in Annapolis was one of those established by the Assembly in 1692. Governor Nicholson obtained the ground for St. Anne's Church, and this church has been on the same site ever since, although the buildings have changed. By 1704, a brick church was completed with a graceful spire, topped with a golden ball. The church grew dilapidated and was torn down in 1774. War delayed the building of a new church until 1792. This second St. Anne's Church was used until it was gutted by fire in 1858. Only foundations and tower were left. A third St. Anne's Church, which is in use today, was finished in 1866.

The rectors of the parish in the colonial period were English, but after the American Revolution, American rectors took over.

The church is named for St. Anne, the mother of the Virgin Mary. The church is built of brick with a tall spire. It occupies Church Circle in Annapolis today. It is a treasure house of history and has a great many beautiful things for Maryland people to see. St. Anne's is noted, too, for the beauty of its music.

In the church today there is communion silver given in 1695-96 by King William III. Records of the church date from the year 1705. There is also a large Bible there, given by Major General John Hammond in the year 1707, a prayer book bought in 1764 and used until 1805, and many other fascinating reminders of the past still remaining to the present day, many presented by former members of St. Anne's Church.

For many years the only public burying ground in Annapolis was the St. Anne's churchyard, originally occupying all the surrounding street surface which now encircles the church, as well as the present church grounds. About 1790 another cemetery was begun on the shores of Dorsey Creek, and it still exists.

One of the oldest tombstones in the St. Anne's churchyard is that of Amos Garrett, the first mayor of Annapolis, "who departed this life on March 8th, 1727 . . .". The stone is located beside the west doorway of the church. Another stone to be seen today is on the other side of the doorway, and is that of Major General John Hammond, dated 1707. One of Maryland's noted colonial men, Colonel Nicholas Greenbury, is buried by St. Anne's Church. He died at the age of seventy in 1697. Also in the churchyard is the tomb of Sir Robert Eden, the last Royal Governor of Maryland. He returned, seeking to recover his land holdings and to live in Maryland, after the American Revolution.

Building Annapolis

Good clay for making bricks was found near Annapolis in the 1600's and was used to build the parish church, as well as a schoolhouse and a statehouse.

Even with Governor Nicholson's planning and encouragement, it took nearly fifty years before Annapolis changed from a "parcel of wooden houses," numbering about forty dwellings in 1700, to a city of dignified townhouses, cozy cottages, and stately public buildings. It did grow, however, and became the chief center of social life in the late colonial period.

The first statehouse at Annapolis was first built in 1697, and a later building was constructed in 1706. This one, too, eventually decayed and was torn down. The present building, designed by Joseph Clark, was begun in 1772. Its roof was originally sheathed in copper until a gale came along and "rolled it up like a scroll." It is the oldest statehouse still in continuous use in the United States. Also, the structure has the nation's largest wooden dome.

The older part of the statehouse contains the Old Senate Chamber, where General George Washington resigned his command of the Continental Army; the Old House of Delegates Chamber; and the Historical and Flag Room. A large addition was made to the building about 1900. In the Maryland Statehouse are many things to see—precious historical relics, as well as busy modern lawmakers in action!

The center of the town of Annapolis is today a remarkable "history in buildings," thanks to its citizens who have preserved so many beautiful and valuable colonial structures. There are brick and cobbled pavements, beautiful doorways, and glimpses of the harbor to enjoy. Every foot along the old streets rewards the visitor with fascinating things to see in Annapolis — Maryland's unique "Ancient City."

(Maryland Historical Society)

The State House, as it looked in the late 1700's.

CHAPTER XX

THE SHAPE WE'RE IN!

LOOKING at a map of Maryland it seems odd that the state of Delaware should not be part of Maryland, and that our state has a "wasp waist" out in Western Maryland. Why is our state so oddly shaped?

Well, if Maryland were its original size, as granted to the Second Lord Baltimore by King Charles I, it would cover part of Virginia, part of West Virginia, Delaware, the present District of Columbia, and a great deal of land that is now in Pennsylvania! The charter of Maryland describes the grant of land as including all of the area from the ocean on the east, bounded by the fortieth degree parallel to the north, extending westward to the "first fountain" of the Potomac River and bounded on the south by the southern shore of the Potomac River. How did Maryland lose so much of these original lands?

Virginia-Maryland Disputes

On the Eastern Shore, in 1663, Maryland settlers began to farm land which was very close to the Virginia-Maryland border. Colonel Edward Scarborough led a band of Virginia men in telling the Maryland people that the land they were on belonged to Virginia, not to Maryland. Scarborough told the people that they must pay taxes to Virginia.

When the governors of Virginia and Maryland heard of this conflict, they met and decided to get the boundary clearly set, in order to avoid trouble. The idea was good, but unfortunately for Maryland, the line laid out by Scarborough and Philip Calvert (the Second Lord Baltimore's brother) was not straight. Maryland lost twenty-three square miles (15,000 acres). By the time the mistake was discovered, it was too late to get the land back.

Since the Potomac River belongs to Maryland, its southern bank being the boundary between Virginia and Maryland, more trouble came when the two colonies could not agree as to which waters in the west were the real source of the Potomac River. Maryland lost this argument, too, when a mistake of geography took away nearly 500,000 acres of land from Maryland and gave it to Virginia. Later

(1863), during the Civil War, this area became a part of West Virginia.

Pennsylvania-Maryland Border Disputes

These losses of land to Virginia were small compared with the slices of land to be lost to Pennsylvania. Shortly after colonists came to Maryland under the leadership of Lord Calvert, they found that some Swedish families were settling on the Delaware River (1638). The Swedish colonists refused to believe that the land belonged to Lord Baltimore and would not pay taxes to his government.

Later, Dutch colonists from New York (New Amsterdam) moved in and took this land away from the Swedish settlers. Maryland authorities protested. Finally, in 1664, English warships captured the Dutch settlements and turned them over to the English government, for in 1664 the Dutch were forced to surrender New York and other Dutch land claims to the English.

Other disputes over land arose when, in 1681, William Penn was granted a great stretch of land to be called Pennsylvania. He claimed that his lands reached some distance south of his city of Philadelphia. Lord Baltimore said, "No!" arguing that the 40th parallel marked Maryland's northern boundary according to the Maryland charter. This parallel, incidentally, almost touches the city of Philadelphia! Penn wanted his grant to stretch far enough southward to give him access to the Delaware River and Delaware Bay. Penn needed a deep-water port and access to the Atlantic Ocean.

Due to the unexplored nature of the Americas, the poor quality of maps, and a very kingly way of giving away vast grants of land to the people in favor of the current English ruler, border disputes were not always settled fairly. So it happened that the King of England gave the land captured from the Dutch and which they had taken from the Swedes to his brother, James, the Duke of York. William Penn was planning a New World refuge for Quakers, and the English Crown owed Penn's father a great deal of money. Penn asked the King's brother for the old Dutch-Swedish lands, near Delaware Bay, and they were granted to him.

Lord Baltimore protested vainly that some of the land was his. Finally, in 1685, thanks to a boundary line laid out by Penn's agents, the case came before the English courts. Maryland succeeded in getting back some of the disputed lands, which are now a part of the Maryland Eastern Shore, but Pennsylvania got the rest. (Later, a part of the Quaker's land was separated from Pennsylvania and was made a part of Delaware.)

Fifty years passed, but time did not end the quarreling over the

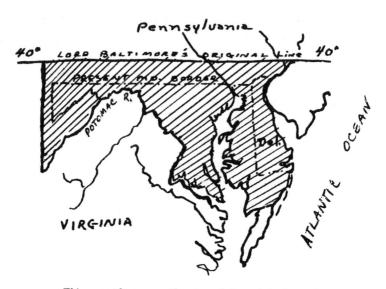

This map shows you the size of the original grant.
Which states took land from Maryland?

Pennsylvania-Maryland border. In the 1730's, a colorful and stubborn character, Thomas Cresap, was one of the settlers living on disputed land. He was a "Marylander" and was able to get along well with the Indians, who called him "Big Spoon" because of his hospitality. It was probably not mere chance that saw this troublesome man settling near the 40th parallel. Possibly the government of Maryland encouraged him to go there to locate his home.

The Indians, too, supported Cresap's claims and, on occasion, warned him of attacks being planned by the Pennsylvanians. Finally, in 1736, he was surprised by men from Pennsylvania, and his house was burned. He was taken prisoner and marched through the streets of Philadelphia. Though wounded, and with a threat that he might be hanged, Cresap, nevertheless, walked cheerfully along with his captors, commenting in a clear voice, "This is the finest city in the Province of Maryland!" He was kept a prisoner in Pennsylvania for a year.

90

More court litigation followed in England, between the Calverts and William Penn. In 1763, the English government sent Charles Mason and Jeremiah Dixon to survey a boundary line. This new boundary was to cause Maryland to lose two and a half million acres!

The line, known as the "Mason-Dixon Line", is regarded as a dividing line between our nation's northern and southern states. Some of the stone markers are still in place along the line. On the Maryland side, the large, original five-mile markers bear the Calvert coat of arms, and, on the Pennsylvania side, William Penn's coat of arms. Mason and Dixon began their work in 1763 and ended their work in 1767 when they were stopped by the possibility of Indian attack. The Indians who had been guiding them evidently had been instructed not to go beyond a certain point.

The north-to-south line dividing Maryland from Delaware is also the work of Mason and Dixon. A re-survey of the Mason-Dixon line was made recently to check its accuracy. It was found that the two 18th century astronomers had done an excellent job of surveying.

And, so the Maryland boundary story is one of English politics, poor maps, Indians, mistaken rivers, and intrigue — a story that explains why the map of Maryland is such an odd shape today.

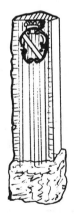 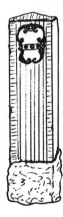

Markers left by Mason and Dixon along the Maryland-Pennsylvania border.

CHAPTER XXI

MARYLAND TOWNS

Baltimore's Beginnings

BALTIMORE had its beginnings in 1729 with the Maryland Assembly's "Act for Erecting a town on the north side of Patapsco, In Baltimore County, and for laying out into lots sixty acres of land. . ." This act was passed at the request of "the leading men of Baltimore County." The act recognized that Baltimore was a good place to load, unload, and sell trade items of various kinds. The new town was to be named "Baltimore Town." The lots were laid out in 1730, on sixty acres bought from Charles and Daniel Carroll. In 1732, the town was enlarged by the addition of ten acres.

Baltimore was needed by farmers, especially those of German extraction nearby, who needed a port of entry nearer to them than Annapolis. The Baltimore location offered a good harbor and water transportation where the Patapsco River branches and empties into the Chesapeake Bay. Seagoing vessels could safely anchor there. Then, too, the Great Eastern Road passed near the site of Baltimore. The road was still rough but it ran through Maryland from Philadelphia in the north to Georgetown to the south. Georgetown was then a small settlement on the Maryland side of the Potomac River. It was located on the fall line where the river became too shallow for ships.

There was not much on the site when Baltimore was first laid out, just a few houses. Opposite Baltimore Town, on the other side of Jones' Falls, Jonathan Hanson had built a water-powered grist mill.

Other towns had grown up near Baltimore. Joppa had developed on the Gunpowder River around a courthouse built in 1709. Joppa was a river port but not ideally located to serve farmers inland. After Baltimore became established, with its better harbor, Joppa lost its business and citizens. It gradually disappeared as a community. Joppa Road still runs to the place and a modern community called Joppatowne is near the site today.

Ships loaded with great cargoes of corn and tobacco from Maryland farms sailed to England. Manufactured items were carried back to Maryland, and gradually, more and more of this trade passed through the port city of Baltimore. By 1756 a Baltimore ship had sailed to the

West Indies with tobacco and corn and had returned loaded with sugar, rum, and slaves.

In 1745 Jones' Town, with its mill and houses, was made a part of Baltimore. Still, by 1752, there were perhaps only two dozen houses in Baltimore, together with two taverns and a church. It took the completion of the Frederick Road in 1760 to give Baltimore a greater volume of trade, more citizens, and more businesses.

German People Bring New Crops and Skills

German-speaking people from Pennsylvania were among the people who came to Maryland to settle and to establish prosperous farms. German-speaking settlers arrived first at Monocacy, in 1734. This first German settlement is near the present city of Frederick. We must remember that there was no united Germany in the modern sense. When we speak of "Germans" we are referring more to their language than to their country of origin. Some of these people came from the Rhineland, some from Switzerland, and some from Alsace and other European areas.

These newcomers to Maryland followed a road cut by sixteen hardy families who, in 1732, had made their way from York, Pennsylvania, to settle in Virginia, cutting the road as they went. For over twenty-five years this was almost the only road that the German settlers of the area had.

Then, as they made their farms comfortable and prosperous with hard work, they began to need markets for the many things they raised and made. These Germans were not only skilled farmers but were masters of many trades. Some could tan leather; some could make harnesses or shoes; some could make hats; there were some who could make glassware, pottery, bricks, and clothing. Among the Germans, too, were millers, butchers, bakers, and carpenters. Indeed, they made many of the things that formerly had to be imported from England. They were to start many Maryland businesses.

In Europe these families had raised grain crops. So, in Maryland, they began to raise wheat and other grains, in addition to the native Indian corn. They raised all sorts of vegetables and fruits and some tobacco.

They were proud of their tidy homes, strong, well-kept barns, and rich fields, and proud, also of their good horses, cows, and other farm livestock. Though the 1700's seem far back in time to us now, the influence of these German-speaking people is still to be seen in the farms of central and western Maryland.

With a trading center needed for the many products of these

German people, the town of Frederick was laid out in 1745. Settlers quickly bought many of the town lots. When Frederick County was set up in 1748, the town of Frederick was made the county seat. Both county and town seemed to have been named for Frederick Calvert, who was to be the Sixth Lord Baltimore.

Trade With Baltimore Grows

Before a road was built, or when there was yet only a trail, the Maryland Germans began to send goods to the port of Baltimore. Horses were loaded with goods — wool, leather, and flax — and led single-file down to Baltimore Town.

Germans soon began to live in Baltimore. There they formed the Evangelical Lutheran Congregation in 1755. The church was to be the center of German cultural activity for many years in the city. In 1785 the name was changed to Zion Lutheran, the name it still bears today. The present church is located at Gay and Lexington streets in Baltimore.

Then the Frederick Road was finished in 1760. It by-passed Baltimore's rival town of Joppa and began to pour an ever-increasing stream of goods into Baltimore.

The German-speaking people had migrated to America because they had suffered much in their own countries, both from wars and from religious persecution. They sought in America a life of peace, freedom of worship, and prosperity. Many of them came to live on Maryland's fertile lands.

Georgetown, A Maryland Town

In 1751 the Maryland Assembly authorized commissioners to "lay out and erect a town on the Potowmack River" on sixty acres of land above the mouth of Rock Creek. It was named "George-town" and later simply, Georgetown.

It was here at the fall line, that large ships could go no further up the Potomac and must unload their cargoes. A tobacco inspection office and a few houses were already there. So eighty lots were laid out and the little port town began to prosper.

As we have said, the great eastern road connected Georgetown with points north and south. Farmers sent cargoes of produce to the Potomac, to be loaded aboard ocean-going vessels at Georgetown. Ships from Europe came in with manufactured items and goods of all kinds. It was from Georgetown that a canal was projected in 1785 that was to have linked the Atlantic coast lands with the rich lands of the Ohio valley.

94

This Georgetown today is in the District of Columbia. There is another Georgetown, Maryland, however, on the Eastern Shore, as well as a town in Delaware by the same name.

Eastern Shore Centers

On the Eastern Shore of Maryland, manors, plantations, and farms spread up the scores of Eastern Shore waterways. Many houses faced the water, and many plantations had their own landings. The rivers and the Bay were the first highways of these Marylanders. By 1674 Cecil County was set up. The town of Elkton is its county seat. Two counties of the Eastern Shore were set up in the 1700's, Queen Anne's (1706) with Centreville as its county seat and Caroline County (1773). Denton is the county seat of Caroline County.

As time went by, more county seats were set up. The town of Snow Hill which was established in 1686, became the county seat of Worcester County when that county was formed in 1742. Kent County, first formed in 1642, selected Chestertown in 1706, as its county seat. Somerset County formed in 1666, had its seat of government at Princess Anne in 1733. In these county seats legal business and courts attracted lawyers, clerks, and officials to the towns, to live and work.

Oxford, on the Eastern Shore, in Talbot County, became one of Maryland's earliest towns. It was started in 1694 and was used as a port of entry because of its good harbor. Near the harbor warehouses, factories, and offices were built. It became a good central point for Eastern Shore people to come to trade. Social life was gay in Oxford for several prosperous families built homes near there. There were taverns and shipping offices. Thriving plantations and farms sent their products to Oxford for sale and shipment. Talbot County was set up by 1662 and the town of Easton was made its county seat. Dorchester County was set up in 1668 and Cambridge was selected to be its county seat. The last Eastern Shore county to be formed was Wicomico County in 1867, which is later than the period we are concerned with in this chapter. Salisbury is Wicomico County's county seat.

In Dorchester County, on the Eastern Shore, were colonists from Scotland who had come to Maryland by way of Ireland. They and their descendents were called the "Scotch-Irish." They built the small town of "Loomtown" (now Woolford). In almost every home the busy Scotch-Irish housewife worked at her loom. From their home country they had brought unusual skills in weaving to Maryland. Soon, so much woolen cloth and good linen was coming from such American looms that English manufacturers began to object to the competition which the American manufacturing offered their English businesses.

It was not long before England passed laws forbidding the sale of American woolen cloth to other than purely local markets. None was to be shipped abroad, nor to be sold to other colonies. This was a hard law to enforce, and the weavers continued to market their cloth, because it was much in demand in the colonies.

(Maryland Historical Society)

Surveyors marking off lots, laying out the town of Baltimore. (Around 1729).

CHAPTER XXII

THE FRENCH AND INDIAN WAR

WHEN France sent men to explore and exploit America in the 17th century, she was possibly the most powerful country in Europe. But the fur trade, not agriculture, interested the French in America the most. For this reason England managed to start colonies and spread settlers at a greater rate than did her rival France.

England was crowded; she had extra people who yearned for land of their own, for opportunity, and religious freedom. England had wealthy families who could furnish money to finance colonies and make them grow. Stock companies were formed in hopes of making money in American ventures.

France held Canada, the lands along the Mississippi River, and Louisiana in the year 1754. She hoped to link Canada to her other claims by a line of forts along the Great Lakes and the Mississippi and Ohio Rivers. This would encircle the English colonies along the Atlantic coast of North American and stop their westward growth. In the western part of North America lay vast stretches of land that few if any Europeans had yet seen. The English claimed much of the land in North America from sea to sea, but the French asserted also, their claims to the land to the west by reason of exploration and settlement.

So, it was truly for the possession and exploration of the entire continent that the French and Indian War (1754 to 1763) was fought. Of course France and England had for many years been at each other's throats, so this war was but a continuation of their contest for power. The French and Indian War started in May 1754, when Virginia militia, under the young Lieutenant Colonel George Washington, attacked Frenchmen in the southwestern corner of Pennsylvania, a location known today as Brownsville, Pennsylvania. The Americans were later surrounded and forced to surrender to the French at Fort Necessity.

The French, in their fighting, since their numbers were so few, joined forces with the Algonquin Indians. Fiercely the French and the Indians descended on every English post, settlement, and farm that lay near.

These raids were so fierce, so cruel, and so merciless that some settlers of western Maryland not only fled to Baltimore but rushed aboard ships in the harbor there. They could not believe that the savage attacks could be resisted and had no wish to see such tortures, such blood, and such death again in their lifetimes. Where did the western frontier of Maryland settlement lie at this time? The small frontier town of Frederick, and settlements in neighboring valleys west of the Catoctin and South Mountains, became for a time the westernmost outposts of Maryland settlers. Some families had actually moved east from Frederick for safety!

Further west was Fort Cumberland, one of the most important forts on the frontier. Later the city of Cumberland was to grow here. Another fort, somewhat east of what is now Hancock, Maryland, Fort Frederick, was built (after Braddock's defeat) as a haven for these remote settlers in case of attack.

Governor Horatio Sharpe of Maryland commanded all the troops on the frontier. He was an efficient man and was one of the best-liked of Maryland's colonial governors. When the British general, Edward Braddock, arrived in Maryland with hundreds of trained English soldiers, he found Sharpe ready to turn over to him plans, supplies, and information.

Braddock took command of the frontier defenses. He felt that his trained soldiers would soon crush the French and their Indian allies. He brushed aside advice from the Americans, though he did select George Washington to serve as his aide. His weakness proved to be his inability to adapt his old-fashioned way of fighting to this new country and this new enemy. He failed, also, to take precautions against ambush that even European generals of that time were using. He moved slowly. He felt that he must build a road and bridge waterways so that his troops could march on the enemy with wagons of artillery and supplies.

Braddock reached the Monogahela River, on July 8, 1755. He planned to attack the French-held Fort Duquesne (this site is now occupied by the city of Pittsburg, Pennsylvania). Fort Duquesne was built on a point of land where the Monogahela and Allegheny Rivers meet to form the Ohio River.

General Braddock marched along an Indian trail toward the Fort. But, before he reached it, he was trapped in an ambush, and his troops were attacked and defeated. He himself was fatally wounded and died a few days later. The British with their glittering buttons and bright coats were easy targets for the Indians and the French, who were hiding behind trees dressed in buckskins that blended with forest colors. George Washington managed to get about half of the original force back to safety. After Braddock was killed, his men deserted Fort Cumberland. Governor Sharpe, hearing of this, rushed to the fort and placed men on guard so that the frontier families would not be unprotected.

George Washington was sent to Winchester, in the Shenandoah Valley of Virginia. He set to work to train new troops, using many militiamen (who are not professional soldiers but citizens trained to act in war or in other emergencies). Washington helped build over a dozen forts in a chain designed to hold the western front along the Allegheny Mountains. These forts, made of split logs, were hollow squares with stout gates. Settlers nearby, in case of sudden raids, could retreat into these places.

George Washington heard families mourn for the farms they had to leave when the French and Indians came through the land. He saw that years of their work had been lost and dreams had been shattered. But finally, by 1760, the French had been defeated by the English, and the frontier quieted down. During most of the French and Indian War period, Maryland gave little assistance toward any organized campaign, but it was more a lack in her government than in her people.[1] The war officially ended with the Treaty of Paris in 1763. The defeated French gave up to the English, Canada and Louisiana east of the Mississippi, except for New Orleans. Several territories held by different European powers changed hands as a result of the war which we call the French and Indian War, but which is also known in history as the Seven Years War. In the peace arrangements Havana (Cuba) was returned by England to Spain and in return Spain agreed to give Florida to England. Some twenty years later, Florida would again be traded back to Spain.

Since colonists hesitated to push westward during the years of the French and Indian War, they had settled down in great numbers to live and work in towns, such as Frederick, Annapolis, and Baltimore. Some took up farmland nearby or worked at whatever tasks were available to them in the towns. The war, thus, had served to speed the growth of Maryland areas just west of Chesapeake Bay.

American Settlers Dissatisfied with British

Frontiersmen, long dissatisfied with the British promises of protection which they felt were not kept, learned a great deal from the French and Indian War. Some Americans grumbled that a government that wanted to profit from its colonies, but left the colonies to shift for themselves against the enemy, was hardly better than no government at all. Even George Washington, loyally trying to protect British land claims with his militia, was irritated with the English government when he had difficulty getting shoes and ammunition for his troops. He heard frontiersmen speak of wanting security from the Indians and the French and desiring access to free land. They talked of protecting and even perhaps governing themselves. When the English won the war, the threat of the French was removed. But, while the colonies were no longer threatened by the powerful outside enemy, pressures from within the Empire mounted steadily greater and the possibility of serious trouble for the colonies appeared closer.

Many things made Maryland settlers push westward. Some had little money to buy land in the east or to pay the low land rents to the Proprietor. So they naturally sought free lands in the almost unexplored west. Then, too, some settlers liked to move about. For those, each new place was more promising than the last, and the next even more attractive.

Settlers were attracted westward, too, by land speculators. As land was settled, its value tended to rise. Towns grew from trading posts. Almost every man of affairs in the colonies had a finger in the pie of land speculation. The larger plantations, moreover, were not always profitable for the land became "worn out," and markets and prices were often uncertain. George Washington himself made a great deal of money from his land ventures, though at one point he became so "land poor" that he wrote to a friend who had asked to borrow two hundred dollars, "I can scarce lay my hands on that amount today myself and may be asking for a loan soon myself!"

So, in 1763, when a royal proclamation abruptly halted the settlement of lands west of the Atlantic watersheds, a great howl of protest arose from the American colonists, both the big landowners and those with little, if any, land. The English crown ordered the lands over the mountains to be reserved for the Indians, until they were willing to abandon their claims through peaceful negotiation. This was well intentioned, but it also proved to be unenforceable. Colonists in considerable numbers continued to migrate in defiance of this edict. Yet, another wedge was driven between the interests of England and those of the English colonists in America.

In a way, General Braddock's road, built to secure English possession of land to the west, did in part, accomplish this. In 1774, when George Washington visited the road that Braddock had built, Washington reported that settlers "in shoals" were swarming down the road to the west. The twelve-foot road, though rutted and rough, was speeding the occupation of the west by English settlers. Many of these settlers, even against the wishes of the English crown, were to occupy and hold lands across the mountains.

1 Andrews, **History of Maryland,** p. 233.

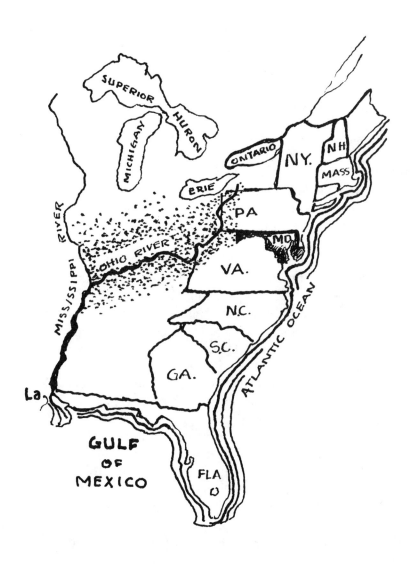

CHAPTER XXIII

MONEY USED IN COLONIAL MARYLAND

THOUGH English pounds, shillings, and pence were officially the currency of colonial Maryland, there was such a shortage of these notes and coins that other kinds of money were used.

We have mentioned the use of the Indian form of money, strings of shells and beads. Barter, too, was often used to avoid the use of scarce notes and coins. That is, one thing was traded for another. Furs were traded for tools, cloth, and salt; corn was traded for meat; services were often paid for with tobacco, livestock, or other items of value.

Even so, storekeepers and factors sometimes had to ask for notes and coins. Tea and manufactured metal products, for example, were usually paid for with cash. Credit was given to landowners, and the accounts were settled up every few months or each year. Today, in Maryland, some mortgages are still payable annually instead of monthly. This is a remaining custom of settling debts after the sale of the crops.

Coins were so very scarce that Cecil Calvert ordered shillings, sixpence, copper pennies, and silver groats to be made. A mint was started in St. Mary's County in 1660. However, the English king disapproved of this, so only a few hundred were made. Some of these coins may still be viewed in the coin collection willed to Johns Hopkins University by John W. Garrett. In this collection is what is believed to be an almost complete set of the coins minted by order of Cecil Calvert. Garrett gave this collection, his beautiful estate "Evergreen," his paintings, and his library of valuable books to the University in his will in 1942.

Since English money was so scarce, many European coins were used in Maryland in the 1700's. Among these were: Spanish dollars called "pieces of eight," Spanish doubloons (a gold coin), Spanish pistoles (also a gold coin), French half-guineas, German pieces of gold, Portuguese and Brazilian moeda, Dutch guilders, Spanish pistareen, and French francs.

Merchants learned to weigh coins. Coins of that day were often made of such soft metals that they sometimes lost weight and value, by wear, or by being pared or filed away. And, since coins were so very hard to get, sometimes the larger ones were cut into halves and quarters. The Spanish milled dollar was often cut into quarters. Our modern quarter of a dollar gets its name from this practice.

A Spanish money mark responsible for a modern United States monetary symbol, the dollar sign "$", came from the practice of coin cutters trying to keep a part of the Spanish mark on each quarter of the coin when it was divided to show that it came from a genuine Spanish dollar. So the sign "$" came to mean "dollar" and is not derived from the combination of the letters "U.S.", as has sometimes been suggested.

Still another kind of colonial money was the "tavern script" which was issued by certain tavern owners. This paper money was as good as the man who issued it. It was his promise to pay a certain amount upon presentation of the script. It was occasionally used in payment for things purchased elsewhere, provided the tavern owner had a good reputation.

Spanish Milled Dollar
(Piece of Eight)

"Two Bits"

"Four Bits"

CHAPTER XXIV

ELLICOTT'S MILLS

IF there were a less desirable piece of land in Maryland than the "Hollow" on the Patapsco River, west of Baltimore, farm owners near it would have said that it would have been hard to find. Yet, three young men, in 1770, looked down into the tangle of great trees, rocks, vines and brush with satisfaction. They had found just what they had been seeking on their scouting trip.

John, Joseph, and Andrew Ellicott were brothers and members of a Quaker family from Bucks County, Pennsylvania. They had come to Maryland looking for a good site for a water-driven mill. A mill required water, fast-moving water which moves down a rather steep slope. A fairly narrow, steep-walled river valley would be easy to dam. All of this was present at the Patapsco River site. Also, land there was cheap, and there would be plenty of room near the mill for houses and other necessary buildings.

The brothers believed, too, that the rolling lands around Baltimore and the mountains could grow quantities of grain to supply their mill. Not far away, also, were deepwater ports and rivers that offered transportation for grain and for the milled flour.

Farmers near the mill site frankly doubted that the brothers would find enough grain grown in the area to make the mill profitable, so many fields had been worn out in raising tobacco. The remaining fertile fields were still being used to grow that popular money crop. It was then that the Ellicott brothers showed their knowledge of scientific farming. They were not only millers, descended from a long line of skilled craftsmen who could even improvise machinery for milling but they knew also, because they were excellent farmers, how to make the land "new" again!

Rather than preach sermons on land renewal to farmers who would probably be slow to believe any new theory, the Ellicott brothers demonstrated their ideas instead. They added plaster (lime) and fertilizer to the fields they owned, and they planted wheat. Soon fine fields of grain were the result. The farmers of the region learned, too, to grow wheat one year, and then to use the land for pasture the next year, and grow corn the third year, after which this sort of crop rotation was repeated all over again. Thus, worn out fields were returned to profitable use, and a new kind of prosperity began for many Maryland farmers. But, before all of this was to occur, the brothers had a great deal else to do.

They returned to Pennsylvania and brought machinery from Philadelphia in May, 1771. To transport this heavy equipment, they used boats to float it down the Delaware River to New Castle. There they loaded the gears, millstones, and iron shafts onto wagons for an overland trip to the Maryland site at the "head" of the Elk River. Here, again, the machinery was loaded aboard vessels for a water trip down Chesapeake Bay and up the Patapsco River to Elkridge Landing. Then, in carts, the equipment was carried to the site chosen for the Ellicott brothers' new mill.

The brothers were helped a great deal by Charles Carroll of Carrollton. Charles Carroll owned Doughoregan Manor, not far from the Patapsco River mill site. He also owned a large tract of land, called "Carrollton", near the town of Frederick. Carroll believed in the young Quakers and in the new ideas they offered to farmers. He helped them to finance their mill and was given in turn a mortgage on a part of their land. He assisted in other ways, too, and let it be known that he gave his support fully to the brothers. As we have mentioned, many German families who were settled generally to the west of the Patapsco and near the town of Frederick were growing wheat, barley, and rye on their farms. They also were to send grain to the mill to be ground into flour.

The first mill building was one hundred feet in length. It was designed to shelter the machinery as well as to store grain and flour. Then, on the east side of the river the Ellicotts built a great house and divided it into compartments for their workmen and families.

Building the mill and the comfortable village around it took about two years. The location was approximately ten miles from the Port of Baltimore. It was a great day in the year, 1774, when wheat produced in the Ellicott's own fields was first milled in this big new mill. The effect on the entire farming area west from Baltimore was tremendous, and this development was of course an important early factor in giving this port town the economic stimulus to become a great city. Several members of the Ellicott family, it may be added, distinguished themselves in later years. Chief of these was, perhaps, Andrew Ellicott, surveyor and city planner, who had much to do with the development of the Federal capital city, Washington, D. C., after the dismissal of the Frenchman, L'Enfant, the first planner-architect.

CHAPTER XXV

TWO HUNDRED YEARS OF PROPRIETORSHIP

IF the entire story of the six Proprietors of Maryland were to be given, it would be an absorbing record of activities and accomplishments. Not everything is known of these men's lives and loves. Here is given a very brief summary of their lives with the generally accepted dates of their births and deaths.

Cecil Calvert, Second Lord Baltimore
First Proprietor of Maryland

Cecil Calvert was born in 1606 and held the title of Lord Baltimore from 1632 until he died in 1675. Cecil Calvert was the son of George Calvert, the First Lord Baltimore. It was Cecil who was granted the charter of Maryland, June 20, 1632 shortly after the death of his father. He carried out his father's plans for the colony of Maryland, sending settlers and supplies to the new land. He was never to see Maryland for himself, however, having elected to stay in England to attend to his many responsibilities. He was, however, the first Proprietor of Maryland, and as such was an absentee landlord.

Charles Calvert, Third Lord Baltimore
Second Proprietor of Maryland

Charles Calvert, the son of Cecil Calvert, was born in 1630 and came into the title as the third Lord Baltimore in 1675. At that time he was Governor of Maryland. He had represented Cecil, his father, in Maryland since 1660. Charles held the title until his death in 1715. As a result of a decision by the English Crown made in 1690, he lost his right to govern or appoint governors to Maryland, but he was allowed to keep his property rights and other benefits in Maryland.

Benedict Leonard Calvert, Fourth Lord Baltimore
Third Proprietor of Maryland

Benedict Leonard Calvert, the son of Charles Calvert, was born in 1677. In 1713 he decided to leave the Roman Catholic Church to join the Church of England. He came into the title as the fourth Lord Baltimore in 1715, but held it for only two months, for he died that same year.

Charles Calvert, Fifth Lord Baltimore
Fourth Proprietor of Maryland

Charles Calvert, the son of Benedict Leonard Calvert, was born in 1699 and came into the title in 1715, after the death of his father. He held the title of fifth Lord Baltimore until his death in 1751. Charles Calvert was given back the power to govern Maryland; and during his control of Maryland, the long argument over the boundary between Pennsylvania and Maryland was settled.

Frederick Calvert, Sixth Lord Baltimore
Fifth Proprietor of Maryland

Frederick Calvert was born in 1731 and came into the title as the sixth Lord Baltimore in 1751. He died in 1771.

He liked to travel and to write. He did not travel to Maryland, however, but felt the colony was a good business to own. It was a venture that earned him a comfortable income each year. During his Proprietorship, the French and Indian (Seven Years) War took place. In 1766, he sold many tracts of the land that he owned in Maryland.

Henry Harford
Sixth Proprietor of Maryland

Since Frederick Calvert did not marry Hester Rhelan, the mother of his son, Henry, born in 1758, the title could not be passed on to Henry Harford. Harford did inherit his father's fortune, however, when Frederick Calvert died in 1771. After attending Eton College, Harford went on to the Exeter College of the University of Oxford, taking a degree in 1776. He lived in England during the American Revolution and managed to get legal title to the proprietorship of Maryland by 1781. He was not supposed to inherit the province but because of his father's will and an agreement reached in 1780 with the legal heirs, he was named Proprietor.[1]

He came to Maryland in 1783 and tried without success to get the government of Maryland to pay him for land taken during the American Revolution. The British government paid him many thousands of pounds, however, and he lived out his life in England at Down Place, near Windsor, and in London. He died in 1834.

---

1 Estate Act of 1781, Record Office, House of Lords, London.

(Joseph H. Cromwell photograph, C & P Telephone Company of Maryland.)

Hampton House, located in Towson, Maryland, was the ancestral home of the Ridgely family. It was built about 1785. It is now designated as a National Historic Site and is open to the public.

YOUR MARYLAND

SECTION II

MARYLAND AND THE
AMERICAN REVOLUTION

Courtesy of the Tourist Division, Maryland Department of Economic Development
Government House, Annapolis, Md. The official residence of Maryland Governors.

CHAPTER XXVI

WHY DID THE AMERICAN COLONIES REBEL?

HAVING followed the Maryland story thus far, and having seen the achievement of prosperity and success, one might wonder why Maryland and her sister colonies decided to fight for freedom from the mother country.

Histories tell us that "the colonies declared war on England because of taxation without representation." *Was* the American Revolution fought because England taxed the colonies and yet allowed them to send no delegate to Parliament in England to speak for the rights and businesses of the colonists? Was it for this reason alone that the Englishmen in America were to turn against England and their King? One might suspect that there was more behind the American Revolution than this single issue.

First, consider that many, many of the people who braved the ocean and the massive wilderness of North America in the 17th and 18th centuries, had strong reasons for leaving England. Some were in fear of religious persecution, and some were in disfavor with the government. Almost all were rebelling against English life in one way or another before they came to America. They wanted a chance for a new way of life and, in general, freedom from various kinds of religious, political, or economic oppression from which they suffered. Even so, when they came to America, they were content to remain within the British empire.

Originally, in Maryland's charter, the King reserved for himself one-fifth of all gold found in Maryland, plus a yearly token tribute of two Indian arrows. Also, the King had agreed that Maryland would be free of the usual forms of English taxation. This promise was broken in the middle 1700's.

England is a very small, island country. Much of its prosperity depends on a steady flow of raw materials from which its skilled workers can make more valuable items to be sold at a profit. For a long time the American colonies were a rich source of supply for England. Furs, grains, tobacco, and many other items flowed from America to England. Back from England came manufactured things, needles, tools, cloth, glass, furniture, and other much needed goods. This was a good exchange balance for many years. Then the time came when American colonies, grown used to governing themselves to a large extent, progressed beyond a simple agricultural economy. They began little by little to create industry and to manufacture products for themselves. Items made in America cost the colonists less and were available more quickly. Many homes not only prepared wool and flax on spinning wheels, but had looms on which to weave sturdy cloth, too. Local iron workers began to make nails, hinges, fireplace bric-a-brac and other items here.

American manufacturing was a challenge to English businessmen. If America kept making more and more manufactured goods, there would soon be less demand for English products. Laws limiting colonial manufacturing were passed in England. Since the American colonists had no voice in the English Parliament, where the laws were made, the legislation greatly favored English manufacturers and other businessmen. Laws were passed which forbade the export of woolen cloth, clothing and hats to any country from the colonies, or between the colonies. So one can see, from this example, how England's laws relating to trade and industry could affect the colonists and why they would feel that they were being unfairly treated.

England, for another example, wanted the colonies to send over raw bar and pig iron, and objected to the growing trend of American businessmen to refine the iron and make iron products. This was bad for English manufacturing. So, in 1750, laws were passed forbidding American businessmen to set up any new furnaces or new mills to process iron. Maryland was an iron-producing colony and exported iron to England and, thus, was directly affected by this new regulation.

After that, more and more laws hampered the growth of American business—unfairly, the colonists often felt. Restricting America's active shipping trade, for example, meant that now American raw materials must be sold only to England, even though other countries might offer better prices and easier shipping routes. This kind of restriction stimulated smuggling and a spirit of rebellion against certain English laws.

Distance and the Practice in Self-Government

Another big reason, of course, for the eventual rebellion of the colonies was that England was 3,000 long, water miles away. Answers and questions were carried back and forth at a very slow rate by sailing ships. It was a clumsy and awkward relationship at best. Also, as one can see from the way that Maryland and Pennsylvania bickered over boundaries, access to ports and land that some proprietors had the appearance of having complete little countries of their own. They were king-like in their power. It was necessary, however, for these proprietors to allow considerable self-government in America and to allow the colonists to have a voice in these governments.

The colonists were a hardy breed of people. They had to be brave and independent in order to leave their homelands, trying to find a better life in such a wild land. Once here, the colonists wanted their own local assemblies to make their laws. The selection of their own leaders to govern them was natural enough. Most colonists, of course, thought of themselves simply as English subjects and did not want a great deal of self-government. Originally, perhaps, the colonists wanted only a voice in the English Parliament so that the American colonies would get fair treatment.

English Enforcement

The navigation and trade laws that Americans objected to had not really been enforced seriously until after the French threat was ended in 1763. England then needed money badly to pay her debts for her seventy-five years of war. Now numerous new inspectors and tax collectors were sent to the American colonies to secure full obedience to the trade and export laws. Not used to this degree of policing and interference, American businessmen were angry at seeing their profitable trade disrupted.

As yet the ordinary citizens in the colonies hardly noticed the taxes on imports and exports; and while businessmen grumbled, no loud objections were raised until, in 1765, England began a more direct and personal taxation of the people.

It was decreed that certain legal papers must bear a British tax stamp. Also, several everyday items imported from England were now taxed. People now generally began to notice the taxes. They began to worry that once Britain began taxing them, there would be no end to additional taxes. The Americans were told by the English government that this was only a way of protecting the colonies, and that soldiers to man the forts and to protect lands acquired in the recent French and Indian War cost money. Yet almost every family now felt the English taxes.

Many Maryland families grumbled but shrugged it off. England was, after all, their country, and its government existed for their protection and well-being. But the provocations increased, and Marylanders grew concerned, even angry. The Maryland charter had appeared to promise no direct taxation from England, and this commitment now seemed to be forgotten. So, in the American colonies, concerned men began to gather and talk. The government of England gave them no voice, they said to one another. If they had no voice in the English government legally, then they would have to find other means to force it to respect their position and their rights, in the matter of trade and manufacturing, and self-government.

American colonists loyal to the English government, who were called Loyalists or Tories, began to be outnumbered by people favoring action against England to force England to give Americans more freedom in trade, and less burdensom taxation. Rebellious Americans were sometimes called Whigs; and there were many such men in Maryland. Men from Maryland, Virginia, Pennsylvania and the other colonies began to write to one another and to meet together as they faced the threat to what they regarded as their rights and liberties.

Some Other Reasons for the Revolution

The colonists of course did not realize the extent to which their struggle would take them, nor did they know that a revolution was coming. Two hundred years later we still find the reasons for the American Revolution complex and sometimes puzzling. Still, with time, certain causes do become obvious.

Adding to the irritation of Americans were those many court cases carried to England which were related to land disputes and boundary difficulties. Sometimes even criminal cases were appealed to English courts. Such intervention by the English government produced long delays and slow, awkward settlements.

Then, too, there was the edict of 1763, forbidding settlement by the colonists west of the Appalachian Mountains. This meant that land was now less available to ambitious, poor settlers and to freed indentured servants; and Americans generally were denied hopes of fortunes to be made in land speculation in that part of the west. Of course the Indian tribes to the west of the mountains hoped that the treaties and promises of the European king would be kept. They hoped that the white men would not take over more of their hunting grounds and village sites. (It was during the time of the American Revolution that the Indian tribes were to try to repel the land-hungry white men from taking the lands that lay between the Appalachian Mountains and the Mississippi River.) Americans protested that much of the guardianship of the western frontier was inept and inadequate.

Another sore point between England and many of her American colonists was the imposition of the established Church of England, and the denial of religious liberty. Tithes (a form of taxation) were imposed on colonists by England for the support of the Church of England. Many colonists, or their parents or grandparents, had come all the way from Europe just to escape this sort of tyranny. People who did not belong to the Anglican church did not like having to pay for its support.

In Maryland, too, quit-rents on land had to be paid to the Proprietor each year, and this, also, was a sort of tax. All of these things, plus the trade restrictions hampering American business, as well as the laws regarding manufacturing, plus the hard times on tobacco plantations as they faced lower prices and unprofitable selling conditions in the English market, added to the woes of the average Marylander. In fact, tobacco planters often found themselves deeply in debt to English factors and commission houses, when tobacco prices were low, as they seemed to be more and more frequently.

New Attitudes in America

Partly because of the kind of person that came to America, and partly because of conditions they met here, colonists were becoming different from the people they left behind in Europe. It seemed that changes were taking place in customs and ideas.

Hard work was necessary to success, and every man and woman in the colonies had to serve a useful purpose. Few could be idle. People learned to work and to respect work. This was an important American lesson.

The average individual gained an importance he did not have in England; moreover, participation in assemblies and in town meetings, and having a part in decisions and voting increased the importance of the individual. It took intelligence and cooperation, too, to survive and succeed in America. In Maryland, for example, every free man had some part of community affairs, was entitled to vote, and had a voice in his government, if he owned only a small amount of property. In 1670, a Maryland law set the possession of fifty acres of land or property valued at forty pounds, as the qualification for men to vote. Many, many men in America owned enough land to vote. Literacy, too, was high compared with that of the ordinary man in Europe. So it was that there came to be a pretty broad base of voters.

In contrast, in England, the upper classes were ashamed to work or to engage in trade, while in America, even the upper classes of society supervised their own businesses and lands in order to make a profit. These Americans found their work quite satisfying. One needed an education in order to work out all sorts of personal and legal problems so the study of Latin, the classics, and law were still valuable. Also, men were expected to operate their local governments. So, in America, through necessity, gentlemen valued education and did not scorn work. They kept their accounts, saw that crops were planted, and often even surveyed their own land. They were virtually forced to engage in business. They took over tasks that in England they could have hired others to do. This gave men habits of self-reliance and independence, as well as pride.

This lack of false pride carried over into other activities. Gentlemen rode their own horses in races, hunted game without beaters to drive it toward them, and were not too haughty to enjoy themselves in sports and contests. Often, too, gentlemen found themselves courting the public with kegs of beer when votes were sought to give them political offices which they wanted.

Military responsibilities were different in America, too. It quickly became obvious that an unsupervised band of militia could become arrogant and corrupt. To prevent this, Americans began the practice of having their militiamen serve regular terms of duty with elected leaders, and so the American militia became less a body of professionals and more one of trained civilians.

But again, it must be pointed out that as the American Revolution approached, Americans did not at first see themselves as a separate nation. True, French agents might be in the colonies trying to stir up feeling against England, but most of the colonists wished only to have a primary voice in their affairs. They wanted direct representation in the English Parliament that made their laws. Above all, they did not regard themselves as lowly persons within a system, but rather as equals with all of the rights of Englishmen at home in England.

Stamps such as these were required on all Maryland legal papers
by the English government. (1765)

(Maryland Historical Society)

CHAPTER XXVII

PRELUDE TO WAR

THE English Parliament passed the Stamp Act in March, 1765. Hearing of this, the Maryland Assembly sent a protest to the King. The Assembly had taxed the people of Maryland to meet not only the normal expenses of the colony but also certain costs of the French and Indian War, including building forts such as Cumberland and Frederick. Now England wanted more money from Maryland, and the other American colonies, to help her pay off English war debts. Possibly the colonies should have been more willing to share in the expense of their defense, but at any rate, they did feel imposed upon. It was a case of Parliament's taking matters into its own hands, without spending enough effort to gain a favorable opinion among the American colonial governmental bodies. In Maryland, where a good deal had been done for the war effort, tempers were rising.

England ignored the protest over stamp taxation and appointed a Maryland man, Zachariah Hood, to be stamp-distributor and tax-collector in Maryland. Angry crowds of men refused to let him get off his ship in Annapolis. He did later manage, however, to get ashore unnoticed. But then some people tore down his house. Hood, realizing the seriousness of the situation, and being fearful that the wild tempers he had helped to arouse might lead to violence, fled to New York. The county court in Frederick, Maryland, absolutely refused to use the tax stamps on its legal papers, and other courts soon followed the example. The *Maryland Gazette* published a "mourning" issue with heavy black lines, a death's head and crossbones where the tax stamp was supposed to be placed.

Groups gathered throughout Maryland, tarring and feathering, or burning, or hanging mock effigies[1] of the Stamp Tax and of Hood himself! In the face of all this uproar throughout the colonies, England repealed the law.

Yet another English law, called the Townshend Act, however, was passed in 1767, taxing glass, lead, paint, tea, and paper. American protests rose again. The colonists formed non-importation clubs and agreed not to buy any of the taxed items.

When the ship, *Good Intent*, came into the harbor at Annapolis, members of Maryland's non-importation club searched it and found taxed goods. They would not let the ship's crew put ashore any cargo at all, but gave the captain fresh water and food and made the *Good Intent* return, profitless, to England.

Note how united the colonists were becoming and how determined they were to stand up for what they believed to be their rights. Thus, Maryland, together with other colonies, helped to fight the English taxes; and in cooperating in this way all were learning to work together.

Again, Americans won the fight to get rid of the Townshend Act, for England repealed all of these taxes, except the one on tea. English lawmakers may have thought that it was such a small thing that the turmoil would now quiet down. If the colonies got used to the idea of paying taxes to England on tea, for example, gradually other items might be added to the taxable list. The colonists were not to be so beguiled[2] and now refused to buy tea, even though some merchants wanted to resume full trade with England.

Committees of Correspondence

To work together better the colonies formed "Committees of Correspondence." By use of these, ideas could be exchanged and news could be passed quickly when action in a particular crisis was needed.

The fastest means of getting messages from one place to another was by sailing vessel or by courier. (A courier was a messenger mounted on a good horse who rode as quickly as he could, changing horses frequently to make better speed.) Through these committees of correspondence, not only was news passed quickly back and forth, but also the colonies were joined together in planning how best to defeat dreaded laws and the hated trade regulations.

On November 28, 1773, a shipload of tea arrived in Boston, Massachusetts. Dressed in makeshift "Indian" disguises, some colonists boarded the ship on the night of December 16 and dumped the tea into the harbor. This was the "Boston Tea Party." The King of England and Parliament took revenge on Boston, officially closing her port until the tea should be paid for. The sister colonies, including Maryland, sent food and clothing to Massachusetts to help the people of Boston. Maryland people loaded ships with food and sent them to towns near Boston. There the cargoes were unloaded into wagons and onto pack horses for transport by land to Boston. Samuel Adams himself wrote later, thanking the people of Chestertown, Maryland, for their help in sending food and clothing to Boston. About this time, four regiments of regular British soldiers were sent to Boston in order to enforce the English laws.

Alarmed at the way the colonies were being treated by England, Maryland suggested that representatives from each of the colonies meet in Philadelphia. It was useless, Maryland men said, for just one colony to fight England's harsh methods (they meant Massachusetts). The opposition of one lone colony against the English rule could be easily squashed. It was only possible successfully to protest if all joined together.

Some British Measures that Colonists Disliked
1763-1773

The following list gives some of the British laws and proclamations which angered American colonists:

Proclamation of 1763. This prohibited settlement or land purchase west of the Appalachian Mountains.

Sugar Act, 1764. This cut import duty on non-British molasses but made enforcement strict.

Stamp Act, 1765. Newspapers, legal papers, and other items, were required to bear a tax stamp. (This was repealed in 1766).

Mutiny Act, supplemented by the *Quartering Act, 1765.* This provided for the quartering and maintenance of British troops in America.

Townshend Act, 1765. This taxed imported glass, lead, paint, paper and tea. (In 1770 the taxes were repealed, except for the tea tax.)

Tea Act, 1773. This allowed the East India Company to export tea to America without paying any tax, except for the existing tea tax.

The "Intolerable" Acts, [3] *1774.*

1. *Boston Port Act.* This closed the port to all shipping and removed the British custom-house from the port of Boston.

2. *Massachusetts Government Act.* This gave power to the royal Governor. Members of the Council were to be appointed by the Governor rather than being elected by the General Assembly as had been formerly done. It also required permission from the Governor for town meetings. His appointed sheriffs were to select juries.

3. *Administration of Justice Act.* This act allowed British officials and soldiers to be tried in a colony other than the one in which they were accused, or sent to England for trial.

4. *Quartering Act.* This directed the quartering of troops inside the town of Boston. It extended the existing Mutiny and Quartering Acts.

The Quebec Act, 1774. This gave religious freedom to the Roman Catholics of the province of Quebec. It also enlarged the boundaries of that province (now under English control, remember) to extend to all of the land southward from the Great Lakes to the Ohio River. This land today is occupied by the states of Michigan, Wisconsin, Illinois, Ohio, and Indiana. The Act, also, imposed English criminal law on Canada.

The First Continental Congress

-The First Continental Congress met in September, 1774. Slowly and through necessity, very able leaders were emerging. Likewise, the habit of working together and of fairly reaching important decisions by a majority vote came to be a fact in America. The members of the First Continental Congress, confronted with England's so-called "intolerable acts," prepared to petition for the repeal of these acts. They asked that these laws which they hated be changed. They decided, meanwhile, not to import anything at all from England. The members of the Congress rejected a plan of permanent union which would leave the united colonies still under the British Empire. It is referred to as the "Galloway Plan." It was proposed by Joseph Galloway of Pennsylvania.[4] Finally, if it were to be necessary, they agreed to meet again the following year.

The American colonies had by this time become a very large part of the market for English manufacturing and exporting firms. These economic factors were certainly important in the disagreement between England and the colonies. Parliament, taking the position that it was master in the Empire, was trying to force its interests by law on the colonies. But the colonists objected to this idea of Parliament's role and were ready to resist the laws as unfair to them. Colonial businessmen believed that they had the right to markets and profits that would logically be theirs if England did not interfere with American trade.

One English law that many of the American colonists did not like, but one that was not irritating to Maryland people, was the rule that only English-owned vessels might be used for trade between the colonies and England. Since many ships and boats were built along the shores of Chesapeake Bay, and these were considered English-owned, this navigation regulation was actually helpful to Maryland shipbuilders.

When the Maryland delegates came home from the First Continental Congress, the Maryland Convention formally approved their work and that of the Congress. The Convention was made up of free men from the counties, united to resist unpopular British laws. Since Governor Robert Eden had sent the legal assembly home, the rebels' Convention became Maryland's temporary government. The Convention urged Maryland people to:

1. Increase wool production to be able to clothe themselves and not be dependent on cloth imported from England. (This action would be in violation of British manufacturing regulations.)

2. Call men together to form a militia and to drill, ready for possible fighting.

3. Join together to support other colonies in their struggle against England.

The Luckless Peggy Stewart

An incident now occured, which is still argued over today— Maryland's own "tea party." Was it a just action? Or was it too harsh a treatment? Here is what happened. A ship, the brigantine, *Peggy Stewart*, arrived at Annapolis. Its owner, Anthony Stewart, decided to pay the tax on the 2,000 pounds of tea that she carried and bring both the tea and other goods quietly ashore. But the news that the ship carried tea quickly spread through the town that day.

Men gathered on the streets and in the taverns. It was pointed out that Stewart had joined Maryland's non-importation society and had promised not to buy forbidden goods from England. Soon, tempers grew hotter and some agitators went to Stewart's house. They were noisy and menacing. There was no doubt that they meant business. "Burn your ship or be hanged right here in front of your door," they shouted.

In the face of these threats Stewart offered to burn the tea and to offer a public apology; and he begged to be allowed to land the rest of the cargo. A few people agreed, but the mob leaders shouted louder. They were keeping the mob excited. Inside his house, Stewart's wife was ill. He dared not resist the crowd for fear of violence to his family and himself. So, he ordered the *Peggy Stewart*, named for his daughter, to be run aground and set afire. In fact, he applied the torch himself. It was October 19, 1774.

The loss to this merchant was considerable, as can be imagined. The tea was only a small part of the very valuable cargo, and the ship itself was worth thousands of pounds. The ship burned to the water, the crowd watching and cheering. It may be asked whether it was right to have punished Stewart so sternly for what he had done. Right or wrong, the *Peggy Stewart* incident demonstrated how determined Marylanders and the people of the other American colonies were at this time.

The Burning of the Peggy Stewart.

What would cause the hot-tempered American colonists to flare into even more open rebellion? So far they were asking only for better treatment from the English government. But the moment came in the early hours of April 19, 1775, when Paul Revere and William Dawes galloped through the Massachusetts night, rousing farms and villages with the shout, "The British are coming!" British ships had brought regular soldiers to compel obedience in Massachusetts to the laws of the Empire. During that long day Americans and British soldiers clashed in bloody fighting at Lexington and Concord.

Meanwhile, in Maryland in this period, 1774 to 1775, the Provincial Convention held several separate sessions in Annapolis. Each county sent representatives to these meetings. A Council of Safety which soon became virtually the government of Maryland was formed and saw to it that the wishes of the Convention were respected and enforced. The people in each county were monitored by a Committee of Observation. Thus, it may be seen that the rebellious Maryland colonists were well organized.

The Governor of Maryland, Sir Robert Eden, who represented Henry Harford, son of the last Lord Baltimore, soon found himself with little power. Eden was well liked in Maryland; but, in June, 1776, after a gay ball attended by leading social and political leaders in Annapolis, he was put on shipboard and was politely returned to England.

More and more of the powers of government were being taken over by the Convention and its Council of Safety. Finally, in July, 1775, what amounted almost to a declaration of independence by Maryland was made. The Convention declared that, if England tried to force Maryland to obey the hated laws of Parliament, then the people would fight force with force!

Americans knew that it would be very hard for England to fight a war when men and supplies would have to cross 3,000 miles of water. Experience gained in fighting in the French and Indian War had given thousands of colonists military training. Men had gained a considerable degree of skill in the use of weapons. Even so, the risks were very great.

Then, too, thousands of colonists in America remained loyal to England; and there was no denying that England was a very powerful country. If the war were to be lost by the colonists, as seemed to many quite likely, those who had rebelled would probably lose their properties and quite possibly their lives. Also, many were fearful that even if the rebellion were successful, the radical mob would rule. How, they asked, could some orderly form of government come out of such a situation? Would there not be greater disorder and dangers until, perhaps, some other European nation took over? Which way should Englishmen in America turn?

It was hard to find good answers to these and other questions. All that Americans could hope for was to try to free themselves from England without falling into the hands of some harsher ruler. Thus, each man who volunteered to fight had hard decisions to make. There would be great risks. He knew that, even if all went well, he would be away from home and from his business for a long time. All the while, too, he would be in great danger; but there was the hope, nonetheless, that he could win for himself and his loved ones a better way of life.

---

1 To burn or hang in effigy means to burn or hang a stuffed image of a person to show hatred or contempt.
2 To beguile one is to charmingly deceive him, or to divert him by amusing him. The word can also mean to cheat, to entertain, to mislead or delude.
3 These four acts applied to the center of resistance in the colonies, Massachusetts. They were known as the Massachusetts acts, or the Coercive acts, but the name "Intolerable acts" is the one most used.
4 Joseph Galloway was born near West River, Maryland around 1729. He studied law and was admitted to the bar in Philadelphia. He remained loyal to England.

Maryland Historical Society
Maryland State Marines, wearing blue hunting shirts.

CHAPTER XXVIII

THE AMERICAN REVOLUTION: BRITISH PLANS

T HE awkward, new, American "states, with no precedent to guide them, had now declared their resentment of English taxes and regulation. Powerful old England stirred, amazed at such antics. The Americans wanted to make their own laws and select their own leaders! More shiploads of British soldiers were prepared and sent out to subdue the colonies.

An early effort was made to split the colonies in half at the Potomac River before the colonists could get their revolution well organized. This was attempted by Lord Dunmore in Virginia.[1] He had been rudely driven from the Governor's Palace in Williamsburg, the capital. If he could gain and hold the Potomac until aid arrived, he would be able to stop the flow of men and supplies through the colonies.

Lord Dunmore planned to send ships up the Potomac to meet with land troops loyal to England. These troops were to march down from various spots farther west to meet the ships. On his way up the river, Governor Dunmore planned to plunder rich plantations owned by two leaders known to be loyal to the American cause — George Washington and George Mason. Dunmore hoped, also, to be able to use Indians against the rebellious colonists.

It was the alert John Hanson of Maryland who turned the land army's hopes of victory into swift defeat. The leaders of the British loyalists in Maryland, who were expected to lead troops to meet Lord Dunmore, were rounded up and put into jail. The ships of Lord Dunmore also met with such fierce resistance that he soon left the Potomac and afterward only tried some raids in the Chesapeake Bay area. So the early plan of this English leader in 1775 failed to split the colonies. But this was just the beginning of the war. It was to be a bitter fight — and a long one.

Later, two main plans for subduing the colonies were used by England. The first was to land troops in New York and cut off the New England colonies by gaining control of the Hudson River. Then troops were to march southward, putting down the rebellious towns as they found them.

When this first plan was not as quickly successful as was hoped, the British decided, later in the war on a second plan. This was to land troops in the southern colonies, hoping to find resistance weaker there. How these plans worked out is told in the following chapters.

Maryland and the American Revolution

The attempt by Lord Dunmore to capture control of the Potomac River and split the colonies was, interestingly enough, the only serious fighting done along the river during the War. Yet Maryland was to play a most important part in the struggle in other ways.

Maryland was to send men by the hundreds and thousands to fight with General Washington. Also, this colony helped with all kinds of supplies. In fact, Maryland and her neighbors were called the "granary of the Revolution." Without the food, supplies, and clothing given throughout the war, the troops of the Continental Army might not have been able to endure to the end. Even so, American soldiers were to suffer terribly from lack of weapons, food, warm clothing, and shoes, as well as from wounds and sickness. It is very hard for us to imagine how brave and how determined these men could be.

1 Lord Dunmore was the Earl of Dunmore (1732-1809). He was born Jòhn Murray in Scotland, the oldest son of a Scottish peer. He served in the British Army. In 1756 he succeeded to the title and estates. In 1770 he was the Governor of New York and, eleven months later, the Governor of Virginia. It was after the revolt of the Virginia Assembly in 1775 that he tried to use British ships and Indians to deal with the insurrection.

During the Revolution, Maryland was one of the "bread basket" states, helping to feed the Continental Army.

CHAPTER XXIX

HOW OUR NATION BEGAN

W HEN the Second Continental Congress met in Philadelphia on May 10, 1775, the rebelling colonies were already at war with the mother country, England. In April at Lexington and Concord, in Massachusetts many lives had been lost. It took twenty days for an express rider to ride from Massachusetts to Georgia with the news of the fighting. The battle for independence had begun. The representatives of the colonies realized, as they met in Philadelphia, that they had serious decisions to make. Every colony was represented except Georgia, which was not represented until autumn when its delegates finally arrived.

John Hancock of Massachusetts was elected president of the Congress. The Maryland delegates to the Second Continental Congress were Thomas Johnson, Jr., Matthew Tilghman, Samuel Chase, William Paca, John Hall, Thomas Stone, and Robert Goldsborough. Of the delegates, one of the most active was Thomas Johnson. It was Johnson who on June 15 nominated Colonel George Washington to be commander-in-chief of the continental forces.

Military leadership was needed. In June 1775 the English and American forces clashed in the Battle of Bunker Hill in Boston. Washington took over the Continental Army and eventually forced the English to leave Boston. On the ships bound for Nova Scotia, with General Howe and his British fighting men, went a thousand Bostonians loyal to England! How sad these people must have felt at leaving their American homes and their hopes for success there.

An Independent Nation?

Too much had happened in 1775 and in the first half of 1776 to make peace likely now between England and her American colonies. The English King had proclaimed, in 1775, that the Americans were "rebels", and he authorized the hiring of twenty thousand German soldiers (Hessians) to crush them. In October, 1775, a thousand Americans were left homeless with winter near, after British warships blasted Portland, Maine. Too much had occurred on both sides to forgive and forget.

Charles Carroll

Samuel Chase

William Paca

Thomas Stone

**Four men from Maryland
signed the Declaration of Independence.**

128

The Second Continental Congress, in 1776, decided that the colonies should be free and independent states. Thomas Jefferson of Virginia was instructed to put the feelings of the Congress into words. The draft that he wrote was taken to the Congress with only minor changes made by John Adams of Massachusetts and Benjamin Franklin of Pennsylvania. The Congress amended some of the things in the draft and then adopted it on July 4, 1776. This is our famous Declaration of Independence. Though the Declaration of Independence was approved and passed in Philadelphia on July 4, 1776, it was not signed on that date. On August 2, 1776, fifty-three members of the Congress signed a parchment copy, while still others chose to sign even later. But, because of the agreement of July 4, 1776, the American colonial era was now ended. The colonies were now states, their citizens no longer subjects of the King of England, but citizens of a new nation!

The original of the Declaration of Independence is proudly kept in the National Archives Building in Washington, D.C. It is one of the most important papers ever written in the history of the world!

What does it say? The Declaration of Independence sets forth ideals of fair government. It lists twenty-seven reasons for separation from England. It tells us that all men are created equal and have the right to life, liberty and the pursuit of happiness. Governments, states the Declaration, are supposed to secure these rights and should obtain their powers only from the citizens by vote, and men should not be governed by the whims or desires of dictators or kings.

Maryland Men Sign

Four men from Maryland signed the Declaration of Independence: Charles Carroll of Carrollton, Samuel Chase, William Paca, and Thomas Stone. Carroll, who lived to a very old age, was known in his later years as "the Signer." By signing the Declaration he risked his great fortune and lands, and his life. The other men signing the Declaration, too, risked all they owned.

Charles Carroll of Carrollton was destined to become one of the great men of America. He contributed a great deal of money to the American Revolution, and he also contributed in helping to form the ideas that were to be written down to form the basis of both our national and state governments. For example, he and others made certain that the powers of government and church were kept separate. The United States of America was unique in having no state religion. Carroll and others made sure, too, that freedom of religion was included in the legal rights of American citizens.

Other American leaders, such as Jefferson, Franklin, Washington, Madison, Jay and Hamilton, regarded slavery as a great evil; and slavery, moreover, did not appear to agree with the ideals of freedom expressed in the Declaration of Independence. But it was a divisive issue, and in order to unite all of the new states the issue of slavery was put aside for the time being. A gradual abolishment of the practice of slavery seemed likely to the writers.

Maryland State Government Needed

Having decided to discard England's rule, Maryland had to set up a government that would give its citizens freedom, but freedom under fair laws. From July 26, 1775, the Maryland Convention had taken over completely the government of Maryland. It was made up of delegates as we have noted, sent to Annapolis by the counties. The delegates were, after that date, to be elected annually, and each county was to elect five delegates.

On June 23, 1776, Governor Robert Eden had left Maryland aboard the warship *Fowey*. The Convention now had undisputed authority. The changeover in government in Maryland occurred with a remarkable absence of unlawful violence.

In the Maryland Convention on June 28, 1776, Charles Carroll had recommended that Maryland join with the representatives of other colonies, in the formal declaration of independence from England. The Convention agreed and issued instructions to the delegates in Philadelphia accordingly.

On July 3, 1776, moreover, the Convention decided that it was time to set up a permanent form of government in Maryland, and decided that a special election should be held. Eligible voters were those of twenty-one years of age who owned fifty acres of land or property worth fifty English pounds.

On August 1, 1776, each county in Maryland chose representatives to a constitutional convention, called to write the first Maryland constitution. The delegates, with this serious task ahead of them, met on August 14, in Annapolis, and elected Matthew Tilghman as president of the Convention. The delegates then selected a committee, by vote, to prepare and submit to the Convention, a State constitution which was to include a declaration of rights. The members of the committee were: Matthew Tilghman, Charles Carroll of Annapolis, William Paca, Charles Carroll of Carrollton, George Plater, Samuel Chase, and Robert Goldsborough. These men set to work to write the first state constitution for Maryland.

The first part of the Maryland Constitution of 1776 was the Preamble. It states that "We, the people of Maryland," intend to write a good constitution for the sure foundation of, and the security of, the State of Maryland.

Then the writers of the Maryland Constitution prepared a Bill of Rights. This section has come down to us with almost no change. The Bill of Rights gave citizens freedom to worship as each decided for himself; also, freedom of speech; freedom of the press; the right to assemble peaceably; the right to have privacy in one's home; the right to petition the government; the right to trial by jury; and the right not to be charged unfair fines, or bail; or to be given cruel or unusual punishments. This first Maryland Bill of Rights is quite similar to those rights enumerated in the first ten amendments to our United States Constitution.[1] Each statement of rights, both state and (later) national, were based on ideas of human rights that had slowly developed and were recognized in England by the time of the American Revolution.

In the Maryland Constitution, the delegates on the committee recommended a "Form of Government," which provided that there should be a governor, to be chosen each year by the General Assembly; who was to serve no more than three terms consecutively.

The legislature, as provided for in this new Constitution, was to be called the General Assembly. It was to consist of a House of Delegates and a Senate. Four men from each county were to be elected each year by the voters, to serve in the House of Delegates; and both Baltimore and Annapolis were each to elect two delegates to this body. The Senate was to be made up of fifteen men, to be chosen every five years. The senators were not to be elected directly by the voters, but were to be chosen by an electoral college. This college was made up of two members from each county and one member each from Baltimore City and Annapolis. The Sheriff to be chosen for a three-year term, was the only county officer locally elected.

The Governor's Council was to be quite a powerful group of men. It was to be made up of fifteen members, elected each year by the General Assembly. When the Governor appointed men to fill State offices, he was to get the approval of his Council on the choices.

Finally, to give equal voice to all sections of Maryland, regardless of population, there were to be two Treasurers and two Land Offices, one each for the Eastern Shore and for the Western Shore; also, both of these sections would have separate Courts of Appeals.

When the committee agreed upon a final version of the constitution, copies were printed. The Convention had the copies sent out through the counties so that the voters might decide whether or not they liked the proposed Constitution. The voters, of course, had to approve or disapprove the final draft. The American Revolution was being fought, and this delayed the final report on the Maryland Constitution. However, by October, 1776, the Convention was able to meet to discuss the proposed Constitution item by item.

Naturally, there were long debates over what should be included. But, by November 3, 1776, a Declaration of Rights was agreed upon. On November 8, the Form of Government was also agreed upon. The Convention then formally adopted the entire Constitution on November 10, 1776.

The finished document had some unusual features in its Declaration of Rights, though its list of rights was quite similar to that of Virginia, Pennsylvania, and Delaware. Among items unique to Maryland was the one that allowed people to vote without paying a yearly fee, or "poll tax." Another unusual feature was in the clause that forbade the taxation of people without money or property. Under this Constitution, the Governor appointed the judges of the courts, and his choices were approved by the Maryland Senate.

Still other unusual features in the Maryland Declaration of Rights were the ones that forbade the granting of titles of nobility, that prohibited any person from holding more than one public office at a time, and that outlawed monopolies. This, also, was the first state constitution to order a rotation of office in the executive departments. Finally, the Declaration of Rights stated that the General Assembly must not declare any item in the Declaration unlawful! The authors of the Maryland Bill of Rights wanted it to be a permanent list of human rights for the citizens of Maryland. For more than two-thirds of a century the Constitution of 1776 served the State with only a few changes. It was first seriously changed in 1838.

State Government Begins

Now that Maryland had a Constitution, the new State government was organized, a legislature was formed and a Governor chosen. He was Thomas Johnson and he took office in Annapolis on March 21, 1777. Johnson was an attorney of great ability. He was among the first in America to insist on American's rights to protest the British laws that he felt were not just. He also was the man, noted before, who had proposed George Washington in the Second Continental Congress to be Commander-in-Chief of an American army. Needless to say, he was an energetic and trustworthy man, a great American and an excellent choice for Maryland's first governor under the new Constitution.

---

1 The Constitution of the United States was not written until 1787.

CHAPTER XXX

MEN OF MARYLAND IN THE AMERICAN REVOLUTION

GEORGE Washington now Commander-in-Chief of the American forces, was well known in Virginia and in other colonies. He had traveled in Virginia and Maryland a great deal to social affairs and to visit friends. He often attended races, balls, and dinners in Annapolis, for example. He had traveled a great deal too, on business as a plantation owner and also as a surveyor. He had explored many a wild western section of the country during his surveys, sometimes investigating land that he wished to buy for a business investment. Also, Washington had military experience. He had organized, trained, and led colonial militia in the French and Indian War.

Now, as Commander of the American revolutionary forces, Washington needed soldiers if he were to resist the ever increasing number of troops being gathered and shipped to America by Britain. The first troops from the southern colonies to come to the General's call for help near Boston were two Maryland companies. To get there, Captain Michael Cresap and Thomas Price led a deerskin-dressed band of sharpshooters 550 miles in twenty-two days. There were one hundred and thirty men, all armed with muskets and Indian tomahawks. Most of them were excellent shots and they knew how to make precious shot and powder count from their experience in hunting game for food.

More than once, Maryland troops were to prove their great importance to General Washington; and, while they did not win the war alone, they could rightly be proud of their courage and fighting abilities! Most of them were young, spirited, and well-disciplined, and their degree of training was unusual in the first days of the war.

In the Battle of Long Island, in August, 1776, British troops in overwhelming numbers succeeded in nearly surrounding the American army. To avoid the fast-closing trap the American army needed to cross over the water to Manhattan Island in order to escape up the Hudson River Valley. But someone had to hold back the British while the main body of the army made its way back to safety. About four hundred Maryland men, led by Major Mordecai Gist and Captain Samuel Smith were chosen for the holding action. Not only did these soldiers stand firm, but they charged the trained British soldiers six times! For more than an hour, this little contingent held off the powerful enemy. Finally a British attack struck from the flank, that is from the side. One group of soldiers was surrounded and forced to surrender. Yet three companies of men hacked their way back through the enemy to the swamp where other Americans, with a withering rifle fire, made the British halt. When Washington had gotten his main army to safety, the Maryland men at last retreated across the stream they had held.[1] They had saved the day, at the cost of over half of their 400 men killed. In fact, only about twenty of the 400 were not wounded! Because of this Maryland troops were henceforth singled out for their courage, and were affectionately referred to as the "Maryland Old Line." Later battles made the name stick and earned for Maryland itself, eventually, the nickname "Old Line State."

At the battle at Monmouth, New Jersey, for example, Maryland troops were called upon again by Washington to hold the enemy forces back in the face of a threatened rout.[2] "We will stop them—or fall!" promised Colonel Nathaniel Ramsey, commander of the Maryland troops. And stop them the Maryland men did. The action of the Maryland men cost many lives, but their courage, nevertheless, was of the greatest importance. Washington knew very well that if his Army were ever to suffer a severe defeat, the Revolution would be over. His genius lay in his ability to avoid total humiliation. As long as he could keep a strong force of men and could move them about, he had hope of final victory.

These first engagements in the summer and fall of 1776 saw Washington and his ragged troops being driven from New York and through New Jersey. The English plan to secure the northern ports and port cities and then march southward appeared to be succeeding.

Howe, the British general, was to win thousands of citizens back to the English government in these early months of the war, saying that, if they renewed their loyalty to England, he would forgive them their part in the rebellion. This offer might have succeeded even better if Washington had not kept on fighting, and if the British had not made other serious mistakes, such as that of not controlling the behavior of their hired Hessian troops. This behavior turned many people from the English government. In December of 1776, Washington was retreating, his forces weakened not only because of battle losses and illnesses, but because many of the enlistments were up and the enlistees were leaving camp and returning home.

It seemed likely that the well equipped forces of British and Hessian troops could not be stopped. In contrast, Washington's penniless army of tattered men sometimes left a trail of blood from their bare feet in the snow. On December 8, these weary men were approaching the Delaware River. The capital city of Philadelphia was now being threatened. To cross the Delaware River, as he must do, and to prevent the enemy from following him, Washington seized every boat he could find.

It was now the dead of winter. The British, according to European custom at that time, did their fighting in the warmer months, with a long rest during the winter season. At Trenton, New Jersey, Howe, thinking the campaign temporarily in recess, left a force of Hessians to hold his position, and then returned to New York. He was sure that he had the rebels on the run now, and the Christmas season beckoned him back to the city. He also left his subordinate, General Cornwallis, with orders to set up winter quarters at Princeton, New Jersey.

Never had matters looked worse for the hopes of the Americans. Washington's army by December 20 numbered about 6,000 men,[3] though many enlistments were to expire at the end of the year. What could his badly supplied army do before then? The General was determined to try to protect the city of Philadelphia and somehow to hold his army together through the coming winter months. He knew that many recruits would join him in the spring. He faced great odds. The men had not been paid. He needed supplies of food, equipment, weapons, clothing, and he needed a place for the winter. He needed, too, time to revive, to organize and to train his troops.

In this, perhaps the darkest hour of the Revolution, Washington's great genius shone through. He chose Christmas night, 1776, as the moment to bring about 2500 men back over the Delaware River in small boats. Muffling all sound, they moved through icy water and floating cakes of ice, to land at a point some eight miles north of Trenton. A blinding snowstorm further helped to hide the march toward the Hessian camp at Trenton. The move was so bold, so quiet, and so unexpected that Washington and his men captured the whole garrison at midnight, as the enemy soldiers were drinking in celebration of their "defeat" of the American army!

General Washington took a thousand prisoners, most of them Germans. These were not only removed from the fighting but some possibly would be useful in exchange for American prisoners taken by the British. Best of all, Washington captured stores of food, arms and clothing that his army so desperately needed to survive the winter. Indeed, the march toward Trenton had been made at the cost of great suffering from the cold and from lack of food.

A British messenger made his way to General Cornwallis, who had gone on to New York, with the news of the capture of Trenton, and the news also was sent to the enemy encampment at Princeton, New Jersey, which began to "hum like a hive of bees."[4]

Lord Cornwallis immediately left New York and, collecting other troops as he went, traveled directly to Trenton. On January 2, 1777, he approached the village with nearly 6,000 soldiers, and with more expected.

General Washington, meanwhile, had again withdrawn into Pennsylvania. But then, daringly, he re-crossed the Delaware River on December 30 and 31, and gathered about 5,000 men near Trenton. Learning of the approach of General Cornwallis, Washington once more drew back to the river, but then suddenly found himself trapped on the east bank with the enemy very near. Cornwallis decided to wait for morning to capture the American "fox" and his troops. Washington, however, did not wait to be taken. He caused bonfires to be built and left a few men at the camp to convince the British that he was still camped. About midnight, he led his army around and behind the British, and made straight for Princeton where he surprised the forces left there. A desperate battle followed, and once more the Americans scored a decisive victory. Five hundred prisoners and great quantities of supplies and ammunition were captured.

Now Washington had General Cornwallis to the west of him, advancing with a large force of British. In the circumstances General Washington elected to turn northward, where he found a good campsite in the hills at Morristown, New Jersey. Because of the cold and the snow the British decided not to attack his position, and withdrew into eastern New Jersey. There the British supply lines were less exposed. With the immediate pressure eased, Washington and his troops stayed on in Morristown until the spring of 1777.

And so the Continental Army had survived. American morale, so low in December, was now much improved. Some historians feel that the battles of Trenton and Princeton were possibly the turning point of the American Revolution. Certainly the Americans had been very near defeat at Christmas time in 1776.

At the Close of 1776

As the year 1776 came to a close it was clear that, despite Washington's winter raid successes, this had been a very dark and dangerous period. Among the early disappointments had been the failure of Canada to join in the rebellion against England.

In an attempt to persuade Canada to join in the fight for independence, Congress had sent a commission to that province. The commission was made up of Benjamin Franklin of Pennsylvania, who was then over seventy years old, and three Marylanders. They were Samuel Chase, Charles Carroll of Carrollton, and the Jesuit priest, John Carroll. John Carroll was later to become the first American bishop of the Roman Catholic Church.

In 1763, Canada had been granted certain unusual privileges including political and religious concessions, and then there had come the Quebec Act of 1774. In view of such liberal treatment, it can be understood why the French-Canadians chose to remain loyal to the British government. The American delegation returned from the long journey to report to the Second Continental Congress. The thirteen American states must fight on without the aid of the Canadians. The American Revolution, nevertheless, was to have considerable effect on the ethnic composition of Canada. During the War between thirty and forty thousand Americans who were loyal to Britain, fled into Canada in order to remain under "the Union Jack." This was a large and important immigration in that it added a large English-speaking population to the French ethnic group in that country.

Winter Raids

During the winter of 1776-1777, Washington continually harassed the British by raids of every sort but would not be trapped into a major battle which might wipe out his American forces. The skirmishes helped to weaken the enemy's military strength and morale.

British soldiers sent into the countryside to gather food for the men and feed for the horses, often were attacked by bands of Americans, who forced them to return empty-handed. For lack of food the British finally had to retire from some of their advanced positions. Certainly the bitter winter weather was helpful to the Americans; and after Trenton and Princeton there was little talk about reconciliation with Britain.

Washington and Marylanders

Washington, a masterly general, was making full use of the situation; and he was good at outguessing his enemy, attacking unexpectedly, and moving his troops rapidly. A strict diciplinarian, his officers and men knew that he was a man to be trusted and respected. American morale was slowly building, and the pride of the Maryland men who served under his command was even greater. These young men were willing to give their very lives, if need be, in their belief that Americans should be free. Washington sorrowfully wrote, in a letter that winter, that of the 1500 young men from Maryland who had joined him, scarce a handful remained. With their lives many had helped buy Washington, and the country, the time needed to gain momentum in the fight for freedom. Many soldiers, too, had been wounded and others had returned home when their terms of service expired. Among the brave Maryland soldiers who gave outstanding help to the General was Tench Tilghman. He served as Washington's confidential secretary and aide-de-camp.

---

1 James McSherry, **History of Maryland**.
2 A rout is a disorganized retreat.
3 John R. Alden, **A History of the American Revolution.**
4 Scharf, **History of Maryland, Vol. II.**

English Foot Soldier

Hessian Fusilier

CHAPTER XXXI

THE AMERICAN REVOLUTION
AND ITS EFFECT ON MARYLAND
1777-1778

IN the spring of 1777 new recruits joined Washington, bringing his army up to a total of 9,000 men.[1] This would have been more encouraging except for the fact that "at least one-half were totally ignorant of discipline and had never looked an enemy in the face."[2] Anxiously, Washington sent out scouts to find out where the British fleet intended to land troops.

When it became apparent that the British fleet was moving toward Chesapeake Bay, it was decided not to defend Annapolis; and stores of weapons and supplies were moved inland away from the Bay. The fleet came sailing up the Bay in August, 1777, and landed the foot soldiers at the head of the Elk River in Cecil County, Maryland. The plan was to attack the Continental Army in force and if possible, to destroy it.

It is little wonder therefore that the wily Washington gave himself what little advantage he could obtain by trying to outguess General Howe. Part of Washington's strategy was to send small bands of fast-moving fighters to harass the British troops, who never knew when they would be suddenly attacked and perhaps ambushed.

To defend Philadelphia, Washington, with his main forces, took a stand on Brandywine Creek in Pennsylvania. The site is about halfway between the head of the Elk River and the city of Philadelphia. Here Washington's army made the British regulars pay dearly, but at last the Americans were forced to retreat. When the battle was over, it was clear that the still untrained and inexperienced Americans, too, had suffered a great deal. Over three hundred of Washington's men were dead and another three hundred were captured. In addition, almost six hundred more were wounded. Yet, Washington had managed to hold the strategic advantage over the enemy. The British dared not get too far away from their ships and from the few positions they held.

In the year 1777, the Americans were gradually gaining strength. Encouraging, was the fact that quantities of supplies were now arriving from France, as well as other forms of financial support from

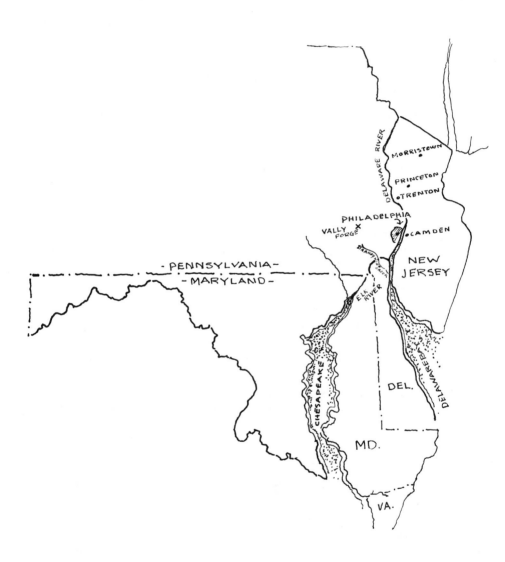

the French and the Spanish crowns. American ships, too, had been successful in intercepting supplies bound for the British forces in America; and, on land, raiders were capturing British pack and wagon trains. Finally, more and more men were enlisting in the Continental Army, and there were now beginning to be many experienced soldiers under Washington's command.

Following the battles at Brandywine Creek and at Whitehorse Tavern, the British were able to take over the city of Philadelphia, but this loss to the Americans was not as serious as it might have been a few months earlier. The control of the Delaware River had taken time and it was not until November 16 that it was all accomplished. There, too, was the fact that General Howe, in seeking to capture the American capital city, had been forced to neglect the important Hudson River Valley, at the very moment when British forces, marching southward on the Americans from Canada, were completely dependent on this control. So it was that the plan to cut off the American's northern states from the rest failed; and finally at Saratoga, on the Hudson, on October 17, 1777, the British were compelled to surrender Burgoyne's army of 6,000 soldiers. Quantities of arms and supplies were captured by the victorious American troops led by General Benedict Arnold and General Horatio Gates.[3]

The Continental Congress had retired from Philadelphia to meet in Lancaster, Pennsylvania, on September 27, 1777. After meeting for three days, the Congress adjourned to meet, on October 1 in York, Pennsylvania. The citizens of Philadelphia who remained, while the British stayed in that city, had mixed feelings about the hard-drinking General Howe and his staff in their midst. The Americans did not fail to notice that General Howe and some of the other military men had brought along their lady friends! Still, there was the fact, too, that the British paid for supplies in good English money, while the Americans passed out Continental currency whose value was doubtful.

During the month of December, 1777, the main body of the Continental Army went into winter quarters at Valley Forge in Chester County, Pennsylvania, about twenty miles northwest of Philadelphia. Here were encamped approximately 11,000 men.[4] It was bitterly cold in the next few weeks and very hard on the men. As yet, the soldiers lacked sufficient food, clothing and comfortable quarters, but even so, Washington and his officers worked to drill and to train the men. Of great assistance in this training was the work of Baron von Steuben, a German officer with American sympathies. How often the Americans must have scowled at the thought of the British wintering comfortably just a few miles away in Philadelphia. Somehow, nonetheless, the men and their officers survived that terrible winter.

The men of the "Maryland Line" were more fortunate and fared better than did the army forces at Valley Forge that winter. They had been ordered to Wilmington, Delaware, in order to guard the area near the head of Chesapeake Bay; and, as it turned out their winter was spent more comfortably, thanks to a lucky windfall. For it so happened that a detachment of Marylanders had managed to capture a British brigantine full of food and supplies.

Medical Treatment at the Time of the American Revolution

It is very difficult for us, today, to understand how very little was known of medicine just two hundred years ago. There was as yet no knowledge of germs or of viruses. Lacking the scientific discoveries that have since been made, doctors and assistants did not know how wounds became infected, nor why and how diseases were spread. Nor was there as yet any anesthesia and this was at a time when surgeons knew only two kinds of major operations — amputations and trepanations.[5] Sterile instruments, sterile bandages, and disinfectants, also, were almost a century away!

Doctors did know that cleanliness seemed to help wounds to heal, and that the dressings must be changed. They realized that diseases spread from one person to another in some way. For this reason, doctors of the Continental Army found that small hospital buildings were better than large ones; for then, at least they could isolate diseases and "fevers."

Hospitals at that time were places to be dreaded, and no one who could be cared for at home ever went to a hospital. In fact, very few hospitals existed in the period of the American Revolution. During the war soldiers were cared for in makeshift military hospitals. These places were, more often than not, dirty, crowded, stinking, and lacking clean air. Typhoid and typhus were lumped together and called "hospital fever," "camp fever," or "jail fever," since these diseases were common when people were crowded into camps, jails or hospitals. In overcrowded hospitals lice thrived, often carrying typhus germs from one patient to another. In those days, to be sent to a prison camp or prison ship was very often a death sentence, because the knowledge of disease control was so limited. During the American Revolution, many Americans died in British prisons. Many died in their own encampments. To Maryland the returning soldiers frequently brought home such diseases as smallpox, which were thus spread through the civilian population in dreadful ways.

Yet, even so, there were conscientious doctors searching, working, trying to make sense of illnesses and trying to improve on methods of treating wounds. It is interesting to note, for example, that the Congress in February, 1777, ordered smallpox innoculation for the Continental Army. The idea was then very new. This was not the safe vaccination that we know today. Instead it was a way of giving the innoculated person a mild case of the disease in order to make him immune. At first some actually died from the vaccination itself, developing severe cases of smallpox, though possibly fewer died than would have done so had innoculation not been given. All in all, it is clear that doctors in those days fought military and civilian illnesses and death with puny weapons indeed!

Among the doctors who served in the Revolution was Dr. James Wilkinson from Maryland. He was, some years later, actually promoted to the position of Commander-in-Chief of the Army. Serving also, from this State, was "the brave Irishman," Dr. James McHenry. Fort McHenry in Baltimore is named for him.

Dr. McHenry had been born in Ireland and had come to America in 1771. He served the Continental Army as a medical officer until he was selected by General Washington for duty as a personal secretary. After the war McHenry served in the Maryland state government and later became a member of the United States Senate. He was next to become Secretary of War in President Washington's cabinet. He retired from this position in 1800 and died in Baltimore, May 1816. McHenry was said to be a good doctor and was genuinely interested in improving the science of medicine. Both McHenry and Wilkinson were both so useful as staff officers that their medical work was shifted to the background.

Of all the medical men of the Revolution, Dr. James Craik of Charles County, Maryland, stands out as probably the most important. As a young man he had served as a surgeon in the British Army. Coming to America during the French and Indian War, he had become acquainted with the, then, Colonel Washington, who soon made him Chief Medical Officer in the Virginia militia.

After that struggle ended in 1763, he bought land near Port Tobacco and built one of Maryland's famous houses, "LaGrange," which is still standing. By this time he and Washington were close friends and he had become the family doctor for the Washington family.

At the beginning of the Revolution, Dr. Craik joined the Continental Army and he soon became Assistant Director-General of the Army's Medical Department, and finally in 1781, Chief Physician and Surgeon of the Army. It was to be this Marylander who attended

General Washington in his final illness. General Washington in his will left some of his furniture to Dr. Craik. This doctor died in 1814 in the City of Alexandria in Virginia, where he had moved to practice medicine, about the time of Washington's death, in 1799.

The French Become Allies

Returning to our story of the Revolution we find that when the British surrendered at Saratoga, in 1777, the French government realizing that now the young United States might have a good chance of winning independence from Britain, decided to make an open treaty of alliance. Now France was actively entering the struggle. France felt that by helping to cut the American colonies away from Britain, not only would Britain lose much power in America but would be less powerful in Europe as well. And so France began to send fighting men and French warships to help the United States openly. The very country that had opposed American fighting men in the recent French and Indian War now joined them in fighting the British. This move on the part of France makes more sense if we remember that France and England were bitter rivals and that in this war, as well as earlier action, France was fighting Britain, her traditional enemy. News that France had become America's ally encouraged our soldiers and civilians. Already, in fact, the young Frenchman, the Marquis de Lafayette, had joined Washington's staff and was contributing his services and some of his personal funds to the Revolution. Now, not only he and other French volunteers who had previously joined the American forces, but also officers and men of the regular French army and navy were to be seen on the streets of Annapolis and Baltimore.

Maryland Women During the American Revolution

While their men were away fighting or in the business of public affairs in Annapolis or elsewhere, Maryland women found themselves more and more taking over the work of running farms and plantations. They helped, too, in other ways. Once General Washington himself wrote to Mrs. Mary Lee, the wife of the second Governor of Maryland, Thomas Lee, to thank her and the women of Maryland for their work. They had sent blankets, bandages, clothing, and food to the encampments at Valley Forge and at Morristown.

In Baltimore, the popular and charming Lafayette, was given a ball. The year was 1780. On hand were women wearing lovely gowns of every color. Silks and satins glimmered in the light from oil lamps and candles. Men in uniform and in formal evening attire danced with the ladies. Toasts were drunk, and music filled the ballroom. But, looking over the gay scene, young Lafayette could only remark, "I cannot enjoy the gaiety of this scene while so many poor soldiers are in want of clothes."

"We will supply them," the ladies promised him.

And they did supply them, for the next morning the ballroom was turning into a clothing "manufactury" by the women. There they made much-needed clothing for American soldiers. Meanwhile, requisitions went out to all parts of Maryland for needed supplies,—shoes, guns, cannon, powder and food.

Maryland Fights at Sea

During the Revolution, Maryland was often at the mercy of British raiders from the sea. At the beginning of the Revolution, Lord Dunmore had harassed the Americans from the lower reaches of Chesapeake Bay. With so little American seapower, the early months and years of the war saw Britain fully in control of the sea. Still, more and more ships were fitted out to protect the shores and to hamper the enemy. Baltimore, in fact, fitted out more privateers than any other American port city along the Atlantic coast. A privateer is a ship which is privately owned but is authorized by a government to serve as a warship. As such they could engage enemy ships in battle and sink them or capture them. Many a cargo, meant for British troops, was diverted to the use of the Continental Army, thanks to the privateers. The privateers, to be sure, usually got a share in the value of the ships and cargo they captured.

To be effective, sailing ships designed for privateering and for running cargoes through the British blockade needed to be built for speed. They had to be quick and maneuverable. With great sails billowing, American ships sometimes chased British ships to the very shores of England during the American Revolution.

Maryland Loyalists

Viewing the American Revolution, one might be tempted to divide everyone into two groups, those Americans fighting for independence, or those loyal to England. The loyalists we might resent and feel that these people were bad. But the question is: was it wrong to be loyal to one's country and to one's king? When the War started, it seemed quite likely that the Americans fighting for independence were simply rebellious hotheads who would shortly be subdued. Also, assuming that, somehow, the Americans did gain their independence, would they be able to bring about a fair and decent government? The decision as to loyalty, then, was not an easy one to make.

During the Revolution, many remained loyal to England. This was the case not just on some Eastern Shore counties of Maryland. And, while quick action by Maryland's revolutionary leaders prevented the Loyalist uprisings from gaining overwhelming strength, by offering pardon to some grumbling citizens and jailing others, yet no doubt Loyalists in large numbers were to be found in every part of Maryland.

The Maryland governor took very direct action in 1777 when he heard that the Continental Army was badly in need of blankets. He had a house to house collection made for blankets! In each household, half of all blankets not being actually used were taken for the Army and paid for in the new Continental currency.

In the year, 1777, new barracks were built at Frederick, Maryland, as well as at the head of the Elk and at Annapolis. The winter of 1777-1778 was again a cold one, and many grumbled about the war, not realizing that brighter days were ahead. Important developments were to come in the spring of 1778.

1 John R. Alden, **A History of the American Revolution.**
2 McSherry-James, **History of Maryland.**
3 Burgoyne surrendered to General Gates.
4 R. Ernest Dupuy and Trevor N. Dupuy, **The Compact History of the Revolutionary War.**
5 To amputate something means to cut it off or remove it. Feet, legs, hands and arms were removed by amputating them. Trepanation is an operation in which the bones of the skull are bored or sawed in order to relieve the brain of pressures caused by an injury that causes a part of the skull to press upon the brain, or pressures caused by blood clots or accumulations of fluids.

The First U. S. Flag, Adopted by Congress June 14, 1777.

CHAPTER XXXII

MARYLAND HAS A PART IN
PLANNING A NEW NATIONAL GOVERNMENT

BEFORE going further with the story of the Revolution, let us see how our present form of government was being "invented" by the Congress. The First Continental Congress had met in Philadelphia, in 1774, primarily to protest the British taxing policies and the Intolerable Acts, but also briefly to consider a possible form of American union within the British Empire. Public opinion was, at first, mostly in favor of the colonies remaining loyal members of the British empire and certainly that was the position of Maryland in 1774.

Yet, when bitter civil war broke out, and when hired Hessian troops were used against the colonists; then American public opinion began to swing toward making a break with England. Other factors, of course, also contributed to developing the spirit of independence and to the action by the Second Continental Congress of July 4, 1776, referred to always since that time as the Declaration of Independence. Four delegates from Maryland signed that important document, Charles Carroll of Carrollton, William Paca, Thomas Stone, and Samuel Chase. All of these men were leaders of great influence and property.

Congress Comes to Baltimore

As the first winter of the war went on (1776-1777), Washington and his troops, as we have mentioned, were forced back toward Philadelphia where the Second Continental Congress was in session; and on December 17, 1776, the threat to Philadelphia was so great that the Congress left Philadelphia to meet on December 20 in Baltimore. There, Congress went on with its work of waging war, as well as designing the form of the new government. The new government was an idealistic concept yet a practical one, too. It was designed to give the citizen liberty, under the exclusive jurisdiction (power) of the newly created State, but one also to make him responsible to the law.

The Congress directed the Revolution from May, 1775, until March, 1781; and during this period managed also to write a constitution providing for a loose confederation, for the final approval of the thirteen states. Since the war created many emergencies, the Congress was forced to go from one place to another in order to remain in session.[1] Its meeting place in Baltimore from December, 1776 to March, 1777, was in a building then located at the corner of Sharpe and Baltimore Streets.

By November 15, 1777, the Dickinson Committee on the Constitution had drafted and had submitted to the Congress the Articles of Confederation. Under the form of union, spelled out in the Articles, the States were completely the masters of their destiny with power to govern themselves. The central government was to act in formulating policy and in an advisory capacity through a national congress representative of the member states. The Articles, of course, must be approved by the states, and it was to be several years before the Articles were to win final approval. In the meantime, the Second Continental Congress continued to direct the affairs of the nation.

---

1 Before 1790 the seat of government for the nation was located at various times in eight different places. These were as follows:

Philadelphia, Pennsylvania, July 4, 1776, to December 12, 1776.
Baltimore, Maryland, December 20, 1776, to March 4, 1777.
Philadelphia, Pennsylvania, March 5, 1777, to September 18, 1777.
Lancaster, Pennsylvania, September 27, 1777.
York, Pennsylvania, September 30, 1777, to June 27, 1778.
Philadelphia, Pennsylvania, July 2, 1778, to June 21, 1783.
Princeton, New Jersey, June 30, 1783, to November 4, 1783.
Annapolis, Maryland, November 26, 1783, to June 3, 1784.
Trenton, New Jersey, November 1, 1784, to December 24, 1784.
New York City, New York, January 11, 1785, to August 12, 1790.

(Joseph H. Cromwell, C & P Telephone Company of Maryland)

Young men, dressed in the uniform of the Continental Army of the days of the American Revolution, parade at historic Fort Frederick, near Hancock, in Western Maryland.

148

CHAPTER XXXIII

MARYLAND DURING THE WAR YEARS
1778-1781

WITH the spring of 1778 the tide of the War seemed to turn. French warships now began to hover off the coast of the United States. The American troops came out of their winter quarters with considerable training, determination, and unity. The British, realizing how easily Philadelphia could be attacked from the water, left that city. In fact, all during 1778 and 1779, the presence of the French fleet on the one hand and General Washington on the other hand were to make the British feel themselves "between the devil and the deep blue sea!"

Early in 1778, France officially came into the American Revolution with a declaration of war on England. Soon Holland and Spain also declared war on England. With these developments, a new confidence was evident among the American states.

Maryland enthusiastically filled a quota of 2,902 fighting men in 1778. Yet, only diligent watchfulness kept Maryland's Somerset and Worcester County residents from open rebellion. Here there were many Loyalists, who did not like the idea of fighting England. Tory galleys and small cruisers operated by the British made it necessary for Maryland to keep a marine force on Chesapeake Bay as well as an active force on the Eastern Shore led by Colonel Richardson. Not until the following year (1779) was this active rebellion suppressed in Somerset and Worcester Counties, where the appearance of the proposed Articles of Confederation, guaranteeing a sound and fair American government made a good impression on the people there. Ships that had been used for patrol duty on the Potomac River, being now of little use, were sold by the Maryland government.

In Annapolis in 1779, action was taken to show Maryland soldiers that their sacrifices were appreciated. A commitment was made to pay officers and men in full for their services when the war should end, and also plans were made to better clothe and feed the soldiers.

Immigration Continues

Maryland had gained some people when a large number of Germans who deserted the British army chose to stay in the state. Interestingly, immigrants from Europe to the United States continued even though the country was at war. There was need for more people to perform all the work arising in a new country. In Europe life was often very hard and the American scene promised hope for new opportunities and a new life.

A considerable number of citizens here and elsewhere, who were loyal to England had moved out; and to offset these losses, Maryland at an early date voted to spend money to spread circulars in England, Switzerland, Holland, Ireland, and Germany, to attract people to the new state. These immigrants could become citizens simply by taking an oath of allegiance.

War to the South

Baffled in the north and threatened in the middle colonies, the British decided in 1780, that their best hope of winning the war lay to the south. British troops in February of that year landed near Charleston, South Carolina, and the enemy proceeded to attack and capture several southern port cities. Yet this plan, too, soon began to go amiss for the invaders. General Cornwallis discovered that the Americans led by General Nathaniel Green were whittling away at his strength. He was losing many men and was being lured far inland. Finally, for lack of supplies and to keep from being cut off from reinforcements, General Cornwallis returned to the coast at Wilmington, North Carolina.

A year of fighting in the south gained the British little, though they still held the port towns of Savannah, Georgia: Charlestown, South Carolina; and Wilmington, North Carolina. As the fall of 1781 began, Cornwallis was moving northward into Virginia, continually harassed and delayed by sharp-shooting Americans, led by Lafayette. Cornwallis fell back toward the Virginia coast where he expected an English fleet to be on hand with supplies and additional troops. Finally, at Yorktown, Virginia, the British general decided to make a stand. He ordered elaborate fortifications to be prepared, and waited for the British fleet to come to his aid.

General Washington Moves Quickly

In the north, General Washington allowed information to leak out to the British that the Americans were planning a huge attack on New York City and other northern positions. But actually Washington planned no such move, only wanting the British forces in New York to stay there. Knowing that the French fleet was nearing the

Virginia coast, Washington very much hoped that the British fleet would move too slowly to save Cornwallis.

As for himself, Washington secretly and rapidly marched southward with his men to join Green and Lafayette who were nearing Yorktown. Sizeable French forces, under Lieutenant-General Count Jean Baptiste de Rochambeau, likewise marched southward from their encampment in Rhode Island. They, too, were bound for Chesapeake Bay. At Yorktown, when this march ended, there were more French than American soldiers! Yet it was General Washington's crafty and intelligent leadership, using his ragged Continentals and his allies superbly that made the seige of Yorktown and the final and glorious victory possible.

Cornwallis, waiting at Yorktown for the English fleet to arrive off the Virginia coast, was dismayed to discover that it was the French fleet approaching! The story back of this momentous development is an exciting and tremendously important one. The French mastery in Chesapeake Bay was the result of the adroit actions of a French Rear Admiral, Count Francois Joseph Paul de Grasse. In a battle with the English in the Chesapeake on September 5, 1781, Admiral de Grasse, with twenty-four ships of the line, had met and battered an English fleet of nineteen ships. The English commander, Rear Admiral Thomas Graves, was forced to return to New York for repairs and for supplies,[1] and the French fleet was left to stand guard in the Bay, ending the hopes of General Cornwallis for needed supplies and men. In fact, the General was now surrounded on the York Peninsula, and his men were dying of fever. Finally, Cornwallis surrendered to General Washington after a short show of resistance. The date of his surrender, October 19, 1781, is a memorable one in American history.

Washington chose a Marylander, Tench Tilghman, to carry the news to the Continental Congress. For his historic trip to. Philadelphia, Tilghman is known as "Maryland's Paul Revere." Tilghman had been Washington's devoted aide-de-camp since the early months of the Revolution.

The list of notable Maryland men who served gallantly in the American Revolution is a long one. It includes certainly the name of William Smallwood, as well as John Eager Howard, Mordecai Gist, Samuel Smith, Tench Tilghman and many others. Black Marylanders fought in the American Revolution on land and at sea.[3] Hundreds of the Maryland volunteers gave their lives in the fight for liberty.

The Treaty of Paris
Though the surrender of Cornwallis at Yorktown ended most of the fighting, it was not until September, 1783, that the peace treaty

was officially signed in Paris. Meanwhile, Marylander Lieutenant Joshua Barney, in 1782, as commander of the *Hyder Ally* attacked a better-armed and better-manned British sloop-of-war, the *General Monk.* He captured the ship and turned it and its cargo over to the American authorities.

In the Treaty of Paris, Great Britain formally recognized the independence of the United States, and ceded to the United States considerable territory then under Canadian jurisdiction, which now is included in the states of Wisconsin, Michigan, Ohio, Indiana, and, Illinois.

When the Treaty of Paris was finally presented to the Congress of the Confederation, that body was meeting in Annapolis, Maryland.[2] The Treaty was ratified by Congress in the Statehouse in Annapolis, on January 14, 1784.

Maryland State Government

Following the Revolution, the government of the state of Maryland continued to operate under the Constitution of 1776. As we have mentioned, there were property requirements for voters. There were also property qualifications for certain state offices. This cut down considerably the number of men available to serve. In fact, Maryland's government was controlled by an "aristocracy," asserts Dr. Verne E. Chatelain, *emeritus professor* of history, University of Maryland. And, another historian notes that, "for all the brave talk of rights of man, some things remained to be done before they were given full effect!"

However, much had been done and done well. Maryland was operating on a solid foundation of law, much of it copied from the familiar laws of England. Maryland leaders were responsible ones and built a representative government that worked well.

Washington Resigns

A small schoolboy recently stood in our Maryland Statehouse. A guide was showing him and his classmates the room in which General George Washington resigned his commission as head of the Continental Army. The little boy stood there thoughtfully for a moment and then asked, "Why did he quit?"

This is a very good question, and the answer is worth knowing. In human history most men who are given authority and power, especially over great numbers of armed men, are inclined to want to keep that power rather than to give it up. The people of the United

Painting by Edwin White   **Maryland Department of Economic Development**

Washington Resigned His Commission in Annapolis.

States then so admired Washington that some even suggested that he be made a king or a permanent president of the nation. But no, Washington had given years of service to his country and to the idea of a great, free nation, governed by representatives of the people themselves. He wanted to hand his powers back to Congress and retire as a private citizen to his estate, Mount Vernon, in Virginia.

This dramatic event in our nation's history took place in the State-house in Annapolis on December 23, 1783. There is a plaque on the floor of the Old Senate Chamber, marking the spot where General Washington resigned his commission.

Following the ceremonies of that day, there were meetings and a beautiful "great ball." It was a happy day, indeed. Washington once more was a free man who wanted most of all to enjoy life on his plantation in Virginia. The place he had left long ago in order to serve his country now could at last welcome him home.

---

1 A most interesting and complete book on the American Revolution and the Battle of the Chesapeake is, **Decision at the Chesapeake,** by Harold A. Larrabee.

2 The American seat of government was located in Annapolis from November 26, 1783 to June 3, 1784.

3 *Portrait of a Free State*, Donald M. Dozer, Tidewater Publishers, 1976, p. 265.

153

CHAPTER XXXIV

CAN THIRTEEN STATES AGREE?

THOUGH the Articles of Confederation were written in 1776, this agreement to cooperate and to form a United States of America was not signed by all of the states for several years. The biggest objection to signing it was that states without claims to western lands did not want to see states that *did* claim western lands become more powerful. Virginia, Massachusetts, Connecticut, New York, North Carolina, South Carolina, and Georgia claimed large portions of land to the west under their original charters.

Two Maryland men, John Hanson and Charles Carroll of Carrollton, proposed that these states give up their claims and allow the United States government to use the land in the west to set up new states when settlement justified this step. This, Maryland and the other states without western land claims felt, would make the states more nearly equal in power. It would also give the central government more power and provide a way, through the sale of lands, for raising money to operate the government.

It was a long and intense argument; but, by 1781, all of the states had agreed to sign the Articles of Confederation. This was a giant step forward in learning to work together and to place some trust in the new United States. The fight to adopt the Articles of Confederation had trained many American leaders to cooperate in solving their problems.

Our "First President"

John Hanson of Maryland has sometimes been called "Our Forgotten First President." The story begins on November 5, 1781, when John Hanson was elected the "President of the United States in Congress Assembled," under the newly adopted Articles of Confederation. This was done because a month earlier on October 19, 1781, with the surrender of Cornwallis and with the adoption of the Articles of Confederation, the people suddenly began to realize that the new United States had become a reality. So, on the last day of meeting, Saturday, November 3, 1781, the historic Second Continental Congress turned public matters over to the "United States in Congress Assembled." And it was this body of men that named John Hanson its first "president" on November 5, in Independence Hall, Philadelphia.

Hanson came from an important Maryland family. He was born at Mulberry Grove Plantation, Port Tobacco, Maryland on April 3, 1721. His family had been in America for some time, his grandfather having arrived in 1643 at what is today Wilmington, Delaware. From Charles County John Hanson had moved to Frederick and while living there, he was sent as a Maryland delegate to the Second Continental Congress. It was Hanson and Daniel Carroll who signed the Articles of Confederation for Maryland on March 1, 1781. Maryland, in fact, was the last state to sign.

George Washington was given the honor of being the first President of the United States to serve under the present Constitution of the United States. He took the oath of office of President, on April 30, 1789, in New York City, where Congress was then sitting. Washington was to serve our nation as its President as ably as he had served it as a military man. Still, in a way, you may call Maryland's John Hanson our nation's first president if you add the words, "in Congress Assembled."

After serving his nation and his state for many years, John Hanson retired. While visiting a nephew at Oxon Hill Manor, he died on November 22, 1783. He is buried at Oxon Hill. His grave lies on the hill above the Maryland end of the Woodrow Wilson Bridge in Prince George's County.

The John Hanson Highway, completed in 1960, is named for this man. As people travel this broad highway, they may ask, "Who was John Hanson?" And Marylanders can answer, "He was the first president of the United States, in Congress Assembled!"

John Hanson

CHAPTER XXXV

WHY DID THE UNITED STATES GOVERNMENT LAST?

R EVOLUTIONS occur, even today. A leader takes over a government by force, only to give way to another who comes along and in his turn takes over the government. Such a leader or dictator rules as he pleases while in office, not necessarily working in the interests of the country. Orderly business is difficult. There may be no sound money system, and injustice is done to individuals. The public treasury can be taken and squandered. Often dictatorships give little attention also to public services, such as roads, schools, mail delivery and police protection. Without a lasting honest system of government the future is uncertain and the nation's people are poor and unhappy.

Fortunately the American Revolution produced no such leaders and results, but led to the creation of a prosperous and stable national life, although these things came slowly and not without great difficulties and periods of grave crisis. One might ask, why this kind of revolution and these results are different from some other revolutions.

English Law Retained

For one thing, the leaders of the American Revolution were intelligent, responsible men who did not throw away law and order. They did not choose one man to lead them as a dictator. Instead, representatives from the thirteen new states set up a governmental system that put the power in the people themselves, to vote and to select their leaders, their laws and the form of government. The control of the military, too, was not given to a military dictator but was kept in the hands of the people through their chosen civilian representatives.

Americans were accustomed to the English system of law, which placed great emphasis upon private property ownership, as well as on fair and just punishment for crimes against personal rights. One writer[1] says that, "The revolution slipped off the skin of British rule as a snake sheds its old skin, leaving the system of laws and courts firm, sound, healthy!"

We owe our present form of government and our personal freedoms to the extraordinary and farsighted Revolutionary leaders, who had the good sense to listen to the thousands of Americans who supported them. We can be grateful that at our nation's beginning, we had men wise enough to lead, unselfish enough to share power, and sane enough to act in the best interests of the nation as a whole.

Even before the Articles of Confederation had fairly begun to operate, George Washington and Alexander Hamilton, and others, saw that the system of government was too weak to be effective. In truth the government of the United States, such as it was, had almost no function except to recommend policy and to advise the states! For instance, the Congress under the Articles could:

(1) Ask the states for money but could not levy taxes.

(2) Debate important matters, but could reach no final decisions for only the individual states could so decide.

(3) Plan for an army but could not draft men.

(4) Object to foreign import taxes on United States goods but could not set up a uniform system of tariffs on imports.

(5) Make treaties with other countries but had no way of enforcing them.

Also, without a strong central government and banking system there was a serious lack of a sound money system. By 1780 the money situation had gotten into such confusion that wheat was used to pay wages and to buy goods. In fact, on that occasion, the Governor of Maryland was paid his salary in wheat. He earned 4500 bushels of wheat!

Quite naturally, the United States was deeply in debt because of the war and as yet had no way to raise money to pay these debts. This was true also of the individual states who were arguing among themselves about lands to the west and about boundary lines. Bands of lawless men were beginning to exploit this situation and to use force to get their way. Without an army or national police force, there was great danger that there would be no central authority or leadership to hold together the loosely joined thirteen states.

States, too, were beginning to enact restrictive tariffs against other states. Other nations were often closing their ports to American shipping.

A Constitutional Convention is Called

At Annapolis, Maryland, in 1786, delegates from five states met to discuss marine navigation and interstate trade regulations. These men talked together and agreed that their new nation was in trouble, and that the Articles of Confederation needed amending. So a call went out to the thirteen states to send delegates to Philadelphia the following year, to discuss and perhaps amend the Articles.

A remarkable group of delegates met in May, 1787, at Independence Hall, in Philadelphia. In all, fifty-five men took part in the Convention at various times and all of the states were represented except Rhode Island. Some historians have called the work at Philadelphia the "completing of the Revolution." Others say that the work of the delegates was in itself a revolution! Most significant perhaps, is the fact that putting aside entirely the Articles of Confederation, a completely new plan of government was considered and adopted— the Constitution of the United States as we have it today, except for later amendments.

By September, 1787, the Constitution was completed. It was not until the year, 1789, however, that the necessary majority of the states had ratified it. The Maryland signers of the Constitution were Daniel Carroll, James McHenry, and Daniel of St. Thomas Jenifer.

The new Constitution created a strong central and national government and divided this government into three departments: (1) the legislative department which makes the laws. (Article I); (2) the executive department which enforces the laws. (Article II); and (3) the judicial department, which is to deal with cases arising out of disputes over the law. (Article III).

An important provision of our Constitution is that it can be amended by a two-thirds vote of each house of the Congress, followed by the agreement or ratification of three-fourths of the states. Article V of the Constitution of the United States explains this and other ways by which the Constitution may be amended. The Constitution gives the United States a strong, central government by making every individual directly responsible to that government. The right to levy taxes, to require men to serve in the armed services, and to enforce treaties are among the features of the Constitution, as well as an implicit[2] promise of the states to obey the decisions of the national government, a commitment not well understood and not faithfully obeyed. Under this Constitution George Washington was elected the first President of the United States, in 1789.

Our National Bill of Rights

Under the new Constitution the national Congress was made to consist of two houses: (1) the House of Representatives, which is the legislative branch of the government, in which each state contributes representatives in proportion to the population of the state. The states with more people send more representatives and so have more votes and power; (2) the Senate, to which each state contributes two Senators. Members of the House of Representatives are usually referred to as Congressmen, even though the Senators are also members of Congress.

One of the first tasks faced by our new United States Congress was that of making the Constitution more acceptable to the states by adding ten important amendments. These amendments, agreed upon by Congress and ratified by the states, are known to us as our Bill of Rights.[3]

The major rights guaranteed to citizens of the United States by these amendments are:

(1) Freedom of worship
(2) Freedom of speech
(3) Freedom from unreasonable search
(4) Right to assemble
(5) Right to petition
(6) Right to jury trial and counsel
(7) Right to summon witnesses
(8) No illegal loss of liberty
(9) No excessive fines or bail
(10) Just payment for property

Within a year (1791) the Bill of Rights was a part of our Constitution. The Constitution has been amended since, but in the main it is perhaps essentially the same document written in Philadelphia in 1787.

1 Frederick Gutheim, **The Potomac.**
2 Implicit: something not written out but thought to be understood; something implied; assumed to be understood.
3 The Constitution of Maryland, written in 1776, contained a similar list of rights.

(Joseph H. Cromwell, C & P Telephone Company of Maryland)

The first monument honoring George Washington to be completed was this one, still standing in Washington County, near Boonsboro, Maryland, a few miles south-southeast of Hagerstown.

YOUR MARYLAND

SECTION III

MARYLAND AFTER THE
AMERICAN REVOLUTION

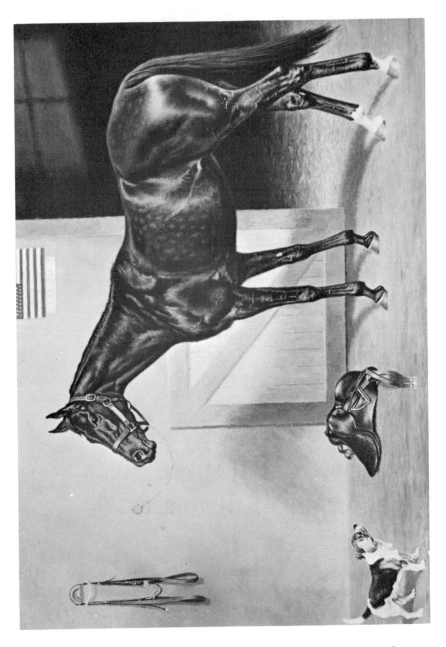

Painting by Richard Stone Reeves.　　　　　Photo courtesy Laurel Race Course

"KELSO"

Kelso is owned by Maryland resident Mrs. Richard C. duPont, Woodstock Farm, Chesapeake City, Md. This horse won the 1964 International Race at Laurel, Maryland, and has brought many honors home to Maryland. In his 6 years of racing, Kelso has earned nearly two million dollars.

CHAPTER XXXVI

MARYLAND GIVES LAND FOR
A NATIONAL CAPITAL

With the war years behind them, the new government of the United States needed a permanent capital. As we have seen, several cities after 1776 had served at different times as the seat of the nation. Functions of government were located in New York in 1789, when George Washington was inaugurated as President of the United States. The following year the government moved to Philadelphia. However, the southern states, in that day of difficult, slow travel, wanted the capital moved still further south.

Since the Potomac River cut through the center of the original thirteen states, it was agreed that somewhere along its length a spot should be selected by President Washington as a site for a permanent capital. Washington chose a location that could be reached by ocean-going ships of the day, and yet one far enough inland to be safe from attack by foreign fleets. This placed the capital away from the coast and nearer to the western settlements, too, reachable by way of the Potomac-Wills Creek-Ohio River route.

The little Maryland port town of Georgetown was on the chosen site. Land on both sides of the Potomac was donated to the United States government by Maryland and Virginia. Later, however, the citizens of Alexandria did not want to be included in the great federal square of land, ten miles long on each of its sides. They asked to be removed from the capital plan. Most of the land Virginia gave was returned to that state in 1846 and later. So it is that *most* of the District of Columbia, also known as the city of Washington, was developed from Maryland land.

In 1791, Congress approved the site, and a French engineer, Pierre Charles L'Enfant was selected to draw plans for the city. It seemed to some, that his plans were much too elaborate for a young, raw country like the United States. But the plan, nevertheless, including recommendation for broad avenues and open spaces has largely been retained. Since so many early cities were built with very narrow and very crooked streets, we may be very glad that L'Enfant was fond of broad avenues and spacious streets.

CHAPTER XXXVII

THE ELLICOTT BROTHERS AND
BENJAMIN BANNEKER

DURING the American Revolution, John, Joseph, and Andrew Ellicott were kept busy, turning out wheat flour and corn meal at their mill on the Patapsco River. More and more grain came in to be ground. The Ellicott's first years had been greatly aided by Charles Carroll of Carrollton, who lived not far away. Their mill was the first in Maryland to produce flour and cornmeal, not at the rate of a few bushels a day, but in quantity. The Ellicotts put the production of meal and flour on a commercial scale.

Once the Revolution was over, the brothers knew that there would be a demand for flour, not only in the local area but with neighboring states and foreign countries, too. So they bought land at the corner of Pratt and Light Streets in Baltimore. There they built a warehouse and a wharf. Andrew's son, Elias Ellicott, was put in charge of the venture.

The Ellicott brothers found that to get their products to Baltimore and to help get grains to their mill, they needed a road. A road was built from the mill down to Baltimore. They later extended the road to the west, to Frederick. Gradually the little town that began with the Ellicotts' mill was to grow into today's Ellicott City, the county seat of Howard County.

The Inventive Ellicotts

Not only did the Ellicott brothers use their wits to build mills, equip them with machinery, and devise wharfs and roads, but as time went on, they also started many other activities in Maryland. For example, they opened a big general store near the mill which became a popular place for farmers and planters to shop and trade.

Of course, the children of the workers needed education. So the three young Quakers from Pennsylvania decided to establish schools. The Ellicotts had brought their families to Maryland from Pennsylvania as soon as they could. They built sturdy houses of stone. Construction continued without a pause as the brothers put up warehouses and other places of work, schools and homes.

Inventiveness enabled the Ellicotts to provide their mill com-

164

munity with a water supply system just as they also introduced, probably for the first time in Maryland, a way of irrigating fields. Mechanically-minded John Ellicott invented a brake for wagons, which helped control the heavy wagons on steep hills.

Among the buildings they constructed and equipped was a mill to grind chunks of plaster (lime) shipped from Nova Scotia, into powder. This, the Ellicotts demonstrated, could be used, along with other fertilizers and certain crop rotation, to turn worn-out tobacco land into producing land. The Ellicotts urged Maryland growers to turn to wheat growing, because it was a profitable crop which left the land productive.

Joseph Ellicott loved to make clocks. He is said to have invented the first four-sided clock made in this country. His son, Andrew, too, was scientifically inclined and very talented, as we shall see. Joseph, the son of the original Joseph who came to Maryland, devised and tried out, in 1789, a steam-propelled boat. The loss of his arm in testing the vessel prevented him from perfecting his design.[1]

Andrew Ellicott

The Ellicott family, following the American Revolution, took an active part in local, state, and national affairs. They even helped with the planning of government activities both on national and state levels.

Andrew Ellicott led a very interesting life. He was an engineer, a surveyor, and an inventor and was always very scientifically inclined. He was to carry out many fascinating projects.

In 1789 he surveyed the land between Pennsylvania and Lake Erie for the United States government. It was on this trip that he made the first accurate measurements of Niagara Falls and the Niagara River. In 1792, he was made Surveyor-General of the United States. He traveled far and wide, going south to survey the boundary between Florida (then a Spanish possession) and the United States. Later, he was sent to extend surveys westward from the Mason-Dixon Line into the Ohio country.

Andrew Ellicott and his friend Benjamin Banneker worked with Pierre L'Enfant surveying and planning the city of Washington, D.C. After Major L'Enfant was dismissed (he was a most temperamental gentleman and left in a temper, taking the nearly completed plans of the city with him), Andrew Ellicott was selected to finish the work.

Many more interesting details about the Ellicott family cannot be told for lack of space, but just a few facts will show the part they had in the development of Maryland.

In 1809, fire destroyed the Ellicotts' mill and many of the log houses. The mill and homes were rebuilt almost immediately. By the year, 1825, the town at the mill had grown to a population of about 3,000 persons. When the Baltimore and Ohio Railroad was constructed to Ellicott's Mills in 1831, the thriving community became the nation's first rail terminus.

The Ellicott family kept ownership of the mills until 1837. In the little city today there are many houses and sites to remind one that the town has played an important part in Maryland's history.

Benjamin Banneker

Near Ellicott's Mills there lived a remarkable man, Benjamin Banneker. He was born in 1731, the son of Robert and Mary "Bannaky." His grandfather had been brought to Maryland from Africa, and was known as Bannka; later, Bannaky. Molly Walsh bought Bannka to help her clear land that she had claimed, near today's Ellicott City. She had been an English maid, an indentured servant sent to Maryland to work out seven years of bondage. Having finally finished her term of servitude, she needed help in making a farm. Bannaky and Molly Walsh after a while decided to marry and among their children was a girl called Mary. Mary Bannaky when she grew up, bought a slave called Robert, from a slave ship. Mary and Robert later on were married and had several children, among them, Benjamin.

The farm came to be called Bannaky's Springs because there were abundant springs of good fresh water on the land. The family made a good living there. They cherished and guarded their status as free people, for all around them members of their race were working in bondage. With knowledge he had brought with him from Africa, Benjamin's grandfather led waters, by means of ditches and little dams, from the springs to irrigate his fields, and so even in dry seasons the Bannakys usually raised good crops of tobacco. Benjamin helped with the farm work. It seemed likely that he would be a farmer all his life.

Using her Bible as a text, Benjamin's grandmother, Molly, taught the boy to read. In the summer of 1743, a Quaker schoolmaster, Peter Heinrich, came to the valley of the Patapsco River. Before long he opened a Quaker school for boys and he invited Benjamin to attend the school. It was there that the spelling of his name became "Banneker." Benjamin in due time became one of Peter Heinrich's most promising pupils. He was eager to get an education and worked hard on the farm and in the classroom. He learned to write and to do simple arithmetic.

When the Ellicott brothers arrived in the valley, they soon met the young Banneker and were impressed with his abilities. Soon he was helping to assemble the machinery of the mill. The Ellicott brothers talked with him, encouraged him, and loaned him books.

A turning point in his life occurred in Baltimore when Benjamin Banneker met a kindly man called Josef Levi. Seeing that Banneker was fascinated with his watch, Levi insisted on giving it to him. Banneker took the watch home with him. In the months to come, he took the watch apart and learned how it worked. In the next three years he spent whatever time he could spare in working to make a clock. Most of the parts he carved from wood. He succeeded in his attempt and made what was possibly the very first striking clock made in Maryland. It ran faultlessly for many years, and many people came to see it. Banneker began to repair clocks and watches and to adjust sundials. He also worked on the very complex clock built by Joseph Ellicott.

Banneker and the Ellicott family were close friends. Books then were both scarce and expensive, but seeing that Banneker was sincere in his desire to learn, the Ellicotts loaned him many of their books on science. He put his amazing mind to work, learning advanced mathematics and other subjects in the field of mathematics and science.

Banneker never married. He led a life of solitary study and thought. In appearance he was a man of medium stature, who stood straight and walked with a tall staff always beside him. In his later years, his hair was white and thick, above a broad forehead. Both his courteous manner and his learning impressed those who spoke to him.

When his parents died, Banneker inherited the farm. To have opportunity to study his books, he devoted only enough time to working the farm to provide for his simplest needs. He became engrossed in the study of astronomy, and spent almost every good night scanning the sky for hours. He built a "work cabin" up on a hill. Inside he had a broad table and shelves for books. Latticed windows let in fresh air. Here he worked over intricate calculations. His fame in the area spread. Banneker's sisters lived nearby and they saw to it that he was left alone and made him comfortable.

This self-taught scientist made a complete and accurate "ephemeris" for the year 1792. An ephemeris is a calendar or an almanac, describing the locations of celestial bodies. His great knowledge of mathematics made this work possible. From 1792 until 1802 he published *Banneker's Almanac*. It was a very successful almanac, and his fame spread throughout the United States and in Europe.

On top of the work cabin on Banneker's land, there was now a window to allow him to study the skies through his telescope. For many years he worked, studied, and wrote there.

Almanacs had many uses in those days. Almanacs gave advice on farming, told when the moon would be full, when the tides would be high or low, and gave the reader an idea of what weather might be expected at certain seasons. If one's clock stopped on a frontier farm, one had only to consult the almanac to see what time the sun rose on a certain date, and then to reset the clock accurately by the sun. Also, for taking a boat trip, one consulted the almanac to find when the most favorable tides would occur.

The weather predictions Banneker included in his almanac were not just guesses. They were the sum of many years of study. Should an observer find for several years that the first two weeks of April were rainy in a certain locality, then he could put this prediction into an almanac. Essays, proverbs, jokes, and other items of interest made the almanac good reading.

At the same time that Banneker was calculating the future positions of the moon, sun, stars, and planets for his almanac, he was asked to help his friend Major Andrew Ellicott, and he agreed. Major Ellicott had been appointed the Chief Surveyor for the new capital city of the United States, Washington, D.C. He was responsible for gathering his own corps of draftsmen and assistants.

Ellicott and Banneker were soon working with Pierre L'Enfant, planning a city with a grid of streets, diagonally crossed by broad avenues. L'Enfant was a very talented man, but he was also not very easy to get along with. He liked to guard his plans and maps, so that selfish speculators would have no chance to buy up land for personal profit. L'Enfant intended to finish his plans, print hundreds of copies of his report, and then release it all over the country at an appointed moment so that everyone would have the same chance to buy property in Washington, D.C. Banneker, as one of Ellicott's surveyors, often worked closely with L'Enfant, to whom he was loyal and courteous as well as being modest, and capable.

But, suddenly L'Enfant was dismissed from the project and left in March, 1792, taking with him the precious plans for the city. An emergency meeting of the Capital City commission in charge of the project, as well as the surveyors and engineers, was called by Thomas

168

Jefferson, now the Secretary of State.

In a recent biography, the *Life of Benjamin Banneker*, author Silvio A. Bedini rejects the legend that Banneker was to help Major Andrew Ellicott reconstruct the plans for the city by redrawing streets and lots from memory. Yet Bedini tells us that Banneker was definitely involved in the survey of the national capital area, "arriving at the site with Ellicott early in February 1791 and returned to his home late in April of the same year."[2] Following the departure of L'Enfant, Major Andrew Ellicott was placed in charge of the over-all project, March 1792. During this year Ellicott and his assistants laid out and divided the squares of the city at the same time that they were engaged in finishing the boundary survey. Papers that could tell us more about Banneker's work with Major Ellicott have been lost, according to author Bedini. Yet it is certain that Banneker did work with Ellicott on the survey of our nation's capital city.

Banneker adopted the Quaker style of dress. With the years his hair whitened. He is said to have looked very much like Benjamin Franklin, with the same features and the same set of the head. Physically, Banneker was active and strong. He was very much loved and respected in the neighborhood of Ellicott's Mills.

On Sunday, October 25, 1806, he died. He had lived a long life in friendship and harmony with his fellow men. He had spent his years absorbed in many important interests, acquiring great knowledge, and doing the work he loved. His is a life of achievement to be remembered.

---

1 Celia M. Holland, **Ellicott City, Maryland, Mill Town, U.S.A.**

2 Silvio A. Bedini, the **Life of Benjamin Banneker**, (New York: Charles Scribner's Sons, 1972), pp. 126-136.

Benjamin Banneker

CHAPTER XXXVIII

CHARLES CARROLL OF CARROLLTON
AND OF MARYLAND

THERE was more than one Charles Carroll in Maryland. But the Charles Carroll who stands tallest in the history of our state and of our nation is the one known as Charles Carroll of Carrollton. He was born in Annapolis, at the town house sometimes called Elkridge. He was an only child and was so frail as a small boy that it seemed doubtful that he would grow to manhood. In fact, throughout his life, he was slight and delicate in appearance and uncertain in his health, yet he was to live to the age of ninety-five!

From his father and his grandfather he inherited thousands of acres of land in Maryland and a substantial fortune. He also inherited certain outstanding characteristics as well, such as the energy and intelligence of his father and grandfather before him.

Grandfather Charles Carroll, sometimes called "The Attorney," was descended from an Irish family, O'Carroll, who could rightly claim descent from Irish kings. This Carroll was a third son, a witty, charming man with a hot temper. Educated in law and statesmanship in London in the 1600's, it was not long before he had a good post in the court of King James II. But he was a young man who longed for adventure, and the English colonies in America appealed to him as a place where he could have lands and a challenging future. Also, because he was a Catholic, he was attracted to Maryland by Lord Baltimore's policy of religious toleration. So it was that this young Irishman left England in 1688 to go to America as Lord Baltimore's Attorney-General for the Province of Maryland. He took a new motto for his coat of arms, "Anywhere, so long as it be free!"

Grandfather Carroll, however, was not destined to enjoy this new freedom very long, for shortly after he reached Maryland, King James II of the Stuart line was deposed in favor of two new monarchs, William and Mary. The government of Lord Baltimore in Maryland was replaced by one which provided for a union of church and state and the established Anglican Church. Never one to hold his tongue, this Charles Carroll was shortly thrown into jail for his outspoken protest against this change. Later he was released from jail and married, but, once again, his outspoken ways landed him in prison, this time interrupting his honeymoon!

Finally, in 1694, when King James II's cause was utterly lost, Carroll decided to keep quiet and was released from jail. Thereafter, he practiced law as a private gentleman for he was a good attorney. When Annapolis became the capital of the province he moved there. In the law and in business he enjoyed success. He owned and operated a trading house and a store in Annapolis, and spent some of his time as a gentleman farmer developing and cultivating some of the hundreds of acres of land granted to him by Lord Baltimore.

Charles Carroll the Attorney-General had a passion for land. He owned about 60,000 acres, all of it in Maryland. In addition to taking care of this land he operated as did some other men of wealth in that day, a banking business lending money at interest.

He and his second wife had ten children, five of whom lived. He never lost his gift, however, for antagonizing royal governors, never quite succeeded in keeping his opinions to himself, and always had a ready Irish reply. He was likeable, impudent, stubborn, and of course, very wealthy. But he never again was to enjoy the freedom of worship and conscience that he had hoped for, although he never stopped fighting for these things. This Carroll died in 1720, still an unbeaten and unsubdued man. His widow who survived him, lived on in Annapolis.

The second Carroll, referred to usually as Charles Carroll of Annapolis was like his father in that he too had a hot temper. He was a likeable sort of person, intelligent, witty, and very shrewd in business. By the time that he reached middle age he had one of the largest fortunes in the colonies.

The continued ban on the Catholic religion in Maryland always made him furious. He was educated in France, as were some other members of Catholic families in Maryland because of legal restrictions by the English government against instruction in Catholic schools. Eventually he married a beautiful young woman, named Elizabeth. In Annapolis he built a home at Elk's Ridge, and it was there that their only child, a son, was born in 1737.

This third Charles Carroll (of Carrollton) remembers his childhood as a very happy one at Annapolis and in the manor, "Doughoregan"[1] near Ellicott City. Briefly he was sent to Bohemia Manor Academy, a school taught by Jesuits. It was being operated quietly and almost secretly to escape the attention of Maryland's Protestant government. A few months here prepared him for entrance into the famous Jesuit college, St. Omers in French Flanders. He was to spend several years in schools in France and in other schools in Europe. He was very fond of the classics, as well as horse racing and playing chess, and along with these interests, he was an expert swordsman and an excellent horseman. He liked wines, too, and was susceptible to pretty women but managed to keep his conduct always within bounds. In fact, he had a rather strict code of behavior and found most young Europeans far too wild to suit his tastes. At his father's urging he studied law and graduated in it.

After nearly sixteen years of study abroad, he returned to Annapolis in 1764. There he found his home empty and lonesome because his lovely mother's gentle presence was gone. She had died in 1761. Perhaps, for this reason, he and his father found themselves even closer than before. It was soon apparent that the third Charles Carroll, although a rather retiring and bashful young man, was very talented in the field of politics. He was unusually well versed in the affairs of government. He had all of his father's and his grandfather's intense concern for religious liberty and good government, as matters most important to human beings. In contrast, however, to the characteristics of his two fiery ancestors with their hot tempers and ready speech, this third Carroll had the ability to reason with others calmly. Being an excellent business man, he was soon absorbed in the problems of managing the family estate. This soon led to an interest in wheat growing and milling, and to following closely the activities of the Ellicott brothers.

About this time Carroll was attracted to a pretty girl, Miss Rachel Cooke, to whom he became engaged. But she, a frail lass, died before the wedding. For the young Charles, life became sad and without color or interest for awhile. In June, 1768, however, he at last found himself a wife. Miss Molly Darnall was 19, he was 31. She was "pretty, well born, educated, good tempered and sensible and had a flair for politics." The young couple were given the Annapolis house by the elder Carroll and he retired to Doughoregan manor.

In the capital city, life for the young couple became a round of teas, races, theater and parties, but Charles still found time for hard work. He was a good accountant and took on most of the burden of managing the vast estates belonging to the family. His own lands were called Carrollton and were located in Frederick County. He began to add "of Carrollton" to his name when he signed it, since there were other living Charles Carrolls. His first child, a girl, did not live. His second, also a girl, was born in 1770, and there was a third girl in 1772.

Carroll became a member of Maryland's Committee of Correspondence in 1774. He was strongly opposed to the Stamp Act and the tea tax. His rebellious mood may have been partly due to the family feeling that the throne of England had been taken from its rightful heirs when James II had been driven from the throne, and non-Catholic monarchs gained power. He did not however, accept a position as delegate to the Congress that had its meeting in Philadelphia in the fall of 1774, though he did agree to go along as an unofficial adviser. Always, it seemed, Carroll worked hard at public affairs but sought no personal power or fame. In that first Continental Congress conservative feelings were dominant and only a few delegates really favored a break with England; but Carroll felt that the final break was one sure to come and that it was desirable. He unquestionably was bitter toward Britain and no longer felt loyalty as a British subject.

A fourth Charles Carroll was born in 1775. At that time only one of the three Carroll girls was still living. In May, 1775, Carroll went to the Second Continental Congress, again in an advisory capacity. He was an unofficial but an important member of the Maryland contingent. He returned later to Annapolis to work in various patriotic committees and also to care for his wife, Molly, who was not well.

When the Continental Congress decided to choose a delegation to go to Canada in an effort to persuade that dominion to join the colonies south of the St. Lawrence against Great Britain, Charles Carroll of Carrollton, along with Benjamin Franklin and Samuel Chase were selected to present the plea of the colonies to the Canadians. Carroll's ability to speak French well, and his Catholic religion were regarded as highly important assets in this first American diplomatic mission to a foreign country. Carroll took along with him his cousin, Father John Carroll. The mission left New York, April 2, 1776 and did not return to Philadelphia until June 11. As previously noted, the Canadians refused to join in the rebellion. Carroll was more insistent than ever in asking for separation from England; and when the Maryland convention met in Annapolis for the crucial decision Carroll was there and the vote eventually was cast for independence.

After this decision, Carroll for the first time agreed to be an official delegate to the Congress in Philadelphia. He later served on many committees and had a reputation for complete devotion to duty. His French schooling, too, it was felt, would be most helpful to the Congress in seeking for a French alliance. He was one of four signers for Maryland, of the Declaration of Independence. The story that he added "of Carrollton" to his signature when someone remarked that "there were many Charles Carrolls in Maryland " is not true. He had been signing his name that way for some time.

Charles Carroll's work for the War Board was valuable, not so much for his military knowledge of which he had little, but because he was a shrewd and intelligent businessman. When General George Washington was harshly criticized, Charles Carroll came to his defense. He was one of the committee sent to Valley Forge to study conditions during the winter encampment there. When Carroll finally left the Congress, in June, 1778, he had accomplished much to make the French alliance possible. He had been powerful in keeping General Washington on as head of the Army, and had proved that Roman Catholics . . . "were as useful and capable public servants as anybody."

One of his proudest accomplishments was his making sure that the new State of Maryland in 1776, granted full civil and religious freedom to Catholics. Much later, in 1789, he insisted on this same religious freedom for the whole country. His cousin, Charles Carroll the Barrister in 1776, wrote the section on the Bill of Rights in Maryland's new State Constitution.

Back home now in Annapolis after many months spent in Philadelphia, Carroll became an outstanding member of the Maryland General Assembly. He showed again that shrewdness as a good businessman and as a capable committee member that had marked his activities in the Second Continental Congress. At this time, too, and unlike many of his colleagues, he strongly urged the creation of a powerful central government for the new United States of America.

But personal troubles now beset Carroll. Within two weeks of each other his father and his wife, Molly, died. He found himself a widower with four of the seven children born to him still living. He must have turned gratefully for forgetfulness to the hundreds of business details that now faced him. The plantations, the companies he owned (the Baltimore Iron Works was one of these), and his work in politics, these were the things that occupied his attention, along with the care of his children.

In 1789 he and John Hanson were elected as United States Senators from Maryland. They met in New York and there saw George Washington inaugurated as the first President under the new constitution. For ten years Carroll continued to work for his country as a member of its government. Then, in 1799, he decided to retire from public service and live the life of a country gentleman.

On Homewood plantation, he built a beautiful Georgian house for his son, the fourth Charles Carroll of the family and his young bride. Baltimore has since grown around this home and it is now on the Johns Hopkins campus. In Baltimore, too, he built a home for his daughter, Mary and her husband, Richard Caton.

Though still an active businessman, he now had more time to spend with his library. All his life he had loved and collected books.

Each good day, also, he rode for miles across his lands. Always he was interested in new ideas in agriculture.

He spent much thought on the question of slavery. He saw that slavery was wrong and that it was against our new government's principles of freedom and equal human rights. He believed, however, that to free all the slaves abruptly was to damage the nation's agricultural system; and, until they were trained for jobs and given land, the black people themselves could suffer. So, he thought that a gradual course of freeing these people would afford a better solution to the problem. Yet, he himself freed as many as thirty slaves at one time.

The National Colonization Society of America was founded in 1816 to send free black people from America to Africa. The Society located a colony on the west coast of Africa. In 1824 it was named Liberia. Several states set up separate colonization societies, among them, the Maryland Colonization Society established in 1827. Charles Carroll was active in the colonization movement. The importation of slaves was forbidden by Maryland law in 1783. The invention of the cotton gin in 1794, however, increased the demand for such labor in the southern states. In 1808 the new American Constitution of the United States forbade the importation of slaves.

It is said that, during the second war with England, the War of 1812, that the glow from the burning of Washington by the enemy in 1814 could be seen from Carroll's estate, Doughoregan. The British had captured Washington, but the young nation was destined to weather this trouble, too. "Our government," Carroll once said in a letter, "is a curious and complicated piece of mechanism of which the world has no example; time will discover how long it will go on without derangement."

In his old age Charles Carroll of Carrollton remained active. He started his days early with a cold plunge, rode for miles, read, entertained, and enjoyed his meals with his favorite wines and champagnes. His grandchildren often came to visit him.

After so many years of religious persecution and criticism, Carroll was now a national hero, honored by all. Hundreds of invitations poured into Doughoregan. He accepted a few when he felt an interest, but was sometimes embarrassed by flattering speeches directed at him. He had the distinction of outliving all of the other signers of the Declaration of Independence. In his later years he was often called "The Signer."

Even at the age of ninety he remained spry, slight of figure, with an unfailing courtliness of manner and a ready wit. He was on the Board of Directors of the Baltimore and Ohio Railroad and was also involved in the plans of the Chesapeake and Ohio Canal Company.

Charles Carroll of Carrollton

In 1828, when construction began, he laid the cornerstone for the Baltimore and Ohio Railway. He was ninety-one at that time. The spring of 1832 found him for a time well enough to ride again, but soon his health began to fail. He lived his last days at the home of his eldest living daughter, Mary and her husband, Richard Caton, in the mansion on the corner of Lombard and Front Streets in Baltimore. The house still stands and is usually referred to as the Carroll-Caton Mansion. It is owned and preserved today by the City of Baltimore.

Charles Carroll of Carrollton died at the age of ninety-five, on November 14, 1832. There is a reference to him in our state song "Maryland, My Maryland," and Carroll County is named for him. The county was created in 1836. His bust and John Hanson's are enshrined in the rotunda of the United States Capitol, in their memory, as Maryland's two most famous men of history.

---

1 Doughoregan is translated "House of Kings." The manor was owned by Charles (the Attorney General) Carroll.

CHAPTER XXXIX

FARMING CHANGES

After the Revolution

W HEN the English first came to Maryland they were delighted to find available a bewildering variety of foods. The new crops they learned to raise, added to ones brought from England, provided a-bundant supplies of food. Then, too, the waters were filled with fish, duck, crab, clams, and oysters; and the meadows and forests with deer, bear, turkey and other kinds of game.

The new settlers experimented to see just what fruits and vege-tables would be successful here. Actually the western shore section of Maryland when first settlements occurred, proved not to be the most productive in the province. Some of this land had a rather sandy soil, excellent for tobacco and certain other crops but easily "used up." Since money could be so easily gotten from tobacco, many fields were put into that crop. Soon it was noticed, however, that each year the tobacco from a given field was smaller in size. It was simple enough, of course, to clear another field and plant there, because land in those first years was plentiful. So, many early tobacco fields were used up and then abandoned.

Later on, it was discovered that the soil could be built up by applying lime to it. This was often produced by crushing and burning shells from numerous Indian mounds found near the shores, and by using the "chalk," or plaster, brought in as ship ballast. Vessels from England normally had less freight and weight on trips to America, than when loaded with tobacco for their return to England. They often needed extra weight, or ballast, in their holds when westbound for America to keep the heavy sails from pulling them over.

Some of the trouble that farmers and planters faced came from their refusal to learn new methods. They liked to farm as they always had; and, as tobacco lands wore out, they found themselves at a loss to know what to do. So there were by the early nineteenth century many acres of tidewater farms and plantations not usable.

New Farming Methods

Across the Potomac in Loudoun County, Virginia, there was a

farmer who, around 1800, had a talent for experimenting in ways to reclaim "worn out" farms. His name was John Binns. He would buy up an old farm at a bargain price and then carefully rebuild the soil until it was again "producing land."

In 1803 he published a book in Frederick, Maryland called *A Treatise On Practical Farming*. It suggested that land should not "be scratched" before planting, but deep-plowed. He also advised the use of lime and the planting of clover in order to add needed chemical elements to the soil; and likewise, the turning of crop fields into pasture lands in certain years in regular rotation. Each third year, he stated, the land might be returned to growing crops. This system of crop rotation did much to save Maryland's and Virginia's piedmont sections, their prime wheat areas.

Wheat

The German farmers of the piedmont region were leaders in agricultural progress. Contour plowing was used to keep water on the land and to prevent erosion. To help keep land fertile, these farmers used manure, marl, deep plowing, and crop rotation. The "maize culture" moved westward. Corn, so easy to raise and to turn into food was most important in the pioneer diet along with wild game, brought down by the long rifle.

The Germans, Scotch-Irish, and Swiss who migrated into Maryland's piedmont region along with a few English settlers, created here a prosperous and stable farming region. In fact, Maryland and Virginia, along with a section of southeastern Pennsylvania, is said to have raised over half of the wheat in the new United States in the period, 1825 to 1860.

Farming Equipment

Very primitive farming tools were used in Maryland's early days. Hoes and pronged forks were used to turn the soil; and crude plows pulled by horses or oxen hardly did more than scratch the surface of the land. These first plows were light and largely made of wood and iron.

Slowly, however, plows were improved by employing a "mold-board" made of cast iron. Mold-board plows were heavier and plowed more deeply, but the cast iron was brittle and frequently would break when plowing a stony field. Still, it was an improvement and was generally used until, about 1840, steel ploughshares became available to farmers. Over in Virginia, John McCormick and his son, Cyrus, shortly after the War of 1812 were turning out these new iron and steel plows and were swamped with orders.

Wheat cannot be left standing when ripe and must be promptly harvested. If it is not, the grain falls to the ground, birds descend to feast, and the crop is lost. Heavy rain, wind and hail can ruin a ripening wheat crop. The problem of harvesting grain was a very worrisome and important matter to farmers. The wheat was cut with scythes, and then brought to the threshing floors. There, the wheat kernels were trodden free from the stalks and chaff,—much the same method as is described in the Bible and used for thousands of years!

There was, of course, a great demand for wheat and flour both in the States and in overseas markets and for that reason, it was a very valuable crop. But, until Cyrus McCormick made a successful wheat reaper in 1831, farmers in general, were forced to use the same slow methods of harvesting and processing grain, that had existed for centuries.

Tobacco Farming

In Maryland's tobacco lands, not only were worn out fields decreasing the income of planters, but there were other causes, too. In years when tobacco brought low prices, growers lost money.

Tobacco "factors" were businessmen or middlemen, who handled for the planters the buying, selling and shipping of the crop to European and local markets. These factors normally operated stores and warehouses filled with goods that were needed on the plantations and farms. These men also extended credit to the planters, who could then obtain supplies in advance of the sale of the tobacco crop.

In bad years, when either the crop was poor or the market price was low, planters found themselves often badly into debt. Even large land owners then were embarrassed and were forced to cut expenses. Small land owners in the same situation frequently had to abandon their farms and move westward, there to start out all over again.

Farm Livestock

Oxen were in general used as draft animals. They pulled plows, tobacco casks, called hogheads, as well as wagons, sledges, grain-grinding machinery and certain machinery at forges. They plodded beside canals towing boats. Even today oxen are used in a few places in Maryland.

Horses of course, were lighter and swifter work animals. They were used not only to do heavy farm work but also to pull carriages and wagons of every sort. They were used for riding, and in gay hunting parties with hounds. Today, we perhaps do not realize how many different kinds of horses there are. Yet, in early Maryland every child knew that some horses were scrubby and sturdy, good for packing supplies and men over rough mountain trails and that others were fleet and swift for racing. Still other horses were bred for weight, bone, muscle and stamina, and these were used for pulling heavy loads.

So you see, horses could be "evolved" (by breeding) for speed or for heavy work, for beauty or agility, or for all-around usefulness. Boys and girls knew as much about horses in early Maryland as today's youngsters know about the various makes and models of automobiles.

Cows were often turned loose in a woods lot to graze, where they were exposed to all kinds of weather and generally to a hard life! Because food and shelter for livestock was scarce in the early days of the colony and especially in the wintertime, the animals were likely to be small and poor in appearance. Slowly conditions improved and small cows, for instance that gave only a pint or so of milk a day were "culled" and herds were bred so that the stock was better. Usually the smaller cattle, including the poorest milk-producing cows were used for meat and the better animals were kept to become good milk producers. At present Maryland dairies milk cows normally give many gallons per day.

Beef cattle are now raised to be used for meat. These animals, too, have been "culled" until only the best ones remained. Beef cattle and dairy cattle are two quite different breeds today.

Poultry, too, including chickens, ducks, and geese, was brought to America at an early period, and, in due time, careful breeding methods served to improve these birds, leading to the production of more eggs, more meat, and more farm income.

Livestock in General

Each plantation or farm eventually contained many kinds of livestock and poultry, and even in the towns, families usually kept chickens and cows as well as a family horse. In the New World the production of many kinds of food products and animals was of course, extremely important. But for these essentially agricultural people, there were many other problems, such as the providing of shoes for the family as well as adequate clothing. Each town and farm became, therefore, literally a factory center in itself, for there actually was very little that could be purchased, even if the necessary capital was available. This applied too, to the problems of housing and shelter, where the same kind of work and planning was necessary if life was to move ahead successfully.

Changing Times

Farming methods slowly changed as the Marylanders adapted to their new lands and found ways to produce better tools and machinery. Better mills for grain and improved plows and the reaper are only a partial list of the developments that took place.[1] In this connection better markets needed to be found and better marketing operations including improved waterways and roads needed to be considered.

---

1 See "Plantations of Later Colonial Days," a Wheeler pamphlet published by the Maryland Historical Society.

CHAPTER XL

EARLY INDUSTRY
(Following the American Revolution)

AFTER the Revolution the new nation set to work to supply its own manufacturing needs. English prohibition having been ended, everything from snuff to nails could now be manufactured freely. Even during the war, cut off by sea blockade and freed of England's restrictions, the United States had already made progress in this direction.

In Baltimore, shipbuilding, supplies for ships (chandlers), freight and passenger transport, warehousing, marketing, combined shortly to make the city one of the nation's leading ports. On the Eastern Shore, weavers could now weave as much cloth as they pleased and this they proceeded to do.

Forests in Maryland were so very plentiful that no one thought much then of conserving them. In fact, wood was generally used for fuel in the homes, as well as in steam engines and manufacturing. It was not until shortly before the Civil War that coal came into considerable use. Coal in Maryland came from the district just west of Cumberland and was floated down in barges, by way of the Potomac River, in the days before the railroads. The supply came in the main from surface coal deposits.

Late in the eighteenth century, a large number of Maryland tobacco planters found their lands exhausted and for this and other reasons, farming was no longer very profitable. They could, among other choices, move further west to a new land, or they might enter trading or manufacturing businesses for a livelihood. When a farmer decided to stay on his land, he needed to learn newer methods and to diversify his crops to meet market demands. He must also be a good bookkeeper and manager. Often, too, he had a handy knowledge of surveying and knew a great deal about land and property laws. The American landowner was an active man. English visitors to Maryland were surprised to find the owners of fine race horses riding them themselves in races.

The Indians of Maryland by the beginning of the 1800's had largely disappeared. Some had moved west into the mountain area of the state and into northwestern Pennsylvania. The old Indian lands had been divided up and sold.

Maryland may well have been the second colony to have a printing press. Massachusetts probably had the first one, and Pennsylvania was soon to be a leader in the number of presses in operation. William Nuthead operated the first Maryland press at St. Mary's City from 1686 until his death in 1695 and was the public printer for a time. His widow, Dinah, moved the business to Annapolis in 1696. She also was a printer although it is said that she could not read or write! Thomas Reading in 1704 is mentioned as "Public Printer."

William Parks in 1727 began the publication of Maryland's first newspaper, calling it *The Maryland Gazette*. This famous paper, often referred to as "America's oldest newspaper," had a more or less continuous publication down to the present time, although there have been periods when it was not issued regularly. By the time of the American Revolution several other printing presses were operating in Baltimore, Frederick, Annapolis and elsewhere. By 1790, Easton and Hagerstown had presses, followed shortly by presses in almost every town. Several of them in this period printed newspapers in the German language.

In the piedmont areas of Maryland and westward, vigorous German ministers were to be found, using their native language in their sermons, and in their everyday contacts with other people. The culture brought over from Europe by the German settlers was a rich one. Music was important with them, as it had been in their homelands. Coming in "church groups" as they did, their religions were very much a part of their lives, as were their simple schools.

Mills in Maryland

On the Honga River in Dorchester County, Maryland was one of the last of the old windmills of the Dutch type, dating from about 1750. When in use, its great rotating sails were blown by the wind and the power was transmitted to mill stones by a series of gears.

Tidal mills were once often used in tidewater Maryland. They got their power from a water wheel that was turned by the incoming and outgoing tides.

Some machinery depended upon horsepower, or on oxen, for turning wheels. Meatgrinders, threshing machines, tread mills and various types of transportation used horses or oxen as a source of power.

Most millers, however, found it simplest to use water power from running streams. There were many water powered mills to be found in every part of Maryland. When a good mill site had been selected and the mill constructed of stone or wood, then the operation depended largely upon the personal talents and energy of a miller. He was often a man of some importance in the area. He might give loans or extend credit. The mill was also a good place to meet and exchange news and ideas.

Early water mills were fairly simple. To make a millpond, which would increase the force of the water for a millwheel, the stream usually was dammed up, and a millrace was constructed. When the gate was opened a millrace filled with water, directing it against a big water wheel and turning it. Inside the mill, gears turned an axle which then rotated millstones in a big box. Wheat went in at the top of the box and came out at the bottom, ground into flour. Removed from the mill, the wheat bran could then be sifted from the flour. Corn was ground into meal in this way, too, as were other grains.

Millers often operated as unofficial bankers for their customers. Sometimes they issued a sort of money, script, which was a promise to pay a certain amount upon demand. Communities quite often grew up around mills. Mill centers performed likewise, other functions. The miller was apt to be a sort of store keeper selling a variety of articles of trade and the mill machinery could be adapted to saw timbers and make lumber. Mill records afford an interesting glimpse into the life of the times, as well as shedding light upon the highly varied business interests of the miller and his neighbors.

Town Life

As Maryland became more settled, little communities began to appear. Each had its particular interests and activities,—perhaps a mill, a quarry, a ferry, an iron furnace, a tannery, or a distillery. Each had its "country store," news center, and church, and then, too, a village school, tavern, print shop and post office. The community was likely to plan most of its own entertainment features such as local fairs, church suppers, and musical programs. Each community, too, had its artisans, tradesmen and perhaps a lawyer or a doctor. Travel was too slow and life was, as yet, too isolated for people to go far to seek any special services. So, usually there was someone in town to mend shoes, to sew, and to tailor clothing, to make and repair guns, to shoe horses, and to do general blacksmithing, not to mention the carpenters, stonecutters, and brick layers. In brief, little communities tended to be self-sufficient just as each plantation had tried to make everything possible for itself in the earlier period.

Western Shore deposits of iron-bearing clay were discovered. The Eastern Shore, too, had its bog-iron deposits and furnaces.

Iron ore was marketed in Maryland in the very early colonial years. In 1719, the government of Maryland in fact offered 100 acres of land free to anyone who would set up a furnace and forge for iron making. English manufacturers very much needed pig iron from the colonies, for there was a serious lack of wood in England to fuel that nation's iron furnaces. Most of Maryland's early iron, however, was low grade ore, and this caused problems in processing it into pig iron.

Iron works were built on Antietam Creek about 1765, and the great Catoctin Furnace near Frederick, was in operation by 1776. These had access to better ores, however, and began to produce quite a lot of good iron. Thus, Frederick County became noted for its gun shops and other iron manufacturing. The cannon and cannon balls made there and at other Maryland furnaces for the American Revolutionary soldiers, in fact, had much to do with the victory finally achieved. Other types of factories also began to appear as, for example, those turning out the thousands of pounds of nails needed to help build a new nation. Every blacksmith was in his own way, too, a manufacturer. He might cut and make nails from long rods or he might shape horseshoes or turn out wheel bands to reinforce wooden wagon wheels so that they lasted longer. He might make hinges for doors and other hardware needed for house construction, and he often created and mended farm tools and equipment.

Glass Manufacture

It is said that it was a Baltimore merchant, Benjamin Crockett, who persuaded a prosperous man from the city of Bremen to come to Maryland. This German, John Frederick Amelung, had the money and the knowledge to set up (near Frederick, Maryland) what was perhaps the finest glass manufacturing plant in existence anywhere among the American colonies. Amelung arrived in Baltimore in August, 1784, aboard a ship especially chartered for the trip. With him, he brought special tools for glassmaking and artisans.

The site of his factory and home was land which he purchased near the Carrollton Manor estate, and he called it "New Bremen." Before long, the factory, houses for the workmen, a school, and his own large mansion were built there. His home had twenty-two rooms and was equipped with every luxury, including an orchestra to play for him when he dined or entertained! Around the mansion were laid out gardens, orchards, and vineyards.

From Amelung's factory came large quantities of flat glass for windows, bottles of many shapes and sizes, jelly glasses, and mirrors. But not all of his products were simply plain and ordinary. He turned out, for example, very beautiful goblets, vases, and many sorts of glass ornaments for public buildings and homes. Production which was begun in 1778, stopped in 1795. Unfortunately, Amelung fell upon hard times and owed more money than he could pay at the time.

The town of New Bremen became known later as "Fleecy Dale," a woolen milling center; and still later it was called Park Mills.

The American Revolution of course emphasized the great need for American industry. The few examples given here serve to show that, while Maryland was to remain an agricultural state for some time, the beginnings of industry were actually taking place.

Old windmill near Church Creek.

CHAPTER XLI

WATER TRAVEL IN MARYLAND

As we have seen, the people of Maryland from the very beginning of the colonial period traveled a great deal by water. There were no roads when the province was first settled, and only a few Indian trails. When roads did begin to appear, they were so rutted and bumpy that journeys overland held little charm for anyone. So those who had to travel much perferred to go by boat. On the water at least one could glide smoothly enough, the weather permitting.

Because water travel was slow, however, the traveler was likely to carry aboard his boat a supply of food for the trip that would keep well,—dried beans, fruits, flour, tea, rice, and nuts. In the early days, travelers by water were even sometimes known to take along a cow for milk, animals and fowl to use for meat, and hens to provide eggs, and a supply of cargo was seldom complete without kegs or bottles of rum, brandy, beer, or wine. Prepared meats could only be taken along if they were smoked, dried, salted, or pickled. Still, there was also the opportunity to catch fish to add to the food supply, and if the trip was well planned, one might be fortunate enough to find a hospitable farmer or plantation owner along the way, who would be willing to offer a meal and a place to rest.

Vessels Used

Shallops and sloop-type vessels were used by early settlers. Most of them were fairly small and built to be moved either by rowing or by sail. The Indian canoe was adopted by the white men. A special type of canoe was to be built in Maryland by Europeans, called the "log canoe." This workboat has low sides which permit easy working of nets and tongs.

On the Eastern Shore of Maryland, Friends, or Quakers, often used canoes in crossing rivers, letting their horses swim beside them. Having reached the opposite shore, they could remount and proceed on their way. Methodist circuit riders, too, sometimes followed this practice.

Ocean-going ships could go all the way up the Potomac to the fall line,—the location of Georgetown, Maryland (later Washington) as well as up the Chesapeake to the head of the Bay. These vessels were beautiful with great, graceful sails.

In the Bay area boats were "the freight trains" or "trucks," of that day. Oxen, pulling loaded wagons or carts were driven right down into the water near the waiting boats where the loads were easily transferred. These cargoes included all kinds of farm products and needed goods.

Winter on the Water

Water travel did not always occur in placid and warm weather. An open boat in winter time could be so cold that the men doing the rowing must put ashore and build a fire to thaw out hands and feet, benumbed by cold. Warmed, they could continue. Trips, using oars, of forty miles a day, were not uncommon.

Storms sometimes tossed small boats wildly, and early colonists soon learned how suddenly the weather might change,—one day perhaps warm, and cold and windy the next! Needless to say, storms on Chesapeake Bay could be very dangerous for people in small boats.

Maryland was abundantly supplied with waterways and these were put to good use. Most of the early manors and plantations had landings and wharves on the water. There were numerous shipyards kept busy building all kinds of water craft, both large and small. Many ocean going vessels were constructed in Maryland, both in the colonial period and later.

Canals Popular Projects

In England, Holland, and Germany, canals were constructed to move great loads easily and cheaply; and in America efforts were made as soon as possible to develop waterways — especially at and above the fall line where the navigable waters ended. The Potomac Company, organized in 1785 by a group including George Washington, had ambitious plans. James Rumsey, the chief engineer, was Maryland's inventor of steamboats. In 1784 he obtained rights to make and sell his steam propelled boat, which used a system of paddles and setting poles; and, a little later, he made a trial of this, the first steamboat at Shepherd's Town on the Potomac. Rumsey was a native of Cecil County, Maryland.

The Potomac Company planned to build a canal in order to carry goods westward from the fall line at Georgetown, Maryland (now a part of Washington, D.C.). Ocean-sized vessels could proceed upstream to that point. (See the map of canals in this chapter.)

Work was begun. Where the Potomac was too shallow for navigation at the falls of the Potomac, canals were built to bypass the

C & O Canal scene, shows entrance to a lock.

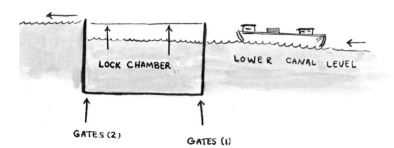

After the gates at (1) were opened, the boat entered the lock from the lower canal level, then the gates at (1) and (2) were closed, water was pumped into the lock chamber, the additional water to the upper canal level. Then the gates at (2) were opened and the boat was towed away on its journey. To lower a boat, the process was reversed.

rough, rockstrewn water. In all, five short canals were planned. This work was finished in 1802. Boatmen then began to bring cargoes down from Cumberland to Georgetown using the combination of river and canal waterways. The downriver trip took about three days and the return upstream about ten days.

Still, the Potomac canal-river system was not completely satisfactory. When the water level of the river dropped, boats often were grounded and damaged. Some years later, a new group organized the Chesapeake and Ohio Canal company. This company planned to build a continuous canal along the Maryland side of the Potomac all the way from Georgetown to Cumberland. Plans were also drafted to carry this canal system westward to the Ohio River, as well as to build another shorter canal to connect Georgetown with Baltimore. The success of the Erie Canal, in New York state, completed in 1825, of course, encouraged other canal projects.

Work began on the Chesapeake and Ohio Canal in 1828 near Little Falls, Maryland. The project, however, was very expensive and very slow, and its success was threatened almost immediately by the plans for the Baltimore and Ohio Railroad. Competition, in fact, became very heated in the struggle to control the right-of-way in the vicinity of Harpers Ferry, and lawsuits and counter suits were filed, while the laborers on each side fought bloody battles. When, finally, these difficulties were settled, the canal was completed, reaching Cumberland in 1850. Beautifully constructed, the canal opened up 184.5 miles of waterway. At certain places it was sixty to eighty feet wide and its seventy-four locks lifted boats a total of 605 feet in elevation on the trip from Georgetown to Cumberland.

Canal boats nearly ninety feet long and fourteen feet wide were used on this waterway. Crews lived, slept and ate aboard. There was a stable, also, on board for mules for the trip downstream and a storage area for mule feed. It took about six days for a boat loaded with stone, coal, whiskey, flour, or grain to reach Georgetown from Cumberland. On the return trip, the boats usually carried lighter cargoes of fish, salt, merchandise, and fertilizer and made the trip in a shorter time. By the 1870's, there were over 500 boats using the canal and carrying about 250,000 tons of cargo a year.[1]

After all the work and expense of building it and the workmen's lives it cost, the Chesapeake and Ohio Canal had only a few profitable years. The railroad was too strong a competitor, carrying cargo more cheaply, and carrying it faster. Floods damaged the canals, and finally, in 1924, canal operation stopped. The Chesapeake and Ohio Canal area today is cared for by the U.S. Department of the Interior, National Park Service.

Chesapeake and Delaware Canal

Maryland's early great map maker, Augustine Herman, said in 1680, that a canal cutting across the land between the Chesapeake and Delaware Bays would save miles of travel on the water route between New York and Baltimore. He was a prophet of what was to come, as the map will show.

A company was organized in 1799, after a survey (in 1769) showed a possible route. Work on the Chesapeake and Delaware Canal began in 1804, but stopped two years later for lack of money. After some delays work began again in 1823, and in 1829 the lock canal was completed. It connects the Elk River with the Delaware River and is over thirteen miles long. Dug to a depth of ten feet, and sixty-six feet wide, the canal originally had four locks.

The United States government in 1919 bought the canal and has since improved it. It today is a deep water passage without locks, which accommodates ocean-going ships, thus saving almost 300 miles and almost twenty-six hours of travel between the Ports of Baltimore and Philadelphia. Ships bound for ports in northern Europe from Baltimore also are greatly aided. Then, too, the Chesapeake and Delaware Canal shortens considerably the distance between the port of Baltimore and that of New York.

The Susquehanna Tidewater Canal

Trade between the western sections of Maryland and Pennsylvania and the market and port town of Baltimore was hampered by lack of adequate transportation. A company called the Proprietors of the Susquehanna Canal was formed in 1783. Work on this canal began in 1803 and it was completed in 1839 by a new group, the Susquehanna Tidewater Canal Company. Again, canal earnings were quite disappointing. When completed, the canal extended from Havre de Grace and Port Deposit (see map) northwestward past the Pennsylvania border to Columbia, Pennsylvania. It was forty-five miles long and had twenty-nine locks. This canal and related connecting canals were at their best in the 1870's. Coal was the important cargo. It is estimated that at that time, approximately 200 boats transported 600,000 tons annually to the Chesapeake Bay. But, again, the railroads in competition were faster and cheaper. Damaged by heavy floods, the upper part of this canal system was closed in 1890 and by 1900, the owners gave up and closed down their operation.

191

Canal Life

A new way of life developed along these canals. Men became expert in handling their bulky, heavy canal boats. They had to know just how to get through the canal locks, how to pass another boat without damage and how to judge the weather.

Families often traveled in canal boats, as well as members of the crew. There were sleeping quarters for the captain, his wife, and children, and also for the others. Apparently, the entire family of the captain usually helped in running the boat, and in preparing the meals in the boat's kitchen.

Normally, mules were used to tow the boats. They were not as easily hurt as were horses, nor so apt to take fright. Sturdy and strong, they were faster than oxen and could move a boat along without much rest for six to eight hours. Fresh mules carried aboard the boat, were then hitched up and the boat continued, until it was moored for the night. Life, of course, was slow on the Canal. A speed in excess of four miles an hour would cause waves that ate away canal banks, and so the safe speed was approximately four miles.

Canal boats in some cases continued to travel through the night, but usually they stopped near a lockkeeper's house, where there were likely to be groceries, mule feed, clothing, and other items. The season of travel was from early springtime until late fall. Of the three major canals mentioned, the Chesapeake and Delaware Canal is the only one still in use.

Boat Building

Almost every sort of boat and ship has been built in Maryland shipyards. Today, boatbuilding is yet an important aspect of Maryland industry; Marylanders still use their waterways for business and for pleasure.

Steam Boats

The steamer *Chesapeake* began regular trips in 1813 to Elk River landing. Here it met passengers who had come from the north by water, having left their ship on the Delaware and having made a short land journey to the Elk River. The steamer took them down the Elk, into Chesapeake Bay and to Baltimore.

William Flanigan built the steamer, *Chesapeake*, in Baltimore. Soon the steamer, because of its speed and good service, put some of the sailing packets out of business. From that time on, until the end of the first World War, steamers were a favorite means of travel on Chesapeake Bay. Their design was varied and often included very elaborate woodwork, trim, and lighting.[2] Steam engines were steadily improved. Some were "sidewheelers" and some "sternwheelers."

Departure from Baltimore meant that there would be a flurry of activity as slaves and laborers loaded casks, bales, and bundles into the hold of these steamers. Lady passengers dressed colorfully in graceful wide skirts, shawls, parasols, chatted with their gentlemen friends. The men were likely to be dressed in top hats, fancy waistcoats, frock coats and the new long trousers.

The Old Bay Line was the last company to continue steamboat operation. It stayed in business almost down to the present day. Yet, in the long run, the steamers, too, went the way of the canals. They were, except for freighters and cruisers, outdistanced by the faster and more economical railroads, bus and truck lines and the family automobile.

1 See Wheeler pamphlet "Canals In Maryland," No. 12A. Published by Maryland Historical Society, Baltimore.

2 For a most interesting look at Chesapeake Bay water craft read **Chesapeake Bay, A Pictorial Maritime History,** by M. V. Brewington.

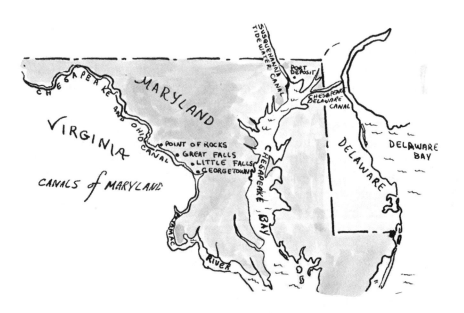

CHAPTER XLII

LAND TRAVEL

INDIAN trails were very narrow but yet sometimes very long paths. Some of them extended all the way from Canada down through Maryland and south into Georgia. There were Indian paths through the Eastern Shore, while others ran down along the Appalachian mountain chain. Swinging quietly along in single file, Indians along these trails traveled great distances in a remarkably short time. They sometimes traded and at other times made war with Indians and whites, often hundreds of miles from their home villages.

Indians traveled both on foot and by canoe. They had trained runners, too, for carrying messages quickly to neighboring and distant tribes. These fleet men of the forest were used in relays when the distance was too great for one man to keep up a fast pace. Oddly enough, the Indians appear not to have discovered the wheel before the Europeans arrived. Since the Indian had long since searched out the easiest and most accessible routes, the white man quickly adopted a considerable number of these early trails.

There were very few road signs in the seventeenth and eighteenth centuries to help the traveler, although, perhaps, a road leading to a ferry might be marked by three notches on a tree along the way, or a road leading to a court house might be indicated by cutting two notches. Other markings, such as a "slip," or slash, cut down the face of a tree by the road might indicate that the road led to a church. Even, today, some roads retain the name "Three Notch Road," because of the fact that they once were ferry roads, and so on. In those days, the traveler, of course, was quite familiar with such markings.

Horseback riding was preferred by many in colonial times, when it was necessary to travel by land, because roads were ordinarily so rough that anyone riding in a cart or coach would suffer severe bouncing. Food, bedding, and luggage were carried along on the trip, either in saddlebags or on a separate pack horse.

Traders who traveled about a great deal, penetrated deep into the forests and mountains, using not one but perhaps several pack horses laden with trade goods. On the return trips, the pack horses were likely to be loaded with furs and other articles of value accepted by the trader in payment for his goods.

There was not much work done in the way of good road building in Maryland until the 1800's. Some effort was made in very bad spots, where the road might cross streams or swamps, to lay logs across, close together, with brush or dirt over them to make for a smoother crossing. This made the road passable, still it was not a very permanent solution for, as the dirt washed away, the same problem developed again.

The carrying of the mails led to the construction of some reasonably good "post roads" between towns and cities. Maryland had some such roads in use by 1695; and then there were "rolling roads," used by the tobacco growers for rolling great wooden barrels or hogsheads of tobacco to the wharves along the water front. Some of Maryland's rolling roads still can be found today. They were narrow, deep, and often bordered by huge trees along their winding way. Even Indian trails were sometimes adapted to this purpose — an interesting part of the Maryland heritage. In the automobile age of today, cars may occasionally travel on highways which once were rolling roads, and where, through the car windows, there comes the fragrant scent of honeysuckle or the pungent smells from tobacco barns.

On both the Western and Eastern Shores, Methodist circuit riders and travelling Friends often went over bog and swampland on horseback if they did not make the trip using the log canoe. When it rained travellers found such shelter as they could, possibly beneath thickly-leaved trees, arriving later at their destinations soaked, muddy, and tired. Sometimes, if they were lucky, they might happen upon a farm house or even an inn, in which to eat, warm themselves and spend the night. But, if those welcome accommodations were not available and darkness came on, then the traveler had to build his own fire and bed down in the darkness as best he could. The camp fire would help to warm and cheer one or give a bit of light. It also was a means for cooking a meal and was a protection somewhat from marauding animals and insects.

The value of a good horse was something well understood by the traveler. A good horse had to be strong, fast in pace, and smooth in "gait," and be able to keep going all day if necessary.

Writers of that day sometimes spoke of riding "a strong black horse," in the same way that today one might comment on the qualities of his car. There were "gentle horses" for young children and older people. There were "trim and frisky" racing horses, which even down to the present time in Maryland delight horse fanciers with their beauty and speed. A "cob" was a "chunky" horse, useful for riding or for pulling a light wagon. "Draft" horses were great heavy animals, and while not fast, were very strong. A farmer with "draft" animals

195

might enter them in weight-pulling contests with other such teams. Maryland, needless to say, has always been a great "horse country."

There were at first no bridges in Maryland, but so many have been built that now this is a land of bridges. If the streams were shallow, horses and wagons drove right across them, "fording" them. If the waterway were deeper, a ferry might be found at a point where travelers must cross. Ferry men charged the traveler for crossing. Eventually, towns and even the state maintained ferry services.

When bridges were built, they were so constructed as to cross the stream at the shortest distance, and, for this reason, they often were located almost at right angles to the roadway itself. In the days of slow-moving traffic, this was usually safe enough. Later, when autos came into use these sharp angles proved to be very hazardous!

Our First Roads

The Great Eastern Road (now U.S. Route 1) was one of the first important north-south roads in the United States. It originally extended from Philadelphia to Baltimore and went on southward to Georgetown, Maryland, on the Potomac. From Pennsylvania it reached northward to New York and Boston. In the middle of the eighteenth century, the Frederick Road was developed from the west into Baltimore. It was connected from the west with the Ellicott's road from Frederick to their mill and then eastward to Baltimore. Then there was "Mr. Digges's Wagon Road," now called Reisterstown Road, which carried traffic from the northwest from Gettysburg and Westminster, into Baltimore. Other roads from Baltimore led northward to the Pennsylvania towns of Hanover and York.

It will be remembered, that, during the French and Indian War, the British general, Edward Braddock (in the 1750's) as he moved westward from the Potomac valley hacked a road through the mountainous frontier for his troops, supply wagons and cannon. Eventually this road especially that part west from Cumberland proved to be most valuable for the nation and for Marylanders, too.[1] All of these roads were in use before the American Revolution, but they were, of course, only dirt tracks.

Lodgings

Generally travelers were welcome to the hospitality of farmers and their families for meals and night lodging, but this generosity was more and more a burden as more people came to use the roads. Even in the colonial period, inns and taverns began to appear along the principal roads for the accommodation of travelers. Still, these were far apart in the early days, and so private homes continued to be havens for the traveling public for many years. For this reason, George Washington, who traveled a great deal, probably did sleep in many Maryland, Virginia, and Pennsylvania homes, that being the custom of that period of history. "The quality of early inns and taverns, moreover, was at best, none too good," one writer comments.

In due time, when stage coaches began to travel the roads regularly, inns somewhat improved, although very few seemed to have separate rooms and accommodations. Besides, the food and drink was usually not very good. Tavern keepers frequently issued "script," as money, when accounts were settled at these places of business. The script was convenient for travelers on the road, but it was only as good in exchange as the reputation of the innkeeper who issued it.

How Fast?

It is very hard for us to imagine how slow travel was in Maryland in the earliest days of the colony, and, for that matter, even down to the American Revolution. Recently, of course, travel speeds have increased tremendously. A man walking makes good about four or five miles per hour; and, at a fast run on a smooth track, from eight to twelve miles per hour. Horses at full speed can go about thirty miles per hour but can keep up this pace for only a very short time. They can trot or pace along for a longer time, at a speed of about five or ten miles per hour. Even so, they need rests, as well as food and water. It is a good horse that can make as much as forty miles in a day's time. Horses pulling a wagon travel at the rate of two to three miles per hour.

A wagon train on good roads, traveling at a steady walk, might make, but not normally, a distance of twenty-five miles per day. On a good road a stage coach might travel at about eight miles per hour. The stage gots its name from the fact that at regular intervals fresh horses replaced the tired ones. Thus, the trip was made "by stages." In 1766, the stage coach from Philadelphia to New York City took two days to make the trip.

In the early 1800's a fast light coach pulled by three horses made the trip from Baltimore to Washington in a day and a half. Also considered very fast was the record of the mail wagon that left Washington at five in the morning and arrived in Baltimore at eleven at night—an eighteen-hour trip!

Mail Service

The very first mail service in Maryland, was, as has been noted,

197

that offered by the captains of sailing ships. A traveler also often might accommodate neighbors or friends and take along letters when making a trip. Servants were often sent to nearby plantations with letters or with written invitations to balls, dinners, and meetings of the hunt.

Post riders on a regular basis in the colonial period first began to take mail from place to place as a private business venture, at a fairly high rate of charge per letter. Arriving at an inn, they would spread out the mail where those expecting letters might come to pick them up. Sometimes, too, traders would carry letters with them to deliver on their trips.

When stagecoaches regularly began to serve towns and cities, mail was sent along with them. But even as late as 1760, mail from Philadelphia to the southern colonies was sent only eight times a year!

Benjamin Franklin of Pennsylvania had became deputy post-master-general for the colonies in 1753 and improved the postal system; and a Baltimore printer, William Goddard, had an important part in starting a national postal system. Goddard hired men on horseback as "post riders" to bring him news stories quickly for his newspaper and to carry both newspapers and other mail to various centers for delivery. The *Maryland Journal* was the name of his newspaper. Goddard and Franklin may be remembered as the fathers of our national postal system.

The first national rural mail delivery service was inaugurated in Maryland in 1899, in Carroll County, Maryland.[2]

---

1 The Braddock Road eventually became a section of The National Road, known much later in the automobile era as U.S. 40.
2 A. E. Summerfield, **U.S. Mail.**

THOROUGHBRED, a Saddle Horse. All thoroughbreds are part Arabian. Used for racing they are the fastest of all horses. They are slim and strong.

CHAPTER XLIII

A NATIONAL ROAD

A Maryland Highway Spurs Western Growth

A highway that was to be the most important in the nation was planned and constructed in the first quarter of the nineteenth century.[1] When Thomas Jefferson was President of the United States, the national Congress in 1806 approved the building of the first federally subsidized road. Previously, the states had built and maintained their own roads, or in some cases, they had been privately constructed. This new highway, however, because it gave a direct route into the west beyond the mountains and would serve many of the new communities being developed there was of such national interest that it seemed logical for the central government to build it. The National Road was to begin near Cumberland, Maryland and was to extend westward to Wheeling, and into the Ohio River country beyond. Already there was a road from the port city of Baltimore as far west as Cumberland, that would serve as the eastern terminus of the federal road. Settlers were thronging from the east to western farms. The new state of Ohio had already been admitted in 1804 into the Union. The Indiana and Illinois territories were being rapidly settled. So it seemed to be good politics in 1806 for the Congress to vote to build a great highway into the west.

The Need

Existing roads from Baltimore westward were clearly inadequate for the ever-increasing traffic. The road to Cumberland, in fact, was crowded with settlers bound for the west and out of the Ohio country already. Wagons, passenger coaches and freight wagons were on the move. In bad weather the existing roads became impassable with mud and bridges were needed to cross many of the streams. A permanent road and also more taverns and inns were needed. Riders carrying the mail wanted to move more quickly and that was impossible over the roads that existed. Travel was so slow that passengers were subjected to much great discomfort. Trade, too, was hampered by the rutted, stump-strewn roadways.

The New Road

Contractors supervised by United States Army engineers, began working in 1811 on the road west from Cumberland, Maryland. The new road was to have a cleared right of way on either side and it was to be thirty feet wide. Most important, it was to be hard surfaced, with a heavy stone layer as its surface. Plans allowed for the proper drainage of the roadbed by making the center of the road a little higher than its edges. This design, it was believed, would help prevent ruts, holes, and washouts.

Bridges were planned to support even the heavy Conestoga wagons that carried as much as six tons of cargo.

Life on the Road

By 1818, the National Road from Cumberland to Wheeling was finished and open to travel. Instantly the road was put to heavy use. Travelers on horseback found the smooth surfaces most agreeable. Smart carriages moved more rapidly along. Wagons with families and their belongings no longer fearing the mud and ruts moved west. Stagecoaches, too, could keep better schedules, and mail wagons and mail riders could more promptly deliver newspapers and mail into the western country. Heavy freight wagons by the scores could move also more easily on the new road.

Soon, too, animals on the hoof, produced west of the Ohio River, began to come eastward to great market centers like Baltimore. Drovers herded horses, mules, cows, sheep, and swine slowly along. At night they stopped to let the animals feed and rest, eventually arriving at their eastern markets.

Boys who worked on the road were called "pike boys." Youngsters began to work on the wagon trains at an early age and many grew up to be drivers. Some men, in fact, spent their entire life working at various jobs along the National Road. To keep the great traffic moving, blacksmiths were needed to shoe horses and repair the wagons. Wagon stands were built and operated to provide pens for animals; and shelter, food, and drink for the drovers. Inns bustled with the work of feeding, sheltering, and entertaining the travelers who were constantly moving along the road. All of these things, as well as other aspects of the problem of dealing with the hundreds and thousands of people traveling on the road, required workers of every kind.

Keeping the road up, likewise made many jobs. It took special

(Joseph H. Cromwell, C & P Telephone Company of Maryland)

An old Toll House stands on Route 40 between Cumberland and Frostburg, Maryland. Here the tollhouse keeper lived, stepping out of his office on the lower floor to collect tolls from those using the old National Road.

skills to keep the stone surface smooth and the bridges in repair. Some men worked "postilions," with two horses. They waited at the foot of the steeper hills to help heavily laden wagons up the long grades. Even six great horses pulling a Conestoga wagon sometimes needed this help.

For those living beside the road, the endless parade of travelers each day provided new interest. From morning to night riders passed. Sometimes, too, there were brightly painted stage coaches, pulled by smart teams of horses. Often drovers passed, driving herds of western hogs to market.

There were other and more harrowing experiences for those who watched the procession go by. There were groups of slaves driven like horses, as traders moved them west. Sometimes they were arranged in pairs and fastened to a long rope to prevent their escape. It was a sad sight.

There were many dangers on the road. There were runaway horses, overturned carriages, and wagons wrecked on icy hills. Bandits sometimes robbed coaches and wagons. In winter, there was deep snow, ice and cold rains to fight. In summer, there was often blazing heat to wither both man and animal.

Then, too, at the wagon stands and inns, arguments and even fights were not uncommon. And as a footnote to this, we might add that whiskey made from corn was only three cents a glass at wagon stands and five cents at the stage houses. Men who drank would frequently fight, hurt and even kill people. But not all was trouble, for at the overnight stops, there was fiddling and dancing in the barrooms to while away the hours; and there were those willing to tell tall stories of adventure and hardships. There were songs to sing. And, when the traveler reached some settlement, he could find amusement in corn huskings, spelling matches, school "programs," frolics and balls, and perhaps a pretty lass to admire.

Rivalries and competition existed among the road boys especially between those called "town boys" and those of the road, the "pike boys."

Toll Houses

The use of the National Road was free until 1828. Then tollgates were built every ten or twenty miles along the road and a charge was made for the use of the road. This money was used to keep the pike in good repair. Toll houses were built for the tollgate keepers and their families. Each kind of traffic paid a different fee. No tolls

202

were charged for local travel or for school children, soldiers or funerals.

Summary

From 1818 until 1852, the Road served as a national highway of great importance. Freight charges dropped, passengers moved more comfortably and faster, and mail service was greatly improved. Work to improve and extend the Road continued. By 1833, it had reached Columbus, Ohio. But, in 1835, the national government decided that road building was not a federal function after all, and it then decided to turn the jurisdiction over to the states. But the highway was finished all the way to Vandalia in southern Illinois. Here construction stopped and travelers going farther westward to the Mississippi River must continue on a dirt road.

In all, the National Road was 700 miles long and built at an average cost of approximately $10,000 a mile. It crossed rivers and mountains. In Maryland, it had to cross Negro Mountain, which is more than 2300 feet high.

It seemed that the old dynamic life of the National Road was ended when the Baltimore and Ohio Railroad reached Wheeling and the Ohio River. Very shortly traffic on the road grew smaller as the number of wagons and coaches dwindled. The railroad could take passengers and freight along more cheaply, more comfortably, and faster. Still, this highway into the west was far from useless or abandoned. In fact, it is still in use today and the automobile age, of course, revived it. On a modern highway map, it is called U.S. Route 40, and while it is much smoother even than when coaches traveled it, it follows much the same route most of the way. Trucks haul freight faster than the old waggoneers ever dreamed of moving. Busses and passenger cars move at speeds today that the old coach drivers could not even imagine. The story of National Road shows that modern life does not simply spring into existence but grows from a rich and intensely interesting past.

---

1 When we mean the years from 1800 to 1900 we sometimes call this "the nineteenth century."

For more information on the National Road read Wheeler Leaflet on Maryland History, No. 12B, published by the Maryland Historical Society. Also you will find most interesting, **The Old Pike** by Thomas B. Searight, 1894.

CHAPTER XLIV

MARYLAND FOLKLORE

As has been noted in an earlier discussion of crime and punishment, Maryland had little of the "witch hunting" that occurred in New England. Perhaps the religious and civil liberties of the colony tended to make men less suspicious and more tolerant. At any rate the few witch's trials held in Maryland showed that there was little public acceptance of witchcraft and magic.

Pirates were a problem all along the Atlantic seaboard and they occasionally threatened the eastern coast of Maryland. Sometimes bands of thieves would arrive by boat in the Chesapeake Bay area to raid homes, especially when owners were away. Occasionally robbers would terrorize the household servants, scoop up silverware and any valuables about, and vanish just as they had come.

Neighboring states, like Virginia and North Carolina perhaps are richer in pirate lore than Maryland. Residents here, however, felt much easier when they learned that the infamous pirate "Blackbeard" had been killed. This pirate's real name was Edward Teach and he had cruised the Caribbean and the coastal waters of the Carolinas, capturing ships and raiding towns.

He was one of the most cruel of a cruel breed of men. He tortured captives and enjoyed their suffering. He stole from churches and homes. He murdered and killed innocent people. He is said to have had fourteen wives. What happened to each in turn would no doubt make fourteen grisly tales, if they were known.

It was in the early 1700's that Blackbeard was fought by the sloop *Pearl* under the command of an Englishman, Lieutenant Maynard. Blackbeard was attacked and both men slashed away on the deck of the pirate ship with broad, sharp swords. One blow from Maynard nearly severed the pirate's head. But, holding his head with one hand, Blackbeard backed away, roaring and pouring blood. Finally, he went down, almost literally "hacked to pieces."

In 1823, Commodore Porter sailed from the Port of Baltimore in the steam galley, *Enterprize*. His mission was to suppress piracy off the coast of Cuba and he led a squadron of pirate-hunting ships. Trade had been hampered by the pirates. Many ships were being captured, the crews killed and cargoes stolen or sunk.

The Rose Hill Mansion of Charles County was the home of Dr. Gustavus Brown, who attended George Washington.

In July, Rogers located and attacked a pirate stronghold near Matanzas, sank a schooner and, as the officers of the vessels under his command claimed, the pirates were killed by angry crew members. Soon the Caribbean was clear of pirates, thanks to Commodore Porter and his fleet. Now the ships from Baltimore and other ports could move more safely.

MARYLAND GHOST STORIES

Now ghosts are not, strictly speaking, historical figures. Ghosts do not actually exist in Maryland but stories about them do; and these are, in a manner of speaking, a part of Maryland's interesting heritage — a part of its folklore.

The Blue Dog

Such a story is the one about "the blue dog" down in Charles County, in the town called Port Tobacco, which may have been named after an Indian queen living nearby whose name sounded something like "Port Tobacco."

Overlooking a garden and Port Tobacco Creek is a home, now restored, known as "Rose Hill." It is a beautiful old house with a columned front portico. The ends of the house are almost entirely made up of enormous twin brick chimneys, serving the many fireplaces within. Yet, because of the great, high-ceilinged rooms of the house, a fireplace could only slightly temper the chill of winter. "No one," comments the writer, Katherine Scarborough, "in Revolutionary days was revolutionary enough, however, to dream of being comfortable in winter."[1]

At one side of the house still stands the kitchen, a separate building. This was constructed apart from the main house to prevent fires from spreading from cooking quarters to the main house. It also kept away the odors and heat of the cooking. At one side of the house was an office used by the man who built the mansion. He was Dr. Gustavus Richard Brown, a jurist and legislator, as well as a physician. Upstairs, a bedroom was set aside and always ready for General George Washington, whenever he visited Rose Hill. He was a frequent visitor whenever he happened to be at Mt. Vernon.

When Dr. Brown, in 1801, died at the age of fifty-six, he was laid to rest in a tomb of stone at the foot of the formal garden in front of the house at Rose Hill.

Down in Port Tobacco, a peddler, so the story goes, drank too much and began to reel about, boasting of a bag full of money that he carried. He left the tavern with his dog and went staggering off up the lane toward Rose Hill. The next day he was found near Rose Hill, lying in the lane, murdered. His money was gone, and his dog was gone.

Local legend has it that the treasure is buried in the woods and that the murderer had planned to return for it. The ghost of the dog, a "blue dog," is said to haunt the scene of the crime keeping away anyone who might seek to search out the treasure. It is said that to the person bold enough to follow the ghost, will some day go the pleasure of being led to where the money is buried. One other thing is reported concerning the blue dog. It is supposed to appear and bark in the night when there has been a birth or a death in the Brown family.

Dower House

The third Lord Baltimore, Charles Calvert, when he was acting as governor of Maryland built in the great forests on his land a house intended as a hunting lodge. This house still stands in what is now Prince George's County; and, over the years it has been enlarged several times until it is now a large and luxurious dwelling. As Dower House grew in size and in beauty, its surroundings were also improved with broad terraces and great lawns. It is said that Pierre L'Enfant, the French planner of the city of Washington, designed the terraces.

During the War of 1812, when members of the Calvert family were still living there, a treasure of gold coin and silver plate is said to have been buried in a lily bed in the garden. The treasure was carried out of the house, so the story goes, through the secret passageway that led from the foundation walls (nearly three feet thick) to a point near the waterfront. The ghost of Elizabeth Briscoe Calvert is said by some to walk in the night, her spirit seeking the lost gold near the end of the passageway.

Tragedy apparently was the fate of a number of the ladies who lived at Dower House. There is another story of the mansion. It relates to a key found inside a locked room, beside a coffin, and of ghostly figures that haunt this part of the house.

More recently, the tale is told of one of the owners who returned unexpectedly by automobile one evening to the house to see as he approached in the driveway, a horseman dressed in armor astride a big horse. This unusual sight disappeared into thin air before the very eyes of the astonished owner, before any pleasantries could be exchanged, the horseman giving only a haughty stare as he vanished.

Today, Dower House is peaceful, in its restored and beautiful environment, a living link with the colonial past of Prince George's County.

1 Katherine Scarborough, **Homes of the Cavaliers.**

Dower House at Dusk.

YOUR MARYLAND

SECTION IV

THE WAR OF 1812

(Joseph H. Cromwell, C & P Telephone Company of Maryland)

Casselman River Bridge, near Grantsville, Garrett County, has been designated a National Historic Landmark by the U. S. Department of the Interior.

CHAPTER XLV

THE WAR OF 1812 BEGINS!

CERTAINLY no Marylander should have to stop and wonder, "The War of 1812, which war was that?" Many of the events related to that war occurred in Maryland and the importance of this State to that struggle was great. Most people do remember that the decisive battle of the war was fought for Baltimore and that our national anthem was written by Francis Scott Key, a native of the state, during the Battle of Baltimore.

After all of the hardships and dangers of the American Revolution, it may seem strange that Americans should so soon again decide to fight another war. Actually, the country was deeply divided concerning the issue of war or peace and a great many Americans violently argued against entering the War of 1812.

There were, of course, causes to be considered. English ships were stopping American vessels in very highhanded fashion. The English justified these incidents, saying that they were searching for deserters from the British Navy and Marine service. A seaman's life in the English service at this time was a hard one, for the hours of work were endless and the discipline relentless and cruel. The result was that many men did slip away, and later, might work aboard American vessels. Americans might not have minded returning a few English sailors except for the fact that sometimes Americans were hustled off as well.

This practice, as might be expected, aroused the American temper to a boiling point. Still, the French also were guilty of similar brutal seizures. French ships were stopping our merchantmen, searching them, and taking off sailors.

America did, in fact, almost enter a war with France over this in 1798. Another reason was that French consuls in several American ports were fitting out ships to fight the British and this endangered our status as a neutral nation. We were, in fact, so close to war that, over in Virginia, George Washington put on his sword, left Mount Vernon, and came out of retirement to command again American forces. He chose John Eager Howard of Maryland as one of his brigadier generals; and, at that point, it seemed almost certain that war would be declared.

At sea undeclared war did begin when the Americans captured two or three French ships. But, following some skillful diplomatic work, the French grew more polite and a bit more careful in their treatment of our shipping. Among the diplomats was the Maryland man, William Vans Murray, who had a great deal to do with causing the war clouds to pass away.

It should be remembered, too, that the United States still felt grateful to the French for their help in our American Revolution. We could not soon forget how important this had been, nor could we so soon forget our bitterness, still lingering, against the English. As the crisis faded, and in the lull before a new crisis was to develop, George Washington died in 1799, at Mount Vernon.

Time of Decision

English injustices, imagined or otherwise, could not be so easily overlooked as those of the French, and over imprisonments and other highhanded English blunders, the debate raged. Ship owners and merchants of New England port cities did not want war because it would ruin their trade. Seafarers, in spite of interference, were growing rich by running goods through the blockades to both England and France.

The American political group, called the "War Hawks," and consisting largely of Southerners and Westerners, urged war against England. They probably wished that a war might give the United States the opportunity of annexing Canada. Their goal was to expand their country, though they publicly claimed that they wanted only to get rid of British influence in the western forts.

For the "War Hawks" this appeared to be the moment to capture Canada, and possibly, Florida, too, while the English were locked in a bitter war with France. Florida, it should be noted, belonged to Spain, but at this time Spain was being overrun, and its foreign policy was dominated by England. The "War Hawks," in 1811 made up a majority in the Congress. It was a tense time. American public opinion probably still favored peace. But there had been recent incidents to fan the indignation of the country. The war party constantly reminded the American people of the fate of the American naval vessel, the *Chesapeake*, which in 1807 had been stopped in the Chesapeake Bay area by a British ship, the *Leopard*. The incident had occurred in American waters.

Captain Barron of the *Chesapeake* had angrily refused to let the English search his ship for deserters. Without warning, the English captain had opened fire and the *Chesapeake's* decks had been raked with cannon shot, almost at point blank range. Deck planks were red with blood as three men dropped and died, and the scene was one of unbelievable chaos. Captain Barron himself was wounded, and seventeen other sailors on board sustained injuries. The guns, rigging and spars of the American ship were wrecked. It was a surprise attack and the Americans had no chance to make a fight of it. The *Chesapeake* was forced to surrender.

News of this outrage had spread across the nation in the months that followed. President Jefferson issued a warning that all British vessels must stay out of American ports and out of American waters.

The crisis, however, was far from being over, for our recent enemy, the British, insisted upon stopping more American ships. The "War Hawks" now constantly reminded the American public of this. In truth, not just men, but entire ships, crews and cargoes were being captured and sailed into English ports to be held as prizes!

The War Hawks, of course, neglected to mention the fact that England was trying to prevent American sea captains from selling food and supplies to France and French allies. In spite of the United States' Non-Intercourse Act of 1806 and the Embargo Act of 1807, many American ships were still engaged in illegal trade, selling food and supplies to both England and France.

The War Hawks, the dominant party in Washington, aside from the tension on the high seas, made use of another alarming report that the British were giving aid to the great Indian, Chief Tecumseh, who was causing a great Indian uprising in the Northwest Territory. Tecumseh was making war on the Americans who were moving westward and taking the Indians' land. So it was that the American Congress, on June 18, 1812, declared war on England and her allies.

The nation was far from being united over this declaration of war. The New England states were so angry that they talked of seceding (withdrawing) from the Union. They knew of the danger of the trade; yet, for high profits, men were willing to run the blockade.

Other Americans, however, reasoned that, perhaps, things might not be too bad. After all, England was busy fighting a war with France and was 3,000 watery miles from our shores. If Britain's 830 warships were free to attack our tiny navy of a dozen or so ships, that would be another matter! Now, the English could only be interested in keeping the French from crossing the English Channel.

In Maryland — 1812

Using the right of free speech, guaranteed to every citizen of the United States, the Baltimore editor, Alexander Contee Hanson, spoke out. He was the publisher of the *Federal Republican,* a popular newspaper. True, being a Federalist and so a bitter foe of the Madison administration, he knew that many would not like what he had to say. He courageously attacked the war policy and the government in Washington for having declared war.

Crowds on the streets in Baltimore on that June day, began to gather and to mutter. In excited voices they discussed the newspaper's remarks about the war. The crowd grew wilder, and finally became a mob. They broke the windows and doors of Hanson's newspaper office and wrecked it.

Violence spread as crowds strongly for President Madison and against the British swarmed through the city. They destroyed everything that suggested trade with Britain—ships, offices, or docks. In their mob frenzy they destroyed property without reason, as they wrecked whatever they suspected of being connected with the Federalist party.

Alexander C. Hanson, however, was a brave man, and he returned to Baltimore to resume publication, July 27, 1812, of the *Federal Republican.* He had been warned that the mob might again try to stop him from saying what he thought, but he gathered together about a dozen friends with guns and guarded the newspaper office.

As night fell, the mob formed again and prepared to attack once more. As the people surged forward, Hanson warned them. Shots were exchanged, and one man in the street was killed and several other members of the mob were wounded.

The police finally arrived, and Hanson and his friends surrendered to them willingly. On the way to the jail, the men were jostled, splattered, jeered, and insulted. The excitement was intense, and even the jail did not seem to be a safe place. Finally, the situation got entirely out of hand. The mob brushed aside the policemen and succeeded in seizing the editor and his companions, whom they beat and tortured.

One of those in support of the editor was General James M. Lingan, a man who had served the United States and the State of Maryland well in the American Revolution! He was killed by the mob. Some of the other Federalists escaped death by pretending to be already dead. In the welter of blood and bodies in the darkness, this was possible.

Just before daylight the mob broke up. Baltimore, this night, had earned a reputation of "Mob Town," which in the years to come would be difficult to live down. From this affair we see that opinions in Maryland about the War of 1812 differed violently.

214

Once in the war, however, Maryland appeared to show more support for the cause than opposition. The State gave men, money, and supplies to help the United States fight the war, in spite of the fact that the first few months of the struggle were going badly. One of the few bright spots for the United States in the year of 1812 was an adventure on the Great Lakes. Several young volunteers from Maryland were involved in the venture and served their country well.

Two of these were Lieutenant Jesse Duncan Elliot and Captain Nathan Towson. In two boats, and with a contingent of fifty Marylanders, they set out toward two enemy ships. Using muffled oars, they rowed the boats quietly through the night. The ships they planned to attack were anchored under the very guns of Fort Erie!

On the British ship, *Detroit*, a lookout stirred, wondering if he heard something. He peered into the darkness and then shouted! But it was too late. The attackers swarmed aboard and, in ten minutes they seized the enemy vessel and its crew. The top sails were hoisted, and the captured warship began to float away from the shore.

The other American force was not quite so lucky. The crew of the British ship, *Caledonia*, saw the Americans and raked their approaching boat with gunfire. Even so, the Marylanders in the party climbed aboard the *Caledonia* and subdued the British crew. They then set out to follow the *Detroit*.

Unfamiliar with the waters, however, the little band of victors sent both ships aground in the Niagara River. There they were too near the hostile Canadian shore for comfort. Captain Towson, on the *Caledonia*, managed to float his ship off. Lieutenant Elliott was unable to free the *Detroit*. So he put his men in boats with their prisoners and burned the ship.

Towson, later on, was able to present his richly-loaded prize, the *Caledonia*, to Admiral Perry. Two vessels had been removed by the raid from the British force. The Americans felt that it had been a successful venture. The price was two men killed and five wounded.

CHAPTER XLVI

THE WAR OF 1812

Blockade, Burning, Battle!

The Years 1813-1814

As the year 1813 began, the British blockade of American ports tightened. British ships, moreover, ruled the Atlantic, and enemy raiding parties struck repeatedly at points along Chesapeake Bay. Many homes and farms in Maryland were plundered and burned; and in the vicinity of the Bay, no family could ever be certain that it was safe. By such tactics the British hoped to discourage the Americans, but, to the contrary, the raids served only to make the people more united and more angry.

The United States government now asked Maryland for a three million dollar loan to help pay war expenses. This money was promptly raised by the merchants of Baltimore, but people generally in the state felt that the national government was more or less unsympathetic to the dangers that they faced. Still, the few troops and raw militia available for defense fought back at every opportunity, although they lacked the strength and means of transportation to attack the enemy, effectively.

On a mild May morning in 1813 a British squadron struck at Havre de Grace, then a thriving town of fifty houses. After firing on the town with cannon the enemy landed. They burned as they went and homes and places of business went up in flames. The few militia were beaten back.

British soldiers took money, silverware, jewelry, food, and clothing away with them. In the heat of the attack also the enemy soldiers had been extremely cruel. In fact, the town and its people had been savagely mauled and hurt.

One defensive position proved hard for the British to subdue. It was a battery manned by "an Irishman named O'Neill." Hotly firing, he poured shot after shot into the landing barges. After one firing of the battery, however, O'Neill, who reacted too slowly, was struck by his own cannon as it recoiled from the shot, and he could not continue to load and fire. Determined not to give up, he went on fighting with two muskets. He loaded and fired as fast as he could and it took a sizeable force of determined Englishmen to capture him.

A hangman's noose for O'Neill seemed certain. However, two British soldiers had been captured in the fight. The Americans sent word that, if O'Neill died, than they would hang their prisoners. Saved by this threat, John O'Neill's life was spared and he was released.

To thank O'Neill for his bravery, the federal government later assured him that the position of lighthouse keeper at Havre de Grace was his for life, and that, thereafter the position was to be retained by the family, provided they were willing to accept it and maintain the lighthouse.

Today, you can see this lighthouse. It stands on the banks of the Susquehanna River, in Harford County, at the town of Havre de Grace. It is probably the oldest lighthouse still in use in Maryland. It is now operated automatically and is important to navigation near the western terminus of the Chesapeake and Delaware Canal. Still standing, too, is the light keeper's home. In its time it has been used as an inn, a stagecoach station, and as a ferry boat terminal.

Kitty Knight, Eastern Shore Heroine

Fear and rumor tend to have a paralyzing effect. Such was the case in May, 1813, when the twin villages of Fredericktown and Georgetown lay in the path of British troops who were advancing up the beautiful Sassafras River. Admiral Sir George Cockburn promised safety to people and property, provided there was no resistance. Only a few local inhabitants were left to defend the town and scattered shots were directed at the enemy. The British soldiers immediately retaliated and set fire to Fredericktown, located on the north bank of the Sassafras River in Cecil County. They then crossed the river and came into Georgetown on the south side of the Sassafras in Kent County.

Houses and precious possessions went up in flames as the British went through the lower part of the little town. Then the attacking force began to climb the hill toward two brick dwellings nearby. In one of these lay an old woman, too ill to run away. A torch had already been set to this house when Kitty Knight ran up, in defiance of the Redcoats who had collected.

"Miss Kitty," to use the name by which she was known to her neighbors, was a thirty-eight-year-old spinster, whose real name was Catherine Knight. After that day she would be remembered all over the Eastern Shore for what she did.

Kitty demanded of Admiral Cockburn that he spare the old woman's house, and he agreed and had the fire put out. Then the house next door began to burn, and Kitty, herself proceeded to stamp out the flames. A young officer joined her and directed that the fire be put out. As the soldiers left Kitty remained behind beating out the remaining flames with her broom. The only buildings not destroyed that day were the church and the two brick houses on the hill.

Admiral Cockburn had blockaded the Virginia and Maryland capes since February, 1813, and for months he harassed the shores of the Chesapeake Bay, repeatedly sending small parties of raiders to burn farm houses and to carry off livestock and to destroy every boat they could find.

British on the Chesapeake - 1814

The Marylander, Commodore Joshua Barney in 1814 had collected a small fleet of twenty-six vessels and barges on the Chesapeake Bay. They had been fitted out in the port of Baltimore and at certain other shipyards in the Bay area. Barney had recruited and trained about 900 marines and seamen. In April of that year, he set out, hoping to carry the fight directly to the enemy and to put a stop to the raids on Maryland.

After a bit of maneuvering and sailing, as luck would have it Commodore Barney found himself face to face with a small force of British ships sailing northward up the Bay. Shots were exchanged on both sides, and then, because Barney knew that his guns lacked the range to compete with the stronger fire power of the enemy, he pulled back into the shelter of the shallow waters of the Patuxent River. Here the bigger British ships could not follow, but on the other hand, Commodore Barney found himself securely bottled up. Still, his forces were intact and his little vessels still safe.

During that summer troops in great numbers arrived to strengthen Cockburn's command. And, at Benedict on the Patuxent, about 4500 enemy soldiers landed almost unopposed. They had picked a vulnerable point well inland and miles from any sizable body of Americans.

Word spread and panic gripped the country-side, for it began to be apparent that the British were aiming right at the capital city of Washington itself!

Maryland and District of Columbia militiamen under General William H. Winder hurried forward to meet this threat but they were no match for the more disciplined enemy, who, besides greatly outnumbered them. Thus, steadily, the Americans were pushed back toward Washington, until, on August 24 they finally made a stand in the nearby village of Bladensburg. Back at the Patuxent the marooned and by-passed Commodore Barney looked over his little fleet with a heavy heart. One thing of course, must not be allowed to happen. The ships and supplies must not fall into the hands of the enemy, who had advantages enough as it was without adding this one. So, with great reluctance, the Commodore ordered his boats destroyed, at just about the moment when at Bladensburg the British onslaught was being prepared for Winder's raw recruits.

Over 2000 additional militia had come up to strengthen those already at Bladensburg. Barney and his marines marching overland, and carrying every bit of ammunition and every gun that they could manage, also arrived in time for the battle.

There was some optimism in the American camp on that morning of August 24, 1814. Some pieces of field artillery had been collected and these guns commanded the approach road. Riflemen stood ready, and officers had issued their orders and stood ready to meet the foe. President Madison at this point arrived to review the troops and to talk over the plans with General Winder. Though no military man, he did venture to suggest several changes, most of which were ignored. Besides, the enemy was approaching now so it seemed better for the President to mount his horse and ride to the rear. A "collation," i.e. dinner party, had been ordered by the beautiful Dolly Madison, his wife, for the victorious American generals when the battle should be over and the victory secured.

The "Bladensburg Races"

President Madison was sure that the city of Washington was secure. After all, 7000 Americans were waiting to meet a British force of 4500. That the British were tough professional soldiers and ably commanded was not to be denied. Still, with so great a number of Americans, it seemed right to assume that the battle would be an American victory.

It did, indeed, appear to be that way, as the firing started. An entire company of British was quickly wiped out by artillery and rifle fire; but the stubborn British came on. They crossed a fortified bridge and captured a piece of artillery. They drove the Americans back.

There the British drive was opposed by more advancing Americans, and for a brief moment the American line held and the battle hung in the balance. At this point occurred a blunder that inexperi-

219

enced troops sometimes make, and that experienced soldiers are likely to exploit. Due perhaps to the last minute change in orders, the front line of the Americans was not promptly reinforced, and the officers gave orders to fall back. This was a serious mistake for the American militiamen were impatient to fight and might have won the day.

As the withdrawal began (and not too carefully organized), the British hurried troops around the flank of the battle line, and this forced a more hasty retreat to avoid the threat of being completely surrounded. Things now happened fast and there was tremendous noise and confusion. Conflicting orders were issued and more mistakes were made. Retreating soldiers now in panic, excitedly broke ranks and ran. Some, it is said, ran all the way home. The retreat lost all order and became a rout. For very obvious reasons the battle is sometimes wryly recalled, even today, as the "Bladensburg Races."

Commodore Joshua Barney and his trained men, however, won praise even from the British. His brave men included black soldiers. Barney's men held their positions until outflanked. Barney himself, downed by a bullet in his hip was captured. Almost immediately he was paroled by the British General Ross. When the battle ended, thirty Americans were dead, fifty wounded and one hundred and twenty were prisoners of war.

At Bladensburg, therefore, the British were triumphant; and it was easy then to march forward to Washington. Dolly Madison, dropping plans for her dinner party had scarcely time to stuff valuables into her carriage and flee across the Potomac into Virginia. Dolly stopped long enough to remove from its frame a portrait of George Washington, which she carried away with her. It was well that the great general had not lived to see this day. He had out-thought and out-fought this same enemy in worse situations. President Madison took a different route, and also left the capital hastily.

The British wasted little time in marching into Washington, after a brief afternoon rest near the battlefield. In the capital city, they proceeded to burn and destroy government buildings. The President's House, hardly completed was partly burned, as was the unfinished capitol building itself. Even many of the precious books and documents of the Library of Congress that could not easily be taken away were destroyed.

On the other hand, the citizens of the town were not abused. Looking at the destruction in the capital city of the United States, General Ross, as he later wrote, felt sorry that the archives had been burned. He realized that in the excitement of his victory he had allowed priceless documents to be destroyed. Yet, this was war and he had little time to spend on regrets. He was quite satisfied this night to be in the captured capital of the United States.

Ross spent only about twenty-four hours in Washington before marching back to his fleet. Just as he was planning to leave in the afternoon of the following day, a storm of hurricane intensity swept the city. He would see at least that Washington weather was bent on bringing some discomfort to the enemy. The storm delayed his departure until nightfall. His plan now was quickly to exploit this overwhelming victory in order really to break the strength and sagging spirit of this upstart new republic. One more decisive encounter, he felt, would most surely shatter all resistance, — an attack in force on the rich port city of Baltimore.

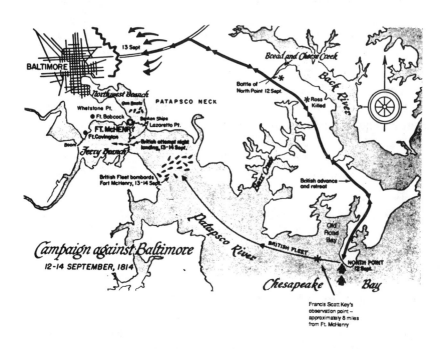

Campaign against Baltimore
12-14 SEPTEMBER, 1814

Francis Scott Key's
observation point —
approximately 8 miles
from Ft. McHenry

CHAPTER XLVII

THE WAR OF 1812

The Battle of Baltimore — September, 1814

IN thinking about the efforts of the British in the Chesapeake Bay to win the war of 1812 and to bring about the final surrender by the United States, one can easily see what the loss of Baltimore City would mean to our young nation. Baltimore was a rich port. It was also a privateering center. In fact, the British called it a "nest of pirates." But, there were even more vital considerations to the United States than the idea, however disagreeable, of seeing the British wintering comfortably in Baltimore. These factors would make the coming battle the decisive one in the War of 1812. The strategic location of Baltimore (and of Maryland, for that matter) was important, controlling as it did the great central route into the West. This location also gave the enemy an opportunity of cutting the nation at its center and making the United States helpless. This was the British theory and the reason for their concentrating their main efforts to gain control of the Bay and its great prize — Baltimore.

Before the final great attack on Baltimore, a Methodist minister of the Eastern Shore, Joshua Thomas, foretold a British defeat. This seemed most unlikely to most people, for had not the British easily cut down the Americans in the recent affair at Bladensburg and Washington?

The attack was, of course, expected and so worshippers in Baltimore were excited but not too surprised when they heard the morning calm rudely blasted by three cannon, booming an alarm. Baltimore congregations on that Sunday morning, September 11, 1814, were hurriedly dismissed and drums began to beat. Horses were ridden at a gallop through the streets. The defenses of Baltimore were ready.

Few people had been idle during the past few weeks. Unknown to the British, Baltimore Harbor had been carefully fortified on its eastern side with gun batteries. Fort McHenry was ready with guns, ammunition and trained men.

A boom of chains and wooden floats closed off the mouth of the north branch of the Patapsco River. It ran from Fort McHenry to Lazaretto Point. Ships had been sunk in the channel approaching Baltimore to prevent the British from sailing right up to the city. (See map.) Men and supplies had been gathered, sea approaches blocked and trenches dug at strategic points to protect the city. Free black men helped with this work. Prominent citizens and their servants worked together building up the defenses of the inner city. Finally, a Committee of Vigilance and Safety acting for the city, selected a leader. General Samuel Smith was to take charge of preparations for battle and was to direct the defense of Baltimore.

About four thousand British soldiers landed on Monday the 12th of September, at North Point, some fourteen miles from the city itself. Major General Robert Ross, riding with an advance party of British men, was shot by a couple of American sharpshooters hidden in trees. He died shortly thereafter. He was an able general and his leadership would be missed very much at the moment that this important battle was about to begin.

Ten miles to the south and east of Baltimore, the fighting began. This battle is sometimes known as the Battle of North Point, but is actually important as a part of the Battle of Baltimore, and the struggle for control of Baltimore and of Maryland. The British seemed triumphant, despite the loss of General Ross, for after a short resistance, the Americans began to fall slowly back. Beating these Americans might be, for professional soldiers, as easy as it had been at Bladensburg, they thought. But the Americans this time were following a carefully planned operation. They were retreating slowly, felling trees across the roads, and generally harassing the enemy. American sharpshooters, too, were steadily firing into the slowly advancing British.

Now the British could see the city of Baltimore. At this point, however, they rudely awoke to the fact that all was not going well. On Hampstead Hill there were twelve thousand troops with plentiful cannon waiting for them. The men they had fought all day had been only an advance skirmish line under the leadership of Brigadier-General John Stricker. He had followed his orders to slow down the British advance and to search out the enemy's strength. The experienced commander of the defense of Baltimore, General Samuel Smith, had planned well. He knew from earlier experience in the American Revolution how to use the sharpshooters and how best to avoid the dreaded British bayonet charges.

The British halted before Hampstead Hill, and sent messengers back to the fleet, asking for more men and guns to be sent to help in the attack.

In the Bay, other British battle plans were being executed. On Tuesday the British sent sixteen vessels into position very close to the inner harbor of Baltimore. Inside Fort McHenry about a thousand men waited. They were under the command of Lieutenant Colonel George Armistead, an officer of the United States Artillery.

Anchored just out of range of the guns of the fort, the British vessels sent shells and rockets into Fort McHenry. Silently the fort took its punishment in the face of the enemy's longer ranged guns— not wasting ammunition by firing into the water short of the British ships. Encouraged by the silence of the guns of the fort, four British bomb-vessels were moved closer, but then the guns of McHenry opened up and drove the enemy back.

Night fell; and, at about one o'clock in the morning, enemy barges, loaded with over a thousand British fighters, slipped away from the warships. Some moved silently by the guns of Fort McHenry. Entering Baltimore harbor, they prepared to use long scaling ladders to overwhelm the fort. They did not know that on the south side of the channel, at Fort Covington, a battery of guns was ready for just such a situation. The British rocket vessels accompanying the barges began to fire their rockets. The Fort Covington guns opened fire. Batteries at Fort Babcock, and at Lazaretto Point fired, too.

For two hours the sky flamed with the glare of rockets and bomb bursts. Cannon boomed, and the houses in Baltimore City shuddered. A British landing barge sank with all aboard. The cries of wounded and drowning men could be heard ashore. The other barges and attackers then "returned with all speed" to the fleet.

Observing this night of battle was a Maryland attorney, Francis Scott Key. He was watching it, in fact, from the British side of the battle! How did this happen? It was because, when the British on their return from capturing Washington, D.C. had marched away to return to their ships at Benedict, Maryland, in the last days of August, they had stopped on the way at Upper Marlboro. There in the county seat of Prince George's County they had rested for a time before continuing on to Benedict. Dr. William Beanes, a medical doctor of Upper Marlboro, had led the local people in capturing and killing stragglers of the retreating British forces. Learning of this, the British had sent back a party of men to take the doctor out of his bed and bring him along as their prisoner.

It was this man that Francis Scott Key had been sent to negotiate for. In a sense, too, Key was an official representative of the United States government, for he had planned his strategy with the knowledge of the American authorities in Washington. Key, with the permission of the President of the United States and in the company of a government agent for the exchange of prisoners, John S. Skinner, traveled to the mouth of the Potomac and under a flag of truce (September 7) went aboard a British ship.

Admiral Cochrane received Key courteously but did not give his approval to the release of Dr. Beanes. However, Key had taken the precaution of stopping at hospitals in Washington and in Bladensburg to collect letters from British soldiers there, who wrote that they had been treated kindly. Finally, after much discussion, it was agreed that Dr. Beanes would be released in return for the good treatment given the wounded and captured men that the British had had to leave behind.

Since the British fleet was planning an attack on Baltimore, however, the doctor, Key and Skinner could not be allowed to leave the British area yet. When the enemy fleet reached Baltimore waters the three men were placed aboard a prisoner of war exchange sloop with a guard of British marines. So it was that when the Battle of Baltimore began, during the night of September 13 and 14, Key and his friends were eight miles from Fort McHenry. Anxiously they watched. Flashes from bomb bursts and rockets could be seen. Darkness, made deeper by low clouds, rain showers and smoke from the battle, kept the group from getting a clear view of Fort McHenry.

Was the American flag in place? Due to the rain, a storm flag was flying over the fort. Around midnight a wave of sound blasted the harbor as the British attempted to land with barges. Key was alarmed. Was Ft. McHenry still in American hands? The morning of September 14th dawned, and then as British withdrew, a huge garrison flag was raised. It was an American flag 42 feet long, 30 feet wide. Baltimore women had carefully sewn it together. Key caught a glimpse of this through his telescope. After twenty-four hours of heavy attack, the fort stood firm. Key was told, shortly after this, that the British invasion had failed; and that, as soon as the British ships were ready to sail, he and the other two men would be free to leave.

Meanwhile, the British army leaders ashore had decided not to attack the well entrenched Americans on Hampstead Hill. So the British land forces fell back and the troops were loaded aboard the ships. By early afternoon, September 15, the British were ready for departure. With that decision to leave, not only was the fate of Baltimore decided, but also that of the war itself.

When Francis Scott Key reached Baltimore, he took the notes

he had jotted down aboard the sloop and composed a poem. It described his feelings as he had watched the bombardment of Fort McHenry and his delight at seeing a flag. Key showed the poem to his brother-in-law, Judge J. N. Nicholson, who liked it very much. Copies were printed, in handbill form. The Baltimore papers picked the poem up[1] and soon it was set to music. So sincere were the words and so well written was the poem, that the song gradually became well known across the country as the "Star-Spangled Banner." It was eventually made the official National Anthem of the United States by an act of Congress, on March 3, 1931. But, we are getting over a hundred years ahead of our story!

The British sailed away in mid-September, abandoning their expedition against Baltimore. It is believed that the gallant and well-planned defense of Baltimore not only saved other Atlantic coast cities from attack, but was the decisive battle of the war and was the factor that the peace commission that fall could not overlook as the terms of the Treaty of Ghent were composed.

So the war closed with "an honorable peace" in the last months of 1814. An agreement was entered into, known as the Treaty of Ghent, which was signed at Ghent in Belguim. The treaty did not answer the questions as to what had caused the war, but did set up joint commissions to set boundaries over which the British and Americans disagreed. The treaty was ratified, that is, made legal by the agreement of two-thirds majority of the Congress in February, 1815.

Though often said to be the war that settled little, the War of 1812 did create a feeling of greater unity in the young nation that was the United States. It increased the control of the Federal government over national life. Also, it stopped, for a time, the power of European events to affect American political affairs.

---

1 The poem was first published in the **Baltimore Patriot**, September 20, 1814.

FRANCIS SCOTT KEY, Maryland lawyer.

CHAPTER XLVIII

FORT WASHINGTON

FORT Washington, located on the Maryland side of the Potomac River, was completed in December, 1809. The fort, whose site had been picked by George Washington in 1794, was designed to protect the new national capital from attack by water.

The rampart wall, about fourteen feet tall, stood above a ditch. The main fort was made of masonry and had a tower equipped with six cannon. A detachment of soldiers was assigned to service the weapons.

During the War of 1812, and shortly after the completion of the fort, the British attacked Washington, but they did not come up the Potomac. Instead they landed far to the rear at Benedict on the Patuxent River, as has been said, and marched from there overland. To mislead the Americans in that campaign as to their real plans for the invasion they did send some vessels up the Potomac to the vicinity of Fort Washington on August 27. Thinking that the enemy was going to attack, Captain S. T. Dyson, the commander, destroyed the works of the fort and withdrew to avoid battle. The small fleet then sailed up to Alexandria where supplies were demanded as a condition for sparing the city, after which the enemy vessels again passed the fort two days later bound for Chesapeake Bay!

Less than two weeks after Commander Dyson had destroyed the works of the fort, the French engineer, Major Pierre L'Enfant was asked to clear away the debris and to construct a new fort, for the British were expected back. This he began to do and worked until fear of invasion died down and the British fleet left for Jamaica.

A new engineer, Lieutenant Colonel Walker K. Armistead took over the work in September, 1815. Work continued until October 2, 1824 when the fort was reported "almost completed," the cost of the new work being over $426,000.

"The fort has been little altered since. It is an enclosed masonry fortification, entered by a drawbridge across the dry moat at the sally port. From above the main gateway, you can see the entire 833-foot outline of the works. Approximately sixty feet below the main fort is the outer V-shaped water battery, begun by L'Enfant, who also constructed the ditch on the southwest face and most of that on the northeast face. All of these features still remain in an excellent state of preservation. A double stairway connects the parade ground with a tunnel leading to the lower work.

"Two half bastions overlook and command the river above and below the fort. Below the ramparts are the casemates, or bombproof, gun positions. From three levels (water battery, casemates position and ramparts), guns could deliver a devastating fire against any enemy coming up the Potomac. The front of the structure built of solid stone and brick masonry is about seven feet thick. On the parade ground are the officers' quarters and the soldiers' barracks. Flanking each of these structures is a magazine. A guardroom containing two narrow cells and the office of the commanding officer are in the main gateway structure."[1]

New gun emplacements with new guns, a better powder magazine and a drawbridge were built in the 1840s. Most of these features can still be seen and the mechanism for raising the drawbridge is still in place. The garrison stationed in the fort was withdrawn in 1853.

But, when Civil War threatened, forty marines in January, 1861, were ordered to the fort for the defense of the capital city. Fort Washington was at that time the only fortification defending the city. It was manned by 4th Artillery troops and other units while another new fort was being built opposite Alexandria.

Fort Washington had become obsolete and was abandoned in 1872. Thirteen years later the muzzle-loading guns were removed and from 1896 until 1921 the place served as headquarters for the Defenses of the Potomac. Interest in it, meanwhile, was revived and more modern guns were installed. When the fort was thought to be no longer useful as a coastal defense it was for a time the headquarters of the 12th Infantry. Finally, it passed from the War Department and was handed from one government department to another, until in 1946 the 341-acre reservation was turned over to the National Park Service for use as a park. It is accessible from Indian Head Road (Maryland #210), five and one-half miles below the D.C. line.

Fort Washington is an outstanding example of an early 19th-century coastal defense, though it was never involved in any defense activities. It is open now to the public daily. Also available to visitors is a small museum and an area for recreation and picnicking.

---

1 U.S. Department of the Interior, National Park Service pamphlet "Fort Washington," 1963.

YOUR MARYLAND

SECTION V

FIFTY YEARS OF PEACE

"Cannon's Inn" by the river.

Patty Cannon's house, still in use today.

CHAPTER XLIX

PATTY CANNON

THERE is a house, so cleverly placed near the Maryland line that part of the state of Delaware is not twenty yards from its porch. In this house close to Reliance, Maryland, at the turn of the century[1] lived a most remarkable woman. She was called Patty Cannon. Her maiden name was Hanley, and some say that her first name was really Martha. She had come to the United States from Canada about 1802, as the bride of Jesse Cannon who died soon afterward.

Patty Cannon was at that time a rather attractive woman, both lithe and buxom,[2] and rather short. Her eyes were large and black. Her hair was thick and "coal black" and swept back from a low but pleasing forehead. Some stories say that Patty was a Gypsy; and perhaps she was. Men were very much attracted to her, though she was obviously not a woman to idealize. Certainly she was not at all the pale and fragile type, in a day when the down-cast eye, the blush, the ever-ready smelling salts were a part of the feminine style of behavior! On the contrary, she was robust, rowdy, coarse-spoken and noisy. It is said, too, that she was expert in Indian wrestling and could grasp even the strongest man by the hand and throw him to the ground. She could whip out a rope from under her skirts and in a flash tie him up helpless.

Her life was, from the beginning, a turbulent one. Amidst the legends and gossip that cling to her name are certain facts. She had a strange power over Ebenezer Johnson, known in that section of the country as the "Pirate of Broad Creek." He met a sudden death in a fight. After he was gone, Patty Cannon joined forces with his two sons, young Ebenezer and Joe. Patty Cannon had a daughter whose husband had been hanged. Eventually Joe Johnson married this daughter. Johnson was a huge, strong, blackbrowed man. He liked to display his prowess by riding in local races on a splendid buckskin horse "Yaller Corn." Some races he won by speed and others by bullying the judges. "Yaller Corn" was famous throughout the Delmarva Peninsula.[3]

Near Patty's house still standing at the ferry crossing on the upper Nanticoke River is a place called "Cannon's Inn." She and Joe Johnson also operated "Johnson's Tavern," which is near the town of Reliance. This last mentioned tavern began to have a sinister reputation. According to the story, sometimes very late at night there would be muffled cries and noises to disturb the peace and quiet of the flat farmlands; and it was said that closed carriages speeding through the night would cross the Delaware line going to the Red Bank Reach, where a fast schooner waited with no lights showing.

By the time the sun rose, however, all again would be quiet at the tavern. No one ever seemed to see the schooner on the Nanticoke River as it slipped down to the Chesapeake Bay, its destination a port on the coast of the Carolinas or even as far south as Georgia. There kidnapped people were sold to dealers.

By this time, in Maryland as elsewhere, it was unlawful to import slaves. In fact, in 1783 Maryland's assembly had acted to make it illegal to bring unfree people into the state to be sold. Maryland was one of the first states to ask the United States government to stop the importation of slaves entirely.

Yet, the trouble was that in the deep South, cotton was just then proving to be a very valuable commercial crop; and to raise it and to pick it required many workers. The rise of cotton, therefore, made slaves very much in demand in the areas where the crop was produced. Slavery in general had been declining until after Eli Whitney invented the cotton gin in 1794 to remove seeds from the short staple cotton. This invention changed the picture, for in the Southern lands now huge amounts of cotton could be grown, "ginned," and sold. England, in particular, welcomed cotton from America to feed its hungry mills.

Patty Cannon and her gang saw the opportunity to act as a source of supply of black workers; and, of course, they didn't worry about breaking every law that came between them and the gold to be gotten from this cruel business. The gang would quietly accept or buy a troublesome slave, for instance, or even kidnap free blacks which they then sold to the slave traders in the South. In Maryland, though slave auctions were yet common enough, there was already a fairly strong public feeling that slavery must end. More and more people were saying that this buying and selling of human beings was immoral and wrong. And, in the face of this attitude slave holders who wanted to make a profit by getting rid of their blacks would sometimes sell secretly to traders like Patty Cannon and then claim later that these black people had slipped away and disappeared. Certainly, however, Patty Cannon and Joe Johnson went far beyond legal buying and selling. Newspapers of that period tell of entire families of freed blacks who simply seemed to disappear, probably kidnapped from their cabins. With more and more Maryland slaves being freed by masters in the face of stern orders from the church and mounting public opinion, and with the price for slaves rising in the South, operators like Patty Cannon became increasingly active in Maryland, Delaware, and Pennsylvania. To be sure, such people had to work secretly and certainly they were without any sense of human decency and scruples.

People began to murmur and there began to be wild rumors about Patty Cannon. It was said that she was responsible not only for many kidnappings, but also for robbing mails, for making and passing counterfeit money, and for the murder of slave traders passing through the area with gold in their saddlebags! With her bold charms, however, and with the clever use of gold, Patty succeeded for years in buying her safety and avoiding the penalties of law she so rightly deserved. Still, there were moments when, as in May, 1822, when her crimes almost caught up with her and when it seemed that she, with Johnson and the others would be caught red-handed. At that time they were charged with kidnapping both slaves and free blacks . The evidence appeared to be pretty clear. Patty, however, went free; but Johnson was not so lucky. He was convicted in Georgetown, Delaware and sentenced to suffer thirty-nine lashes as well as to have his ears nailed to the pillory and portions of his ears cut off. The sentence was carried out on June 4, 1822 except for the mutilation of his ears. This part of the sentence was ordered not to be carried out by the Governor of Delaware.

Seven more years went by, with the reputation of Johnson's tavern growing darker and darker. Its ill repute spread like a stain across the Delmarva peninsula. Then, quite by chance, something else happened. A farmer was ploughing his orchard, near Patty Cannon's house. He noticed that the ground near a clump of briars and brush was sunken. He dug at this spot and found a chest. When the lid of the chest swung open, he saw to his horror that the chest held the bones of a man. He reported his find. Those investigating wondered if these were the bones of a trader who had disappeared suddenly ten years before. Both the trader and gold he carried had vanished completely.

In the same area were discovered three other skeletons. One of these was that of a child with a fractured skull. Cyrus James, who as a child had been raised by Patty Cannon, now guided the search. Whatever his motive—whether he was afraid now for his life at the hands of the gang, or whether his conscience had begun to worry him, the facts finally began to come to light of a long record of crime.

The Archives of the state of Delaware today reveal the evidence and the conclusions that were made at that time. Patty Cannon was arrested.

Johnson's Tavern finally was searched and a most unusual tavern it proved to be. In an upstairs closet, a trapdoor was found in the ceiling. From this, a ladder could be lowered. Climbing into the attic, the searchers found a prison.

Built into one end of the attic was a cell made of two-inch-thick white oak planks. It was very strong and nearly soundproof. There was no outside window. However, in the massive oak door, made of five thicknesses of white oak, there was a small iron-barred window. In the cell itself was a bucket of water and a dipper. But, more interesting to the law enforcement men, there were chains with leg irons, strongly bolted to the walls. This was where Patty Cannon and Johnson had hidden the people they had kidnapped or bought.

Another apartment, not open to the public, was found in the tavern. It was a very small cellar room. This dark place could be entered only through a false floor of a ground floor closet. Searchers shuddered to think of the uses that the cruel Patty may have made of this place. On April 13, 1829, the records of Sussex County, Delaware, show that Patty Cannon was charged with murder. "Yes." Patty Cannon confessed, she had killed eleven people and had helped murder at least twelve others!

Facing her now was all of the evidence; her trial, without doubt, would result in her execution. So, in her cell in Georgetown, Delaware, she made the number of deaths to her credit an even twenty-four by taking poison. With this grim action, the story of Patty Cannon closed on May 11, 1829.

It is interesting to note that, despite the break up of the Patty Cannon gang, kidnapping and trading did not completely stop. As late as 1849, the February 27 issue of the *Baltimore Sun* tells of a black mother and her eight children carried off in the night by kidnappers; and there were other such cases in Maryland at the time of the Civil War.

The Patty Cannon house stands about twelve miles from Federalsburg near Reliance, Maryland. It is a private home now. Near it looms a giant black oak tree that furnished shade even in the time of Patty and her gang. Some distance away, over the fields, stands a small building. It is part of what once was Johnson's Tavern.

Across the state line in Delaware is a state-maintained ferry site now called Woodland.[4] It was here that the gang loaded schooners. In the woods, across the river, local legend says, more victims of Patty Cannon are buried. Still standing there is a big frame building known as Cannon's Inn. Beside the inn, is a white frame church. In its graveyard the dates, 1820, 1842, and 1844 appear on the flat, raised grave stones. By one tall, very old gravestone, is a very tiny grave. Here, in 1962, a baby was brought to rest by the side of a relative three generations removed.

It is possible, in journeying to the Eastern Shore for one to feel as though he has taken a step back in time. There are old homes and farms which stand almost unchanged after many generations. Well painted buildings and cultivated fields tell the visitor that people here work hard. When one talks with them, he finds them friendly, and many have an old-fashioned grace of speech and manner.

For all its strange details, one of the oddest of all of the facts about Patty Cannon is that, until quite recently, the story of her life has been "buried." Historians seem to have buried Lucretia P.[5] Cannon as neatly as she buried her victims! There have been some newspaper stories and a sensational book or two, but this notorious woman is not mentioned in most historical accounts of Maryland — almost as if authors have been ashamed to recite so sordid a chapter of cruel and inhuman acts. Possibly, also, these writers have been reluctant to point the finger at Maryland law enforcement officials, who were so "oddly idle" in stopping her activities.

Such writing perhaps tells something about history, for without much doubt, there are writers who prefer to further a cause, or to tell an agreeable story, rather than to bother too much about the truth. Every record available should be checked if one wants the truth and every story compared with every other for these facts. Students of history must also sometimes be like detectives, too!

1 The 1700's were ending, the 1800's beginning.

2 Lithe: supple. Buxom: plump and good to look at, healthy and cheerful.

3 "Delmarva Peninsula," is the name of the long Eastern Shore peninsula between the Chesapeake Bay, the Atlantic Ocean, and Delaware Bay. It is a combination of the names of the three states—Delaware, Maryland, and Virginia.

4 The Woodland Ferry crossing was formerly called "Cannon's Ferry."

5 A writer of a pamphlet published in 1841 gave the names, "Lucretia" and "Alonzo," to Patty and her partner in a story about their activities. The names, "Patty" and "Jesse", however appear in the Delaware records.

CHAPTER L

MARYLAND, A PIONEER IN RAILROADS

I N New York State the Erie Canal was being finished in the year 1825. It was to be very successful and it was obvious that it would compete with the National Road. This would not only decrease business along the Road but also in Baltimore City and the Port of Baltimore. It was a situation that needed prompt action, if the early advantages gained by the building of the great central highway into the West were to be kept.

True, improvements had been made in the National Road, such as permanent bridges, better surfacing and road alignment. Also, there was a canal scheme for the Potomac valley, with the new canals paralleling part of the road from Baltimore to Cumberland. This had long since gained public approval and now seemed likely to be begun soon. Still, it would be a long, expensive project and it was doubtful whether it could compete seriously with the Erie Canal.

So, with northern ports beginning to draw trade away from Baltimore, businessmen were worried. Some new action was needed, one that would result in moving people and freight more quickly and easily from one part of the country to another. It was clear that something must be done in order that Baltimore might continue to be a growing and prosperous city. Because of this need local merchants, bankers and other business leaders met for a conference one day in the year 1827. They had an interesting idea. Experiments, especially in England, had suggested the possibility that building a road on rails would greatly speed up the flow of traffic and volume of goods. There was talk of hauling trains of wagons or cars along on these rails.

Now, at that time, when a person spoke of a "rail road," they meant a road with tracks of wood or sometimes of stone. Along these tracks, one horse could move a carriage with small wheels that on a common road would require ten horses. Also, the use of rails would prevent that jouncing, dusty, muddy, exhausting ride that passengers endured in stagecoaches and other vehicles at that time. Instead, one would glide along in a most pleasing way.

The bankers and merchants of Baltimore decided to build such a railroad. They formed a business corporation, to be known as the

Baltimore and Ohio Railroad Company and got permission to operate initially in Maryland, Pennsylvania, and Virginia. The new idea so appealed to the public that in just twelve days, every share of stock issued by the corporation had been sold.

On July 4, 1828, a great celebration was planned, for then the first stone supports for the railroad were to be placed into position. People sensed that something unusual and spectacular was about to happen.

Early on the day of the parade, cannon boomed, and crowds gathered to watch the marchers who met at the corner of Baltimore and Bond Streets. By eight in the morning over 5,000 people were parading westward toward the center of town. More thousands came to Baltimore to take part in this event. Buildings were gay with flags, balloons and bunting. Pretzels, pies and doughnuts were sold to the crowds by pretty girls wearing hoopskirts and bonnets.

In the parade itself were floats representing many trades. Artisans were actually at work at looms, printing presses, and other machines. Over fifty trades were presented in this way. The most spectacular float, perhaps, was the one carrying an entire twenty-seven-foot vessel.

Ninety-one-year-old Charles Carroll of Carrollton was there in an open carriage to take part in the ceremonies. He was beloved and respected in Maryland and one of the last of the signers of the Declaration of Independence still living. He was now generally known as "The Signer."

Finally, west of Baltimore, on a small ridge near Gwynn's Falls, the parade stopped. There, with prayers, music, speeches and cannon volleys, the first stone of the B & O was laid by Charles Carroll, who firmly turned the first spade full of earth. "I consider this among the most important acts of my life," said the Signer. ". . .second only to my signing the Declaration of Independence, if second even to that."

A night of noisy gaiety followed the return of the marchers and spectators to the city. There were special showings of the new "magic lanterns," as well as fireworks, concerts, and banquets, before the celebration ended.

The Actual Building of the Railroad

The engineers hired to build the railroad had an unusual problem. They were working without precedents to guide them and so they did not quite know what they were doing; but then, neither did anyone else at that time. The engineering problems were new and so, had to

237

be solved only by rules of common sense and invention.

The engineers did know that they must have fairly level ground for the railroad, and also, that they must design gentle curves, and make as gentle a grade, or slope, as possible. They must provide a roadbed that would not settle or wash away from under the rails; so crushed stone and gravel were laid over the leveled earth. Crossbars of wood, or railroad ties as they have come to be known, were then put in place.

After this the rails themselves could be laid. But how should rails be made, and of what shape, size and material? Wood was then plentiful and could easily be made into rails, but wood wore out so very quickly in use. So, engineers and construction men decided to plate the wooden rails with iron. With light cars to ride these rails, this idea worked out pretty well. Rails made of stone were experimented with, but the work involved in making rails of stone made this type of rail impractical. The initial cost of building the railroad was $17,000 per mile—a cost that did not include the cost of the rails.

One of the reasons for picking a route from Baltimore to Ellicott's Mills for the first section of the railroad was that the latter town was also on the Patapsco River. One can see that often railroads and highways follow river valleys. River beds have been both eroded and filled in by action of the water and have flood plains that are fairly level. Also, the flow of rivers is generally gently sloping down from higher to lower levels in this part of the country. Also rivers cut down through hills and mountains, creating gaps and openings in ridges.

Other reasons for building the railroad to Ellicott's Mills was that it lay west of Baltimore in the direction in which the merchants and bankers of Baltimore needed to route the new railroad. Also, the busy mill town would provide a ready-made market center from which grain and milled flour could be brought to Baltimore as soon as the railroad reached the mills.

The whole idea of the use of rails was to carry heavier loads under easier conditions and at faster speeds, and so there was need for strong bridges and well built road beds to support the weight of the loads to be carried.

On May 22, 1830, a thirteen-mile-long stretch of double track railroad was opened to Ellicott's Mills. At first the new railroad carried only passenger traffic in cars designed by Mr. Ross Winans. These were in appearance much like the horse drawn vehicles of the period. Horses were used to pull these cars along the rails. The novelty of this smooth and relatively fast (eight to twelve miles-per-hour) ride attracted literally hundreds of riders. There was no doubt about

238

public support of this new venture. In September of that same year the B & O began to offer freight service, and almost immediately ten times as much freight was offered to the railway as could be carried with the available equipment.

This was a year that was to be a very important one to the new railroad. Not only was the experiment with rails proving successful, but, at this time, also, another significant development in motive power was to be introduced. But, before discussing the B & O's new kind of power, let us look at the progress then being made with a new kind of power elsewhere.

"Steam Wagons," and "Road Locomotives"

Inventors at this time were busy, as is usual with their breed, with all sorts of fascinating projects. They were very interested in the possibilities of creating power by using steam.

As everybody today realizes, the steam engine of the 1800's brought a great change in manufacturing, travel, mining, transport, and human progress. Even before 1800 steam engines of great sizes and weight were being used to pump water from flooded mines. Such early engines were so gigantic, however, that it seemed improbable that they could ever be used to propel land vehicles.

James Watt, a Scottish inventor, in 1765 developed an improved steam engine which, it was thought, would be useful in propelling water vessels, for in ships the power plant did not have to be either very small or very light.

Several inventors were working at this time, however, to find a way to power a land carriage with a steam engine. A Philadelphia wheelwright, Oliver Evans, in 1787 was granted the right by the General Assembly, to manufacture and operate steam wagons in Maryland.

It took Evans thirteen years to get one built. Public opinion, however, was so strong against the use of steam wagons on the roads, that he was almost persuaded to give up the idea altogether. Still, he stubbornly defended his ideas by predicting that "the time will come when people will travel in stages moved by steam engine from one city to another, almost as fast as birds can fly—fifteen or twenty miles per hour. . . ." Poor Evans was laughed out of Maryland.

But this American inventor persisted in his experiments and in 1804 he succeeded in building a working scow for the Philadelphia Board of Health to be used as a harbor dredge. The scow was fitted with wheels and, powered by a steam engine, was driven from Evans' shop to the water! Evans deserves credit, then, for having developed

This railroad car used horse power.

Sail power for rail cars proved
to be "upsetting"!

the first steam-driven vehicle to move on land in the United States.

Yet, the public was not impressed with the idea of steam-driven land vehicles. This was partly because they were at that time huge, clumsy, noisy, and dangerous machines. They were like stage coaches fitted with steam engines. Horses stared and ran away in panic when confronted with such steam-snorting, top-heavy devices. The vehicles were ruled off the highways as a public hazard.

The idea, however, of a steam engine, even though heavy and clumsy, fitted to run on rails, still continued to challenge inventors. With a smoother roadway than could be provided by the uneven and muddy highways of the early 1800's and with rails to support the great weight of the engine, the "steam locomotive" might be practical after all. In England already the locomotive, or "iron horse" as it was sometimes called, was rapidly being developed into a means for transporting people and freight over railroads.

Many, especially in Europe, were beginning to see that this type of power had a future. As one could see, the horse had been bred to the peak of perfection, and could not be made a great deal faster or stronger. But no man could predict what future the "iron horse" might have. A delegation of engineers from the United States in 1829 went to England to see for themselves what possibilities there might be if steam-driven engines were run on rails.

Meanwhile, as far as the B & O Railroad was concerned, horse-power had proved to be a reliable, if somewhat slow, means of locomotion. Experiments with railway carriages propelled by sails had come to grief when one such car upset and threw the passengers, including the visiting Governor of New York, into a ditch! And, yet another experimental car, propelled by a horse walking a treadmill, also literally ran into trouble by bumping a cow and going off the track.

A school book of the period, Peter Parley's *First Book of History*, said about Maryland that ". . .the most curious thing about Baltimore is the railroad. This consists of iron bars laid along the ground and made fast. One horse will be able to draw as much as ten horses on a common road. A part of this railroad is done," wrote Parley, and "If you choose to take a ride upon it you can do so. You will mount a car, something like a stage, and then you will be drawn along by two horses at the rate of twelve miles an hour." Such was his description in 1835 of the early progress of the Baltimore and Ohio Railroad.

Peter Cooper's "Tom Thumb"

What a grand future the railroads would have if a powerful, self-contained power plant could be found. Into this situation now enters Peter Cooper, a New York merchant with his engine, the "Tom Thumb." He was to be the man who proved to the B & O that a steam locomotive was feasible. The *Tom Thumb* was a light locomotive weighing about one ton, which Cooper had assembled, using his own design, probably the first such locomotive built in America. The year was 1830.

People for miles around came to marvel at the *Tom Thumb*, speeding from Baltimore to Ellicott's Mills at twelve miles-per-hour, pushing a twenty-four-passenger car. It took only an hour to cover the entire thirteen mile route! True, there was some inconvenience to the passengers seated in the carriages of the train, for they had to use umbrellas to ward off the sparks and smoke from the engine. Often, too, these shields caught fire or blew away, and it was not unusual on these early trips to see the passengers beating each other wildly, trying to keep clothing and hats from burning!

The curiosity aroused by the *Tom Thumb* and the evident popularity of the railroad had made the stage coach companies jealous. They were worried lest the railroad soon swallow up all of their passenger traffic. So they decided to challenge the little steam engine to a race. On one track the steam engine, with one car loaded with passengers, hissed as steam power built up. On the other track, one of the stage company's most powerful big grey horses snorted, ready to draw a coach along the second track. The signal to start was given.

Though the big grey horse took the lead right away, Peter Cooper calmly built up steam and sent the little *Tom Thumb* forward. It chugged into Ellicott's Mills ahead of the galloping horse. On the way back a leather belt came off the steam engine. Cooper stopped the *Tom Thumb* and quickly replaced the belt. Then he tried vainly to catch up with the horse-drawn carriage but he was too far behind. So, in that first contest to Ellicott's Mills and back, the little steam engine lost to the horse. Looking back, however, one can see that the horse really lost, for soon the locomotive would be more and more improved. In fact, within a year the B & O changed to steam power.

Happy with the success of the *Tom Thumb*, the railroad now offered a prize of $4,000 for a new and improved locomotive. Soon thereafter, an engine called the *York*, which could pull fifteen tons at the amazing speed of fifteen miles per hour, won the prize. This engine was built by a York, Pennsylvania, watchmaker, Phineas Davis. It was in operation in 1831.

Another famous early locomotive was the B & O's *Atlantic*. This train pulled odd-looking double-decker "Imlay" coaches—which looked very much like stage coaches—only with a top deck! Again, the passengers suffered some inconveniences. Ladies, wearing dainty gowns and wide hats with feathers, gentlemen in tophats and tight breeches, would climb aboard, smiling and clean. After the trip, they were often scorched and sooty, with eyes streaming from the wind, cinders and smoke. The engineer and the fireman stood out in the open in wind and weather but at least were spared the sparks and smoke! Still, despite these and other problems, the speed and glamour of these early railroad vehicles attracted ever more passengers.

The railroad in 1831 was extended to Frederick, Maryland, located amid rich rolling hills near the beautiful Catoctin range. The small community soon jumped rapidly in growth and took on the appearance of a city. Large increases in passengers and freight resulted from the extension of the road to Frederick. As many as fifty and sixty people a day, as well as hundreds of barrels of flour, tons of granite, firewood and bark, went regularly to Baltimore. Car loads of groceries, oysters, iron, dry goods, bricks and other goods came back to Frederick. Soon regular daily round trip service was begun between Baltimore and Frederick.

It was the locomotive, the *Atlantic*, that led the introduction of the railroad into Washington, D. C. The first train to enter the capital city on the B & O's new railroad line arrived on August 24, 1835. Though it was a very hot day, even without one's clothing afire, everyone riding the new train seemed happy on this gala occasion. The train had made the unheard of speed of twenty-five miles per hour on parts of the trip! The total running time from Baltimore to the "District" was a mere two hours and ten minutes! Evans' prediction had come true. People were now traveling between cities "as fast as birds can fly!"

While Railroads Grew

On the very same day (July 4, 1828) that the Signer, Charles Carroll, turned the first spadeful of earth to mark the beginning of the B & O railroad, the President of the United States, John Quincy Adams, at Georgetown on the Potomac turned the first shovel of earth to begin the Chesapeake and Ohio Canal.

Thus the race for western trade routes was on and at first it seemed the canal company would win. Of course, more was known at that time about building canals than was known about building railroads. In fact, the railroad lines reached Point of Rocks, and later, Harper's Ferry, a year behind the canal construction. After that, however, the railroad forged ahead to reach Cumberland, Maryland in 1842 — ahead of the canal by eight years. In the long run, the speed and power of the steam engine won the race for the railroads, but construction problems were great for both canal and railroad builders.

The contest between the two was a bitter one. Bloody fights frequently broke out between the rail and canal workers. Using every means they could, the canal owners tried by legal suits to cause stops and slowdowns in railway construction. Yet, it was clear to most people that steam power would eventually win. It was in 1830 that the legal battle between the canal and railroad was settled, though some cases lingered on until the 1833. Then, "out of court" and for a price, the canal owners settled their claims. The settlement was expensive to the B & O and it appeared that the canal company had "blackmailed" the railroads. But whatever the price paid by the railroad, it was probably worth the cost to reach the rich valleys past Harper's Ferry. The legal settlement helped to open the Shenandoah Valley of Virginia to the railroad, as well as the Great Valley of Maryland, with profit to Baltimore markets and to the Port of Baltimore.

Having disposed of the canal competition, the railroad still faced the task of building a railroad through the mountains. Also, the low-powered steam locomotives seemed hardly strong enough to face the grades of the mountains and this, too, slowed the progress of the rail lines. At long last, after many problems had been met and solved, the railroad, moving over rivers, valleys and mountains, finally did reach Wheeling, West Virginia and the great Ohio River by 1852.

Railroad building, the cars and the locomotives cost for those days, great sums of money. Yet with every dollar spent and with every additional mile of track added, more and more trade from the west poured into Maryland. Baltimore City hummed with activity. Mills and manufacturing concerns of all kinds were busy. Ships from all the world crowded into the Port of Baltimore. Shops and offices prospered.

It was not long also, before the railroad passengers were better protected from weather and wind; and from the smoke and cinders of the locomotive itself. The first of the famous "Pullman" cars, in 1858, even enabled passengers to sleep enroute. True, in the mid-1800's railroad travel was not as safe as it is today. Hundreds of people each year died in derailments and other accidents. With time the safety of rail travel increased. By 1868, travelers could eat in comfort in dining cars, and, by 1872, improvements in sleeping cars enabled passengers to go to bed more comfortably than before. By this time, too, rail travel for first class passengers had become quite luxurious. Even the less costly "day coaches" gave the traveler more speed and comfort than ever before.

Looking backwards, that 1827 decision of Baltimore businessmen had had far reaching results for Maryland. It had been the basis for keeping the continuing allegiance of the West. It had also helped lead the way in many ways to the developing prosperity and growth of the great city of Baltimore. The railroad had richly fulfilled the hopes and dreams of its founders.

The B & O Railroad was the first in America to use steam power. Here is one of the B & O's most famous locomotives, the "Atlantic," pulling two Imlay coaches.

(C & P Telephone Company of Maryland)

The first B & O train to arrive in Cumberland on November 1, 1842, may have been the *Memnon*, shown here. The town became a great railroad center.

CHAPTER LI

FIFTY PEACEFUL YEARS

BETWEEN the War of 1812 and the Civil War there was a great deal of growth in population, towns, transportation, and industry in Maryland. Yet this period has been given less attention by writers than it deserves. With no dramatic battles, no heroes firing cannon or sinking ships, and just the ordinary details of everyday life to record, a student may not recognize the fact that this is an important span of history which can throw light on many of our customs, laws, and habits of life today.

Certainly the early nineteenth century reflected some customs no longer existing now, as for example, duelling which was still a practice. South of Queenstown on the Eastern Shore "Slippery Hill" was a well known duelling ground, as was a spot near Bladensburg, near the Nation's capital. Duelling was illegal, but it persisted almost up to the time of the Civil War!

Towns

We have mentioned the early beginnings of Annapolis, Baltimore, and Frederick as well as how centers of trade on the Eastern Shore, began. When the Cumberland Road, later to become the main road feeding into the National Road, reached Cumberland, Maryland, in 1811, that rural village, too, grew rapidly.

Hagerstown, also, was growing faster in this period. It had been founded by Jonathan Hager at the time of the French and Indian War on land granted to him by the Fifth Lord Baltimore in 1739. It was a small town until the roads to the west were improved. It grew faster when, in 1867, the Baltimore and Ohio Railroad arrived. Fifteen years later two other rail lines had reached Hagerstown.

Today, Hagerstown, located in Maryland's Great Valley between two beautiful mountain ridges, is a distributor of produce from surrounding rich farmlands. It is unique in its production of pipe organs. Important businesses of the city include the manufacture of furniture, trailers, vinyl pipe, rainwear, books and diesel engines; brick making, production of ice cream and leather goods plus many other items.

Annapolis, which grew rapidly in colonial times, had by the nineteenth century lost its lead as a port city to Baltimore. It had become a rather quiet and drowsy place except when the legislature was in session, until the Naval Academy moved there in 1845. Then the city began to take on a trim nautical look and its business again began to pick up.

After the Civil War and the development of the Eastern Shore railroad system, Salisbury, Maryland grew rapidly. With the introduction of refrigerator railroad cars, Salisbury's large sources of fresh fruits and vegetables became easily marketable.

Baltimore

Baltimore's English, Irish and German merchants built a brisk trade in tobacco, corn, wheat, and flour and the city even in the eighteenth century became a principal United States port. The beautiful Baltimore Clipper ships were used to carry much of the city's trade with foreign ports well down to the time of the Civil War. These ships had a clean, uncluttered deck and a sharp bow. Their hulls were sleek and narrow. The ship rode deep in the water and carried towering masts, with not only the usual large sails but many topsails. They were fast ships and their cargo space was limited because the hulls were built narrow and sleek for speed. Between one hundred fifty and two hundred tons was usually all they could carry. But their speed enabled them to outdistance warships and let them slip into the ports of warring nations, which needed goods of all sorts desperately and would pay high prices for them.

Maryland ship builders shortly after the middle of the eighteenth century, using the basic design of the speedy Bermuda sloop, had begun to turn out numbers of larger ships, rigged as schooners. These "Baltimore Clippers" were beautiful to see and until after the War of 1812 were the fastest ships afloat. In the 1830's and 1840's, New England also began to build clipper ships with even more space for cargo. These Yankee Clippers, too, became famous and ranged the oceans of the world, but for over seventy years, the Baltimore Clipper was America's leading vessel. The average small American boy dreamed of those ships, of "long black Baltimore schooners under a cloud of snowy-white canvas, reaching across the wind."

In Baltimore the years, 1818 and 1819, were bad ones. In '18, there was a national financial panic that ruined many a local businessman. The stock of the Baltimore Branch of the Bank of the United States dropped to one-third of its former value in a few weeks.

In 1819, yellow fever plagued the poorer sections of the city and business activities came almost to a stop. The city was quarantined,

247

and the northeastern hills of the city were dotted with tents used to isolate plague victims. Doctors did not know that the mosquito was carrying the disease from person to person.

Still, before another ten years had gone by, and with canal and railroad projects prospering, business again began to grow. Baltimore in 1830 had a population of 75,000, as compared with 40,000 at the time of the War of 1812; and it continued to be a leader in trade and in export.

Government Reforms

In the fall of 1809 bills in the Maryland General Assembly were passed, doing away with the law that required a voter to be the owner of considerable property. In 1824, the law forbidding members of the Hebrew faith from holding public office also was repealed.

The year 1837 saw a great many new laws made to strengthen democratic gains and to improve government in Maryland. (1) The office of Governor was made elective and the term was fixed at three years. (2) The Senate of the legislative body was reorganized, and now every two years, one-third of the Senate was to be elected by the people. (3) The counties were given delegates in proportion to to their population. (4) The terms of office of County Clerks and Registers of Wills were reduced to seven years.

With these changes fifty years of complaints about unfair government practices were somewhat soothed. These reforms in effect took the power in the state government out of the hands of a few men and handed it over to more voters.

Almost forgotten is a General Assembly vote of thanks to our troops from Maryland in 1850, for valiant service in the "War with Mexico," a war that was fought over rival land claims in the Texas Territory.

The Black Marylander

What the Europeans were after—the labor of the captured black—was obtained. With this labor came much of the original progress of the English colonies. It was the work of strong, skilled, dark hands.

In America the African learned new customs and laws, a new religion and a new language, as well as how to do the many tasks awaiting him. Much of the agriculture of the country, especially in the South, depended on his labor. Slave rebellions were always expected and feared, but though often rumored, actually violence never occurred on a large scale. The white man was armed and there were strict laws, too well enforced to allow the slave to defy them. Then too, unfair as slavery was, the black servants often grew up believing that they owed loyalty to their owners. Serfs in Europe were taught the same philosophy.

History shows that black people in Maryland fared better than some of the African workers further south. Remember that from the beginning of their importation into Maryland, there were free blacks in the colony, and there continued to be many here. These people proved to be so important a part of the pool of workers that, in 1859, a convention of slaveholders refused to encourage the idea of passing a Maryland law to expel free blacks from the state. On the contrary, the convention recognized that these free workers were essential to business in the state.

It cannot be stated whether black people held in bondage in Maryland were treated with kindness or with cruelty; actually both sorts of treatment existed. Slavery, it should be recognized, was not good for either the slave or the master, for its psychological effects were bad for both. On the Eastern Shore plantation where Anna Ella Carroll grew up in the 1800's, the blacks appeared to be well treated. Yet, just a few miles away to the north, Frederick Douglass, born into slavery himself in this same period, saw many scenes of brutality and cruelty. He told of these events in his later writings and lectures in the mid-1800's.

Generally speaking, black people in the "border" states such as Maryland had a somewhat better life than those in bondage in the deep South. The Maryland plantation was generally operated by the family of the owner, while in the deep South there was much absentee ownership, with the plantation workers often left to the mercy of a merciless overseer. So, partly because of the laws restricting his actions and partly because of a better feeling between the races, there were very few incidents or uprisings in Maryland involving blacks Slavery existed in the state for a little over two hundred years and yet the only serious uprising that apparently is recorded was an incident, thought to be spontaneous, in St. Mary's County, on April 7, 1817, when there were "several outbursts" involving about 200 slaves. No one was killed, though several people on both sides were injured, and two houses were sacked.

The great bulk of the importation of Africans occurred in the eighteenth century. Before that, immigration was fairly light. After 1800 the importation of laborers from Africa was discouraged by most of the governments of the world, including the United States, which after 1808 forbade international slave trading.

In Maryland it is especially true that black families have been here for a long time. As early as the year 1712 there were reportedly 8,000 blacks in Maryland and about 38,000 people of European descent. From that time the importation of black workers increased. They were brought in freely until 1780, when a heavy tax was imposed. Then, three years later, the importation of black slaves from Africa was entirely forbidden by Maryland law.

From the beginnings of our national life in 1776, probably the majority of the leaders hoped for a gradual ending of slavery in the United States. They realized that slavery was not in agreement with the ideal that all men were created equal and entitled to the free pursuit of happiness. With the invention of the cotton gin in 1794, by Eli Whitney, however, as noted before it became profitable to grow cotton in the South and land owners demanded captive African workers. So the national hope for gradual abolition faded.

Freeing enslaved people was no problem in those states having only a few people in bondage. But abolition was a problem in the Southern states where so much of the agriculture depended on having enough low-cost labor to work the great fields and where blacks made up a much higher percentage of the total population. So, slaveholders made excuses for keeping men and women in bondage. The slaveholder argued that the black was physically able to stand the Southern climate better than other workers; that he was better off learning the white man's ways and religion, and, after all the Bible sanctioned slavery.

Anti-slavery forces succeeded in preventing the spread of slavery westward into the area north of the Ohio River, but the institution did spread south of the Ohio to the west, into Kentucky, Tennessee, Mississippi, and even onto the plains of Texas. With cotton becoming such a profitable crop, the price of good field hands moved sharply upward. This was especially true after the forbidding of more importation of slaves from abroad in 1808, though this law was certainly not always obeyed.

Within the United States the trading of slaves was still legal. Many people, even in the South, regarded the slave dealer with scorn and contempt, but this did not stop the business. One history[1] states that slave trading was the "cornerstone of the South's economy involving perhaps $150,000,000 in 1859-1860." In Maryland, where farms and plantations had more blacks in bondage than were needed, there was the temptation to sell away excess workers. It was realized that it was not morally right to break up long established homes and families. Where, as happened often, the slaveholder preferred to free his black workers, he still knew that they had little chance for successful lives in the hostile society of that period. Free blacks also ran the danger of being kidnapped by criminal gangs to be sold in the South.

Yet there were many people in Maryland who wanted an end to slavery. The Quakers or the Society of Friends, were perhaps most active in demanding aid to blacks in bondage. As early as 1700, they were speaking out against the evil and were insisting that all Quakers free their blacks . In 1784 the newly-formed American Methodist Church, with a large membership in Maryland, spoke out against slavery. As a result, many wills were written containing instructions to free slaves, and, by 1860 due to all these influences, the state had almost as many free black people (84,000) as it had slaves (87,000). Maryland had at this time fewer slaveholders and slaves than any other Southern state.

The Maryland and the American Colonization Society

The American Colonization Society was established in 1816 to relocate black people freed in the United States. Colonies were planned for the west coast of Africa in the area known as Liberia. This idea found strong support in Maryland. A separate Maryland Colonization Society was begun in 1827. Both private and state funds were given to aid the project. The Maryland colony was a little over 250 miles down the coast from Monrovia where the American Colonization Society had begun relocation work. It declared its separate independence in 1854 but joined Liberia as "Maryland County" in 1857. This was shortly after the Monrovian settlers had helped the Marylanders battle the local Grebo people.

An interesting story is that of Dr. Samuel Ford McGill.[2] This young man was the son of a Monrovian colonist. Since white physicians could not seem to survive the climate and diseases of that part of Africa, the Maryland Colonization Society decided to finance the training of an acclimated African, for the colony needed a doctor. Samuel McGill volunteered to undergo medical training though he knew that he would face obstacles and discrimination in any medical school he might enroll in. This was especially true if he were enrolled in a southern school. On the other hand, the Maryland sponsors were reluctant to let him study in the northern United States where he would be in contact with abolitionists and northern ideas of resistance to the whole institution of slavery.

Sure enough, McGill was not able to attend a medical school in Baltimore for very long, in 1836, before his classmates refused to let him go on. His sponsors sent him north to study under a physician in Vermont and later he studied at Dartmouth College. He was an outstanding student, even mastering the study of Latin by means of much self-directed effort. By 1840, Dr. McGill was the colonial physician of the Maryland colony in Liberia and held that post for many years. He was to do other important work there as well.

But colonization was not to be the answer to the problem of what was to happen to the freed slave. American blacks did not like the idea of leaving the United States and not enough volunteered to go to Liberia to make much difference in conditions here. So, though over $300,000 was spent over a period of twenty years, only about 1500 American black colonists were ever actually settled in Liberia.

There is an odd ending to this story. In 1931, the League of Nations investigated reports of slavery and forced labor being inflicted on the native blacks by the Americo-Liberians. The reports were found to be true. Steps taken to abolish the practice of slavery in Liberia were successful by 1936 and today, the nation is one of the world's most promising black republics.

Laws Affecting the Status of Africans in Maryland

Mention has been made of the colonial laws designed to prevent Caucasions and blacks from marrying one another. There were other measures passed both in colonial days and later in the early days of statehood. These were designed to help slaveholders capture runaway workers, to prevent the free movement of blacks in bondage, and to prevent slaves from owning and inheriting property. All of these laws restricted the freedom of action of the slave.

Free persons of African descent in Maryland found life very difficult for there were many laws to hamper them, too. All too often, free blacks were kidnapped and sold into slavery again. Then too, they were abused in business, had property damaged and generally were harassed at every turn. Even so, free black people in Maryland progressed by determination and hard work. Early in the 1800s schools were set up in Baltimore for adult free Africans and later, opened to a few boys. A Catholic organization also started a school for black girls.

Inventions and Technical Progress

The first Baltimore building to be lighted by the new "illuminating gas" was Peale's Museum. By 1820 gas lighting was being used occasionally in the city and, by 1860, a gas lighting company had been organized and many of the city streets and homes in Baltimore were lighted by gas.

A telegraph line in 1844, with service available between Baltimore and Washington was built by Samuel Morse, the inventor of the first telegraph service in the United States. Electric lights, too, came soon after their invention in the 1870's by Thomas Edison, to Baltimore, and this was followed shortly thereafter by the electric iron.

The sewing machine created an entirely new era after its invention in 1843 by Elias Howe. Some years passed before it was accepted but the results were significant indeed. Handsewn clothing gradually gave way to clothing made on the sewing machine. More important still, was the fact that with this machine for the first time clothing could be manufactured rapidly and in quantity. Ready-to-wear clothing is a huge industry today, the growth of which is due largely to the sewing machine. Steam power was applied also to this industry, and, as has been noted, steam power revolutionized, too, both land and water transportation.

The change from a slow way of life in which machinery played a small role and the horse, was important—to a faster way of life with steam engines, electricity and all sorts of new inventions—that is the drama of the nineteenth century.

The Baltimore Scene

To a small boy or girl in the 1800's the streets of Baltimore must have been a fascinating playground. Carriages and horses were the regularly used way of getting around the city; and even when the electric street cars came shortly before the twentieth century, horses were stationed near hills to help them to the top. Horse-drawn fire engines often plunged through the streets, pouring smoke from their steam pumping engines. In different parts of Baltimore, crowds of youngsters often followed "their" favorite fire engine to fires.

Since automobiles were not on hand to threaten lives, children played around their city homes with more freedom than now. There were often wonderful things to watch: the little German bands, the waffle wagons, the organ grinders, and the one-man bands. There were wild-game peddlers with ducks and geese to sell. There were men with oysters and crabs to sell; and peddlers sold live or cooked diamond-back terrapin, nuts, and other foods.

Tobacco was used in several ways. It was used in the form of snuff; and it was also made into "plugs" as chewing tobacco. It was smoked in the form of cigars and also smoked in pipes. Sometimes, too, it was used as medicine.

Water pumps were to be seen in most public squares. Some had flat iron dippers beside them for the public to use. Many householders still had to carry water from the public pump to their homes. Back fences were whitewashed by boys or hired men. Housewives and their maids still "beat" rugs to clean them.

Hanging in the doorway of a butcher's shop in 1890 in Baltimore, one might see an entire bear or a deer. The customer asked the butcher to cut meat for dinner from this protein-in-bulk display. Near the post office a black man called Jim "shook" a refreshing, delicious lemonade for sale.

By 1884, stepping stones that had helped one get across the muddy gutters were disappearing. Modern pavements and sewers were making it possible to get across the street without them. Pavements were made of cobble stones or stone blocks.

In the 1880s and '90s, a sixteen year old lad could work as a general clerk and make from one to two dollars a week. Remember, prices were different then. One could buy a nice dinner for twenty-five cents.

As late as 1899, a "coach and four" was still a fashionable vehicle. Owners made sure that the harness was kept shining, the horses selected carefully to match, and groomed until they gleamed. These coaches and carriages were expensive. A good coach might cost about $2,000 and its sets of harness another $1,500. A carriage such as used by a physician might cost from $600 to $1,000. Doctors liked to drive fine horses and could be seen going at a fast pace to make calls on their patients.

All the homes that could afford it had some sort of stable for the family horse and carriage. There were livery stables, too, in every part of Baltimore, many run by horse-loving Irishmen. To keep the horses company, sometimes a goat was kept in the stables.

It is perhaps understandable why people look back to "the good old days." Life then did have a charm and a quiet pace. There were so many things to marvel at. People stayed up all night in Baltimore to witness the coming of the first cable cars. They were thrilled at the sight of the first large street car moving along without horses or any motive power in sight.

Today, more than ever, we have a world of things to marvel at. And, looking back is one way of getting perspective. It helps us to notice, to wonder, and to be thrilled by our world and its people.

---

1 Frederic Bancroft, **Slave Trading in the Old South**.

2 Acknowledgement is made of the article by Penelope Campbell, "Medical Education for an African Colonist," published in the **Maryland Historical Magazine**, Vol. 65, No. 2, 1970.

CHAPTER LII

JOHN BROWN CAPTURES AN ARSENAL
AND A SCHOOLHOUSE

NOT far from Harper's Ferry, Virginia, on the Maryland side of the Potomac River, about two dozen children settled down to study. If they had trouble keeping their eyes open, it was not surprising. This Monday morning, October 17, 1859, was one of those gloomy fall days. The clouds pressed down on the mountains. There was a raw edge to the wind. The schoolmaster muffled a yawn himself at the thought of a long, quiet day ahead, full of readin', writin', and 'rithmetic.

The occupants of the schoolhouse could not know that they were living a day to be studied by many future students. As yet, no one in the school knew that John Brown, his two sons, and twenty men had slipped down out of the Maryland hills the night before. Armed with guns and Bowie knives, they had come, under the cover of fog, to the covered bridge that led to the town of Harper's Ferry.[1] The men had cut telegraph wires and captured the bridge watchmen.

On the Virginia side of the river, they had turned out the lights on the bridge and in the town. Moving swiftly in the dark, they had overcome the armory gate watchmen. Next, they took the buildings and the United States arsenal[2] itself. Not a shot was fired and the town had slept on, unaware that John Brown and his raiders had seized the arsenal!

Brown was a tall man, about sixty years old. Though his shoulders were slightly bowed, his figure was wiry and strong. Long, rough, white hair and a full beard surrounded "the face of a hawk." His burning eyes revealed the excitement of this moment. He, John Brown, was now ready to head up armies of slaves and sympathizers and force the South to free every slave. He felt sure that the slaves would rush to follow him. He was fanatical about this, and so strange, in fact, were his actions, that it seems doubtful that John Brown was entirely sane.

Back in Kansas a territory from which he had recently fled, he was wanted for murdering five men in cold blood. He was charged, too, with kidnapping slaves and smuggling them to freedom. For some months he had been a fugitive in hiding, but now he felt his moment had come. With all of the rifles and plenty of ammunition from the captured arsenal, he planned to lead the slaves to form a new nation. Since early July, he had been plotting his course and it felt good to go into action. His first objective was to capture the arsenal, and now that that step had been successfully taken, he felt sure hundreds of slaves would now rise up and join him at Harper's Ferry.

Back at the school house, the pupils and their schoolmaster knew nothing of all this. Their first inkling of trouble was the sound of horses and men outside, the jangle of trace chains and the screeching of slowing wheels as brakes were applied. The children's eyes grew round with fright when several men came in the door carrying pikes and guns. In no time, it seemed, the schoolhouse was full of big, wild-looking men carrying in boxes of ammunition and guns. The schoolmaster, recovering somewhat from his first surprise, and thinking of his children, asked if he might send them on home. The man giving orders objected, but the schoolmaster persisted and finally convinced the intruders that it was all right to let the children go. No one would believe their story at any rate until it was too late. The schoolmaster, they kept with them as a hostage.

Over on the Virginia side of the Potomac, about two miles from the schoolhouse, things were beginning to go wrong for John Brown. Workers were coming to work at the arsenal. One by one these men were captured and quietly herded inside and guarded. But rumors were beginning to fly through the town. Some people fled from Harper's Ferry, hearing that a whole army of anti-slavery men were taking over. A few began to hunt for guns and to think about organizing and defending themselves.

More news was on its way out of town. John Brown had finally let a train leave Harper's Ferry at 6:30 in the morning, after he had kept it there for five hours. Even so, when the train stopped an hour later at Monocacy Junction, the conductor, A. J. Phelps, could get no one to believe his story. For two hours, he continued to wire the railroad headquarters in Baltimore, before he at last convinced the outside world that something strange was going on at Harper's Ferry. The B & O officials then notified the War Department in Washington.

About this time, too, messengers had reached nearby Charles Town, then a part of Virginia. The militia unit there was ordered out and soon was marching to Harper's Ferry, its members armed with every sort of old gun and sword imaginable. The militia surrounded the abolitionist-held arsenal grounds and waited for more help to arrive.

Brown's men holding the schoolhouse soon learned that Brown himself and the others at the arsenal were surrounded and outnumbered. No aid had come from slaves or northern anti-slavery sympathizers and hopes for an uprising were evaporating. The raiders at the schoolhouse concluded that the best thing for them to do was to save themselves. So, much to the schoolmaster's relief, they left.

Meanwhile, down in Harper's Ferry, the noose was tightening for John Brown and his men in the arsenal. At first, full of confidence, he ordered his men to hold out saying that soon slaves and anti-slavery sympathizers would be there to help. But early on the morning of Tuesday, October 18, a company of U.S. Marines commanded by Colonel Robert E. Lee, captured John Brown and his men after a brief but bloody fight.

The strange happenings, however, were not entirely ended. The school children had, by this time, told their parents. One father, a farmer, hearing of the events at Harper's Ferry, decided there might be some connection to all that was going on. So, he hitched up a horse and went to Colonel Robert E. Lee.

Lee acted quickly in hopes of capturing the other raiders, and promptly sent a part of his company to the schoolhouse. The place was quiet and the raiders were gone; yet, proof of the truth of the schoolboy's tale was in the grim presence of two hundred carbines, two hundred revolvers, two hundred fifty pounds of gunpowder and quantities of cartridges, all stacked in the schoolhouse!

By the end of that Tuesday, five citizens of the town and a Marine lay dead, and nine citizens and another Marine had been wounded. As for John Brown's abolitionists, ten were dead and five of those taken prisoner had been wounded.

The next week, on October 25, 1859, John Brown and his men were brought to trial at Charles Town, Virginia. It was an odd trial. Brown lay on a cot in the court room part of the time. He was suffering from fatigue, ill health, and a poor memory, he said. Yet, he would not let his attorney reveal to the court that there was a history of insanity in his mother's family. John Brown told the court only that he wanted to free the slaves and take them to Canada.

The jury sat through all the strange speeches and heard the evidence for both sides. Then they left the court room and for half an hour the courtroom buzzed with low conversations. Finally, the door opened and the jury returned to the courtroom and took their places. The verdict was, "Guilty."

John Brown and six of his band (another had been found) were hanged. His name spread far and wide after this. Songs and poems were written about the Harper's Ferry raid. Anti-slavery people thought him a hero. Southerners, always worried about the possibility of a slave uprising, were very bitter about him. The news, the gossip, and the bitter feelings that John Brown's raid had roused added to the ever more difficult problem facing a nation, part of which was for slavery, and part against it.

The guns were removed from the little schoolhouse. When the schoolmaster again faced his students, they could talk about the exciting events of the past days, and they could ask whether this was just one raid, or whether it would be followed by others. Would there be peace, or was it possible that men would fight about this slavery question? Even the children on that Maryland hill overlooking Harper's Ferry could not help but wonder if there would be more fighting and violence over slavery; but they could not then realize that the story of the events they had experienced would be of historical interest to pupils like themselves in years to come.

---

1 Harper's Ferry was then in the state of Virginia. Later, the area became a part of a new state, West Virginia.

2 An arsenal is a place where guns and military equipment are made or stored.

John Brown

258

CHAPTER LIII

A MARYLAND LADY

Anna Ella Carroll

THERE was nothing to show that the baby girl born in a plantation mansion in Somerset County, Maryland in the summer of 1815 would become an unusual person. Anna Ella Carroll was the name given to the little girl sleeping in dainty billows of white linen. To be sure, her father would one day become governor of the state.

Nor, was there any possible reason to think that a small boy of six, who slept in that year on a cornhusk mattress and a bearskin, in a western territory called Illinois, would join forces one day with this newest arrival in the home of a famous Eastern Shore family. With serious deepset eyes and a shock of black hair the boy grew very tall and very strong in the years that followed. His name was Abraham Lincoln.

Yet, these two children were destined to grow up and to become known to national leaders, and they eventually would plan together and make decisions that would greatly affect American history.

Anna's mother, Juliana, was, before her marriage, a Miss Stevenson. She is said to have been blessed with a dazzling fair skin, dark red curls piled high on her head and serious blue eyes. Anna's father, Thomas King Carroll had met his wife-to-be in Baltimore. When Thomas made Juliana his bride, he took her home to a great house, called "Kingston Hall." They drove up to the house, so the story goes, in a coach drawn by six white horses. The family coat of arms was painted on its doors. Both the coachman and footman had new green livery, as did the troop of outriders that kept them company. At Kingston Hall, they drove down an avenue of Lombardy poplars and tulip trees. There were approximately one hundred and fifty slaves in new green and gold uniforms to greet them. Kingston Hall was a "simple gentleman farmer's home" . . . but there were twenty-two rooms! Floors shone; glass windows were curtained with lace; and rugs had been brought to the Hall by clipper ship from the Orient. It sits today, as it did then, on the banks of a stream, off the Annemessex River, about ten miles from the town of Princess Anne in Somerset County.

The front of the mansion faces the stream. A walk edged with boxwood led down to the water landing where the boats came in, often bringing visitors and supplies. The land approach to Kingston is by a long lane. In the house itself the original great beams fastened with wood pins still remain. The 6,000 acres granted originally to the family had shrunk to 2,000 acres by the time that Anna was born.

Juliana found her days busy, indeed, nursing the sick, tending the newborn, teaching, and generally supervising the work done by house and field slaves. While busily engaged with all of this, she managed to have eight sons and daughters; Anna was the first of the eight to come.

News of her birth may have diverted the minds of her kinfolk, the Nehemiah Kings, over at "Beverly" in Somerset County, from the grand plot they were hatching. The story is that they planned to help Napoleon Bonaparte to escape the fever-ridden island off the coast of Africa where he had been sent in exile and to bring him to a secret place at Beverly. The Kings were friends of Napoleon's brother, Jerome.[1] However, the plot failed to materialize, for Napoleon died before he could be rescued.

Even as a child, Anna was expected to learn many things. Though she had no hard labor to perform, yet, she was taught responsibility for others. When she grew up, she would care for her family, for her home, and for scores of servants. This was a heavy burden in her earlier years.

Now that the cotton gin had been invented, slaves were much needed in the southern cotton fields. Cotton was making men rich. Yet, Anna's family felt it inhuman to sell their slaves for work in the southern cotton fields. To separate a mother from her children, or a man from wife, was, for Anna, unthinkable. But for the Maryland plantation owner, it was becoming more and more a problem to feed the increasing number of workers, especially when tobacco was no longer so profitable a crop. Anna was taught, too, to feel very strongly about freeing blacks without seeing to it that they had homes and jobs. The blacks who eluded Patty Cannon and other slave catchers lived a poor life, trapping and fishing for food or living in the Baltimore slums with an occasional work day in waterfront activities.

Perhaps, because Anna was the oldest of the children, she was her father's constant companion. She often sat in his study, where she was allowed to read the heavy law books, the Shakespearian plays, and books on philosophy and history!

She had a chance, too, to listen to her father's visitors; and often she got down the law books from the shelves to help him make a telling point in those long talks. After a while, she became clever at

260

putting two and two together in legal arguments. Her memory was very good.

Her geography did not come just from books, but from long talks with her father and from the trips she took up and down the rivers and the Bay. On a globe her father shuwed her where the ships she saw on the Bay were bound, perhaps to South America, or Africa, or to the Pacific Northwest, or to the Orient.

She often heard her father speak of a plan to return black people to Africa. The American Colonization Society was begun in 1816.[2] The Society's chief Maryland promoters at that time, besides her own father, were Francis Scott Key and Robert Goodloe Harper. Her father was for a number of years the president of the Maryland branch of the Society. In the spring of 1824, Anna waved him off to Philadelphia where the Society met to make plans to take freed slaves to the African country of Liberia.

By the time of her tenth birthday, which was August 29, 1825, Anna was an attractive and somewhat sober and intense little girl, quick to anger but quick also to love. Her eyes were expressive and blue; her nose was freckled, and she had a square-shouldered strong little body.

Anna was now acting as her father's secretary, reading newspapers, and clipping and filing items about the Colonization Society, plans for a Panama Canal, shipping news, items on the new steam engines, roads, canals, and scores of other subjects in which her father was interested. This, in itself, thanks to her memory and appetite for information, was an education unusual for a girl in that period of Maryland history.

Politics was a subject always being discussed in the family. The most important thing for a politician, as she learned from her father, who served a term as Governor when she was fourteen, was to stand for principle. One must believe in right, search for truth, and always act honorably. If there was one principle Thomas King Carroll believed in, it was the need for unity in "the Union." Any other idea for him was treason. Local or personal wishes must be put aside. If the states became widely separated from each other, and if they quarrelled and hindered each other, then foreign powers could gain control of them. United, the states could be strong, and the people free and prosperous.

So it was that by the time her father became governor, that Anna had in her mind the ideas she would use the rest of her life. In body and manner, too, she showed the intelligence and charm that she would keep to the end. She was now a short and slim young lady with a small waist and small feet. It is doubtful if she was a natural beauty. Her skin was very fair, her hair brown except in the sunshine, when one might detect a glint of red in it. Her eyes were large and blue. Her attractiveness was due to her intelligence, her warmhearted ways, her quick wit, and her flashing smile. With these qualities there was also the combination of endless energy and enthusiasm, tempered by a soft voice and good manners. Coming from one of Maryland's finest families, she was naturally known to scores of prominent people both in Maryland and in Washington, the capital city.

Because her father, whom she adored, increasingly neglected his own affairs for those of the public, the family fortunes were steadily decreasing. Anna's gentle mother, Juliana, was worn out trying to manage the plantation and take care of the workers. At length, she became ill and for awhile Anna's father came back from Annapolis and devoted himself to his wife and his farming, but, unfortunately, he acted too late to save his estates.

In the circumstances, Anna decided to set up a school to help bring in some money. With typical energy she set to work. She was almost overwhelmed with pupils, when in 1834, her school for girls was opened. At this time, too, her future might have ended right there in Somerset County, for several distinguished men proposed marriage; but she decided to stay single.

Not yet twenty, her life was set for quite a different course now. She went to Washington to hear speeches, and to meet interesting public men including explorers and many senators and congressmen. She had been told, when she asked how she might help James Reynolds with his proposed scientific expedition into the South Pacific, that she could help by talking because women's words were the "threads of public opinion." So she began to talk and to write.

In this period of her life, she wrote many long letters to her wide circle of family and friends. But, as far as her friend Reynolds was concerned, in the long run he did not head the exploration; instead, another was sent and the purpose of the expedition was changed to a military, from a scientific one. Disappointed, she wrote appeals and scores of letters. But, for Anna this experience was not all lost, because it gave her the idea for a fascinating career. Why should she not become a person who through letters, friends, and writing, would mold public opinion toward worthy projects? After all, for Anna, the need for a challenging as well as a well paying profession was very real.

Kingston Hall and half of its slaves in 1840 were sold to pay off debts. The arrangement was that these slaves were to remain on the plantation under the new owners. The Carroll family moved about fifty miles away to Warwick Fort Manor on the Choptank River.

Anna had a plan now to become the family bread-winner, though her sisters were alarmed. They wanted to know if she was going to become one of those "strongminded women!" While she denied this, it is a fact that she intended going to Baltimore to support herself, and that is just what she did. In the spring of 1840, she crossed over on a steamer to Baltimore, at that time, the third largest city in the nation. She lived in a "refined boarding house." Her writing and public relations work went well; and she not only earned a living in a genteel way, but won considerable influence as well. By 1846, the family was once more in better financial shape, largely due to her efforts. During the next fifteen years, Anna, though usually in the background and always in every way a lady, became well known for her talent in writing and in shaping public opinion. Her signature "A. E. Carroll," by 1861, had come to be highly respected when attached to the letters and articles that occasionally appeared in the public press.

The Union that she and her father so loved was now in grave danger. During the period of her lifetime, the nation had been held together by compromise, largely by letting in a slave state each time that a free state was added to the Union. But compromises no longer seemed to work, and the forces for and against slavery were growing more and more angry with each other. The southern states were threatening to pull out of the Union and to form their own government. Southerners feared the growing power of the northern states, who since 1850, had become more numerous than the southern group. The North and South argued over other issues, too, like the question of tariffs.

In the North, manufacturing, shipping, and farms were not in need of the cheap labor that slaves provided. This, plus the fact that so many fiercely believed slavery a great evil made the Northerners bitterly opposed to slavery and to the introduction of any new state added to the Union being a "slave state."

Maryland, on the dividing line between North and South, is sometimes said to be the "northernmost Southern state," and, the "southernmost Northern state!" Anna Ella Carroll knew the political conditions in her state as well as anyone and she feared that if the General Assembly of Maryland met, it would vote to secede. Maryland's Governor Hicks, too, feared the secession movement and felt that the Union must not be divided. So with Anna's help, and despite heavy pressure, Governor Hicks managed to delay the meeting of the legislature and prevented the decision that would have proved disastrous to the state.

1 Jerome Bonaparte, the younger brother of Napoleon Bonaparte who ruled France, came to Baltimore after Napoleon was deposed and exiled. In Baltimore, Jerome met beautiful Elizabeth Patterson, daughter of one of the wealthiest men in the city. They were married on Christmas Eve, 1803. Further details may be found in the "Dictionary of American Biography," published by Charles Scribner's Sons, New York, 1957.

2 Scharf, **History of Maryland,** Vol. III, p. 320.

Anna Ella Carroll of Maryland

YOUR MARYLAND

SECTION VI

MARYLAND DURING THE CIVIL WAR

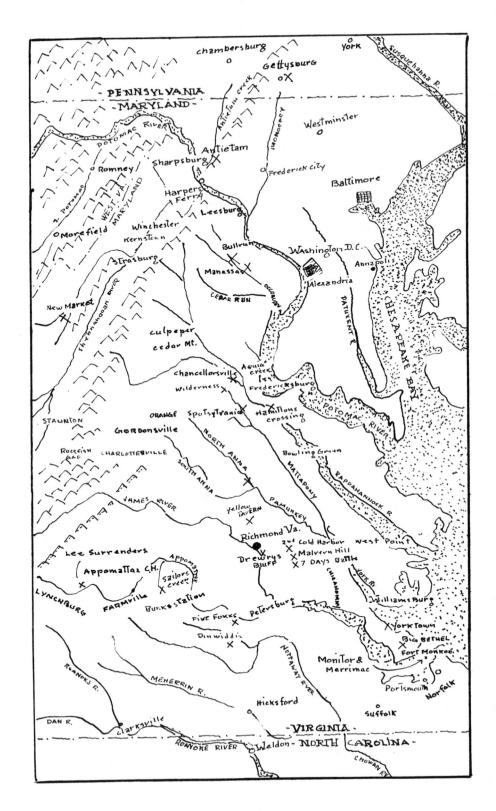

CHAPTER LIV

IN MARYLAND AS WAR NEARS

GENERAL Winfield Scott was old in 1861 but his mind was still alert. To Anna Ella Carroll, the young Maryland lady, General Scott was "Uncle Win," and they were good friends.

The General was an imposing man. Brass buttons gleamed down his ample front, and gold epaulets topped his broad shoulders. He had an honest, sympathetic face. Lively blue eyes twinkled from beneath his craggy white brows. His white side whiskers were bushy. But, for all his kindly appearance, his was one of the keenest military minds in the country.

For years Anna had listened to this staunch old patriot and had talked and sometimes argued about the state of the Union and what should be done about it. With her wide knowledge of railroads, gained by writing for the railroad companies, and her grasp of geography, Anna understood the General's stories of the Mexican war, and his thoughts on past battles. His ideas on conditions in various parts of the nation were fascinating to the young woman.

General Scott was correct in saying that the seceding Southern states must be, and would be, cut away from the West and from their port in New Orleans. He saw, too, the danger that England might possibly come to the aid of the South should the Southerners appear to be winning their battle to withdraw from the Union. After all, England did need cotton for her mills.

It was General Scott who was to write to Abraham Lincoln, when war broke out, advising a tight blockade of the Southern coastline. The old general knew that the South had few factories and must import guns and many other things in order to fight. Lincoln was to thank him for this suggestion and was to follow the General's advice.

Meanwhile, as has been noted, Anna was working closely in 1861 with Maryland's Governor Hicks. She wrote to members of the Maryland legislature, searching out their feelings about the action of the South in secession. She knew at that moment that the issue in Maryland was still unsettled and that if the legislature met while still undecided, there was great danger that it might vote to join hands with the Confederate States of America. She wrote newspaper articles, though not revealing the fact that the author of the articles was a woman, in order to swing the public to the view that the Union must hold together. In the meantime Governor Hicks delayed the meeting of the General Assembly.

Baltimore "Secedes"

War! That was the cry after Confederate guns boomed in South Carolina firing on Fort Sumter in Charleston Harbor. President Lincoln called up the militia for a term of just three months. He hoped within that time to put down the rebellion.

Rumors began to spread that Union troops would be coming through Maryland on their way to defend Washington. Or, because of the uncertainty as to Maryland's position, maybe they would come for the purpose of occupying the state. April, 1861, in Baltimore was a time of great tension. On April 17, at 2:00 P.M., troops did begin to arrive at the railroad station in Jones Falls Valley called the Bolton Street Station. From there they had to march to "Camden Station" to take the "cars" to Washington. Under near-riot conditions the troops, largely Pennsylvania militia with some Federal artillery units, moved through the streets of downtown Baltimore.

The next day, a Baltimore mob jeered Northern soldiers of the 6th Massachusetts Volunteer Regiment that was bound for Washington. The mob forced the railroad cars, which were being towed by horses to the rail line across town, to temporarily return to the station. Excitement grew as the soldiers set out again, this time on the march, to get to the Camden B & O station and the train for Washington. Mob violence is a dangerous thing. By the time the troops had reached Pratt Street and were turning westward, everyone was tense. A shot was fired by someone, and the green troops were ordered by equally unseasoned officers to turn and fire a high volley. The crowd went wild. Shots rang out and a soldier fell to the ground dead.

Then, under attack, with stones thrown and ugly shouts filling the air and the men of the crowd attempting to pull the soldier's guns from their hands, the militiamen began to fire back. City policemen came running up and helped calm the people by getting between the crowd and the soldiers. So, finally, after great confusion and some bloodshed the troops got through to their train for Washington. But the events of the day had served to arouse people in Baltimore to a fever pitch. The more they thought about it the more angry and determined they were that Northern troops should not again move through the state or into the state. Virginia had seceded, Union troops were occupying Harper's Ferry. By Monday, April 22, Baltimore people had succeeded in stopping troops from moving through the

City. It was a situation that could easily lead to secession. Certainly Mr. Lincoln's government had to act quickly in order to prevent Maryland's rebellion.

Armed citizens were busy organizing themselves and drilling. The South rejoiced, thinking that Baltimore had seceded. Though not officially it had done so in fact. Some of the people of Baltimore wanted to join with the South, others wanted to stay with the Union. If Maryland should secede, not only its factories, ports and railroads would be put to the use of the South, it seemed that April, but also the capital city of Washington would soon surely be lost to the Union.

How narrow a margin between Union and a separate system of states! The United States would quite possibly never have become the great nation we know today, if Maryland had seceded. But many who loved the Union were working to prevent this. In the critical hours that followed Baltimore's halting of troop movements, the Mayor of Baltimore, George William Brown, met with Lincoln in Washington. Together with old General Winfield Scott and some of Lincoln's other advisors, they worked out a compromise plan to get troops from the North to Washington without going through Baltimore. The tension then began to subside.

Maryland! My Maryland!

When Baltimore was very nearly joining the Confederate States of America on her own, without waiting for the rest of Maryland, a young Marylander, James Ryder Randall, far away from home, learned of the clash in the streets of his native city. He felt so strongly for the South, that he worked through the night on a nine-verse poem, "My Maryland."

Randall was a teacher at that time, at Poydras College, Louisiana. His pupils encouraged him to send the poem to the New Orleans newspaper *Delta*, where it was first published on April 26, 1861. News of the poem spread rapidly through the Southland, and then into Baltimore City. There it was set to a melody already quite familiar to many by two young ladies, Jennie and Hettie Cary. The poem-song became instantly popular. Long afterwards, in 1939, it was officially made our state song by the Maryland General Assembly.

If we study the words which Randall composed, we can see that Maryland was being urged not to submit to Union occupation, but to join the Confederate cause. As it turned out this is just the opposite of what finally happened.

Northern troops continued to bypass Baltimore until the city quieted down. The Maryland General Assembly, when finally it did meet, avoided the decision on secession. Perhaps the Union was the important thing after all, or perhaps the great amount of sympathy for the Southern states was being forced to yield to superior Northern military power. At any rate, the vote was to remain united. Governor Hicks, in a letter to Anna Carroll, dated January 19, 1862, wrote: "I feel that I have acted for the good of my state and my country and am content . . ." Governor Hicks was one of those who still hoped for peace between the South and the North.

Whatever the reasons that brought about Maryland's decision, the results, as will be seen, were tremendously important. Maryland was certainly strategically placed in relation to the nation's capital city and to the great route into the Ohio and Mississippi valleys. It is probably true that the Union would have had great difficulty in surviving at this point, without Maryland.

My Maryland.

James R. Randall.

1. The des-pot's heel is on thy shore, Ma-ry-land, my Ma-ry-land! His torch is at thy
2. Hark to an ex-iled son's ap-peal, Ma-ry-land, my Ma-ry-land! My Moth-er State, to
3. Thou wilt not cow-er in the dust, Ma-ry-land, my Ma-ry-land! Thy gleaming sword shall

tem-ple door, Ma-ry-land, my Ma-ry-land! A-venge the pa-tri-ot-ic gore That
thee I kneel! Ma-ry-land, my Ma-ry-land! For life and death, for woe and weal. Thy
nev-er rust, Ma-ry-land, my Ma-ry-land! Re-mem-ber Car-roll's sa-cred trust, Re-

flecked the streets of Bal-ti-more, And be the bat-tle-queen of yore, Ma-ry-land, my Ma-ry-land!
peer-less chiv-al-ry reveal, And gird thy beauteous limbs with steel, Ma-ry-land, my Ma-ry-land!
member Howard's war-like thrust, And all thy slumb'rers with the just, Ma-ry-land, my Ma-ry-land!

CHAPTER LV

THE CIVIL WAR BEGINS — 1861

To understand the Civil War and Maryland's part in it, one needs at least an outline of the entire war. If the following story of the war seems to range far away from Maryland, then, remember that men of our state fought on both sides of the struggle. Remember, too, that Maryland men were present at many of the battles we shall mention.

As we have seen, John Brown's raid, in 1859, alarmed both the South and the North. The publicity that followed the raid made Northern citizens even more determined to free the people enslaved in the South. Southerners, in turn, became more determined not to give up their unpaid laborers. They became more afraid, too, of uprisings.

Some Western states had been given the right to have slaves; but other Western states were not. "We'll secede (withdraw) from the Union (United States)," the Southern states began to say. "You can't," the Northern leaders replied. So a second big argument raged. The first was over the right to have slavery; the second over the right of states to decide for themselves whether or not to secede.

1861

On March 4, 1861, Abraham Lincoln was inaugurated the sixteenth President of the United States. Photographs of the time show the dome of the Capitol only half finished and the streets of Washington deep with mud. The development of the capital city was still an uncompleted project.

On April 12, Southerners demanded that Union troops give up Fort Sumter at Charleston, South Carolina. The Union men refused. The Southerners then fired the first shots of the Civil War.[1] The following day, President Lincoln, learning that local law officers would not jail the rebels who fired on Fort Sumter, called up the militia, over 75,000 men. He at first called for enlistments of only a three-month term of duty.

When the actual firing began at Fort Sumter on April 14, a Maryland lady, Anna Ella Carroll, did a most extraordinary thing. She urged President Lincoln and his military advisor, General Scott, to arrest certain people and to hold them without trial, in order to prevent Maryland from joining the southern Confederacy!

With the future of the Union in danger, whether or not this was fair, or within legal bounds, did not matter too much to the practical Miss Carroll. Possibly influenced by her advice, President Lincoln did suspend the writ of *habeas corpus*[2] in Maryland on April 27, 1861.

Command of the Northern forces was offered to the brilliant officer of the United States Army, Robert E. Lee. Though saddened at the thought of a war between the states, Lee was to refuse this offer and go to his home state of Virginia to join the Confederate Army.

Lincoln had only General Winfield Scott, a brilliant man, but an old man, when the war began.[3] Scott advised a tight sea blockade of the South. This, he told Lincoln, would eventually strangle the Southern states through lack of food, war supplies, and clothing. Lincoln sent every possible vessel, loaded with guns, to patrol the shores of the Southern states.

Two feelings were shared by both armies, Northern and Southern. One was a feeling of impatience to go ahead and fight and get the war settled. The other was a feeling of deep reluctance to see Americans fire on Americans. In Maryland, the war created many *very* difficult decisions. Many families were divided, brother against brother, with some going to join Northern armies and others heading south to join Confederate troops!

After much confusion and many delays, at last Union troops advanced to fight. They perhaps thought that the advantages were all theirs and that it would be very easy to defeat the Southern forces. People from Washington actually came out to watch the fighting, bringing picnic lunches. Scores of carriages stopped on the hillsides near Manassas Junction, Virginia, to witness what for them was to be almost a "sham battle." How wrong they were!

It was in this First Battle of Bull Run that the Confederate general, General Thomas J. "Stonewall" Jackson got his nickname. The Union forces soon found the battle no picnic but a deadly fight to the death. Roads back to Washington soon became a tangle of fleeing civilians in carriages, troops running for their lives, and wagons loaded with wounded, suffering men. Shaken by this debacle, the defeated Northern forces returned to Washington.

Meanwhile, in the West the war went better from the start for the North. At Wilson's Creek, a Southern force was defeated, and considerable Missouri territory was saved for the North. Then, with "two small fights," General George B. McClellan threw back the

Confederates and helped to keep western Virginia under Union control.

In May, 1861, delegates from twenty-five Virginia counties were sent to a meeting in Wheeling. These men decided to call a convention to meet in June. This June convention was attended by representatives from forty western Virginia counties. The convention members voted to secede from the State of Virginia and voted to remain a part of the United States. Fifty-five counties joined together to form a new state, West Virginia.[4]

In Washington, Lincoln now saw that it would be a long and serious war. He called up half a million men to serve in the Union armies.

The War in the West

Events in the southwestern part of the nation were moving fast. It was felt that, if southwestern states should decide to join the Confederacy, there would be no stopping the flow of guns and supplies from Mexico and through the Port of New Orleans. To prevent this the capture of the Mississippi River for the Union was necessary. The Confederates, however, had the river well fortified.

In September, 1861, Anna Carroll was sent by Lincoln westward with an Army officer, Lemuel Evans, as her escort. She was sent to observe matters in the West and directed to return to Lincoln with information and ideas. She visited many of the Union army positions west of the Alleghenies. Then she went on to Chicago, Illinois; and later to St. Louis, Missouri. In making her inspections of the camps she insisted on looking over every part of them. It was not an easy task for a gentlewoman, for the camps were often described as "pigsties."

She talked with Sherman, Grant, and other generals in the West, none of whom saw much hope for success in a campaign for control of the Mississippi. Gunboats had been prepared, but they were low, slow, armored devices. Most of them had but one gun, facing forward. They could attack in one direction—downstream, but then might not be able to sail upsteam against the current.

What the high-ranking Union officers thought when they first met Miss Carroll may be imagined. They seemed to find her keen and able, however, and she had been sent west by Lincoln himself.

There was the germ of an idea that Anna began to consider as she talked with the army leaders. Though the Confederate forts on the Mississippi were strong enough to fight off an attack from the river, they might not so easily defend themselves on the landward side. Poring over her charts, the Marylander thought she saw the answer. A river did flow from the south-southeast into the Mississippi — the Tennessee River. It flowed in a generally northward direction, while the Mississippi flowed in the opposite direction. Attack by this route was simple and obvious. But, perhaps the river was too shallow. Anna checked with a river pilot. "No," he said, "The river is not too shallow for the gunboats." So she decided that the Tennessee River would offer a route to take Union troops down behind the Mississippi River forts. These soldiers might then march across and strike the forts from the poorly defended land side.

After telling her escort, Evans, of her idea, Anna Carroll on the evening of November 12, 1861, sat down and wrote to Mr. Lincoln, as well as to General Winfield Scott and Attorney-General Bates. She made her suggestions. This attack, she said, was the key to the war in the West. If the nation were to be spared a long and bloody war, a decisive blow must be struck very soon. With the capture of the South's main railroad into the West, the Confederacy would be cut away from the West.

---

1 Definition of terms: The Northern forces were also called "Union" forces or "Yankees" or "Federal" forces. These represented the United States government. Southerners were known as "Confederates," "Johnny Rebs," and represented the seceding Southern states under a new government formed there, which was named "The Confederate States of America."

2 The writ of **habeas corpus** is the right to be accused of a specific misdeed or crime, and then the right to an open trial; there proof of wrong-doing must be given, and, if it is not, the accused person must be set free. This prevents the imprisonment of citizens for false or unproven charges.

3 Note that in wartime the President of the United States becomes the Commander-in-Chief of all armed forces.

4 West Virginia entered the Union on June 20, 1863. It was the thirty-fifth state to enter. Charleston became the state capital.

A Union soldier.

A Virginia cavalryman.

CHAPTER LVI

THE CIVIL WAR YEARS OF 1862 AND 1863

By the end of January, 1862, the rough-mannered, tough, Union general, Ullysses S. Grant, was ready to attack. Following the plan suggested by Anna Ella Carroll and approved by President Lincoln,[1] Grant took troops and a few small gunboats up the Tennessee River (see map). He captured Fort Henry, Kentucky, and then took Fort Donelson, Kentucky. As Miss Carroll had predicted, this route allowed Union forces to attack Confederate forts on the Mississippi River, on their weak, landward side.

The Battle of Ironclads

In March, 1862, a Confederate ironclad ship, the *Merrimack*, steamed into Hampton Roads, Virginia, an anchorage which was in Union hands. The *Merrimack* proceeded methodically to blast the wooden Union ships there to splinters! Cannon balls fired at the ironclad ship simply bounced off its iron sides. Suddenly the Union navy men were alarmed. What was this new kind of warship? Was there nothing that could stop her? Would Washington, D. C. itself be attacked next?

Then, in one of the most amazing stories of the Civil War, the small Union ironclad, the *Monitor*, just barely completed and not yet proven out with test runs, came steaming up. How it managed to reach the area at that time is quite a story. The ship was scarcely seaworthy and had very nearly sunk to the floor of the Atlantic on its way southward. The two ironclad ships met in a strange duel. The *Merrimack* was finally forced back into her Norfolk harbor. She was never to come out again, for Union forces captured her berth before she could be repaired.

This historic battle between the first ironclad warships clearly showed navy men all over the world that the day of the wooden warship was at an end.

The Peninsula Campaign of 1862

General George B. McClellan was still in command of the Army of the Potomac for the Union in 1862. Lincoln often rode out from

Washington to talk with him but the two men did not seem to be able to understand each other. McClellan prepared and prepared, but never seemed to get ready to move and fight. At least that is the way Lincoln and some of his military advisers felt. But Lincoln did admit that "Little Mac" was very popular with his men. They believed in him and resented the remarks so often made against him.

General McClellan was finally ready to act. He sailed off to Yorktown, Virginia, with a large body of troops and much equipment. He was determined to capture the very capital of the Confederacy itself, Richmond. He stayed at Yorktown for about a month and then marched to Seven Pines. There, by May 20th, he was in sight of the city of Richmond. He stopped to prepare the troops still more for the coming campaign. In a heavy rainstorm, the Confederates attacked. Heavy losses were suffered on both sides, with the Union troops getting the worst of it. The famous detective, Pinkerton, serving as McClellan's intelligence officer was apt to imagine more troops facing them than were actually there. Also discouraging to McClellan, was the fact that the Confederate general, Joe Johnson, was replaced by the brilliant and crafty, General Robert E. Lee.

To keep more troops from being available to enter Virginia in support of McClellan, General Lee sent off General Thomas "Stonewall" Jackson into the Shenandoah Valley of Virginia which blends into the Great Valley of Maryland. But a little later Jackson was quietly recalled with his troops to rejoin Lee in the defense of Richmond. Together, in the Seven Days' Battles of June 25 to July 1, they pushed General McClellan back to the James River in Virginia. There McClellan took shelter under the guns of the Union navy.

New Orleans

Meanwhile, a retired admiral, David Glasgow Farragut, had returned to active duty in the Union navy as Flag Officer. He had been given command of the West Gulf blockading squadron. He had, in April, attacked and captured the great port and city of New Orleans. He captured as well, Fort Jackson and Fort St. Phillip. This dimmed the hopes of the Confederacy of getting help from England. The Confederates had hoped that England's need for cotton for her mills might cause her to aid the South. But, with the Port of New Orleans closed and the blockade of the Southern coast working well, shipment of cotton almost completely stopped.

The War in the West

If the Union forces could cut the Confederacy away from the West by capturing the entire Mississippi River, the South would be completely encircled and cut off from the world. The South could be starved into submission for lack of supplies and weapons. So, General Grant moved up the Tennessee River to a log meeting house known as Shiloh. It is a place located in Tennessee, very near the southern boundary of that state, and close to the Tennessee River. This was to be the site of one of the most terrible battles of the Civil War. There each side had over 1700 men killed; each side had 8,000 men wounded; and hundreds of men on each side were listed as missing in action. April 6 and 7, 1862, were desperate days. Grant gained a partial victory, forcing the Confederates to retreat.

Action in the East

However, in the east, the action now shifted to northern Virginia. At Manassas Junction, Union troops were again beaten, on practically the same battlefield as in 1861, by the Confederate troops (August 29-30). Once more, too, the Union army had to retreat to Washington to tend its wounded.

In September, Lee now moved many men into the Shenandoah Valley of Virginia and the Great Valley of Maryland. He desperately needed a great victory to try still to persuade England that the South had a chance to win separation from the North. Lee also had high hopes at this time of winning Maryland over to the side of the South.

Anna Ella Carroll

In Washington, the Maryland lady, Anna Ella Carroll, continued to work for Lincoln. Many a night she and the President watched over incoming telegraph messages for news of the progress of the fighting. Miss Carroll's writing talents and her grasp of legal matters were put to use for her country. She wrote continuously, papers on the powers of the Presidency, letters, speeches, plans, and opinions. Few of her readers realized that the author of these writings was a woman. Her Union sympathies made her unpopular with some people on the Eastern Shore of Maryland, for many of her old neighbors felt that the South was right.

Though her brilliant mind was recognized by many in Washington, including Abraham Lincoln, it was not thought proper to openly recognize the work of a woman in government and military matters.

She was kept behind the scenes and received scarcely enough money from the government to pay the printing bills she made in doing her work and to pay her living expenses.

The Slavery Question

More and more people in the year 1862 were urging President Lincoln to free the slaves. Lincoln had hoped to first make some definite plan for their future. Miss Carroll had freed her own slaves some time before, but only after training them to make a living and finding work for them. She did not think, as some people did, that bands of free blacks would roam the city and country, robbing and killing. She did remember, however, their poverty and fears when freed in Maryland with no home and no way of earning a living. So she advised President Lincoln to plan for the future of American blacks and this he agreed to do.

Lincoln, in a conference on May 12, 1862, with seven congressmen, pointed out that it was no kindness to release slaves as free men into communities where they would not be welcome and where they might not get land of their own. He believed that land might be secured for them if a colony were to be started in Central America, possibly in the area that is now Panama. He showed the congressmen a box of food and trade products, including mahogany, coffee, coconuts, and bananas, which he said were, "from Miss Carroll." Then Lincoln added, "This Anna Ella Carroll is the top of the Carroll race. When the history of this war is written, she will stand a good bit taller than ever old Charles Carroll did."

During the summer of 1862, Lincoln asked Anna to write out a paper explaining carefully the Central American relocation project. But, the pressure of events forced the President to move more swiftly than he wished in the matter of freeing slaves. By August 25, the capital city of Washington was in danger of capture by the Confederate army. Plans were made for the evacuation of the capital if necessary! Lee advanced into Maryland on September 3 and tried very hard to make the state a Confederate stronghold. It was then that Lincoln promised that, if the Confederates were pushed back across the Potomac, he would issue an executive order to free the blacks held in bondage in the rebelling states of the South.

Lee's 1862 Invasion of Maryland

As one reads about the Civil War, it is easy to see that the Confederates seemed to move their troops more quickly than did their foes, much as George Washington had done in the American Revolution. Union troops, on the other hand, were moved so slowly and carefully that many opportunities for defeating Southern armies appeared to be missed. The Union leaders continually gave General Lee time to get his positions fortified and to gather or to move his troops.

The campaign of September, 1862 was a good example of this. As the Confederate forces began an invasion of Maryland, Lee ordered General Jackson to capture Harper's Ferry, and then to rejoin him. By chance, a copy of Lee's orders fell into the hands of the Union army, which was again under the command of General George McClellan. From reading the orders, McClellan knew that the Confederate army was divided. But, even so, after the victory of the Northern forces on September 14 at South Mountain, west of Frederick, McClellan moved with agonizing slowness. Lee had time to get into position at Sharpsburg, Maryland, behind Antietam Creek, and to bring up his troops from Harper's Ferry.

After waiting two days, on September 17, 1862, McClellan attacked. By this time, Jackson, the visitor at Harper's Ferry, had hurried back to rejoin General Lee. The bloody battle of Antietam, sometimes known as the Battle of Sharpesburg, has been called by some a Union victory. But the fact is, there were dreadful losses to both armies. The Union forces lost 12,000 men and the Confederates lost 11,000 men. Surely our country had never had such heartbreaking days. How would this bitterness ever be healed?

The Year 1863

"I, Abraham Lincoln . . . as of January 1, 1863. . . .all persons held as slaves within any state . . . now in rebellion . . . shall be then . . . forever free." President Lincoln's proclamation was an Executive Order which freed thousands of enslaved blacks in those states which had seceded from the Union. Oddly enough, in some Union states this left the practice of slavery still technically legal. In Maryland, slavery did not become officially outlawed until November 1, 1864.

At first this seemed a wonderful day for black men and women. But though they rejoiced to be free, at last, still the abrupt end of their servitude left them with serious problems. They were completely unprepared for freedom. They were freed without jobs, homes, or plans for their future. They needed many things very quickly— such as education, jobs, and housing. However, each year thereafter saw the black citizens making some gains, and learning and progressing, despite many obstacles.

General Lee withdrew his troops to the Virginia side of the Potomac River soon after the battle at Antietam Creek, in September 1862, and the Union forces did not follow him right away. In December the Northern army did try to cross the Rappahannock River at Fredericksburg, Virginia, but found itself facing well dug-in Confederate armies. In this battle the Union army lost 13,000 men.

In the Western states, the news in this year was generally better for the Union. Flag Officer Farragut had one end of the Mississippi River bottled up. After the capture of Island #10 and the capture of Memphis, Tennessee, that great river was held by the Union, almost from end to end, and the Confederacy was all but surrounded. In the West near the Mississippi River, only a part of the state of Mississippi still remained in Confederate hands.

Spring came with suffering increasing on both sides. The South was strangled by the tight Union blockade; it lacked food, supplies, weapons, and clothing and its railroads were almost completely disrupted. So scarce was food that prisoners of war held in the Confederate prison camp at Andersonville, Virginia, were almost living skeletons when freed at the end of the war. Many, not even so lucky as this, died of starvation and disease behind the prison walls.

During the Civil War, Clara Barton began her work of locating missing soldiers and obtaining medical supplies and nursing care for the wounded. She was later (1881) to found the American National Red Cross. Her house, the "Clara Barton House," is located on Oxford Road, Glen Echo, Maryland, in Montgomery County. It has been named a National Historic Landmark.

The war had so far cost both the Union and the Confederacy thousands of men. What gave the North the advantage in this situation, however, was the fact that the Confederacy could not replace its limited manpower as could the Union. Besides, all hope of English help for the Confederacy had now faded away.

In May, 1863 the Union general, "Fightin' Joe" Hooker, attacked General Lee at Chancellorsville and at Fredericksburg, Virginia. The Confederates may have won these battles but with great losses. It was at this time that General "Stonewall" Jackson was accidentally shot and killed by one of his own Confederate men, and as Lee said, he had "lost his good right arm."

In the West, the last Confederate stronghold on the Mississippi River was Vicksburg, Mississippi. General Grant crossed the river to avoid an unfavorable battle ground in the swamps north of Vicksburg, and then marched his troops southward. His gunboats ran through the cannon fire of the fort and joined him, ferrying his troops back across the river to the east bank to attack Vicksburg by land from the south. He fortunately crossed the river in time to stop a Confederate relief force headed into Vicksburg. The city was in a state of seige until July 4, 1863, when, starved out, it surrendered.

General Lee, realizing that sheer numbers were winning the war, despite his well fought battles, headed his Confederates into Maryland, June, 1863, in a march aimed at Pennsylvania. There he might be able to replenish some of his supplies, and, if lucky he might even capture important cities like Philadelphia and Baltimore. General Hooker followed with his troops. President Lincoln, feeling that Hooker lacked decisiveness and that more speed was necessary, replaced Hooker with the bewhiskered, hot-tempered, General George Gordon Meade. The tall and lanky General Meade settled his floppy hat on his head and set off to pursue the Confederates.

General Lee raided southern Pennsylvania and then moved southeastward, threatening major Northern centers of population. But at Gettysburg, Pennsylvania, 75,000 Confederate soldiers met over 82,000 Union men in the first days of July, 1863. It was "the most famous single battle in American military history," and the three-day conflict may have been the decisive battle of the War. Even Grant's victory at Vicksburg could hardly compare with it, great as had been that triumph. Death struck down many more Americans on both sides. It is important to note, that, as in 1862, the paths of both Southern and Northern armies were through Maryland— Frederick and Hagerstown figuring prominently in both campaigns, just as would be the case once more in 1864.

Heartsick, Lee withdrew in the hot July weather. With him, in jolting wagon trains, went his wounded men. There were no hospitals for them. There was, in fact, very little help for them at all. For Union soldiers wounded in battle there were at least a few crude, makeshift field hospitals. One man, who lived to tell the tale of the battle, described such a hospital:

"It was dark," he wrote, "And the building was lighted partially with candles. All around . . . lay the wounded men, some cursing and swearing and some praying; in the middle of the room, there were some ten or twelve tables with just enough (room) to lay a man on; these were used as dissection surgical tables and they were covered with blood . . . By the side of the tables was a heap of feet, legs, and arms."

Supplies of ether, morphine and laudanum were soon depleted. Whiskey was then almost the only pain-killer available, and there was not even much of that to be had. Army surgeons and medical aides of both armies tried to help the suffering and dying men.

Official reports of the three-day battle show that the Confederate army had nearly 2,600 men killed, nearly 13,000 wounded, and over 5,000 captured or missing. The Union army had 3,000 men killed nearly 15,000 wounded and another 5,500 missing or captured.

Lincoln at Gettysburg

In time, the raw horror of the battle at Gettysburg was covered over. Neat rows of graves stretched across the fields, green with new grass in a huge national cemetery. In November, 1863, the cemetry was ready for dedication. Abraham Lincoln was invited to attend. For two hours he listened to one of the most polished speakers of that time. Finally, it was Mr. Lincoln's turn to make "a few remarks." He rose, tall, gaunt, and sad. Lincoln took only a few minutes to give what has come down in history as one of the greatest speeches ever delivered. Simply and quietly, he said:

"Four score and seven years ago, our fathers brought forth on this continent, a new nation, conceived in Liberty and dedicated to the proposition that all men are created equal.

"Now we are engaged in a great civil war, testing whether that nation or any nation so conceived and so dedicated, can long endure. We are met on a great battlefield of that war. We have come to dedicate a portion of that field, as a final resting place for those who here gave their lives that that nation might live. It is altogether fitting and proper that we should do this.

"But in a larger sense, we can not dedicate—we can not consecrate—we can not hallow—this ground. The brave men, living and dead, who struggled here, have consecrated it, far above our poor power to add or detract. The world will little heed, nor long remember what we say here, but it can never forget what they did here. It is for us the living, rather, to be dedicated here to the unfinished work which they who fought here have thus far so nobly advanced. It is rather for us to be here dedicated to the great task remaining before us—that from these honored dead we take increased devotion to that cause for which they gave the last full measure of devotion—that we here highly resolve that these dead shall not have died in vain—that this nation, under God, shall have a new birth of freedom—and that government of the people, by the people, for the people, shall not perish from the earth."

What Lincoln said was that our United States of America and our hope of a government run by people would fail but for the bravery of soldiers on the battlefields. But, in that year the war was not yet over and the time for healing all the bitterness and hatred was indeed far off.

In the western arena of the war Union troops marching toward eastern Tennessee continued to gain ground, although at great cost. Finally Grant and his generals at Chattanooga were again able to deliver a crushing blow to the South. The Confederates retreated, their forces all but shattered.

---

1 Years later, Assistant Secretary of War, Thomas A. Scott, told Congress that he was directed to take the "plan presented by Miss Carroll in November, 1861, for a campaign upon the Tennessee River and thence South" to the Union armies in the West.

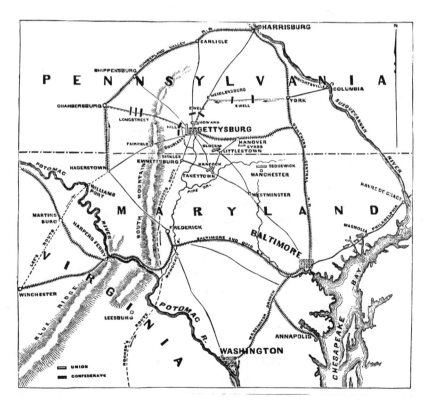

(Maryland Historical Society)

Position of the Confederate and Union forces, July 1st.

CHAPTER LVII

THE LAST YEARS OF THE CIVIL WAR, 1864 AND 1865

PRESIDENT Lincoln kept General George G. Meade in command of the Army of the Potomac but decided to bring General Grant east to be supreme commander of all Union armies. Some criticized Lincoln for promoting Grant, claiming that he drank heavily and was a rough, graceless man. Lincoln replied, "What brand does he drink? I'll give it to some of my other generals!" Whatever his personal habits, no one could deny that Grant won battles.

Grant left General William T. Sherman in charge in the West, with orders to drive from Chuckamongo-Chattanooga toward Atlanta, Georgia, where important rail lines met. For himself General Grant planned a steady, relentless drive with General Meade, from the Potomac valley southward toward Richmond, Virginia.

The South, hurt, weakened, shut off from the world by the ever stronger blockade, fought on desperately. Unwilling to quit, Southerners thought of the Confederacy as their beloved country, for which, if necessary, they would die.

Just how fierce the Southern troops were, General Grant found out early in May, 1864, after his Union troops had gone two days journey into a tangle of thicket and swamp called the "Wilderness," south of the Rappahannock River and west of Chancellorsville, Virginia. The Confederates attacked through the thick underbrush and the battle was terrifying. To add to its horror, fire broke out and raged through the dry brush, burning many of the wounded on both sides to death. Grim, tired Union forces counted 17,000 casualties by the end of that second terrible day.

Unlike other Union generals before him, however, Grant did not fall back to Washington to recover. He gathered his wagons and soldiers and moved out, not northward, but once more southward to chase the retreating Lee. After more fighting at Spotsylvania, Grant once again marched by the flank, around General Lee's force, ever deeper into Virginia.

A short time later, at Cold Harbor, close to Richmond he attacked and in ten minutes lost nearly 5,000 men; but, nothing appeared to shake him from his implacable determination to destroy Lee and the Confederacy. He seemed almost inhumanly able to take blow after blow from the desperate Confederates and still fight on. Finally he reached the James River and then moved toward Petersburg, where the Confederates had decided to stand fast in order to protect Richmond. The campaign had started in May and now it was the summertime. Meanwhile, in August, Mobile, Alabama, was taken by Admiral Farragut and General Sherman crossing the Chattahoochee River, the Confederate's last good line of defense protecting the city of Atlanta, Georgia attacked and took that Southern stronghold. Then began the famous "march to the sea" in the course of which Sherman burned and wrecked almost everything in his path. He also seized and destroyed guns, cannon and such horses and food as still remained in that part of the South. It had never been just a war between soldiers, but this time the people (civilians) were made to suffer even more terribly. By Christmas, Sherman was in Savannah, Georgia.

Petersburg and Richmond in Virginia, were finally about all that remained to the Confederacy. All through the winter, Richmond resisted. Grant tried in every way to take the city. He had his siege troops make a tunnel under Confederate lines around Petersburg and set a massive charge of powder to destroy every resistance. The plan was for Union soldiers then to pour through the opening made by the blast and attack. The explosion went off as planned, but before the attackers could move up, the Confederates closed the break and held on to their lines. While all this was going on, the Confederate, Jubal Early, invaded Maryland once again, fighting near Frederick and to the rear of Washington.

Maryland Engagements

The Battle of Monocacy Junction was fought in Maryland on July 9, 1864. General Early advanced to Frederick and then southward toward the capital city of Washington. Union troops at Monocacy Junction, a short distance south of Frederick, under General Lew Wallace attempted to stop Early. The Confederates won the battle, but the day's delay at Monacacy cost Early the chance of capturing Washington, because more Union troops were able to move in to protect the city.

Many small engagements were fought in Maryland. Raiding parties of considerable size sometimes captured towns and exacted money from the residents. Raiders also occasionally crossed Maryland on their way into Pennsylvania.

Harper's Ferry in Virginia, just across the Potomac from the Maryland side, was a valuable and popular prize which changed hands several times. Rails and canals in Maryland were attacked to disrupt troop and supply traffic all through the war. Canal waters were sometimes diverted for this same reason.

Prison Camps in Maryland

During the Civil War, Maryland was the site of two grim prisons for captured Confederate soldiers.

One such prison was Fort McHenry in Baltimore harbor, headquarters of the Union general in charge of troops occupying Maryland. Usually prisoners were kept here for a short time before being transferred to larger prisons elsewhere.

After the Battle of Gettysburg, in July 1863, over 6,500 prisoners were crammed into Fort McHenry. Generally, however, it housed about two hundred and fifty to three hundred and fifty prisoners. Living quarters were described as "filthy" and disgraceful for men to live in. Hospital quarters were a little better. Food was very plain and was not appetizing!

Camp Hoffman at Point Lookout in St. Mary's County, became a place of horror and death for thousands of men. Its history in the beginning, however, was not that kind, for Point Lookout had been the site of a summer resort before the Civil War. The United States government, in 1862, rented the land and buildings to be used as an army hospital. A building with an odd shape arose. Hallways radiated out from a central structure like spokes from a wheel. Patients arrived at the hospital, then named the Hammond General Hospital, in August of 1862. Only a few prisoners were held there until early the next year. After the Battle of Gettysburg, in July 1863, when the North captured a large number of prisoners, a prison camp was ordered built on Point Lookout. When ready for use, it was known as Camp Hoffman.

As the war went on, conditions at Camp Hoffman grew worse and worse. The men were cold, hungry, dirty, and disease-ridden. Blankets and clothing were frequently not given to them, even though sometimes relatives sent such items to the camp. The water was impure and added to the diseases of the camp. In the summer of 1864, an attempt was made to improve the disgraceful conditions. But little improvement was made and the guards continued to be very cruel. In the summertime swarms of mosquitoes and vermin added to the misery of the men.

It is only fair to mention that prison camps in the South were no better and that confinement in most prison camps, North or South, was a terrible ordeal and often led to great suffering and even death. However, since supplies and food were available to the North, there does seem to be less excuse for the dreadful conditions in Northern prisons.

For the most part, Point Lookout's Camp Hoffman was a prison for enlisted men, while captured Confederate officers were generally sent to Fort Delaware located on an island in the Delaware River.

At one time, in April, 1865, as the Civil War was ending, there were over 20,000 men crowded into the prison at Point Lookout. Mercifully, the war ended soon afterwards, and the men were paroled and allowed to go home. There is a marker at Point Lookout today on the spot where at least 3,400 prisoners died and where thousands of others suffered terrible hardships.

Maryland "In the Middle"

Maryland in the Civil War was in a most uncomfortable position. People of southern Maryland and the Eastern Shore, many of them slaveholders, and many Baltimore people as well, favored joining the Confederacy. But there were many, too, who favored the Union as we have seen.

The attitude of its citizens, plus the important geographical position of the state, being what it was, Union troops occupied Maryland throughout the war. This made sure that Maryland would not take an active part in the fighting. Even so, many men did manage to go south to join the Confederate forces. Spies and sympathizers moved through southern Maryland frequently during the war. The Northern authorities took severe and sometimes unjust measures to insure that no rebellion would succeed in the state. President Lincoln felt forced to suspend several of the Constitutional rights of the people in Maryland.

The Last Months

Finally hoping to draw Union troops away from Richmond, General Lee sent forces northward up the Shenandoah Valley, once more under the command of General Jubal A. Early. But, by now, the valley was too heavily held by the North and the Southern raiders were forced back.

1865

Early in 1865, Fort Fisher on the North Carolina coast fell to the Union fleet commanded by Admiral David Porter and in April of that year, Sherman's troops took Raleigh in that state. At last on April 26, General Johnson was compelled to surrender to Sherman.

The "War Between the States" was now about ended. In Virginia, Petersburg had eventually fallen and also Richmond. Lee at long last surrendered to Grant at Appomatox Court House, Virginia, on April 9, 1865. The South was shattered—its business wrecked; its plantations burned and deserted; railway lines torn up and the cities in shambles. Thousands of families mourned for soldiers who would never return home. Thousands more did come home, though often wounded and sick. Prisoners, too, were released. The treatment of these, by both sides had been disgraceful. They had been allowed to starve and suffer from cold and disease, in places filled with vermin and filth.

Black Americans, however, at last were free and the United States was no longer a divided country—at least in the political sense of the word. The Civil War had been a cruel and costly one for both the North and the South. Tired, dazed, citizens were grateful that the war was over.

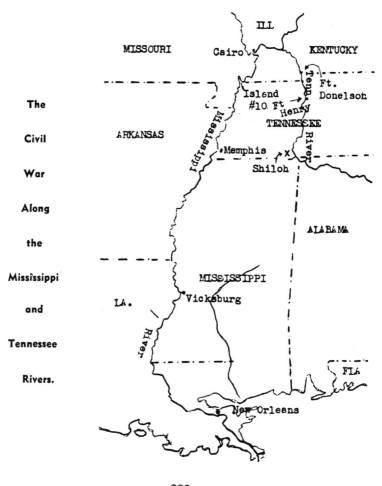

The Civil War Along the Mississippi and Tennessee Rivers.

CHAPTER LVIII

LINCOLN'S DREAM

PRESIDENT Abraham Lincoln felt a strange sense of fore-boding. This was strange, really, because for the past five days he had called on friends, chatted with visitors, and everywhere he went he had joined in celebrating the end of the Civil War. Lincoln could not explain his uneasiness. It was April 14, 1865. Perhaps he was just tired out from the long and anxious years of the war. Perhaps it was the reaction to his trip a few days earlier to Richmond, Virginia. Perhaps his mood came from the deep sorrow in his heart over the loss of his son Willie. He decided to lie down for a rest.

He dozed off and dreamed. In his dream he seemed to see himself in a coffin, lying in state in the White House. In another room, he dreamed, he could hear women wailing.

When Lincoln woke, the dream troubled him. He mentioned it to his wife, Mary Todd Lincoln. "Do we have to go to the theater tonight?" he asked her. Mrs. Lincoln then showed such obvious dis-appointment that he said, "Well mother, it's all right; we'll go." He wished that General Grant had been able to come to the theater with them. Instead, they were planning to go with young Major Henry R. Rathbone, an attache from the War Office and Major Rathbone's fiancee, Clara Harris. Still, a visit to the theater might cheer him up. And so, that evening Lincoln, his wife, and his two young guests, sat in the Presidential box in Ford's Theater on Tenth Street, N.W. in Washington.

John Wilkes Booth, a twenty-seven year old actor, had rehearsed this evening carefully, though he was not to be a member of the cast of the play "Our American Cousins," that was playing at Ford's Thea-ter that night. Booth was a handsome, young man. He had shining, dark hair, large dark eyes, and a drooping mustache. Now, just as Booth had planned, he sauntered into the theater where he was well known. He saw that the President's guard had left his place. The door opening into the small hall that led back to the President's box was not watched. Booth entered the hall and propped the door shut. Now he looked through a hole he had bored earlier that day in the door of the box. He wanted to see the location of the people there.

Booth waited now, a small pistol in his hand. He knew the play well. As soon as he heard a wave of laughter, he knew that only one person was on the stage. He stepped into the Presidential box, aimed his gun, and fired at the back of the President's head.

Major Rathbone leaped up; the women sat stunned and shrank back in their chairs. Booth dropped his gun and drew a dagger. Shouting the Latin words for "Thus ever to tyrants!" he stepped to the front of the box. Rathbone tried to seize him, but Booth slashed the officer's arm and leaped for the stage. Booth's spurred boot tangled in a hanging as he dropped to the stage. He landed hard, and his left leg broke with a stab of pain. The audience did not realize what was happening until Mrs. Lincoln cried out, "The President has been shot!"

Booth, half-limping, half-hopping, got across the stage and out the stage door entrance. He reached his waiting horse. He was so excited that he hardly noticed the pain in his broken leg as he galloped towards Maryland. He knew the state well and planned to make his escape down roads he had traveled before.

The young man riding down the dark Maryland roads was not a criminal. He was an actor and came from a family of fine actors. His brother, Edwin Thomas Booth, who was born in Maryland, was one of America's finest actors. John Wilkes Booth had been born on a farm in Harford County, Maryland, May 10, 1838. He had grown up in Maryland and attended school in his home state and in Pennsylvania. The Booth family had been known as an eccentric one, some of the Booths were rather strange, and some were addicted to alcohol, yet other Booths were quite responsible and talented persons.

All through the Civil War, Booth had very much sympathized with the Confederacy. He thought of the Confederacy as his country, although it is not too clear why he felt that way. He felt that Lincoln had ruined the Southern people, and indeed, he blamed Lincoln for bringing on the War. Booth felt that now he would be cheered, just as an actor is who gives a fine performance, everywhere in the South as a hero. Booth had long plotted against the President. At one time he and others had planned to kidnap Lincoln and hold him as a hostage to be exchanged for all the southerners taken prisoners by Northern troops.

Now that his plot had been successfully carried out, Booth felt easier for he was now in Maryland, but the pain in his leg was now very sharp. It was a piece of luck, he thought, to get across the Anacostia River bridge without being stopped by the soldiers there. His companion, a twenty-one-year old man, David E. Herold, also had negotiated the bridge safely.

Meanwhile, another intended assassin had been busy that night. Lewis Paine, a member of the group of plotters with Booth and Herold,

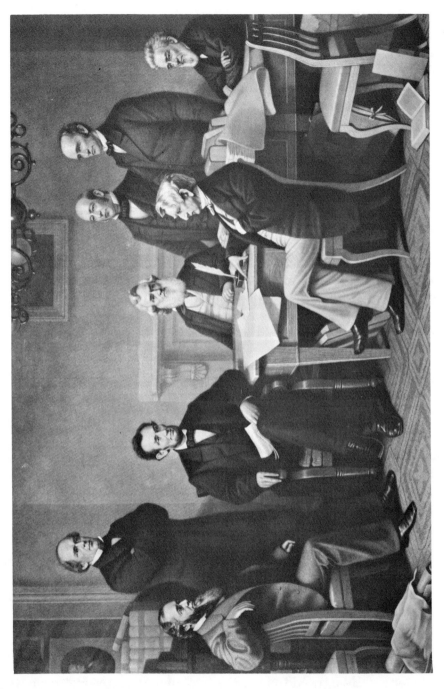

A painting by Francis B. Carpenter   Courtesy Library of Congress

The first reading of the Emancipation Proclamation before the Cabinet.

had entered the house of William E. Seward, Mr. Lincoln's Secretary of State. Seward was in bed recovering from a neck injury. He was stabbed but not killed. Paine was able to escape from the house. Another member of the group plotting the assassination was George A. Atzerodt, of Port Tobacco, Maryland. He might have been actually one of the assassins, too, but at the last moment rejected the idea and left Washington. Later, he with some of the other plotters would be captured and tried.

As the first thrill of excitement left him, Booth began more and more to suffer from his leg and riding added nothing to his comfort. He rode on toward the place where he was to meet Herold—Lloyd's Tavern in Surrattsville, Maryland, now known as Clinton. The conspirators had all planned to meet at the tavern, but only Booth and Herold turned up. They told Lloyd, who ran the tavern, about their "success." At the tavern Herold and Booth were able to obtain a rifle, and also some whiskey and other supplies, after which they rode on into the night. But Booth's pain, increased and it seemed that with every footfall of his horse the ends of the broken bone in his leg grated together. Finally he realized that he had to get to a doctor. He recalled that he had met a Dr. Samuel A. Mudd who lived somewhat beyond T. B., near Bryantown. It was very nearly on his way to go by the doctor's home.

Back in Washington, everything was confusion and at first little effort was made to follow the murderers. Booth, of course, had been recognized at the theater. Early on April 15, the President died. Since Stanton, the Secretary of War was slow in taking action, the Washington Chief of Police started men off after Booth. Soon police, citizens, and finally soldiers, were searching the roads leading out of the capital city. The President's body was brought to lie in state in the White House just as he had dreamed.

Very early on the same morning that Lincoln died, Booth and Herold reached Dr. Mudd's house. That afternoon, with his leg splinted and his mustache shaved off, Booth left the doctor's house. He took a pair of crutches with him. The two fugitives crossed part of a swamp and by midnight reached a friendly house near Bel Alton, Maryland, where presumably they were expected. They were now just a few miles from the Potomac River. The owner of the house was Samuel Cox, a rich plantation owner who sympathized with the Confederacy. He agreed to help the two men cross the Potomac River into Virginia but they must hide nearby until Friday, April 21.

Behind them, swarms of men were searching for clues to the whereabouts of the conspirators and huge rewards were now being offered for their capture. Some of the plotters who were known to have been associated with Booth were now in jail. Martial law had been proclaimed in Maryland and soldiers patrolled all of the roads, while gunboats searched the Potomac River. No more than three people at a time were permitted to travel together, and passes were required to travel. The government under the circumstances momentarily expected an uprising of southern sympathizers. Excitement was intense.

After Booth and Herold had lay hidden away for several days, on the first try at getting across the Potomac they were turned back when a Federal gunboat was sighted. The fugitives were wet, cold, and hungry after being hunted through the swamps like animals. Booth could not understand it. Here he, John Wilkes Booth had just killed the man who was to blame for the Civil War! Why should he be hunted like a beast of prey? Some days later, Sunday, April 23, Booth succeeded with his companion in getting across the Potomac. In Virginia, the two men rented horses and made their way to a Dr. George Steward, who had been mentioned to them by Dr. Mudd. They were fed, and Booth's leg was treated there, but then they were promptly sent on their way. They crossed the Rappahannock River near Port Royal in Virginia, April 24, and felt safer. They decided however to hide quietly at some farm home for a while until the excitement died down, and then they would go further south. They decided upon the farm of Richard Garrett, who lived about three miles south of Port Royal, Virginia. After several days Union troopers came on April 27 to this place. The troopers surrounded the barn in which Herold and Booth were hiding.

The barn was set afire to force the men out. Herold surrendered. Booth was killed, whether he was shot by his own hand or by that of a soldier, it is not known, though most historians believe that he committed suicide.

The companions in the plot were tried, eight in all. Four men, including Dr. Mudd were sent to prison. Mrs. Mary Surratt[1] who owned the Lloyd's Tavern in Maryland and managed a Washington boarding house where the plotters had met along with Atzerodt, Paine, and Herold were all hanged on July 7, 1865, for whatever parts they may have played in the assassination plot. Booth's body was finally brought to the Green Mount Cemetery in Baltimore in 1869.

Booth had died, still unable to understand why he was not immediately hailed as a hero. Actually, his violent reaction to the defeat of the Confederacy helped to set the clock backwards and pave the way for harsh treatment of his beloved Southland. In trying to help the South he had helped to kill more than the President of the United States. Gone as well were Lincoln's hopes for a peaceful reconstruc-

-tion of the Southern states. Lincoln had planned to return the Southern states to the Union of states with the least possible harshness.

Lincoln had planned, too, to help the freed Negroes to become educated and relocated on their own lands, if possible. His death meant the end of these plans for healing the wounds of the War, including fair treatment for the Negroes. Ahead for the Southland were many years of harsh treatment and suffering. Revengeful measures were adopted which resulted in the loss of political rights for years. In the South a reign of oppression was begun.

The state of Maryland was in the odd position of having remained a part of the Union, which meant furnishing men and materials to the support of the North, while at the same time many people in the southern counties sympathized with the Confederacy and tried to help it. Due to this leaning toward the South, Maryland shared in the years after the War, in much of the oppression dealt out to the defeated Confederate states! Maryland was ruled by the military throughout the War and it was, in fact, not until January 31, 1866 that the Federal military rule was finally withdrawn. Then only was civil government returned to Maryland.

In the midst of the War, the Maryland Constitution in 1864 was rewritten. It reflected only the feelings of the men then in power in Maryland, the Unionists. The Constitution called for a strong oath of loyalty to the United States by every State official. Men who would not take this oath, because they sympathized with the Southern states, could not hold office in Maryland. According to the *Baltimore Sun*, three-fourths of Maryland's voters were not allowed to vote, due to the strict and searching loyalty tests at election time in the years following the adoption of the Constitution of 1864.

This feature among several others made the Constitution of 1864 very unpopular with the people of Maryland and in 1867, as soon as Maryland had regained control of her own affairs, another Constitution of Maryland was drafted and then ratified. It is the Constitution under which Maryland is governed today, though it has, of course, been amended many times.

The unpopular Constitution of 1864 had good features such as the abolition of slavery in Maryland, for example. This clause was retained in the next Constitution. Also, the 1864 Constitution provided for a uniform state system of education in Maryland. It also gave the state a Lieutenant-Governor and brought back the office of Attorney General. Since the man holding the post of Lieutenant-Governor was not popular in 1867, that post was abolished in the Constitution of 1867. In the 1867 Constitution, the hated loyalty oath was softened. The writers reached back to the Constitution of 1776 for their Declaration of Rights. It was a conservative Constitution.

It was April 2, 1867 when President Andrew Johnson declared the rebellion officially over, and this was two years after General Lee's surrender at Appomattox. These years might have been quite different if John Wilkes Booth had not succeeded in murdering President Lincoln.

Yet, despite the battles, the bitterness, and the postwar injustices, this new Union of America somehow held together. Never again was our nation to be divided so violently. The effects of the Civil War and the Reconstruction period that followed, however, were to last many years after the guns were silenced.

---

1 Researchers now doubt that Mrs. Surratt was guilty of plotting the crimes.

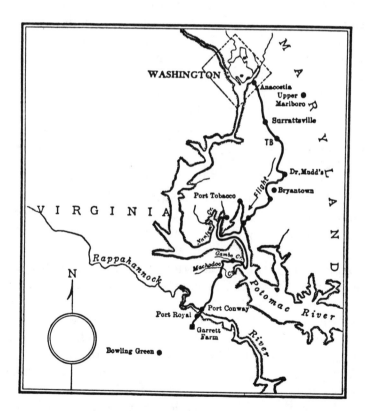

Booth's Escape Route

CHAPTER LIX

ANNA ELLA CARROLL

THOUGH disappointed in 1863 at not getting her plans accepted for a program for freed black people, Anna Ella Carroll worked on. She was having difficulty, just then, too, in getting money to live on. But Miss Carroll continued to write throughout the War for Lincoln. She wrote many statements, decisions, and prepared a number of pamphlets for him. Though everyone close to the President knew of her work and worth, she continued to be invisible as far as the public was concerned.

An artist, Francis B. Carpenter, of New York, came to the White House in Washington in 1864 to depict Lincoln and his cabinet members at the moment of the signing of the Emancipation Proclamation. Carpenter did a great deal of research work before he touched a brush to the canvas. He had Lincoln and his associates go over that historic moment many times. He planned the large canvas carefully so that everything in it would have a meaning.

In the picture he portrayed an empty chair with a folder of maps and notes, like that carried by Miss Carroll, leaning against a leg of the chair. Some feel that this was Carpenter's way of pointing to the fact that Miss Anna Ella Carroll of Maryland was "the great unrecognized member of the cabinet."

Though still not given public recognition for her war work, Anna Carroll in 1864 was given a good position in the Interior Department. About this time, too, she began to write for the *National Intelligencer*, a newspaper reporting national news, as well as news of Washington and of Congressional activities.

On April 10, 1865, as mentioned before, Lincoln returned to Washington from Virginia. The war had ended and now he could work for reunion. Lincoln wanted lenient steps to be taken so as to avoid further bitterness, and generally to lessen tensions promptly. Attending a play in Ford's Theatre on April 14, he was shot by the actor, John Wilkes Booth. The following morning Anna wrote in the *Intelligencer*, "As we go to press at five o'clock this morning, the President is still alive but is rapidly sinking."

After Lincoln's death, Anna left Washington to rest with her sister, Sally, in Pikesville, Maryland, where she was well known for a story that had preceded her there. It appears that Anna had seen a lady in tears on the steps of the Capitol building and learned that the woman's husband had been unjustly jailed as the result of a decision made by a court in a martial law case in Maryland. After listening to the story, Anna had told the woman, Mrs. Charles T. Cockley, a resident of Pikesville, to wait. Anna had re-entered the capitol building and shortly came back with a pardon from President Lincoln himself!

Anna Plans a History

Back again in Washington, later in 1865, Miss Carroll decided to continue writing for the *Intelligencer*. Some three years later she was sent on official duties to Texas by President Grant. She felt at this time that surely her work on the Tennessee River campaign would be formally recognized. She hoped, too, that a pension would be awarded her.

She was very busy in the years following Lincoln's death. She had decided to put her personal knowledge of the war years to good use by writing an accurate history of that period. She spent many hours on this project.

Romance

Anna, in 1870, met again the fine-looking Texan who had so long ago escorted her to St. Louis for President Lincoln. He was now Judge Lemuel D. Evans. He wanted very much to have Anna for his wife.

She was young-looking for her fifty-four years, still petite and trim of figure. Her manner was as gracious and gentle as always. Her auburn hair was beginning to be frosted with white. Though she was greatly attracted to Judge Evans, Anna was unable to tear herself away from the interesting life she had always led in Washington. Perhaps, too, she liked her solitary life. The Judge understood her feelings, at any rate, and remained devoted to her.

The years passed rapidly by until, in 1874 she lost her father; and three years later death took from her that steadfast friend, Judge Evans.

The Disappearing Papers

Anna was not one to give up easily. As a matter of principle, she continued to work to get recognition on the work she had done and to obtain money owed her by the government. At long last, in

1880, a bill (HR 7256) was written which was all that Anna could desire. The Military Committee of the House of Representatives of the United States heard General Bragg make a report. The Committee drew up a bill that said: "Be it enacted that the sum . . . given by the government to the major generals of the United States Army be paid to Anna Ella Carroll from November, 1861, the date of her service to the country, to the time of the passage of this act, and further payments of the same amount as the pay . . . of a major general in the United States Army be paid her in quarterly installments to the end of her life, as a partial measure of recognition of her services to the nation."

Anna felt very happy in the beautiful spring days that followed. President Garfield had just been inaugurated; and visitors and admirers came often to her rooms at Termont House in Washington. She was deeply involved in her final great work, her history of the Civil War. In her closet she kept the writing she had done so far, together with records, letters and notes on the war.

Yet, public reward was not to be hers after all. Gloom swept the city of Washington with the news that President Garfield had been shot to death, and only four months after he had become President! For Anna, too, gloom descended. Her Bill, H.R. 7256 was mysteriously removed from its place among the measures to receive Congressional approval. Another bill was put in its place which simply directed that her name be placed on the pension rolls by the Secretary of the Interior so that she might be paid $50 a month for life "for the important military service rendered the country by her during the late Civil War!"

Anna's friends, furious, descended upon the capitol building to corner members of the Military Affairs Committee. Anna, in her disappointment, became very ill. Her brother and sister came and took her away. Slowly she recovered. Her first words were, "My papers. Where is the trunk with the papers?" But the trunk and Anna's papers had disappeared, never to be found.

Anna's Last Years

For five years Anna was an invalid, trying to recover from her illness and her disappointments. It was 1886 before she recovered enough once again to begin to write. Her youngest sister, Mary, by that time had found work as a government clerk in Washington; and the two of them were able to set up a modest home at 973 New Hampshire Avenue, and later on 21st Street, N.W. There in Washington, Anna passed her last days in comfort, surrounded by affection.

Members of her family and friends called often. Newspaper editors and many men and women of prominence, came to relive with her some of her memories of Lincoln and of the Civil War. She was seventy-eight years of age when she died on February 19, 1893.[1]

The moon was full the night her sisters took her body by steamer across Chesapeake Bay to Maryland. At dawn, friends and neighbors from Eastern Shore homes met the steamer at Cambridge. From the dock, they went to the chapel of Old Trinity Church. There, as she had wished, Anna was buried. Near her grave is a monument marking the resting place of her father, the former Maryland governor, Thomas King Carroll. In the same quiet cemetery, there is a monument marking the grave of her brother, Doctor Thomas King Carroll.

Today, one may go to the restored Trinity Church, seven miles southwest of Cambridge, Maryland. In the churchyard will be found the markers of the Carroll family of Maryland. On each Memorial Day, a flag is placed on the grave of this great Maryland lady, who was without doubt one of Lincoln's most brilliant military advisers and talented writers. She is perhaps, one of Maryland's most remarkable women.[2]

---

1 Miss Carroll was born August 29, 1815, and died February 19, 1893.

2 The work of Miss Carroll remained all but unknown, in spite of a book on her life published in the late 1800's, until 1938. Her story and many documents were found by the writers, Sydney and Marjorie Greenbie, who wrote a definitive biography of Miss Carroll, **Anna Ella Carroll and Abraham Lincoln**.

Artist's sketch of Old Trinity Church near Cambridge, Md. In the churchyard the stone marking the last resting place of Anna Ella Carroll reads: "Maryland's Most Distinguished Lady — A great humanitarian and close friend of Abraham Lincoln. She conceived the successful Tennessee Campaign and guided the President on his Constitutional war powers."

The Smithsonian Institution

A two-wheeled vehicle sometimes used in 1900.

300

YOUR MARYLAND

SECTION VII

MODERN MARYLAND

CHAPTER LX

WHAT IS THE "BIG DIFFERENCE?"
(A Comparison of Maryland Before 1900 and Maryland Today)

THERE is one great difference between our life today and life before 1900. This one factor really impresses upon us that we have advanced, in a very short time, from a fairly simple way of life to one of considerable complexity.

Was it Lighting?

Is that big difference the fact that every child, woman, and man before 1900 lived a much darker life? Homes were lit by wax candles, lanterns, and lamps that burned oil. In houses built mostly of wood, there was constant danger of fire. Another danger was that one's clothing or hair could be easily ignited. Death from burns was not unusual.

At Dower House in Prince George's County, one lady of the house, carrying an oil lamp, stumbled on a stair, spilling oil over herself and setting herself afire. She died as a result of this accident.

But, no, it was not the lack of easy, brilliant lighting. People simply went to bed early if they could not afford to spend money on candles or oil.

Was it Heating?

Was the greatest difference between life before 1900 and now the difficulty in heating homes? When you think a moment you will realize that heating homes in winter was a great deal of work. Stoves were not very common until after 1900. They had to be constantly attended, had to be fed quantities of wood or coal, shaken occasionally, and cleaned of ashes. From hut to mansion, fireplaces were used for heat. The difficulty in heating with fireplaces is that, a burning fire needs air. Air enters the fireplace and escapes with smoke, and, unfortunately most of the heat goes up the chimney. So, a cozy fire tends to warm one's front and leave one's back chilly. There was always a chill draft feeding the fireplace, sweeping along the floor. This perhaps explains why highbacked chairs and settles, highbacked benches, were so popular in fireplace days.

302

People got around this to some extent, however, by dressing warmly in winter. Men wore heavy boots or hightopped shoes, long stockings, heavy trousers with vests, coats and cloaks added. For women, warm petticoats, layer upon layer, topped by a woolen or linen gown that swept the floor, helped keep away the chill. So, you see, people were not as carefree as we are today about heat in wintertime. Still, with a good deal of wood chopping, fuel carrying, fire tending, and planning one could manage to keep warm.

Was it Diet?

Was the biggest difference between our ways of life the food? Food preparation was a lot of work in 1900. Food came into the house from the market, from the plantation, or from one's own kitchen garden in a rather rough state. Kitchen gardens were quite popular even in town. It was nice to be able to pick corn, beans, carrots or peas and pop them in a pot. Since quick-frozen products were not available in 1900, each vegetable, fruit or berry could only be enjoyed when it came into season.

When vegetables came into the kitchen, they had to be washed, and there was a great deal of peeling to be done. Meat, eggs, and milk had to be bought almost daily in the summertime. Even in spring houses or cool pantry rooms, without refrigeration most food could not be kept very long. Only after the first World War were there very many iceboxes.

Bread, cakes, pies, and other baked foods were made right at home. Often, too, in the kitchen there was a churn for making butter; and, outside, many a home had a pasture lot with a cow mooing there. Every morning and night she had to be milked, the milk strained for dust, hairs, and other odds and ends, and then set into a spring house or a cellar to keep cool. Cream that was not used while sweet was allowed to sour and was churned into butter or heated and made into cottage cheese. Up in Maryland's piedmont area German housewives made tasty cheeses and baked wonderful flaky things to eat.

Almost every household preserved foods for later use by drying and curing. People stored such produce as potatoes, apples, carrots and cabbage in "root cellars" where temperatures were steady.

There was certainly a big difference in methods of cooking and storing food but that was probably not the most important difference as compared with our lives today.

Was it Sanitation?

Life was quite different before 1900 in that even in the icy winter one had no cozy, heated bathroom. In most homes a trip out to the back of the yard was necessary. Or, perhaps one used a tastefully decorated china pot which must be emptied later. Not a fragrant subject so we won't dwell on it, but still, a true fact of daily life.

Was it bathing then? That, too, was quite different then. Basins, with a pitcher of water, were kept in bedrooms. Hot water could be brought from the kitchen. Tubs could be brought up and placed before a bedroom fire. By 1900 inside bathrooms complete with tubs were more common. Yet, in most Maryland homes Saturday night really was "bath night" with a tub of water near the kitchen stove serving the family.

Laundry, including all of the clothing, sheets, towels, and everything else, had to be washed by hand. And, there was not a vacuum, a dishwasher, an automatic clothes dryer, or a floor waxer to help the housewife. Though, perhaps she had a maiden aunt who would help, or a maid, or a hired girl.

For all this inconvenience and hard work, however, keeping clean probably was not the "big difference."

Was it Education?

Schooling, until 1900, was really rather rare. Only the few could at first afford to educate their children past the elementary school stage. But, almost every parent hoped for more education for his children.

Churches often did a great deal to educate children. The Jesuits were famed for their teaching, and there were some small Jesuit schools in colonial Maryland. There were special schools sponsored by Protestant churches as well. Reading, writing, arithmetic, and Latin were taught. Most girls were taught at home. There were a few private schools and academies for boys of white families. Black people were seldom able to attend school.

The groundwork for a system of education in Maryland was supposed to have begun even before the first settlers arrived! Edward Palmer in the 1620's planned to "erect an academy." This generous Englishman purchased an island in the Susquehanna River for that purpose. The island is called Garrett Island today but was known then as Palmer's Island. It is located where the Baltimore and Ohio Railroad bridge crosses the river. Here, Palmer wanted to build his little college and have it ready when the first settlers should arrive.

Unfortunately the people he sent to put his plans into action were not faithful to his trust in them and were either unwilling or unable to build the school.

In October, 1694, the Maryland Assembly passed an "Act for the encouragement of Learning." Matthew Page Andrews in his *History of Maryland: Province and State,* mentions this fact, noting that surprisingly few people signed by "making their mark" and suggesting that this proves that elementary education must have been available in the colony. He also tells us that though Governor Francis Nicholson did encourage the beginnings of a college in Annapolis, the school, which was then called King William's School, did not actually open until 1701 after Nicholson's departure. This school later was to become St. Johns College. King William's School was the third school of its type to be opened in England's American colonies.

Education for black people was frowned upon. Some church groups, however, held classes so that they might learn to read religious books. A few schools were opened in Baltimore in the early 1800s to educate black students but these reached few people.

By 1900 many Maryland people might get some education but even elementary education was hard to find. There is much more opportunity for education today! As early as 1864, however, Maryland legislators had been giving education serious thought. That year the members of the state legislature, pressured by the national government, set up a statewide school system and a state board of education. At this time the Civil War was in progress and the system did not prove to be very effective. In 1864 there was less than one high school to each county.

Experience was to show that a state-administered school system, once Federal pressure was removed, did not meet with the approval of citizens. So, after 1867, control of local schools was handed back to county school boards. In 1870, the State Board of Education was reestablished to provide county school boards with assistance, advice and certain standards.

It was necessary in the 1800's and early 1900's to give children long summer vacations so that they might help with farm chores and crops. There were fields to be planted, berries to be picked, and livestock to be cared for. Youngsters who lived near Chesapeake Bay also helped with oystering, crabbing, and fishing. So, education had to be carried on in the winter months.

These conditions afford a big contrast to those in education today. Yet, education is probably not the chief difference between those days and ours.

Were Politics So Different?

Looking back we can see some significant developments in politics about 1900. Black men had the right to vote but did not normally use it. The Irish and other new immigrants had the right to vote, but, again were sometimes prevented from doing so. Sometimes force was used to keep them from the polls. During the last half of the 1800's, there was much discrimination against certain people by reason of race, nationality, or religion.

There was, for example, the "Know Nothing Party." This in the 1850's was a sort of dictatorship right here in Maryland. The Party, using terror, force and tricks controlled votes, offices and thus also, the government. Despite present day faults in politics, it is unlikely anyone would like to return to those "good old days!" Yet, despite the people who used votes and power for their own reasons, there were still many honest and dedicated Maryland men in public office, seeking to build a decent and just social order. Of historical interest in those old days were the political torchlight parades and speeches, street fights and free flowing beer at election time.

Even so, it was not the political life of that day that made the big difference for most, in a Maryland citizen's daily life.

Was it Communications and Travel?

A very big change in our lives since 1900 has been the increase in the speed of communication and travel. In 1900 the fastest way to travel and carry mail was by railroad. There were a few hand-operated telegraphs. To places with no telegraph line or railroad, news, mail and people had to move by road or waterway at perhaps five miles per hour. There was no radio, telephone nor television.

The Big Difference

A most important difference, it seems to this writer, was in life itself. At the beginning of the twentieth century, for example, the average life span was only about forty-six to forty-eight years. Today the average life span is much greater, about 76 years.

The Maryland death rate in 1900 per 1,000 population was 14.7 (the U.S. rate was then 17.2).

The Maryland death rate in 1990 per 1,000 population was 6.8 (the U.S. rate was 8.7).

The life expectancy for males in the U.S. in 1900 was 46.3 years.

The life expectancy for females in the U.S. in 1900 was 48.3 years.

As of 1990 the life expectancy for males in the U.S. was 71.1.

As of 1990 the life expectancy for females in the U.S. was 79.

(Statistics from Tables 82, 83, 105, 106 and 107, *Statistical Abstract of the United States, 1991.*)

In earlier days Maryland babies by the thousands did not survive their first year of life. Mothers also often died in childbirth. Physical dangers were many. One might be kicked by a horse, drown, fall under the wheels of carriages, suffer fatal burns or gunshot wounds or cuts from sharp tools such as axes.

Sicknesses were more likely, too, to be fatal. Baltimore, for example, had many epidemics. In 1819-1820, thousands died of yellow fever, and there were other epidemics of various kinds that swept the city from time to time.

Illnesses were many and often mysterious because of lack of medical knowledge to deal with them. There were only a few herbal remedies and brews for use to protect one from various ailments; and there were few good doctors who could correctly diagnose problems of health. Few schools of medicine for training doctors existed in Maryland or elsewhere and all of these had many shortcomings, indeed.

Baltimore, A Medical Center

Yet the fact remains that Baltimore has long been a leader in medical training, treatment, and research.

An interesting sidelight in Maryland medicine is the fact that John Archer of Harford County, Maryland, was awarded the first medical diploma in America in 1768. The great Medical School and Hospital founded in 1876 by Johns Hopkins, a wealthy banker and merchant is a case in point, too. Hopkins gave money to begin the school, where students might be taught and where they might gain experience in a hospital. Today the Johns Hopkins Hospital and Medical School at Broadway and East Monument Streets is famed the world over, as is the University on North Charles Street, which also bears his name.

Significant, too, was the establishment in Baltimore even earlier (1807) of the University of Maryland's College of Medicine. This College later produced also a school of dentistry (the oldest school of dentistry in America, founded 1840), as well as a school of pharmacy, established in the 1870s. The present University of Maryland including the non-medical colleges on the College Park campus and at Catonsville, grew from these Baltimore beginnings.

Development of medical knowledge and instruments has been very recent. For example, it was 1819 before even a very simple form of stethoscope was invented. It was not until May 1, 1801, that James Smith began the practice of vaccination in Baltimore.

Before 1830, diagnosis of diseases depended mostly upon listening to a patient's account of his symptoms, looking at his tongue, and the inspection and thumping of the outside of the body.

There were no clinical thermometers until those, almost a foot long, were made. These clumsy instruments required a full five minutes to register a patient's temperature. Pocket sized thermometers were perfected by 1868.

Though Leeuwenhoek saw bacilli in 1683, it was 1840 before the germ theory of communicable diseases was clearly stated. It took the Frenchman, Louis Pasteur and the German, Robert Koch, to really begin our modern bacteriology with their work done in the last half of the 1800's. Other brilliant "microbe hunting" doctors were to bring their knowledge of bacteria to the United States in 1878-79.

From then on, a burst of medical progress followed. More was learned of the body. More information was learned about germs, bacteria, viruses and the antibiotics that could be used to control them. There were more studies made, more records kept, and more pictures drawn. Instruments were improved and much progress began to be made in the 1900's in medicines. Laboratory work improved, too.

In 1895, Roentgen had discovered X-Rays and their use in photographing the inside of the body from the outside! This helped doctors spot foreign objects, fractured bones, and diseased organs. Later, X-Rays were found useful in fighting diseases. There were martyrs to X-Ray however, for the radiation danger of this new medical discovery was at first unknown.

The first hypodermic syringes made their appearance in 1853. Medical education now began to undergo a change to keep pace with the new instruments and discoveries.

It was October, 1846 when in Massachusetts, anesthesia was first used in the United States. Surgery was at that time a "last resort" since so many patients died after surgery from shock and from sepsis (infections). Very, very slowly, antiseptics began to be accepted. Doctors scoffed to think that infections were caused by organisms too small to be seen. Joseph Lister, an English surgeon, in 1867, published a new paper on "Antiseptic Principles During

Surgery," which was received with raised eyebrows! Lister used carbolic acid to mist the operating field and to cleanse his hands and the instruments. Cleanliness gradually began to be appreciated and the instruments, the surgeon's hands and the patient himself were then kept as clean and free of germs as possible during surgery.

In 1881, again Lister led the way to fewer deaths in hospital wards, with his paper on preventing the deadly fever that so often followed childbirth.

Soon, there followed the modern art of dentistry; and later, psychiatry, to treat mental illnesses and to promote mental health. It was found that insanity was often the result of infection by syphillis, high fevers of long duration, or oxygen starvation of babies at birth. Continued use of alcohol in any form, whiskies, wines, brandies, and rum accounted for many cases of insanity.

It was discovered that some of the mentally troubled could be helped to overcome their fears, to exercise self discipline, and so avoid an unhappy life and thus return to a busy, useful life instead.

City engineering played an important part in public health. For example, after the year 1914, when the sewage system in Baltimore was completed, fatalities began to drop dramatically.

Yes, a big difference was health, length of life. We have medical and health mysteries to solve today but in this century much progress has been made. All of the other things, light, heat, food, clothing, education, communication, transportation and politics are of less importance to a population than having more years of life to live. Years in which we can contribute to our community and find happiness.

Not everyone will see longer life and medical advances (or any one item) as *the* most important change in the lives of Maryland citizens. Certainly there is room for debate when we compare everyday life in colonial days or in 1900—to everyday life today.

CHAPTER LXI

TOBACCO GROWING IN MARYLAND

WHEN the first European settlers came to America, they found that the Indians had a custom of smoking the leaves of an American plant. The plant was called "tobacco" because of the Y-shaped pipe (*tabaco*) in which it was sometimes smoked. Pipes were made of clay, wood, or of soft stone. One fork of the pipe was inserted in one nostril and the other fork into the other nostril! Tobacco has the botanical name *nicotiana*, after J. Nicot, who introduced tobacco into France. It belongs to the nightshade family of flowering plants, as does the petunia, potato, pepper, eggplant, and tomato.

Sir Walter Raleigh is said to have promoted smoking in England. King James I reacted to his first knowledge of tobacco by saying that it was "loathsome to the eye, hateful to the nose, harmful to the brain, . . . and dangerous to the lungs."

The Indians believed that tobacco had certain uses in religious ceremonies, in promoting good health, and in "sealing" promises made between tribes. In religious ceremonies or in negotiations between Indian groups a pipe of tobacco was gravely smoked by the Indian men. When tribes made agreements, the leaders would sit together to "smoke the pipe of peace," indicating an end to war or a future of good will. During some ceremonies the pipe was used, together with prayers, to ask for good luck and good crops.

The use of tobacco soon spread throughout South America and Europe and even to the Far East. Two centuries ago most fashionable English gentlemen carried with them a snuffbox containing dried tobacco which had been ground to a powder. This they daintily placed in each nostril and apparently enjoyed inhaling it, despite the great sneeze that always followed!

The soil and climate of Maryland proved to be well suited to growing tobacco. With tobacco very much in demand in Europe, it became a profitable crop. It could be raised in little space, so the first settlers found that less time was needed to clear away trees in order to grow tobacco than to grow many other crops. Also, tobacco kept well and could be shipped in a fairly small space. Best of all, to the colonist's mind, in England it brought money to pay for the many manufactured items that were needed back in Maryland. Because there was so little manufacturing here, most of such items had to be brought from Europe.

By 1775, three-quarters of all Chesapeake Bay shipping was made up of tobacco. As early as 1639, England was importing 1,500,000 pounds of tobacco a year from her colonies — chiefly from Maryland and Virginia.

As Good As Gold

Coins were scarce in the new American colonies. A system of trading one thing for another (barter) was used a great deal. Tobacco was well suited to this method of exchange. It became as good as gold and was used to pay for goods and to pay for services. Tobacco was an accepted form of "money" in the colonial period.

Tobacco was extensively grown in southern Maryland. Great fields of tobacco there made the owners prosperous, and they were soon able to afford many goods from England, and even luxuries.

Problems Arise

Since writers like to dwell on the glamorous life of great plantations, it is a little hard to realize that, in Maryland, small farms were more numerous than large ones. The small farm was the most common of all types of land ownership. Both the large and the small farms benefitted financially from tobacco growing. It was, and still is, the popular Maryland "money crop."

Naturally growers rushed into the production of as much of the valuable "golden leaf" as they could. This in time caused the price of tobacco to fall. Growers sometimes found themselves with tobacco crops unsold at the end of the season and found that they owed their "factors" (business agents) a great deal of money. Growers often ordered goods through their factors, planning to pay them off when the tobacco was sold.

Also, Maryland farmers discovered, tobacco quickly exhausted the soil. Growers found that they must plant the tobacco in new fields every year or so. Later, they learned to rotate crops in a four-field system, but even so it was hard to maintain tobacco production without the use of fresh land every so often. Today tobacco growers know very well just what "cover crops" and what fertilizers must be used to replace chemicals taken from the soil by tobacco. They can grow tobacco year after year in the same fields. Still, with all its problems, tobacco growing in the colonial era was probably the easiest way for people in southern Maryland to make money.

Kinds of Tobacco

Virginia tobacco growers found that they could import tobacco seed from South America and raise tobacco of better quality and size than that raised by the Indians of Virginia and Maryland. One kind of tobacco grown was "Orinoco." The original seed came from near the Orinoco River in South America. The flavor of the Orinoco tobacco was strong. It came to be extensively grown in Maryland. Other types of tobacco were also developed.

Today, Burley tobacco is the most widely grown single type in the United States. Another type, often grown in Maryland is called "Maryland," and it is in great demand by leading American tobacco companies.

Tobacco Transport

From Maryland roads one can see old mansions which many years ago were important on the tobacco plantations. On the waterways of Maryland even more can be seen. Plantations, preferably, were built on waterways because tobacco was shipped to market in good condition by water, while that brought from farther inland was often crushed or torn on the way to the shipping wharf. Naturally markets in England paid more for tobacco in good condition. The plantations built near the water had wharves which accommodated oceangoing ships. Thus, the tobacco was rolled right aboard the vessels in barrels without damage to the valuable leaf.

Less conveniently located planters had to pack their tobacco into giant barrels called hogsheads, slide an axle through the center, and roll the great casks down to the wharf of the nearest plantation owner, or to a port town. To pull the casks along, oxen, mules, and men were used. West of Baltimore today, there is a road still called Rolling Road, which in the 1700's was used as a pathway along which tobacco casks were rolled to the wharf on the water front.

Tobacco Farming Methods

While machines have replaced men and mules to a considerable degree in tobacco growing, yet tobacco is planted and raised in much the same way as in colonial times.

The tiny tobacco seed is planted in March or April in protected beds. From an aircraft, for example, in the early springtime in Maryland, you can see here and there in many sheltered locations the white-covered squares of tobacco beds. The bed is made up of a wooden frame with a white, lightweight cloth tacked across its top. The frame of the bed is only three or four inches high and it protects the tender seedlings from frost or too much sun until they are big enough to be transplanted.

In June the young plants are ready to be set out in the fields. The plants are carefully set, usually by hand, about three feet apart, in small hills of earth. The best time for transplanting is after a rain when the soil is damp and soft.

Now the tobacco farmer keeps the soil loosened, kills off weeds and watches for insects or fungi that might affect his crop. As the plant begins to flower, or just before it does, the farmer "tops" the plant by cutting off the top. This insures that what remains will become a better quality of tobacco. Later, side shoots or "suckers" are removed to improve the leaves for sale.

Three or four months after transplanting, the crop is harvested. It is allowed to wilt in the fields for a very short time after cutting and is then gathered up and hung in barns to dry or "cure." The curing process takes from four to eight weeks depending on weather conditions and on the kind of tobacco being dried.

Now the leaf is dry and brittle, and it will crumble easily. But it must be sorted and packaged into what are called "hands." This step is necessary before the sale of the tobacco. The tobacco farmer waits for damp, warm weather. He allows the leaves thus to absorb moisture and become pliable enough to be handled. Such weather is called "tobacco season."

All of this work and more is necessary in growing tobacco profitably. Tobacco growers say that their year has a thirteenth month called "Tobaccuary," which is made up of all the extra hours they have to work. It does take about four hundred man hours to grow an acre of tobacco, compared with perhaps only eight man hours needed to tend an acre of wheat.

Tobacco is still one of Maryland's chief staple crops, one on which many families depend for a livelihood. The tobacco auctions at Upper Marlboro, at Waldorf and at Hughesville are nationally famous. Most Maryland tobacco is grown in the five southernmost counties on the Western Shore of the state.

Smoking and Health

In 1959 the Public Health Service of the United States examined the evidence linking smoking and certain serious illnesses. Its findings were made known to the public. The studies showed that there was a definite connection between smoking and lung cancer.

Later, studies of hundreds of thousands of people have shown that not only is smoking a cause of lung cancer, but that it shortens the smoker's life and can be blamed for much heart disease, emphysema, and bronchitis! The golden leaf of which Maryland has been so proud has been found to be very harmful to the smoker's health.

Studies indicate that all regular smokers suffer some ill effects to their health. Statistics reveal that smoking is not a gamble. The more one smokes, the shorter one's life, and the more one is apt to have lung cancer and other cancers of the respiratory (breathing) areas. However, a smoker may improve his health and lengthen his life by stopping smoking and allowing his body to repair the damage.

Studies show that young people begin smoking because it is a symbol of adulthood. But by 1970 the trend among persons in their teens to smoke showed a decrease in the habit. It may be that modern young people are recognizing the damage to their health, caused by cigarette smoking. The damage is linked to the amount of smoke inhaled. For this reason, most cigar and pipe smokers usually suffer less damage than cigarette smokers.

If the tobacco habit is bad for one's health why do people continue to grow tobacco for manufacture of cigars, pipe tobacco, and cigarettes? For one thing, the campaign against the tobacco habit is recent. Also, the crop is still a profitable one. Possibly, too, growers and tobacco manufacturers do not yet believe the evidence against smoking.

At any rate, a distinguished health expert, Dr. E. C. Hammond of the National Cancer Institute, in Monograph 19, published January, 1966, "Smoking in Relation to the Death Rates of One Million Men and Women," gives the following table. From over 400,000 men, Dr. Hammond selected 36,975 "matched pairs" of men. The pairs of men were alike in background and habits, except for the fact that one member of each pair smoked a pack or more of cigarettes daily, while the other member had never smoked regularly.

The results over a three year period is summarized as follows:

Age Group	Never Smoked Regularly		Cigarettes Over 20 a day	
	Number of Men	Number of Deaths	Number of Men	Number of Deaths
40-44	3,410	15	3,410	40
45-49	10,468	59	10,468	192
50-54	9,583	123	9,583	252
55-59	6,534	135	6,534	323
60-64	3,990	150	3,990	254
65-69	2,083	98	2,083	193
70-74	747	64	747	98
75-79	160	18	160	33
Total	36,975	662	36,975	1,385

CHAPTER LXII

MARYLAND'S BLACK CITIZENS

WITH the Civil War raging, on September 22, 1862, President Abraham Lincoln issued the famous Emancipation Proclamation. This was just after the costly Union "victory" at Antietam. Effective January 1, 1863, Lincoln's proclamation, as we have noted, freed all people enslaved in the states rebelling against the government of the United States. Oddly, the proclamation did not free people in bondage in Maryland, because it was not one of the states which had seceded. Not until November 1, 1864, was slavery actually ended in Maryland with adoption of the State's new constitution. This Constitution of 1864 in addition to prohibiting slavery, said that persons supporting the Confederacy were to lose the right to vote and to hold public office.

Two years later, the Fourteenth Amendment to the Constitution of the United States (Civil Rights Act of 1866) gave freed men the rights of citizenship. The amendment states that no state should deprive any person of life, liberty or property without the due process of law. The next amendment to the Constitution (Fifteenth Amendment) gave black men the right to vote. This was reflected by Maryland law in 1870 when black men were given the right to vote. Interestingly enough, up until 1810 in Maryland, free black men had had the vote.

In a recent study of black people in Maryland politics, research showed that since black men regained the vote in 1870, they usually voted with the Republican party and helped keep the two-party system in our state.[1] In the years covered by the Callcott study (1870-1912) it was found that few black people were elected to public office in Maryland. Today there are many Maryland people of African ancestry in public office.

In other Southern states, black voters were prevented from using their vote by both legal and illegal methods. In Maryland, however, open terrorist tactics were not as popular as in the "deep South." There were some illegal activities but frankly secret groups such as the Klu Klux Klan seem not to have been widespread in Maryland. There was prejudice to be sure, but at least the appearance of legality was maintained.

In modern times, still another important ruling was to affect Americans of African descent in Maryland and across the United States.

It was the Supreme Court ruling made May 17, 1954, that the segregation of races was illegal in the United States.

After the Civil War

After the Civil War people in the United States who had been held in bondage were suddenly faced with the problem of earning a living. Most had not the land, tools, money or training to do this. They were faced, too, with the problem of earning a place in a society that was often hostile to them and one which was unwilling to give them their full rights of citizenship.

Black people, who had so long been denied education, immediately began to seek schooling. People sympathetic to their hopes sent teachers and money into the southern states . Schools and colleges were started. There was by no means equality of opportunity as yet, but black leaders came forward to help with educational projects. Funds and volunteers were gathered by sympathetic white citizens.

Toward the end of the nineteenth century and in the early twentieth century, however, laws were passed in many states that forced white and black people to live, work, study, travel and play separately. It was the practice of segregation. This condition continued down to the 1950s.

Black Men in American Military Service

During the American Revolution a number of black men accepted the British offer of freedom in exchange for service against the rebelling American colonists. The war offered them the possibility of freedom should the British win. On the other hand, the American Continental Army, at first did not want black men to enlist on the theory that they would not be able to become disciplined soldiers. Gradually this attitude changed and in January 1776, General George Washington agreed to accept free black men into the Continental Army. By 1778 the Second Maryland Brigade, for example, had sixty men of African descent in its ranks. In 1780 a Maryland law was an admission that black men made good soldiers, for it made free black men liable to being drafted into the State militia. It also allowed for the recruitment of black men still in bondage with the consent of the slaveholder.

317

During the Civil War, black men served on both sides of the conflict. In the South black men helped build defenses, raised food and provided much useful labor. As Union forces entered the South a large number of black men flocked to the Union commanders and offered their services in return for their freedom. There were varying policies concerning black volunteers. Yet, many black men were helped to freedom in this way. They, in turn, helped Union forces with their work. In the later stages of the war, black men served in Union services as soldiers and sailors.

Before the end of the Civil War, commanders on numerous occasions commended their black servicemen for their courage and ability.

Both World War I and World War II saw black men serving their country with courage and honor in the armed forces. As women were accepted into the military services, they too worked together as Americans in an integrated military. Again, in the Korean War the black American soldier, sailor and airman performed bravely along with his comrades of other races. Young Americans of many racial backgrounds served in Vietnam, fighting side by side.

Prominent Maryland Men and Women

A most distinguished Marylander was Frederick Douglass. He was born into slavery in Talbot County, Maryland, in 1817. He was descended of both black and white ancestry. As a child he was starved and ill-treated by a slavewoman, "Aunt Katy." This treatment was allowed by his master. He once saw an overseer shoot and kill a black man when the man plunged into a creek to escape a whipping. For Douglass, injustice and cruelty darkened many of his boyhood days. He grew tall and strong and, at the age of sixteen, he objected to a whipping. He was sent to Baltimore and hired out by his master there to work on the Baltimore docks. He turned most of his wages over to his master. He longed to learn to read and while he was in Baltimore he did manage to do so. He treasured the one ragged book on oratory (public speaking) that he owned. At the age of twenty-one he escaped to the North.

In the North he improved his education and rapidly grew to be a famous speaker, author, and later on, a newspaper editor. His work was directed toward the improvement of the life of black people and, of course he worked for the abolition of slavery. All his life, in fact, he worked for the freedom of black people but he steadfastly refused to advise the use of violence to bring this about.

This remarkable man, in time became a United States Marshall; and he served for a time as the United States' Minister to Haiti. Also, in another period, he served as Recorder of Deeds in the District of Columbia. He made his home, during his last years, on an estate called Cedar Hill in Washington. Many people came to him there for advice and help. He died in 1895.

The story of Benjamin Banneker (1731-1806) has been given earlier in this work. He became, you may remember, a well-known almanac author, a surveyor, an inventor, and an astronomer. Also, in a later chapter the life of yet another important Marylander will be presented, that of the adventures of Matthew Henson, the Arctic explorer (1866-1955). Another prominent black Marylander was Frances E. W. Harper (1825-1911). She was a lecturer and a member of the powerful Women's Christian Temperance Union movement. Still another well-known representative of the black Marylander, was James W. C. Pennington (1809-1870), who was born a slave on the Eastern Shore of Maryland, and who, after his escape to freedom became an outstanding preacher, and author.

In some respects the most remarkable of these black leaders and the subject of several books was Harriet Tubman (1815-1913). She had escaped from an Eastern Shore plantation when she was twenty-five years of age. She determined to help others escape, too. It is said that she led over three hundred people to freedom. So effective was this Maryland woman that a reward was offered for her capture! During the Civil War she lived further adventures as a nurse and a secret Union agent. Afterwards she helped many black people to obtain schooling and was always ready to extend a helping hand. One of the last things she did before she died was to found a home for the aged. Harriet Tubman spent her lifetime doing remarkable work.

Another able spokesman for freedom was Josiah Henson (1789-1883), who was born a slave in Charles County, Maryland. In 1828 he became a preacher and was an outstanding worker and supervisor on the plantation where he lived. Like many black people, he had become convinced that to be successful he must give loyal and diligent service to his owner. At last, however, he realized that slavery was not a duty, nor an obligation to be endured permanently. He crossed into Canada in 1830. Eventually he was to tell his story to the famous writer, Harriet Beecher Stowe. Henson is thought by many to have been the character called "Uncle Tom," in her novel, *Uncle Tom's Cabin*, published in 1853. This book was widely read and did a great deal to stir up public opinion against the practice of slavery in the United States. Henson preached, lectured, and wrote for many years.

He came to be known and loved as Father Josiah Henson. He published autobiographical books in 1849, 1858, and 1879.

No story of Maryland history would be complete without mention of a nationally-known family called Murphy. A most important project was begun on August 13, 1892, when a four-page sheet was printed by the Reverend William M. Alexander, pastor of the Sharon Baptist Church in Baltimore. He operated the little paper, which he called the *Afro-American*, in order to advertise his church and community enterprises. Reverend Alexander was "a better pastor than publisher,"[2] so he sold the paper to a Mr. John H. Murphy, Sr.

John Murphy was a man who earned his living by painting interiors. In that day people used a kind of paint called "whitewash" on their walls to make the rooms bright and clean. Murphy was the superintendent of the St. John AME Sunday School. He had been printing a small paper in his cellar to aid Maryland Sunday schools. With $200 borrowed from his wife Martha, he began to build what was to become a great newspaper chain!

He soon merged the original paper with another small paper; and, slowly, the *Afro-American* grew. At the age of fifty-two, Murphy decided to turn entirely to newspaper work and for twenty-five years he devoted himself to this work. When he died at the age of eighty-two in 1922, he left a successful publishing business to his sons, George, John, Daniel, Carl, and David.

It was Carl Murphy who became President of the Afro-American Company. This was the company that was to publish the *Afro-American* in Baltimore, Washington, Richmond, Newark, and Philadelphia. The Murphy family has had a great influence in the state of Maryland and in the nation. Generation after generation they excel in church and community activities, and in their publishing businesses.

Today the publisher of the *Afro-American* is John J. Oliver, Jr. The newspaper employs over 190 persons. In Baltimore the *Afro-American* owns its own buildings and printing plant. It is located at the intersection of Druid Hill Avenue and North Eutaw Street. It has a circulation of over 150,000 copies. Each copy of each issue carries the words of Frederick Douglass: "We are Americans and as Americans we would speak to America."

Finally, in our mention of some of the well-known Maryland men and women, we come to the story of Thurgood Marshall. He was born in Baltimore, on July 2, 1908. After years of study, experience in law and politics, he rose to become Associate Justice of the United

States Supreme Court in 1968. He was formerly the Solicitor General of the United States. After over twenty years of service, Justice Marshall retired in 1991.

The Future

It was not until after World War II that black Americans began to receive their full legal rights and opportunities. Rapid progress has been made. Patiently, persistently, Americans of African descent have worked for equality in education, employment and in living conditions.

Census figures in 1990 reveal that over 12% of the total population of the United States are black people. In Maryland census data indicates that about 25% of the total population of the state is of African descent. Census figures show, too, that like other Americans, black people are leaving rural areas and are moving into cities.

Even though Maryland has come through a period of change, the state in general has enjoyed a peaceful desegregation of the races. There has been some conflict in the state. From July through September in 1967 there was unrest, destruction of property and other violence in Cambridge, Maryland. In the following year, during March and April, violence occurred in Baltimore City. This outbreak lasted less than a week.

The actions of some crowds are not always tied to causes. At times young people expend their energy in response to mob psychology. It is interesting that so often riots occur in the spring.

There have been other minor incidents but Marylanders in general have been able to make the changes without violence that are right and necessary. There are now increased opportunities for African-Americans in the work place, in housing and in education. Today Maryland citizens work, play and learn together.

Other immigrants to America faced oppression and discrimination. Chinese, imported to work on the giant railroad-building projects of the 1800s in California, suffered many injustices. The Irish, who migrated to eastern port cities of the United States, were often denied jobs, cheated and taunted for being Irish. Italians, too, faced much discrimination. They came in great numbers to many cities of the northeastern United States, including Baltimore.

The "image" of the black American has changed greatly since World War II. In Maryland, as in many other states, there is a large black economic middle class and an impressive black economic upper class.

Unfortunately, and unfairly, the news media focus on urban events which may involve minorities. These might be drug trafficking, violence and murders involving black citizens. This is quite misleading and does a great deal of damage to the image of African-Americans.

For generations now, Marylanders of African descent have owned land, have entered the professions of law, the ministry, medicine and university teaching. Political office is now another option for black men and women. Certainly Maryland businesses, schools, hospitals, manufacturing and transportation benefit from skilled African-American employees. Today in Maryland we see young people studying and working together to build a better state and a better nation for all citizens.

---

1 *The Negro in Maryland Politics, 1870-1912*, by Margaret Law Callcott, Johns Hopkins Press, Baltimore, MD, 1969.

2 *Good News for You!* Afro-American Company, Baltimore, MD, 1969.

CHAPTER LXIII

RELIGION IN MARYLAND
A Comparison of Maryland Religions

CHURCHES in Maryland and around the world share certain ideas. These concepts are belief in a God, a supreme being. Church books and leaders advocate that their church members be good people who are honest, brave, truthful and who help people in need.

At churches and temples there are people to offer advice, to help people in need. Most religious organizations support orphanages, hospitals and homes for the aged. Many churches send teachers and medical workers to other lands. The purpose of most churches is to encourage and educate their congregations and to reach out to the community.

This remarkable fact of life is often ignored but it is very real. Religions have had a great deal to do with shaping our history. Since churches are so important in history this chapter will sketch in a very general way the religions in Maryland.

One of the oldest religions represented in our state today is that of Judaism. People who share this religion are known as Jews. The history of the Jewish people and their religion goes back over 4,000 years! It originated with a nomadic group of people known as Hebrews who lived in areas along the eastern end of the Mediterranean. It is the parent religion to most Maryland churches, for in our state many of our citizens belong to Judaic or Christian congregations. The Hebrew language is used in Jewish books and early documents.

The Jewish people believe in one deity and have a strict code of behavior. They refer to their places of worship and study as temples or synagogues. Generally Jewish congregations reserve Saturday as their day of rest, study and worship. The basic holy books of the religion are what is essentially the Old Testament of the Bible and the *Talmud*.

Christianity as a religion began almost 2000 years ago and is based on the teachings of Jesus. The holy book of the Christian churches is the *Holy Bible*, which is made up of the Old Testament and the New Testament. Christians share many beliefs and ideas in common with the parent religion, Judaism, but they vary on a number of points, too.

The Catholic Church used to be the only Christian church. In the year 1054 A.D., there was a split and the first Christian church found itself divided into the Roman Catholic Church and the Orthodox Church.[1] The Roman Catholic Church is the one that most Maryland Catholics attend. This church is headed by the Pope in Rome, Italy. The Christian churches, except for the Seventh Day Adventist Church and a few other denominations, have chosen to use Sunday for their day of rest and worship.

In the sixteenth century there was a move to resist the authority of the Roman Catholic Church — a movement known as the Reformation. Martin Luther was one of the first men to voice openly this protest against the authority of Rome. New Christian groups, like Luther's own Lutheran congregation, formed. These came to be called Protestant churches. Protestants, to be sure, share many beliefs of the parent church, the Roman Catholic Church. Members of Protestant churches, too, believe in Jesus and his teachings, and regard the *Holy Bible* as their basic religious book.

One of the Protestant religious groups that found a home in Maryland was the Society of Friends, whose members are often called Quakers. It is a religious group which advocates peace and whose members like very plain religious meetings without trained priests or clergymen.

The Presbyterian church, popular in Maryland, is a Christian church favoring a more elaborate program of worship services. Teachings are based on Biblical doctrines. It is a conservative church. The Protestant Episcopal Church and its ritual has much in common with the Roman Catholic Church. It was formerly the Anglican Church or Church of England, the official "established" church of England.

Puritans were yet another group who came to colonial Maryland. Puritanism was a very strict religious organization. Its members were intolerant of other religious groups. Puritanism, as such, died away in Maryland.

The Baptist Church is popular in Maryland. It got its name from the practice of baptizing new members by total immersion in water. Methodist churches, also popular in our state, had early beginnings in Maryland.

The Lutheran Church arrived in Maryland with German-speaking people. Another Protestant denomination, the Moravian Church, too, came here with German immigrants who settled in the Piedmont section of Maryland. Amish church members, sometimes called "Mennonites" left Switzerland and Germany for America. The Old Order Amish is the main church body. These are peaceable, religious, agricultural people who believe in a plain life. They avoid luxury and even many conveniences. There are groups of Amish in Maryland and other states.

As you can see, the differences in the Protestant churches are mostly in their rules for their members, the church service rituals and in their varying ways of admitting new people to membership. All, however, have many concepts in common.

Early Maryland Churches and Ministers

Much has been written about members of the Roman Catholic Church who helped to settle Maryland. It is important to understand their contribution to the history of our state. We must not, however, forget the contribution of other religious groups who also did well here. About 40% of all Maryland citizens today are members of Christian churches, including the Catholic church. Around 5% of Marylanders are affiliated with the Judaic temples. The remainder belong to other religious groups, such as the Moslem faith, adherents to Buddhism, or to no specific church at all.[2]

Possibly the very first minister in Maryland was one representing the Church of England, the Reverend Richard James, who joined Captain William Claiborne on Kent Island in 1633. Captain Claiborne, you will remember, was the Virginian who had a trading post on the island as early as 1631.

When colonists sent by Lord Baltimore settled at St. Mary's City in 1634, members of both the Roman Catholic Church and those of the Protestant faith set up places of worship. You will remember that with the *Ark* and the *Dove* were two Jesuit priests, Fathers Andrew White and John Altham. By 1638 there were five Jesuits in Maryland.

In 1648 and 1649 Puritans from Virginia came to Maryland, with Lord Baltimore's permission, and settled on the Severn River near the present site of Annapolis. Puritans were those people who, in the time of Queen Elizabeth I and the first two Stuart rulers of England, opposed the traditional religious forms and wanted simpler church services and customs. As Puritans had done when they gained control of the government in England, in Maryland they also enforced their own kind of toleration—and were most intolerant of Catholicism! They forced Catholics to abandon public religious services and they also denied Catholics many religious, educational, and political rights. If Catholic parents were able to afford the expense, sons of these families were sometimes sent abroad to be educated.

It is not quite certain when the first Quakers arrived in Maryland, but they were active here by the late 1650's. As early as 1661 "meetings" of the Society of Friends were being organized in Maryland. One of the English founders of the denomination, George Fox, visited Maryland in 1672 and began the "Maryland Yearly Meeting." This was the second such "meeting" set up in America. William Penn, himself a member of the Society of Friends, visited with a congregation on the shores of the Choptank River in December, 1682.

One may still see the Third Haven Meeting House, near Easton, Maryland, on the Eastern Shore. It was constructed in the years 1682-1684 and is said to be the oldest surviving wooden church in the United States.

Wenlock Christison, a pioneer advocate of religious freedom, lived in Talbot County. The story of his experiences in Massachusetts and his coming to Maryland reveals the religious intolerance of that time. He had been persecuted for his beliefs in England, and then, later on, in New England. There, in the 1650's, the Society of Friends were not allowed their own worship. Wenlock Christison was given twenty-seven "cruel stripes" on his bare body for speaking out for his Quaker beliefs.

Christison was turned out of prison at Plymouth, Massachusetts. It was midwinter, and he shivered in his thin clothing as he made his way to Boston. But there he found no haven either. He was told that he must leave and that if he returned he would be executed for being a Quaker. Stubbornly he returned and stubbornly he refused to change his religious principles. He was brought to trial for this before the Governor of Massachusetts and said ". . . I refuse not to die!" The judges and the Governor, though they did not execute him, were determined to humiliate him. He was tied to a cart and made to walk behind it with two other Quakers and was "whipped through three towns."

Christison eventually came to Maryland. Here he was given land for a plantation in Talbot County by Dr. Peter Sharp, a Calvert County physician. In Maryland he became quite active in politics and finally had found a place where he was to be able to live in peace. Christison died in 1679.

Presbyterians

The Reverend Francis Makemie came to the lower Eastern Shore of Maryland in 1683. He founded the first Presbyterian congregations in America.³ These first church groups were located at Rehoboth, Snow Hill and at the (now) Pocomoke City. In all a total of five congregations were formed by Reverend Makemie and included others at Wicomico and Princess Anne. At Rehoboth, Maryland, one may see a square brick church on the banks of the Pocomoke River. It is said to be the first Presbyterian Church built in America.

Among the Presbyterians, children sat with their parents in church and took part in the services. The sermons were very long and were made to seem even longer because the early churches were unheated in winter. It was not until the early nineteenth century, around 1820, that the idea of having a Sunday School for young people was developed in Maryland. The idea appears to have been first used that year, at the Falling Waters Presbyterian Church, originally founded in Virginia in 1745. This congregation is presently located near Spring Mills in Maryland. The minister's mother put the idea into practice.

Though a Reverend Hugh Conn worked in the North Point area of Baltimore County in 1715, it was not until 1761 that a Presbyterian congregation was organized in Baltimore by Scotch and Irish merchants of that city.

The Presbyterian Church showed new patterns for that time. Henry H. Garnet, who was born in 1815 into slavery on the Eastern Shore of Maryland in Kent County, was brought north when his entire family managed to escape. His study and work resulted in 1842, in his being ordained to the Presbyterian ministry. He was much later appointed as the United States Minister to Liberia in the 1880's. Unfortunately he died there shortly after his arrival.

Old Trinity Church

A beautiful Maryland church and one of the first Protestant churches built in the Province is Old Trinity. It is located not far from Cambridge, on Church Creek in Dorchester County. It is considered to be one of the three oldest church buildings in the United States, which is still in its original form and used regularly. It was built before 1690, although the exact date is not known. The church records were destroyed by fire. Missing from the original equipment of Old Trinity, too, is a very old Bible and a communion set sent to Maryland by Queen Anne of England. The Queen's chalice, however, still remains.

The work of restoring the church was begun in 1953. It was then crumbling away, as might be expected, because of its great age. The efforts and generosity of the Old Trinity Association, and that of

Shown here is the Chapel of the University of Maryland, College Park Campus.

Colonel and Mrs. Edgar W. Garbisch, carried the work through to completion in 1960.

In the churchyard of Old Trinity are the graves of Maryland's former Governor, Thomas King Carroll, as well as those of his son, Maryland's "beloved physician," Dr. Thomas King Carroll; and of his daughter, Anna Ella Carroll. Here also are the graves of several officers who served in the American Revolution.

The Roman Catholic Church

The Lord Proprietary gave orders strictly forbidding religious arguments aboard the *Ark* and the *Dove*, as the colonists came out to Maryland. After the settlement was begun at St. Mary's City there was unusual religious toleration during the first years.

By the early 1700's, things had changed. There was still toleration in Maryland for members of some Protestant churches, but members of the Roman Catholic Church were unfairly treated in many ways. Catholic priests were forbidden to hold public worship and were not supposed to baptise children into the Catholic faith! All members of the Roman Catholic Church by 1740 were required to pay double taxes; and Catholics were largely prevented by law from holding public office and from voting, thanks to a 1718 ruling. Now a part of this oppression was due to the Protestants' dislike of Catholicism itself, or "Popery" as they called it; and part was due to the fact that Catholics were thought to favor the Stuart family of English royalty, which by that time had been driven from the throne.

Because of this treatment, Catholic priests and church members avoided public worship. They "went underground" — attending services held privately in homes or in other convenient, non-public places. As late as 1800 it is estimated that there were less than 3,000 Catholics and only a half-dozen Jesuit priests in Maryland.

Early Catholic Churches

The Jesuits had a brick chapel on their land at their headquarters on St. Thomas Manor, and at St. Inigoes Manor, in St. Mary's County. Little chapels of worship were set up in the homes of the wealthier Catholics. The more wealth a Catholic might have, the finer chapel he could build. There was, for example, an elaborate and lovely chapel built earlier in 1636, at St. Mary's City. This is today possibly the oldest Catholic church site in all of the thirteen original colonies, as well as the oldest in the country in continuous possession by the

Jesuits. When, in 1704, Catholics were forbidden to worship publicly, "St. Maries" was closed and its bricks removed to other Jesuit property. In 1785 land for a new church was selected and the present church was completed in 1788. This Catholic shrine has one of our nation's oldest cemetaries beside it. The men of the nearby Patuxent Naval Air Test Center, together with residents of St. Mary's County, have been working since 1950 to restore the church.

Maryland has a rich Catholic religious heritage. The first American bishop of the Roman Catholic Church was the Right Reverend John Carroll of Maryland. He was consecrated Bishop in 1790, with a diocese that then included the entire United States!

Bishop Carroll invited priests to come to Baltimore in order to plan the first English-speaking seminary—a school for training candidates for the priesthood. In 1808 the cornerstone was laid for what became St. Mary's Chapel on Paca Street in Baltimore. Hidden away and scarcely known to the public, this little chapel is a gem of early architecture and is still used by priests and seminarians.

Just outside the walls of St. Mary's Chapel, Mother Seton's "Sisters of Charity" order was founded. There her first school for children was started. She later moved her school to Emmittsburg, Maryland, where she was made the Mother Superior of her order of nuns. This order is known today as the "Daughters of Charity in the United States." Mother Seton was beatified by the Pope of the Roman Catholic Church in 1963.

The oldest convent in America is located near La Plata and Port Tobacco, in Charles County. It is called Mount Carmel and was established in 1790. Carmelite nuns came first to Chandler's Hope, a large home near Port Tobacco, but on October 15 of that year they moved to the nearby Mount Carmel location. The order was begun by three Charles County women of the Matthews family who were members of the Carmelite order, and by a fourth nun, an Englishwoman. The Americans had gone to Belgium originally to take orders as nuns and had then returned to their native America.

These four nuns stayed at Mount Carmel for forty-one years and then at the invitation of Bishop Carroll they moved in 1831, to Baltimore. The Mount Carmel convent and chapel are being restored by a group formed in 1935—called the Restorers of Mount Carmel. Seven acres of land have been purchased surrounding the restored convent buildings for the purpose of creating this historic shrine honoring the first order of nuns in the United States.

The Catholic Church has long had black communicants and in 1836 a chapel was built by the Oblate Sisters in Baltimore for the purpose of serving black church members. A mission was set up in Baltimore in 1857 and later, in 1864, a church was built in that city to serve a predominantly black congregation. Today there are numerous Catholic churches in Maryland which have a largely black membership. Most Catholic churches have an important percentage of black members. Also, several black priests have been ordained in Maryland and a number are at work in the various Catholic parishes of the state. In recent years, older separations of the races have been removed and the trend is for persons of all races to be welcome. Catholic schools have long been open to all children of Catholic persuasion, regardless of racial background.

There are so many beautiful churches in Maryland that the state might easily be known as the land of great churches and of great church history. In fact, there is material for several books just on the denominations and churches of Maryland alone. Mention, of course, should include the first Roman Catholic cathedral in the United States, begun in 1806 in Baltimore. Bishop John Carroll himself laid the cornerstone, at a time when about half of all Roman Catholic Church members in the United States lived in Maryland. Maryland is still a state which is a leader in that church's activities in our nation.

Bishop Carroll was a great and very active churchman, for he helped found the religious order called the Sisters of Charity; and he was a prime mover in founding Georgetown University, in 1791, which was located then in Maryland, but is now in the District of Columbia. Bishop Carroll, who in 1808 became the first Archbishop of Baltimore, died in 1815. He is buried in the cathedral that he helped to build— the Cathedral of the Assumption of the Blessed Virgin Mary, in Baltimore City.

Moravian Churches

A spring of fresh, cold water was the reason for locating a church near Graceham, Maryland. The spring allowed church-goers to quench their thirst and provided water for their horses, too. Graceham Moravian Church was begun by Jacob Weller not long after he arrived in Maryland, about 1742. On the same site occupied by today's church, the first Moravian church in Maryland was built in 1749.

The first Moravians to come to America settled in Pennsylvania about 1741. They were of German background and they believed in living lives of goodness and simplicity. They brought with them "brass choirs." In 1752 trombones were added to the other brass instruments in these choirs. It is an unusual and very vigorous kind of church music. It can be heard today at the mother church in Bethlehem, Pennsylvania, and on occasion, at Graceham Moravian Church in Maryland.

The Protestant Episcopal Church
(Formerly the Church of England)

An Anglican clergyman, the Reverend William Wilkinson came to the Province of Maryland, probably in the year 1658. He preached to a congregation which was to become the St. George's Poplar Grove Parish in St. Mary's County. This gives that Anglican church a good claim to being the oldest in Maryland[4] for it was founded shortly after the founding of Lord Baltimore's colony.[5] Earlier a Protestant group had built a chapel in the county, but it was not at first served by a minister. Thomas Gerard, a Catholic, in 1642 was found guilty and fined 500 pounds of tobacco, for taking the key and books of a Protestant chapel located on his land. This tobacco money was ordered to be set aside to help support the first Protestant minister who should come to Maryland.

Under the Royal government of Maryland an act was passed in the Assembly in 1692 to establish the Church of England, sometimes called the Anglican Church, as the official religion of the colony. Thirty parishes were laid out. A tax to support this church was placed on everyone regardless of his religion.

It was in this same year that St. Anne's Church in Annapolis was founded. King William III of England presented communion silver to St. Anne's, and it is still there in use today. When one visits Annapolis he will see the present church structure, built on the site of the original St. Anne's. This building is made of red brick of a warm, rosy shade and is gracefully proportioned. To the left of the entrance there is a marble slab whose faded carving reads: "Here lieth interred the body of Mr. Amos Garrett, merchant, chosen first Mayor of Annapolis . . . Born 1671 in Southwark, London, England. Died in Annapolis on the 8th of March 1727 at the age of 56."

The Reverend Thomas Bray, Commissary of the Church of England, in 1699 collected books to form parish libraries and to start a central Anglican library in Annapolis. He came to Maryland to help in the development of the young parishes in the province.

The Anglican Church was disestablished, that is, it was declared to be no longer the official church of Maryland under the provisions of the first State Constitution of Maryland in December, 1776. This left the former Church of England parishes in a sort of legal vacuum. So the property and operation of the church were made the responsibility of eight men from each parish. The Vestry Act of 1779 set up certain legal procedures for what had formerly been the official church. It provided for giving to the members of the former State Church the church property; and the management of the church was placed in the hands of an elected group of persons, the "vestry." The members of the vestry were to be elected each Easter Sunday by the church members.

A new name for the former Church of England in America was decided upon at a conference held in 1783 in Chestertown, Maryland. The church would now be the Protestant Episcopal Church. The Reverend Thomas John Claggett of Maryland was chosed to be the first bishop of the newly reorganized church. He was consecrated in 1792.

In Cecil County, Maryland, Bishop Stone ordained the first black person to be a Deacon in the Episcopal Church, not only in Maryland but in the entire South (in June 1834). The man was William Douglass. The Bishop praised Douglass for the sermon he gave to black church members that afternoon when the St. Stephen's Parish Church was given over to them for their services. Later, on February 14, 1836, Douglass became a priest of the Episcopal Church. In the years that followed he wrote a book of sermons and a church history. For twenty-seven years he worked as the minister of St. Thomas (African) Church in Philadelphia. He was born in Baltimore in 1805 and died May 22, 1862.

Another prominent Marylander, the Reverend Doctor George F. Bragg was to serve that same Philadelphia church for fifty years. Reverend Bragg wrote a book titled *Men of Maryland*, published in 1914.

Baptists

In a walnut and oak grove on Chestnut Ridge in Howard County is the first Baptist church built in Maryland. After meeting for a time at the home of Henry Sater, the congregation with Sater's aid built a brick church on land Sater had donated in 1742. The church is called, not surprisingly, "Sater's Baptist Church." The deed to the congregation states that the land was donated for a meeting house and burying ground, ". . . .forever to the end of the world." The Baptist Church was a popular one in the state and its membership grew.

In 1835 the Reverend Moses Clayton, a black minister, came to Baltimore to found a Baptist Church in that city. It was February, 1836 that he organized what was to be the First Baptist Church. The growth of that church continued, particularly under the direction of Reverend Harvey Johnson in the 1870s.

The Lutheran Church

As early as 1729 some of the German settlers coming to Maryland from Pennsylvania were members of the Lutheran and Reformed churches. These people were Germans only in the sense that all of them spoke the German language. At that time there was no united Germany as we know it today. Both of these German denominations at first used a single church building near Creagerstown, Maryland. Later the Reformed Church congregation moved to Frederick and that city has become a center of Reformed Church activity.

In Baltimore the first Lutheran Reformed Church congregation worshipped as early as 1756 in the "town clock church." Dr. Wiesenthal, an early Maryland leader in medicine and anatomical research, was prominently identified with Baltimore's Lutheran beginnings.

The Methodist Church

Today some of the Methodist churches in Maryland are reviving the practice, on occasion, of holding services at the edge of Chesapeake Bay with a minister speaking from a boat to the people on the shore. This practice began with the early preaching of Robert Strawbridge who, about 1760, preached some sermons in this way in the Annapolis area. The first Methodist place of worship in Maryland is where the Reverend Strawbridge preached in a small log chapel on Sam's Creek in Carroll County.

Organized Methodism in America dates from the year 1771, when Reverend Francis Asbury began his work in the United States. In Baltimore he succeeded in getting a meeting house built in the year 1773. Construction of the Lovely Lane Meeting House was started in 1774. Baltimore has always been an important center of Methodism. In the large Lovely Lane church in Baltimore, there is a section devoted to the historic papers and objects relating to the history of Methodism in America. Lovely Lane Museum is located on St. Paul Street and is open to the public.

So many Marylanders came to support the Methodist Church, that our state was often referred to as the "Garden of Methodism."

One of the early Methodist workers on the Eastern Shore was Joshua Thomas. He came to be called the "Parson of the Islands." He was born in Somerset County in 1776 and grew up in poverty on the islands of the lower Chesapeake Bay. While visiting a camp meeting of Methodists in 1807 the young fisherman became converted to Methodism and was soon a Methodist "exhorter." In 1814 he became a local preacher. It was in this year that he accurately predicted that the British fleet attacking Baltimore would be defeated. Parson Thomas died in 1853 after many years of preaching. He is buried beside the Deal Island Methodist Episcopal Church, located in the lower Bay area.

Methodism appealed to Europeans and Africans. Several prominent Methodist preachers in Maryland were black men. A first society of black Methodists was organized about 1797 and was served by a black minister, Daniel Coker. Born in Frederick County in the latter part of the eighteenth century, he was one of those ministers ordained by Bishop Asbury. He worked in Baltimore and helped in the organization of the Sharp Street Methodist Church (1802) and operated a very famous church school, which was often called "Dan Coker's School." He was a leader, too, in the Philadelphia convention which resulted in the organization of the African Methodist Episcopal Church in 1816. He was elected to be its first bishop but decided to decline that post. Reverend Coker left America in 1820 for Liberia and later went to Sierra Leone where he built a church and raised his family.

When the American Revolution split American churches away from their home church headquarters in Europe, there followed a time of confusion. The leaders of the Methodist Church, in 1784, in a Christmas conference in Baltimore, gathered at the Lovely Lane **Meeting House. There the separate churches were merged into one national body, known as the Methodist Episcopal Church.**

During the Civil War the Methodist church again found itself divided. The churches split on a North and South basis and it was to be many years before they began to draw together again. In 1939 all were reunited under the original name, the Methodist Church. This church was to merge with another denomination in the late 1960's to become the United Methodist Church.

An unusual Methodist church is the one called the Stone Chapel, located just off Reisterstown Road in Baltimore County. It is of Greek Doric design and was completed in 1862. Its congregation first met in the home of Joshua Owings. Then a first stone chapel was built on ground bought in 1785. It is said that the son of Joshua Owings was the first native American to be ordained a Methodist minister in the United States.

Lloyd Street Synagogue

Cathedral of Mary our Queen

Church of the Redeemer

(Maryland Dept. of Economic Development)

Hebrew Congregations

There were apparently few Jewish people in Maryland in colonial times. However, there is seldom to be found any record of actual persecution of this religious group. Laws in Maryland did definitely favor members of the Christian religions. Jews who were members of the Hebrew congregations were prohibited from voting or holding public office in Maryland until 1825.

The Baltimore Hebrew Congregation was chartered in 1829, and in 1838 the Fells Point Hebrew Friendship Congregation was started. Today almost every Maryland community of any size has a Hebrew temple, and many of the leaders of our state are of Hebrew family background.

Religion in Maryland Today

There have been mentioned here only some of the larger denominations in Maryland. There are many other religious groups with very interesting histories. Our state is rich in unique places of worship.

Two sects that have emerged with Maryland connections and that have won national attention are those of George Baker and G. M. Grace. George Baker was known as the head of a popular church and was nationally known as Father Divine. G. M. Grace was called Bishop Grace, or Father Grace, and headed missions of his religious group in various parts of the country. Both of these religious organizations were most active in the 1940's.

A great deal has been written about historic church buildings, yet surviving more strongly than the buildings are the congregations themselves. People hand down their faith, their hopes, their ideals, and their responsibilities to the generations following them. In religious life as in our secular lives, we today learn from past events and in turn hand our hopes and beliefs down to succeeding generations.

---

1 The Holy Orthodox Catholic Apostolic Eastern Church is another title of the Orthodox Church.

2 *Statistical Abstract of the United States, 1991,* Table 76 and 80.

3 These were the first regularly constituted Presbyterian congregations. There is some evidence of still earlier Presbyterian activity in Charles County between 1658 and 1662.

4 **Maryland Historical Magazine,** XXI, No. 1, March 1926.

5 The student must keep in mind the fact that an Anglican minister, the Reverend Richard James was at the Kent Island post with William Claiborne prior to the time of Lord Baltimore's St. Mary's City settlement; and it is thought that he was the first Anglican to preach in Maryland.

Recommended reading:
Maryland Historical Magazine, Volume XXI, No. 1, March 1926, the article by Bernard C. Steiner, "Maryland's Religious History."

CHAPTER LXIV

MATTHEW HENSON AT THE NORTH POLE

APRIL 6 is set aside in Maryland as the official Matthew Henson Day. But who was Matthew Henson and what happened on April 6th? This is our story in this chapter. It is a tale of action, danger and adventure.

Henson, an African-American, was born on his father's farm in Charles County, Maryland, August 8, 1866. The Henson family was threatened by an illegal band of terrorists called the Klu Klux Klan, and were forced to sell their farm and move away. Matt was quite small when they made the move from Charles County to Washington, D. C. Matt grew up there in the Georgetown section. His mother died while he was very little, and his father entrusted him to the care of an uncle. By the time he had completed the sixth grade in school, however, he was homeless and had to go to work in a small restaurant in order to eat. He stayed there for just a short time, sleeping on the floor at night. Then Matt decided that he would seek work and adventure on the sea. He walked all the way to Baltimore and began to stay around the waterfront. Until the mid-1800's many ships were propelled by sails. In Baltimore Matt found a place as a cabin boy on a sailing ship.

The captain of the ship liked Matt, taught him mathematics and navigation and let Matt read books in the captain's cabin. Matt soon learned all of the skills of the sailor, too. He learned how to climb into the rigging and to operate the lines that operated the huge sails. He learned how to do the many things necessary to help keep the ship seaworthy. It was a hard life, but one in which Matt took justifiable pride.

Matthew Henson became an able seaman while still in his teens. He sailed for five years aboard the *Katie Hines* and saw many exotic world ports. In 1885, following the death of the captain of the ship, to whom the youngster was devoted, he left the *Katie Hines* and decided reluctantly to seek work ashore. He was now a master mechanic and a good carpenter, and he hoped to find steady employment.

Unfortunately for Matt, finding a good job was not easy. He even went to Buffalo, New York, and worked there as a night watchman. Later on he tried several other jobs, but found none very interesting or rewarding. Finally he came back to Washington, D. C. and became a helper in a store which sold men's hats and furs. Here he met a young Navy lieutenant, Robert E. Peary. Peary asked Henson to go with him to Nicaragua in Central America, as his valet. Matt liked the idea of adventure overseas. So, in November, 1887, they left New York.

The purpose of the Nicaraguan expedition was to finish surveying a mid-American canal route. The proposed canal was to extend from the Atlantic to the Pacific through Nicaragua, to allow ships to sail from ocean to ocean without going all the way around South America first. This was, of course, long before the building of the Panama Canal. Once there and at work, Henson was soon asked to leave his duties as valet and become a member of the survey crew. Again, the work was not easy, but it was important and interesting, and Henson liked that. In the summer of 1888, Peary and Henson were back in the United States. Henson renewed his search for an interesting job. Peary asked Henson to keep in touch with him.

A year or so went by and then Peary contacted Henson. Peary wanted Henson to go with him on an exploring expedition to the icy waters and highlands of Greenland. This was the Peary expedition of 1891-1892. Again, in the years 1893-1895 Henson was asked to go with Peary on other Greenland expeditions. Though called Peary's manservant, actually Henson was an invaluable and loyal aide. Henson mastered the art of driving a team of dogs hitched to a sled. Sleds pulled by dog teams provided the best means of transportation over the ice and snow in Arctic regions. The Eskimoes in the region thought of Henson as one of themselves because of his dark skin. He had an unusual talent for making friends with the Eskimo people and he learned to speak their language well. He learned from them how to make igloos of ice and snow as well as ways of building and repairing the dog sleds. He was devoted to Peary and became expert in the techniques of exploration of Arctic areas. Always, when Peary asked for volunteers for difficult tasks, Henson stepped forward. In the art of staying alive and traveling in the Arctic, Henson excelled. Peary explored Greenland for several years, learning for one thing that it was an island and not part of an Arctic mainland. In the ten years between 1892 and 1902, Peary made many trips into the Arctic, aspiring now to be the first man to reach the North Pole. Henson was always included on these expeditions. After the end of the expedition of 1902, Henson, liking the travel involved, worked as a porter on a railroad. During these years he met a young woman, Lucy Ross, while visiting in Chicago. They became engaged to be married. But, before this could take place, Peary called for Henson again for his 1905 expedition. This Arctic exploration was aimed straight for the North Pole! In 1902, Peary and Henson had gotten further north in the Western Hemisphere (84°16°27″) than any other men. On that expedition, Peary had finally turned back sadly feeling, at age forty-six and after sixteen years of Arctic exploration, that he would never reach his great goal. Peary hoped to achieve for the United States and himself the honor of being the first to reach "the top of the world." Yet another trip was planned.

With Peary, now nearing fifty years of age, on his 1905-1906 expedition were three other white men and Henson. Matt was thirty-nine years old at this time. The expedition leader planned to use his carefully-thought-out "Peary system." This involved getting as far north as possible in the ice-breaker ship the *S.S. Roosevelt*, then sending out teams of men with dogs and sleds to clear a trail and to set up igloos with caches of food and fuel. Peary and his team of five men were to follow and in this way would be fresh enough to make that last dash for the North Pole. Open gaps, or leads of deep black water lay between them and their goal. These had to close together in time, or else Peary, Henson, and the four Eskimo men with them would not have time and supplies to reach the Pole and still return alive to the ship. On this expedition Peary reached a north point of 87°6′, farther north than any other man had ever gotten. But, then weather and open water stopped him from reaching the North Pole.

In 1908, still another expedition set out. Once more Henson went with Peary, and again the "Peary system" was used. The commander was now a Navy Admiral. The weather and the water conditions were a bit more favorable this time. Months and years of planning and effort were finally beginning to count in their favor when, on April 4, 1909, an advance group, consisting of the Admiral, Henson, and four Eskimo men, found themselves just sixty miles from the North Pole. In the next two days they overcame seemingly impossible problems, and arrived on April 6, 1909, at 89 degrees 57 minutes 11 seconds. . .about three nautical miles from the Pole. Camp was made here and Peary, accompanied by two of the Eskimoes went on some ten miles further for another reading. The sextent showed that the party had passed the Pole. They made their way back and forth across the area several times and took other sextant readings to be sure that "at some moment during these marches and countermarches I had passed over or very near the point where north and south and east and west blend into one."[1]

Back at the camp site Peary handed Matthew Henson the flag of the United States and Henson planted it firmly in place, within sight of the North Pole. Peary took pictures of Matt and the Eskimo men. On their return trip, the open leads of water, for a change, were a minor problem, and storms held off. They regained land and the

Admiral wrote in his diary: "My life work is accomplished." After twenty-three years of effort the prize was won for Peary and his men, and for the United States.

After their return from the North Pole, Henson seldom saw his commander except to receive orders from him. Admiral Peary was honored for his great explorations. Another explorer later claimed to have been the first to reach the Pole, and this tended for a time to dim Peary's triumph, but the claim was later found to be untrue.

It has been said that Henson was neglected by Peary after the Polar expedition. It is true that the two men were estranged when Henson made a lecture tour soon after his return. Peary felt that Henson was included in the agreement he had made with the other men which gave Peary the only rights to speaking and publishing the story of the expedition. Henson had not signed any agreement, however, and so believed that he might lecture and write freely. Peary had been ambitious all his life to become famous and he did not like to share the honor of reaching the Pole. Yet Henson had always been loyal to his old friend and had given up much to go with Peary and had been his staunch and enduring companion through all the northern travels. Fortunately, later on the two were again on friendly terms, although they did not meet again for some years. The Admiral wrote a preface to the book that Henson wrote, *A Negro Explorer at the North Pole*, published in 1912. An author's study of Peary's papers, made recently, revealed also that Peary wrote several letters of recommendation for Henson.

There had been a deep bond between the two men, though at that time there was a great difference in station between an Admiral and a black aide. In 1920 when Peary lay on his deathbed, he sent for Henson. Henson went to him and they talked together at last. Not long after Henson's visit, Peary died. When Henson heard of Peary's death, he went into another room so that his wife, Lucy, would not hear him weep.

Though honored by members of his own race, Matthew Henson was to live for twenty-eight years quietly, almost unknown to the public. But Henson was not discouraged. He worked at a Customs House post that an explorer companion obtained for him. He felt that one day his work would be recognized. Once Henson said to Lowell Thomas, the world-roving writer and radio reporter, "History will take care of that. God will see to it, and God has plenty of helpers." Little did Henson know that a helper was to work most of his life to see that Henson's work was known. That helper was Herbert M. Frisby of Baltimore, Maryland.

Frisby, now Dr. Herbert M. Frisby was born and raised in a slum section of Baltimore. He worked his way through elementary and high school and then through Howard, Columbia, and New York Universities, as well as other graduate schools. Dr. Frisby had learned as a boy of the black who was a member of the Peary expedition. "I'm going to be the second black to go to the North Pole," the boy had exclaimed; and forty years later he actually was to realize that ambition. All his life Dr. Frisby worked to focus attention upon Henson; and he was able to get Henson recognition while the explorer still lived.

Henson was seventy years old when he retired. At last recognition began to come to him. In 1937 he was selected to be a member of the famous Explorer's Club. In 1945 the Congress of the United States presented him with a silver medal "for contributing materially to the discovery of the North Pole." Henson often dropped in on the Explorer's Club and spent many of the happiest hours of his retirement there. Dr. Frisby went on working, too, in his behalf. When in 1954, Henson was almost eighty-five, he accepted an invitation to go to Washington, D.C., to lay a wreath on Peary's grave. On April 6, of that year, forty-five years after reaching the North Pole, Henson was the guest of President Dwight D. Eisenhower at the White House.

When Henson died in 1955, his wife, Lucy, insisted on giving half of his insurance money to the Explorer's Club. She explained that she wanted the Club to have the money because Henson had spent so many happy hours with the Club members there.

A special mission was flown by a United States Air Force plane, on August 12, 1956, in order to drop a memorial on the North Pole itself in honor of Matthew Henson. Dr. Herbert M. Frisby dropped the memorial, and in so doing realized his boyhood dream of becoming the second black to go to the North Pole. Frisby's life has been an adventurous one, modeled after his boyhood hero, Henson. He combined a life of teaching with a life of Arctic travel, most of it at his own expense, and a life of working for recognition for Matthew Henson. Dr. Frisby has completed twenty-two missions into the Arctic and Polar regions, and in the summer of 1970 he was in Russia's Arctic circle area on yet another mission.

Among the honors Dr. Frisby and the people helping him have won for Matthew Henson is a plaque, mounted in the main hall of the beautiful old statehouse in Annapolis, Maryland. Henson's native state honored him in 1961 with formal ceremonies led by Governor J. Millard Tawes and other officials, and attended by Matt's widow, Lucy. On the plaque, Matthew Henson is recognized as "co-discoverer of the North Pole." Maryland also has set aside April 6 as Matthew

Henson Day, and a school in Baltimore City is named for this great explorer.

Henson's fame does not decrease the credit due to Peary, yet it recognizes Henson's invaluable assistance to Peary. When the team of six men raced back from the Pole over the Polar sea toward land, Peary's age showed. Due to his great expenditure of energy he now had to ride the sled frequently. Henson said of that journey later: "(Peary) was practically a dead weight, but I do not think that we could have gotten back without him, for...he was still the heart and head of the party." Nor should we forget Peary's efforts at fund-raising, his life of dedication and the organization and leadership of the man. Today we honor both men and are proud that it was not one, but two great Americans who first went to the "top of the world." [2]

Henson did not have an easy life, nor did his devoted friend, Dr. Frisby. Yet both men lived happy, adventurous lives. Both had few advantages in their youth except for good health and intelligence. With determination, regardless of problems, handicaps, failures—each was successful. The story of Peary, Henson and Frisby leaves us with much to admire.

---

1 Peary, *The North Pole*, p. 291

2 Recently there were debates over whether or not Peary and Henson had actually reached the North Pole. To answer these the National Geographic Society in 1989 commissioned the Navigation Foundation to check. It was found that the party did indeed reach the Pole and camped within four to five miles of it.

Matthew Henson

Dr. Herbert Frisby

CHAPTER LXV

AVIATION IN MARYLAND

MARYLAND skies, so clear one day and so hazy the next, invited the attention of a young attorney in the 1780's. Peter Carnes spent many an hour with his head tipped back. He marvelled at the flight of birds, at the feel of the winds, at the clouds banked high over Chesapeake Bay in the summertime. He envied the gulls he watched, as he stood looking over Baltimore Harbor.

Carnes was not content just to watch from the ground. He had read that in France, flying balloons had become quite a popular sport. He was determined to fly a balloon. First trying this, then that, he finally succeeded in getting a balloon sewn together. He knew that if he could get the great bag filled with hot air, it would lift. Yet, he found that he had to be very careful or he would set the whole contraption afire from sparks.

By June of 1784, however, he had mastered the art of filling the balloon with hot air. In Bladensburg, Maryland, he carried out the first documented, unmanned balloon ascent in America. Now, in Baltimore, there were chuckles at his efforts. He was determined to fly in his balloon. But when the time came, Peter Carnes was disappointed. The balloon, though buoyant with hot air, ready to fly, and tugging at its rope, was not big enough to lift his weight.

Smiles grew to laughter. "It will never fly, old man," his friends teased. "A splendid idea and all that, but come along now and have a glass of wine with us. It just won't work." But, rubbing a sooty hand across his face, tipping his hat askew, Carnes stayed by his bobbing balloon. "It will work," he thought. "It's just that I built it too small. A much greater volume of hot air is needed to lift my weight."

As though echoing his own thoughts, a voice beside him said, "Don't be disappointed, Mr. Carnes, sir. I know it will work. It's just that, well, you're too heavy for it."

He looked down and then smiled at the lad beside him. It was thirteen-year-old Edward Warren. The boy was eyeing the balloon and the sky above it. "I'd certainly like to try it."

"But Edward, it's too dangerous!"

"But wouldn't you have ropes to it?"

"Well, yes," and Carnes stirred. It certainly was a tempting idea. The boy would not weigh half as much as an adult. Edward

344

looked a bright and daring lad, but, of course, it was risky. The two decided to take the risk, and, on June 23, 1784, near where the Baltimore Washington Monument stands today, young Edward Warren ascended in a balloon over Baltimore!

This was the first recorded flight made in the United States by a human being. It took place 157 years before the Wright brothers' flights.

Dirigible Flight

Much later, another flight over Baltimore was recorded in the newspapers. Lincoln Beachey, an entertainer, made headlines by his appearance in 1850 at Electric Park in Baltimore with a dirigible! Electric Park is now Belvedere Avenue between Park Heights Avenue and Reisterstown Road.

Riding the warm July air, the daring Beachey flew right over the city of Baltimore. People watched in awe as he crossed the city, ambled out over the harbor, turned back and found Electric Park. There, he tossed ropes over the side, vented a little of his sustaining gas and sank to the earth. He was cheered as the first man to fly over Baltimore in a dirigible.

Balloons Used During the Civil War

A balloon, constructed and flown by the inventor, Thaddeus Lowe, was used in Maryland during the Civil War. It took fifty men to inflate, tow, guide, and guard the balloon. Hydrogen generators were used to make the hydrogen for its gas. The balloon served as an observation post to see Confederate activity across the Potomac. One location was near Mattawoman Creek and others were near Poolesville, Maryland, and Harper's Ferry, West Virginia.

In the fall of 1861, the Confederates were trying to blockade the Potomac River in order to stop ships from moving between Washington, D.C. and places along Chesapeake Bay and beyond. This, and the need to know what the Confederate forces were doing across the Potomac, led to a request by General Joseph Hooker for an observation balloon. Thaddeus Lowe loaded his balloon, his ground crew and his equipment onto boats. Then, hugging the Maryland shore line, he reached the mouth of Mattawoman Creek.

When Lowe's balloon ascended, he could see the campfires of Confederate troops on the opposite shore. He spotted Confederate gun batteries at dawn over three miles away in Virginia.

There were four balloons, including Lowe's, used in the Washington area and on the Potomac River during the Civil War.

Wright's Fly Heavier-Than-Air Machine

Only three newspapers in the entire United States believed the report when news was telegraphed that the Wright brothers, Wilbur and Orville, had flown an airplane at Kitty Hawk, North Carolina, on December 17, 1903!

The First Successful Plane Built in Maryland

Oddly enough, it was again a boy who dared to challenge the Maryland skies in 1909. Charles F. Elvers, in a barn on his father's farm near Owings Mills, spent months puzzling out a design for a biplane. How should he brace the wooden framework? How should the wires go to hold the thing together? Once he had all these problems figured out, there followed hours of work making the framework and sewing on the fabric covering. Now came the biggest question of all, would it fly? And, could someone, who had never before been up, fly it?

Yes! It did fly. It was the first plane built in Maryland to copy successfully the Wright brothers' feat of flying a heavier-than-air machine under its own power.

First Army Aviation School

Still in operation is a small flying field known as College Park Airport. Private planes park there, helicopters use the field, and small planes drone in and out. Yet, for all its quiet appearance, it is historically important, for this little airport is the oldest in the United States in continuous operation. It might be called the birthplace of the United States Air Force and "the world's first military airport."

When the Wright brothers showed the quality of their airplane to officers at Ft. Myer, Virginia, the Army decided to buy it. Lieutenant Frank P. Lahm was ordered to locate a good flying field. When the Army bought the plane, it was a part of the contract that the Wright brothers would teach two or three Signal Corps officers to fly. A flying school was to be started.

While free ballooning, Lieutenant Lahm saw a tract of land that seemed level and open. Later, he rode his horse over the acreage and found that it would indeed be a good site for the school. So, during the early fall of 1909, the Wrights moved their military model of the

Wright Flyer into College Park airport. Hangars were built and training began.

Lieutenant Lahm soloed (flew alone) October 26, 1909. There, on November 3, Lieutenant G. C. Sweet flew as a passenger from College Park airport. He was the first Naval officer to do this.

After the airport at College Park was enlarged in 1911 by buying more land, more "firsts" occurred. The first bomb sight was tried out there in 1912. In June of that same year a machine gun was fired at College Park from an airplane.

The Army kept College Park Airport as their flying school until August 12, 1918. That was the year when the field was used for the first Air Mail flights. Another important moment came in 1925, when at College Park Airport, one of the world's earliest successful helicopter experiments was accomplished.

In 1928, the airport came under the management of George C. Brinkerhoff, who operated it until 1962. For over thirty-four years "Brink" taught students, sold planes, and carried passengers far and wide on charter trips. During World War II, he ran a nonscheduled airline out of the field, using Douglas DC-3 twin-engined aircraft. Today the airport is owned and operated by the Maryland National Capital Park and Planning Commission.

Early 1900s in Aviation

As we look back to 1909, we realize that it took a brave person just to ride in one of those early flying machines. Only the wing, tail surfaces and controls were covered. The occupants of the plane sat out in the open exposed to the rush of air, amidst a "bird cage" of wires, struts and wings.

A little engine turned two propellers by means of a chain drive. (The Wrights were originally bicycle shop men!) The clumsy propellers were of the pusher type and shoved the plane forward through the air. The wings got their lift from the air passing over the curved top surface of the wings.

It took a brave man to sit calmly near the thrashing propellers and the roaring engines, the air rushing by him as he hurtled along at forty miles per hour or more! Crashes were not unusual.

In 1918, the Aviation Section of the Army Signal Corps became a separate unit called the Air Service. Three years later, Brigadier General William (Billy) Mitchell was to conduct historic tests in the lower part of Chesapeake Bay. He hoped to prove to military leaders, especially to the Admirals of the Navy, that aerial bombing was a deadly fact of modern life, and must be considered seriously. In the tests, Billy Mitchell and his pilots loaded their small planes with the largest bombs they could haul into the air and headed for the target area off Tangier Island, where an old battleship had been moored for the test. The pilots sank the huge ship. At that moment in the fall of 1921, the airmen were proving that battleships were no longer safe from everything except heavy shore batteries and other battleships. Oddly enough, it was in this same general region though about a hundred miles further south, in Virginia's waters, that the *Monitor-Merrimack* battle during the Civil War had been another historic turning point, ending the day of the warship made of wood and beginning the day of the ironclad.

The Great Air Meet

Flying and flyers attracted great public attention and admiration in the year 1910. Just outside Baltimore, at Halethorpe, in early November, there was scheduled a memorable event, the Halethorpe Air Meet. There, Baltimorians marveled as the French pilot, Hubert Latham, November 7, 1910, flew his powerful "Antoinette," with its engine of fifty horsepower.

"Every tall building was a grandstand", a Baltimore newspaper reported. Wearing a smart linen duster, Latham flew to Fort McHenry, crossed right over Baltimore harbor, over downtown Baltimore, Patterson Park, and Druid Hill Park. Finally, in a blaze of glory, he came "through the thin air" back to Halethorpe "where the other aviators rushed up to congratulate him."

The "Lord Baltimore II"

After the air meet, dozens of Baltimore youngsters worked, by trial and error, to build planes. They wanted to lift from the ground and ascend up into the magic air. Few flights were successful, but at least one, we know, was completed.

The plane was called "Lord Baltimore II." (We do not know the fate of the "Lord Baltimore I.") The young builders were Edward R. Brown, Don Swann, and Clyde Loose. All they had to do, once the plane was built, was find a field long enough to try a takeoff. They located such a strip near the old, wooden, Light Street bridge.

The flight scheduled for May 17, 1911, was widely advertised throughout the city. Crowds gathered. The plane was brought to its makeshift runway. Citizens shivered as they viewed the airplane made of fabric, sticks and wire. Would this be another one of those fatal crashes? After all, this thing had been built by youths, not by mature men.

348

The earliest Fairchild aircraft, the FC-1 introduced in 1926, was the first airplane with an enclosed cabin and folding wings. It achieved a top speed of 97 miles per hour.

The Martin "Clipper." Flown by Pan-American across the world.

An Air Force TM-76B MACE tactical range ballistic missile built at the Baltimore Division of The Martin Company.

The motor roared and dust flew! Men held the wings, straining to hold the plane back until the engine was running at nearly full throttle. Then, at a signal, they let go. Anthony Jannus at the controls sent the airplane down the runway. Slowly it accelerated and then took off! A cheer went up from the crowd as the odd contraption climbed into the sky.

It circled bravely out to fly above the harbor. Then, as the plane turned back, the crowd held its breath. This was the most hazardous part. Steadily, young Jannus steered the awkward craft down, down, closer and closer to the ground. Would he crash, they wondered? But no, he touched down in a perfect landing.

World War I Pilots

Not until 1917 did aviation begin to stride forward under the stimulus of a need for it in the war, and government funds poured into research and manufacture. At first planes were used for aerial spying on enemy lines and positions. Later, weapons were invented to make aircraft into bombers and fighters. In 1917 the United States entered World War I, the "war to end wars." There were eight Maryland men among the very first one hundred war pilots recruited by the United States.

Though no complete airplanes were constructed in Maryland in World War I, the state did contribute a most important part of the machines of the period. About seventy-five percent of all aircraft propellers used in the war by the United States and her allies were manufactured in Baltimore, Maryland.

After the Armistice on November 11, 1918, aircraft design was very much changed. Pilots now no longer sat exposed to the wind, but were strapped into a cockpit, in a covered fuselage. In front of them were new instruments—such as the airspeed indicator, the altimeter and the compass. There followed a most exciting decade of progress in aviation.

Fairchild Corporation

Little realizing, perhaps, that they were starting a great Maryland industry, two men in Hagerstown began to build airplanes. It was 1925, and they had only a small wooden shed, combined with a garage, to work in. Yet, Ammon Kreider and L. E. Reisner, with their very first handmade aircraft, entered and won the Scientific American Trophy Race!

Encouraged, they fell to work to make more planes. About one hundred planes later, in 1929, the Sherman Fairchild interests bought the control of the Kreider-Reisner works. Fairchild built a plant at Hagerstown which, for that time, was very modern and spacious. Soon Fairchild planes became very popular with pilots. The Maryland-built planes performed well, and each year became faster, roomier, and more comfortable.

During World War II, Fairchild Aircraft developed a primary training plane and manufactured these in mass production for the training of Army Air Corps pilots. Later, their engineers developed a "flying boxcar" plane named the Fairchild "Packet." This was a big cargo plane with two engines, and with two long tail booms supporting the rudder and elevator controls. Trucks could drive into the great door at the back of the plane. Other innovations followed.

Soon the company, then called the Fairchild-Hiller Corporation, began to design and build missiles. Today, Fairchild is a leader, not only in aircraft, but also in the field of missiles and spacecraft.

Glenn L. Martin

As early as 1909, out in Santa Ana, California, an intense young man was working in an abandoned church building to build an airplane. His mother often helped him with the fabric sewing, and by holding a lantern for him at night. Day and night he toiled over engines, the wooden parts, and the balky bracing wires.

In addition to building a plane, according to known aircraft designs of his time, Martin added many new ideas of his own, and improved on the current designs. He saw a great future for flying boats. "Why build runways," he reasoned, "with so much open water around?"

After considerable success with building planes, Martin decided that he would like to be nearer Washington, D.C. The capital city was the best market place for planes for the armed services. He began looking for a new factory site near water and near Washington, and where there were plenty of skilled workers and adequate raw materials. It seemed to him that Middle River, near Baltimore, Maryland, just fitted his needs. So, in 1929, he moved there.

In the years that followed, Glenn L. Martin's company poured forth aircraft in great numbers, designed to fit military needs. One, called the "B-26" was a very fast two-engined bombing plane, widely used during World War II. He built the giant seventy-two-ton "Mars" flying boats, and the Navy PM-1 (1930) and P5M "Marlin" of the 1950's.

351

The Martin Company, Glenn Martin announced in December of 1944, was making a gift of money to the University of Maryland, for setting up a school in aeronautical sciences and to pay for research in aeronautics. In the next year, Martin added to this sum, as did the State of Maryland. In 1947, the Glenn L. Martin College of Engineering and Aeronautical Sciences opened with smart new buildings and with one of the best wind tunnels in the country.

Glenn L. Martin led an active, inventive, successful life in the field of aviation. In his later years, he devoted much thought and money to helping the industry of aeronautics that he had done so much to bring about. Glenn L. Martin died in December, 1955, at the age of sixty-nine.

The Martin Company and American-Marietta Company were joined in October 1961, to form the Martin Marietta Corporation. The corporate offices are located in Bethesda, Maryland. Martin Marietta Corporation produced exciting vehicles to be used in space and various devices to be used in the Space Shuttle program, a manned transportation system which began operation in the 1980s. Martin Corporation is working on systems to be used in national defense. In Baltimore parts are made for a number of commercial and military aircraft, fan reverser assemblies for jet aircraft engines and many other items. Oddly enough some of the company's largest money making products are materials mined and processed, used in paving roads and used in various manufacturing processes.

Perhaps one of the most unusual "products" of the company is in the field of pure research. The Martin Company, in 1955, set up an institute for advanced studies at Ruxton, Maryland, where scientists from many nations can work in a serene setting to advance man's knowledge of the universe, exploring such subjects as mathematics, the biosciences, physics, chemistry and metallurgy. This, it seems, is very much what the company's founder, Glenn L. Martin would have liked. Martin Marietta Laboratories, too, employ some 100 scientists and workers to devise new engineering techniques for all five of Martin Marietta's companies.

Captain Philip V. H. Weems

It is a strange fact, but a true one, that a man born before the first airplane flew is now helping plot trips through space. Philip Weems was born in 1889 and was raised on the family farm in Tennessee. He came to Maryland for his college education, entering the United States Naval Academy, at Annapolis, in 1908 and graduating in 1912.

Right away, during his Academy days, Philip Weems became fascinated with celestial navigation. His first sea duty after graduation, aboard a survey ship, gave him a good chance to practice the use of navigational instruments. He served at sea aboard battleships, troop transport and destroyers from 1914 until 1919. This was the period of World War I.

He stayed ashore a year then on Navy duty, and it was that year, 1920, that saw him win a place on the American Olympic Wrestling Team. Wrestling was just one of his athletic interests, for Weems also loved swimming, football, and boxing; and though he had an active mind, he was also interested in keeping his body fit and alert.

He then alternated time ashore with sea duty and by 1928, had become quite well known for his work in navigation. Just what work needed to be done? In those days, ships were beginning to move faster than ever, aircraft were now rapidly being perfected. A navigator could no longer spend a great deal of time consulting heavy books and making complicated calculations. Things were beginning to move too fast for that. Weems' main work was in simplifying the navigator's tasks. When Richard Byrd, later made an Admiral, flew over the South Pole in 1929, some of his charts and instruments had been developed by his Naval Academy classmate, Philip Weems. Early in the 1930's Weems began to write textbooks on air navigation and other books that aided the air and sea navigator.

There followed active years ashore and at sea. Weems wrote, studied and invented all the while. In October of 1932, he was given command of the *USS Hopkins*. In 1933, he published his famous *Air Almanac*, used by both the United States and Britain as a standard navigational reference. In May, 1933, Weems, now a Lieutenant Commander, was lowering the flag of the *USS Hopkins* and going into retirement. He foresaw ahead years of study, invention and writing. But, ten years later his country was at war and called him back to active duty. In July of 1942 he returned to the Navy.

For three years, Weems served on the dangerous and demanding convoy duty that herded ships across the seas to supply war needs. For his service as Convoy Commodore, he was awarded the Bronze Star Medal. As another mark of honor, the Navy, in 1945 awarded the fifty-six-year-old Weems the wings of a Naval Air Navigator. Finally, in 1946, Weems, now a Navy Captain, again retired.

During his busy life, Weems has been aided and encouraged by his wife, Margaret Thackray Weems. He met her in 1908 and they were married in New York City in 1914. She was born and raised in Johnstown, Pennsylvania. While raising their two boys and a girl, Mrs. Weems also found time to organize firms to market the products of her husband's busy mind: books, air navigation instruments and training courses. Captain Weems founded the world famous "Weems System of Navigation." Weems and his wife for many years lived in an historic house in Annapolis, Maryland, near the State House and not far from the Naval Academy.

Captain Weems has worked out ways by which astronauts may navigate their craft across the vast wastes of space. He kept to his original idea, that of making navigation ever more simple to perform, without the sacrifice of accuracy. From sea to sky to space, Weems has helped us find our way.

Maryland Aviation

From the balloonist, Thaddeus Lowe, who hung over the Maryland shore of the Potomac to spy on Confederate military movements, to the American Flying Club of Baltimore—our state can boast of many early aviation activities. The AFC was one of the very earliest flying clubs in the country. The club was successful in getting Logan Field at Dundalk established. It was Baltimore's first airfield.

As aviation grew, Maryland kept up. In 1925 crowds watched as the Army's Lieutenant James Doolittle broke a world speed record. He was in an international race at Baltimore's Bay Shore Park and averaged a fantastic, for that day, speed of 232.57 MPH.

Baltimore turned out by the thousands to cheer Charles A. Lindbergh and his frail little "Spirit of St. Louis" when he visited Dundalk Field in 1927.

Few people, even then, could have possibly imagined the progress in air travel in Maryland today. They would have trouble believing their eyes if they had looked into the future and had seen our giant USAF Andrews Air Force Base with its jet planes, or the huge Baltimore-Washington International Airport, where "jets" bring people from all over the world to Baltimore, as well as gigantic loads of airfreight! In Maryland, too, is located the Goddard Space Flight Center at Greenbelt, Maryland. It would be very hard for old-time pilots to foresee that in such a short time, Americans would not only fly through the air, but also through space to the moon!

World War I "Jenny".

CHAPTER LXVI

THE NAVAL ACADEMY

T HERE are at least two things that attract a visitor's attention in Annapolis, Maryland. The first is the colonial atmosphere of the town. The city is, in a way, a living museum of early Americana, from its rolling brick walkways to the unique State House, whose wooden dome towers above State Circle. All through the town charming colonial homes have been preserved. Some are open to the public; and many are still in use as private residences. There is an ancient tree on the lawn of St. John's College where, legend has it, Indians met with the colonists to agree to a treaty. In brief, Annapolis is most unusual, and has a distinct colonial atmosphere.

Secondly, a visitor quickly notices not only the students from St. John's College passing by occasionally, books beneath their arms, but many young, fine-looking Navy midshipmen[1] in the town, and many officers of higher Navy rank. Also, to be seen are Navy enlisted men and professors with a nautical swing to their walk. These live, work, teach or study in Annapolis because the United States Naval Academy is located there beside the Severn River.

The local citizens who are accustomed to all these sights and people, appear scarcely to notice them. Their attention, rather, is on the marketing of products of farm and waterway, or upon selling or buying equipment and supplies for use on the farms or on the water. Also, there are many in the city who attend to government affairs, since Annapolis is a center of city, county and state administration. It is Maryland's capital city.

We have seen how Annapolis grew from a "parcel of wooden houses" to a sophisticated colonial center of government and social life. But how and why, for instance, did the Naval Academy come to Annapolis?

Near the Academy site there used to be a stone windmill. It was used before the American Revolution to grind grain into meal and flour. With favorable winds, this mill could grind eight bushels of grain an hour. The mill site was not to remain undisturbed, however.

After *H.M.S.*[2] *Leopard* attacked the *U.S.S.*[3] *Chesapeake*, a new fort was built here in 1808. Fort Severn, as it was named, was to serve as a protection for the capital city during the War of 1812. Standing there at the end of the town, it protected the city from the British fleet that cruised regularly up and down the Bay. Inside a fourteen-foot-high stone wall there was a parapet three feet below the top. On this were mounted eight guns whose business-like muzzles commanded water approaches to Annapolis. In the center of Fort Severn was a brick powder magazine, and outside the fort, on the shoreward side, was a furnace for heating red hot shot to fire at the wooden ships of the enemy, if need be.

There was a great deal of concern in the early 1800's with the lack of regular naval vessels and well trained officers and men to man them. In fact, there was little, if any, methodical training for officers in the United States Navy. What the young midshipmen learned for the most part was at sea with some tutoring from older seamen. Schools had been set up at Philadelphia and at Norfolk to try to correct this situation. Better facilities and instructors, however, were needed.

Secretary of the Navy and distinguished historian, George Bancroft, suggested that all instruction of midshipmen be carried out in the same way that young men were being trained for the Army at West Point. The Secretary suggested Fort Severn as a good site for such an academy. The fort had been little used for some time by the Army. So, on August 15, 1845, the fort was formally turned over to the Navy Department.

Old Fort Severn became the United States Naval School. Its first Superintendent, Commander Franklin Buchanan, assumed command of the academy on September 3, of that same year. With seven other officers and about forty midshipmen, Commander Buchanan organized the academy's first class on October 10, 1845.

The first classes of midshipmen appear to have been an unruly lot. They often engaged in dueling, brawling, drinking, poker playing, and occasionally in fighting with the townspeople. This condition came to an abrupt end in 1850, when a harsh code of regulations was put into effect and enforced.

Those first courses included gunnery, naval tactics, engineering, chemistry, mathematics, astronomy, French, and English. All were useful subjects for these young officers-to-be at that time. Sail was giving way to steam; ordnance was changing; and there was much to be learned and quickly. The academy's entrance age requirement was "from 13 to 16 years."

Originally, the program for midshipmen included one year spent at Annapolis, and then three years at sea. Afterwards, they returned to Annapolis for their fifth and final year. In 1851, the Naval School was formally designated the United States Naval Academy, and a Board of Visitors first met at the Academy. Eventually a four-year, uninterrupted curriculum was begun, with intensive training at sea with the fleet during the summer recesses replacing the years previously spent at sea.

As the Civil War drew near, sympathies in Maryland wavered between the Union and the Confederacy. In the Eastern Shore counties and the counties of southern Maryland, where there were numerous slave-holding landowners, sentiment tended to be pro-Southern. The more northerly and westerly sections of the State on the other hand, tended to side with the North. Because of these divisions, the *U.S.S. Constitution* on April 24, 1861, sailed north to Newport, Rhode Island, with 151 midshipmen aboard. These young men sadly parted with their Southern classmates, who planned to go to the South to join Confederate forces.

Just five days prior to this, Franklin Buchanan, then Commandant of the Navy Yard at Washington, believing that his native state (Maryland) would withdraw from the Union, resigned his commission in the United States Navy. (He was later to play a most dramatic role as the Confederate captain of the armored fighting ship the *Merrimac*.)

General Butler "Captures" Annapolis

Anxious days followed with local public opinion becoming more and more pro-Southern. In April of that year, also, the 8th Massachusetts and the 7th New York regiments arrived under the command of Brigadier General B. F. Butler. Maryland's Governor Thomas H. Hicks, protested that these troops might touch off riots and fighting like that in Baltimore on April 19. But, though the excitement was intense in Annapolis, the troops did disembark from the transports in the harbor without conflict. The presence of these troops in the capital city, it may be added, was one of the reasons why the State legislature, faced with the decision as to whether or not to secede from the Union, decided to meet in Frederick, Maryland.

Acting coolly in this period of emergency, General Butler dispatched most of the troops to Washington by rail, but he himself stayed in Annapolis to await the arrival of reinforcements. On May 16, however, he left for Baltimore taking a large troop contingent with him. The Maryland situation stabilized somewhat then for Governor Hicks was able to influence the legislature to forego any rash decision, especially in view of the presence of numerous occupation troops.

Though Annapolis was used as a mobilization point in the Civil War, it was to serve mainly as a place to care for wounded men. The facilities both at the Naval Academy and at St. John's College were to be used as hospital sites. Annapolis also served as a reception point for prisoners. These were at first kept in a camp behind St. John's College, but later were moved three miles west of town, to Camp Parole.

After the Civil War

Following the Civil War the midshipmen returned to Annapolis to find the Navy changing over from wooden ships to the "iron-clad" and then to steel ships. Also, the service was converting from sail power to steam power and installing many improved weapons.

The growth of the Academy after the war was slow at first. The 1886 class numbered only twenty-five graduating students. In 1899, following the Spanish-American War, there was a graduating class of fifty-three, and, in 1905, a class of 114 midshipmen graduated. The buildings were remodeled and enlarged at this time in order to take care of the much larger classes. The graduating class of 1907 numbered 350 men.

John Paul Jones

In the year 1913, John Paul Jones' body was entombed at the Academy at Annapolis. The life of John Paul Jones, the great early naval hero in America, is a fascinating one. Why is he so revered by American Navy men? It is a story that goes back in time to the days of the American Revolution.

Born with the name John Paul in Scotland, he left home at the age of twelve, sailing as a cabin boy to Fredericksburg, Virginia. In 1766, he became chief mate on a brigantine vessel engaged in the slave trade. For two years he sailed on slavers; then, sickened by the trade, he took passage for home on a ship bound for Scotland. During this voyage, the master and the mate of the ship both died and the twenty-one-year-old John Paul took command. He brought the ship safely to port.

This won for him command of his own ship, one used for trading with the West Indies. At Tobago in 1773, John Paul killed the leader of a crew of mutineers. Rather than wait in prison for trial, he escaped, added "Jones" to his name, and returned to Fredericksburg. The English, after this, called him a pirate and a fugitive from justice.

All midshipmen learn to sail.
(U.S. Navy photograph)

The midshipmen "hat toss" after graduation at the Naval Academy.

(U.S. Navy photograph)

Academy Color Guard. *(U.S. Navy Photograph)*

Women midshipmen will wear this Working Blue uniform when attending classes and while off-duty at the Academy.

(U.S. Navy photograph)

In 1775, when the American Revolution broke out, Jones joined the new Continental Navy in Philadelphia. As a captain he cruised the West Indies and captured and sank a great many British ships. He rose to the rank of Commodore and was given command of a fleet of ships. His flagship was the *Bonhomme Richard*. In September, 1779, he battled, and captured, the British man-of-war *Serapis*. By 1781, he was back in America supervising the building of the largest ship in the Navy, the *America*.

The end of the American Revolution did not end his adventures. He was sent to Paris on a government mission. Later, he entered Russian naval service and fought the Turks. In 1790, he retired and went to live in Paris.

Two years later, the United States appointed him United States Consul to Algiers; but, before his commission arrived, John Paul Jones died.

Our American Ambassador to France, General Horace Porter, many years later, in 1899, became interested in the fate of the body of John Paul Jones. Jones was the great hero of the American Revolution and of our first Navy. For six years, General Porter searched old records until he found that John Paul Jones had been buried in a lead coffin in the St. Louis Cemetery in Paris. He arranged to have the body returned to America.

Since 1913 John Paul Jones' body has rested in Annapolis. It lies now in a specially-built crypt beneath the dome of the beautiful Chapel. Many visitors, who come each year to the Naval Academy stop at the chapel to see the tomb of this hero of our early American Navy.

The Naval Academy Yard Today[4]

Through the years the Naval Academy has reflected the changing needs of the United States Navy. Enrollment has climbed, buildings have been built, and new courses have been added. During both World War I and World War II the Academy hummed with activity as it trained hundreds of midshipmen for service as officers of the Navy.

Today the Naval Academy Yard occupies 300 acres of land. On this land are 219 major buildings and extensive fields for drill and for sports. Located in a beautiful setting, the grounds are well suited to the Academy's mission of training midshipmen for life afloat and inspiring them with the seaman's love of salt water. In front of the Academy the Severn River widens as it enters Chesapeake Bay. Great oaks shade the massive granite buildings. And, here and there in the "Yard" are monuments to naval heroes, as well as cannons and other weighty souvenirs of the history of the American Navy.

Air View of the U. S. Naval Academy.

Annapolis Waterfront Today.

361

Bancroft Hall is, of course, the center of midshipman activity. There they study, eat, and sleep. The Hall is a community in itself with a post office, medical and dental quarters, a soda fountain, a bookstore, tailor shop, barbershops, recreation rooms, a tremendous galley (in naval terms, the kitchen of the ship), and a vast mess hall, where the entire brigade is served at one sitting.

There are now some 4,300 midshipmen in the Brigade of Midshipmen. Each lives an active life. From the time the midshipmen rise in the morning until time for sleep, a planned routine is followed. The Academy's rigorous discipline distinguishes it from other American colleges, excepting, of course, the other service schools.

Academy Superintendents

The Academy is headed by a Superintendent who is invariably a naval flag officer with wide fleet experience. From the first Superintendent, Commander Franklin Buchanan, who took command on September 3, 1845 to today's Superintendent, Rear Admiral Thomas C. Lynch who assumed command June 15, 1991, each Superintendent has contributed to the progress of the Naval Academy.

The fifty-four Superintendents have brought to the Academy a determination to turn out officers morally, mentally and physically prepared to serve their country in the Navy or Marine Corps. The men and women upon graduation will be able to take on the responsibilities of command.

The Academic Program

The Naval Academy today is much more than an excellent professional training establishment. It is an academic institution providing a broad liberal education and offering over twenty major programs of study. The curriculum, though demanding, offers many choices. Each midshipman is challenged in terms of his or her aptitudes and interests.

The day is long past when every line officer could be expected to be, and to know, everything desired in a naval career. The Academy, therefore, does not give every graduate the same program but undertakes to produce individuals who will collectively possess a wide range of knowledge of great value to the modern Navy.

Following World War II the academic program was changed so that midshipmen might use previously earned college work and might take on elective courses. In 1963 the first civilian academic dean was appointed. Indeed, Dr. A. Bernard Drought, who assumed full-time duties at the Academy on July 1, 1964, was the first civilian dean to be appointed to any service academy. Today the dean is R. H. Shapiro, who works with an outstanding faculty of over 600 military and civilian members.

The greatest academic change, however, waited for the 1969-1970 entering class when "core" courses were cut to a minimum to make room for more than 300 elective courses. Every midshipman is now ordered to select one of the over twenty major programs of study.

Women Enter the Academy

In October of 1975 the Congress of the United States approved the admission of women to the United States Naval Academy. Women must meet the same requirements as male applicants with only minor exceptions. The Secretary of the Navy authorized the Academy to accept 80 women into the 1,250-member class of 1980. The first women to become midshipmen entered on July 6, 1976. There are 450 women midshipmen today.

Academy Traditions

Not all is study and drill at the Academy. There is the traditional and glamourous June Week. This event-packed week began with the first Superintendent's authorization of "the Great Naval Ball," now called "the Farewell Ball." Among the events of June Week today are the Ring Dance, the Color Parade, and of course, Graduation with its hat-throwing finale.

There are more sports than can be listed here for midshipmen and athletic training of all kinds. Leisure time may be spent in dozens of different ways, making music, presenting plays, enjoying hobbies, writing for Academy magazines, debating, in all over seventy such activities are available.

During the winters the midshipman is busy with classroom and laboratory work. Summer finds the student on training cruises. Throughout the year there are several leaves and liberties (days off) to enjoy.

Visitors will find the Academy grounds and the Preble Hall Museum well worth visiting.

How to Become a Midshipmen

To be eligible for selection to enter the Academy, the applicant must be between seventeen and twenty-two years of age; a citizen; single and remain single while at the Academy. The prospective midshipman must be physically and academically qualified.

If the candidate meets all of these requirements, then he or she must obtain a nomination. These are available by Presidential appointment, Congressional appointment, appointment from the regular Navy or Marine Corps, from the Naval Reserve or Marine Corps Reserve, from the Honor Military and Naval Schools, from Naval Reserve Office Training Corps units and by appointment from qualified alternate nominees and competitive candidates. For details, write to: Candidate Guidance Office, United States Naval Academy, Annapolis, MD 21402-5018.

Before a young person applies, one may avoid disappointment by being certain of one's ability to meet the entrance physical examination requirements. Then too, each applicant should learn just what prior education or experience is needed to meet the Academy's scholastic requirements.

Midshipmen receive four years of fine college education and a world of naval experience. They are paid enough to provide themselves with uniforms and with other necessities while at Annapolis. After graduation they know that they will serve their country in a leadership role with reasonable certainty of a useful, interesting, and adventurous future.

The Academy's Future

The Academy has now undergone a seventy-three-million-dollar construction and renewal program. Michaelson and Chauvenet Halls were renovated by 1968. The 650,000-volume capacity Nimitz Library which overlooks the Severn River, was completed in 1973. Rickover Hall, an engineering and laboratory complex, was finished in 1975. All equipment needed for computer-aided, multi-media education is available. Today all academic areas are air conditioned. Private funds were donated to build a new Sailing Center offering midshipmen recreational facilities. The new Lejeune Physical Education Center was completed in 1981. Dahlgren Hall has been converted (with private funds) to the Academy's version of a student union center, a recreational facility. Alumni Hall, completed in 1991, can seat 6500 people.

Here in Annapolis, these and other buildings provide facilities to train the leaders of our nation's Navy and Marine Corps. These young people come to prepare themselves for lives devoted to their nation, to follow the Academy motto—"Not Self, But Country."

1 A midshipmen is a student in training at a college for duty as a Naval officer.
2 H.M.S.—His Majesty's Ship (in this case King George III of England).
3 U.S.S.—United States' Ship.
4 For detailed information on the United States Naval Academy see the current catalogue of information, or write the Public Information Office of the Academy.

CHAPTER LXVII

THE TREASURE OF CHESAPEAKE BAY

ALONG the extensive shorelines of Chesapeake Bay, watermen reach for treasure with tongs. Tongs are long-handled rakes hinged like scissors. The fishermen "feel" along the bottom, close the teeth of the tongs and hoist the awkward handles upward. Grasped in the tongs are what they seek—a treasure of Chesapeake Bay—oysters! Every year watermen seek this valuable and delicious shellfish.

When the first colonists came to this region they found that the Indians depended upon oysters as an important part of their diet. So plentiful were the oysters once, that they were very cheap and were enjoyed by all who wanted them. In fact, it seemed that oysters would always be plentiful in Chesapeake Bay waters. But in the decade from 1880 to 1890, a new invention was brought to the Bay, called the oyster dredge. These machines in a single operation dredged up oysters in great quantities, and in the process destroyed many oyster beds. Almost too late laws were passed to prohibit dredging, just in the nick of time to prevent the total ruin of the oyster industry. Even so, the results of this "oyster orgy" are still felt.

Today Maryland's marine police constantly scan the waters of the Bay to help watermen and to keep oyster beds producing. Shells are now returned to the Bay floor to provide a place for new oysters to grow. Only oysters at least three inches long may be harvested.

The Maryland Marine Police force has developed from the earlier State Oyster Police, begun in 1868. These first officers, however, were apt to take their duties very seriously, enforcing their orders with a one-pound, quick-firing rifle mounted on the forward deck of their police boat. But they used, as did everyone else at that time, sails for motion. The first patrol boat was a bugeye launched in 1894, with the unusual name of "Brown Smith Jones." That year, the Governor's name was Brown, the state Comptroller as a Mr. Smith and the Treasurer of Maryland was a Mr. Jones.

Today, of course, the Marine Police use powerful boats sheathed in copper. Patrolmen check for water pollution, locate missing boats and

Looking eastward one can see the William Preston Lane, Jr. Memorial Bridge spanning Chesapeake Bay as it appeared in the summer of 1970. The pilings of the second span are seen projecting out into the Bay to the left of the original span.

(Joseph H. Cromwell, C & P Telephone Company of Maryland)

Two graceful bridges now span Chesapeake Bay, as this photograph shows.

persons, and sometimes recover the bodies of drowned persons. They count waterfowl, and supervise the planting of oyster shell and seed for the State. In addition, they answer all types of questions, give directions, warn boat owners of unsafe weather and water conditions, and come to the aid of watermen and sportsmen in times of danger. There is the problem of crime on the water as there is on land. The Marine Police are trained to meet the problems of stolen boats and equipment. The men of the Marine Police have varied skills. Some fly helicopters, many pilot the various police vessels, and others are trained in the use of scuba diving gear. To help prepare men for such a variety of tasks, a Maryland Marine Police Academy was established in 1963. The comparatively few men making up the water police force, enforce conservation regulations and Maryland law along 2,000 miles of shoreline and in the over 2,400 square miles of tidal waters. In their work they use many cruisers, several airplanes, helicopters, hovercraft and many outboard boats. The police are now called the Natural Resources Police with over 200 officers engaged in work on the Bay and Maryland's inland waters. Officers are trained in many skills, law enforcement, rescue, medical aid and some in underwater diving.

Watermen of Maryland

A waterman battles ice in winter, heat in summer and all year the winds, tides, sunshine and storms of the waterways. The waterman of the Chesapeake Bay uses a work boat with low sides, a culling board, pairs of tongs and a light hammer. By starting early and working hard all day he harvests his oysters. These he takes to a "buy boat" or to an oyster house, then pockets his money and returns home, to repeat his efforts all over again the next day. Once the oyster season is over, waterman may work on shore at various jobs or businesses, or they may stay on the water, catching crabs and fish for sale.

Why, one may wonder, do watermen gather in oysters, using an implement such as tongs? This is a tool nearly 200 years old, and is truly an antique! The answer is, of course, conservation. Though considerable oystering is done on the Western Shore of the Chesapeake Bay, the greater amount is done in the hundreds of inlets and shore-side oyster bars of the Eastern Shore.

Clams are harvested by a clam dredge which is pulled along the bottom of the Bay. It is called a "hydraulic dredge" because water is sprayed over the dredge, releasing clams from the mud. The clams are then lifted aboard on a moving belt. Market sized clams are lifted off and smaller ones dropped back into the water. Again, conservation has been learned the hard way. The clam dredge is a new invention (1950). It was the product of an Eastern Shore waterman, Fletcher Hanks.

Dredges, at first, operated without controls and special laws. Unfortunately, this resulted not only in ruining the clam flats but in dredging up and ruining many oyster bars as well. By the time laws were passed, considerable damage had been done. Still, the oyster industry has managed to survive and is gaining back slowly some of its earlier productivity, thanks to recent conservation measures. Good work recently has been done, too, in conserving the clam crop, though clams are still dug all year round.

By the middle of May or sometimes as late as the middle of June, enough crabs are in the Bay to make catching them profitable for watermen. Using salted eels for bait (these are caught earlier and packed away for use) the men bait and drop overboard a long line. They let the line "fish" for a while, then go back along to the buoy that marks its beginning and start pulling it up over a roller device. With a net, the crabber dips up the crabs before they come out the water.

Crabbers go out before dawn, since crabs hold on to bait and come up best very early in the morning. More or less feeling one's way about over the water in the dark can be a problem. One problem has been solved by law again. It is the marine rule that if there is a crab line on the bottom, the next crabber cannot lay a baited crab line across the first one. This, and other rules, help watermen work and help preserve the valuable marine life in the Bay.

Fishing

The State of Maryland leads the nation in the production of striped bass (rockfish). Over a million dollars a year is paid to Maryland watermen for fish. The value of clams, crabs and oysters sold in 1990, for example, amounted to more than another five million dollars in income.

Commercial fishermen use nets. For a few kinds of fish a "gill" net is used. This is a net the fish can stick his head through, but when he tries to back up and get out of the net, his gills catch and he is trapped. Bigger catches are made by big nets called seines which are dragged through the water by boats, then closed around the fish and hauled aboard the vessels (seiners).

Looking Back

Before fine highways made it possible for trucks to take the farmers' grain crops to market, schooners, bugeyes and skipjacks nosed into every navigable stream, all along the Eastern Shore. A look at a map of the Eastern Shore will show that it is a land laced with waterways.

A scale for weighing wheat was sometimes set up on shore. After the wheat was weighed, it was carried in bags out to the vessel. There it was poured down into the cargo space (the hold). If a dock were handy, the work was easy. Then, too, sometimes when a dock was not available, wagons could be rolled into the shallow water beside the boat. But many times a barge was needed to take the wheat from shore to schooner. Wheat loading was back-breaking work indeed! Finally, the captain would float his vessel off at high tide, heavy with wheat, and carry it off to market in Baltimore.

The Log Canoe

From four to seven separate logs are used in the building of the Chesapeake log canoe. The skill to construct such boats is almost a lost art today. It took craftsmanship and "woodsmanship," too. First, the builder had to hunt through the forest for just the right tree to use for the center log (keel log). He wanted a big, straight tree.

This type of canoe has knees! The builder, when he cuts down the keel log tree, trims it to save the curved places where limbs grew out of the main trunk. These he uses later to make the knees of the canoe. After shaping the keel log with an axe, two or more trees are selected and used as "garboard logs." And now he needs two additional logs. These must be naturally curved and just the right size to fit the width of the canoe he wants to make. To fit these logs together takes time and talent. Iron or wooden pins are usually used to fasten the carefully shaped and cut logs together. The builder must now carefully make the sheerline and the trim.

When colonists came to the Chesapeake Bay area they saw the excellent canoes used by the Indians which had been formed from single logs. The Indians burned and chipped away the inside of the log and shaped the outside to make a light, slender water craft. The natives used paddles to move the vessels along. The colonists wanted larger boats, however, so they invented a way of using several logs to form a canoe. The Chesapeake log canoe is an American invention.

The canoe is strong, fast, and well suited to the shallow waters of the Eastern Shore. Masts were placed in the canoe in such a way as

Annapolis, Md., U. S. Naval Academy midshipmen learn to handle sail on Chesapeake Bay.

to leave the middle of the vessel clear for oyster tonging and crabbing work. There is no boom to get in the way and the sail of the log canoe can be (with practice) furled by one man. It was designed as a working boat; and by 1800, watermen were using over 6,000 of these log canoes in the Bay. Builders were making about 175 a year; and there were, at that time, about two hundred or more such builders.

A few log canoes are still used as racing craft especially on the Miles River. Races were held at St. Michaels on the Miles as far back as 1840. The Civil War stopped these races and they were not resumed again until 1924 when they became a yearly event, the Miles River Regatta, of the Miles River Yacht Club.

The Bugeye

The bugeye looks like a miniature racing yacht, but to yachtsmen and watermen, this craft has certain features that mark it unmistakably a product of the Bay.

Just when the Civil War was putting an end to log canoe racing, the bugeye was "born." It was designed to provide a vessel large enough and powerful enough to pull a dredge over oyster bars. It was a vessel from fifty to seventy-five feet in length, with low sides to let watermen haul dredges or nets into the vessel easily. Since the bugeye was intended for use in the shoal waters of the Eastern Shore region, it "drew little water." That meant that the boat did not extend very far down into the water. The bugeye had a center-board that could be moved, too, instead of a fixed keel.

The sails of the bugeye were a plain jib, a fore-and-aft at fore, and a mainmast. These could be easily worked and usually one man could sail the ship while the rest of the crew worked at handling the dredge, culling the oysters hauled aboard. The sails were cut cleverly to be taut and thereby keep the boat evenly trimmed and not prone to heel over and roll.

Since Maryland law forbids the use of engine-powered dredges, the sail-powered bugeye is still worked on the Bay, a part of the world's largest working sail fleet still in existence. This fleet includes sloops, skipjacks and other types of sailing boats. The bugeye is still seen on the Bay, not only working, but in use as a sports vessel, well liked for its nice handling and graceful lines.

Skipjacks

The skipjack is presently the working boat used in dredging for oysters in the Bay. The State law, limiting oyster dredging to

371

men working from sailboats, so that oyster beds will not be over-harvested, virtually outlaws powerboats. Powerboats must use tongs, not dredges in oyster fishing.

The skipjack has masts that are raked back. The hull is low, long and sleekly curved. The main mast is almost sixty feet tall. As can be imagined, this boat slipping through the water is a beautiful sight.

Maryland law forbids the building of new skipjacks any larger in size than ten tons. Here again the idea is to protect the oyster beds. Unfortunately, fewer and fewer skipjacks are being built.

Recreational Uses of Bay and Waterways

One of the state's fastest growing industries is—tourism! Our abundant and beautiful waterways play an important part in this. There has been an amazing growth in recreational boating in recent years. City dwellers desert their towns for the Bay, for beaches, and for rivers almost all year long in Maryland. Waterside vacation cottages, marinas, and beach hotels are especially popular in summer.

The Bay and our many streams provide ample room for fishing, cruising, boating, swimming and waterskiing. Marinas and boat-builders are doing a good business. The Eastern Shore is feeling the impact of easier access since the opening of the $45,000,000, Chesapeake Bay Bridge in 1952. This bridge was renamed the William Preston Lane, Jr. Memorial Bridge in 1967 in memory of a Maryland governor. A second, $112,000,000 span was opened in 1972.

Thousands of people each year are attracted to the Eastern Shore town of St. Michaels by the Chesapeake Bay Maritime Museum there. It is the goal of the Museum to gather together, and place on exhibit, examples of all the vessels that have been used on the Bay. At the Museum one may see Indian canoes made of a single log, Chesapeake log canoes, a Bay lighthouse, and hundreds of other items of interest. Exhibits range in size from models in cases up to full-size ships.

Mountain lakes and streams, too, provide a variety of recreational water space. Deep Creek Lake in Garret County is a very popular recreational area with water skiing in summer and snow skiing in the winter. Many other activities may be engaged in there in the forests, on the beaches and along the pleasant streams. An excellent airstrip offers facilities for the aviation-minded visitor. Good roads and campsites attract many people to Garrett County each year.

From mountain stream to ocean beach, Maryland can offer water-lovers an assortment of activities.

CHAPTER LXVIII

MODERN MARYLAND

MARYLAND, one of the thirteen original English colonies, has some areas that have drowsed through the years with little change in their pleasant way of life. Still, generally in the state, rapid changes are occurring.

Population, for example, has increased considerably in the past few years. By the year 1970 nearly four million people lived in Maryland. The 1990 census count revealed that Maryland's population had grown to a total of 4,781,000 persons. Much of this population increase is centered near the cities of Baltimore and nearby Washington, D.C.

In recent years, Maryland has changed rapidly from an agricultural state to one in which most of the population earns a living in industry, manufacturing, research, teaching, government work, and transportation.

Industry

Industry in Maryland is led by "primary metals," that is, the process of changing metals from their original state to one in which they may be used in manufacturing. The process of making iron ingots from iron ore, for example, or of using iron to make steel, is work in primary metals. In Maryland there is the manufacture of transportation equipment, food processing and the manufacture of chemicals and allied products, as well as of electrical machinery, equipment, and supplies. Literally hundreds of items are made here, including many fabricated metal products.

Maryland is a center for missile manufacture, rocket research and electronics development and manufacture. The presence of the giant Goddard Space Flight Center at Greenbelt has attracted many companies to the area that are engaged in designing and making computers, space launching and tracking machinery, as well as space vehicles.

Transportation

Five Class I railroads serve Maryland. The State of Maryland runs three commuter lines (MARC) and five freight lines. These railroads,

(Joseph H. Cromwell, C & P Telephone Company of Maryland)

This picture of the Calvert Cliffs Nuclear Power Plant, was taken in the summer of 1970, and shows the nuclear energy power station being built.

(Baltimore Gas and Electric Company)

In this photograph Unit One (right) is shown. This unit was placed in commercial operation May 8, 1975. Unit Two (left) went into operation in 1977. The total cost of the Calvert Cliffs Nuclear Power Plant came to over $750,000,000.

together with connecting lines, give Maryland excellent direct rail transportation to every city in the nation.

Truck transportation in Maryland, over state and interstate highways, is available to provide fast freight transport and many specialized services. There are carriers, for example, which are able to carry structural steel, heavy machinery, liquid and dry products in bulk, and cargoes that need temperature control or refrigeration en route.

There are several dual highways linking our national capital with nearby cities in Maryland. One is the Baltimore-Washington Expressway; another is the John Hanson Highway which connects Washington with Annapolis; and still another is one of the most beautiful highways in the country, the Washington National Pike, which connects Washington and Frederick. Also of interest is the busy Capital Beltway, opened on August 16, 1964. Two other highways of note are the John F. Kennedy Highway (Route 95) extending from Baltimore to the Delaware line, and the Blue Star Highway (Route 301) which crosses the Eastern Shore.

Since steps were taken in 1898 by the General Assembly to improve Maryland roads tremendous improvements have been made. Today's highway system is an excellent one. For example, two bridges now cross Chesapeake Bay. The second span of the William Preston Lane, Jr. Memorial Bridge opened for traffic in July 1972. Also, in 1977 the Francis Scott Key Bridge opened. It crosses the Patapsco River to the south and east of Baltimore City.

The Baltimore Harbor tunnels, like the bridges, are great engineering feats. The first Baltimore Harbor Tunnel was opened to traffic at midnight, November 29, 1957. It is 6,300 feet long with sixteen miles of approach expressways. It helps the motorist drive rapidly around congested areas of the city. The cost of the tunnel was $130,000,000. It has been so successful that another one, the Fort McHenry Tunnel, was built. It opened in 1985. These tunnels, the Baltimore Beltway, the Jones Falls Expressway and the Harrisburg Expressway, all help drivers move rapidly in the Baltimore area.

Air transportation in Maryland is served by four large airports and over forty smaller ones. Largest is the Baltimore-Washington International Airport which offers international jet freight and passenger services and many other aviation services. BWI connects Maryland with the world. It is an aerial port of entry where U.S. Customs Service officers clear passengers and freight in, and out, of the United States.

In Western Maryland, Hagerstown Municipal Airport offers passenger and air freight services. On the Eastern Shore, the Salisbury-Wicomico County Airport and the airport at Easton have airline services. The aerial spraying of crops is an important aviation business on the Eastern Shore.

Maryland may well boast of having one of the nation's busiest waterway systems. The Port of Baltimore has over forty-five miles of waterfront. It is among the four largest ports in the nation for foreign trade. The Port can serve vessels carrying automobiles, steel, coal, grain, oil and containers of cargo. There is service to every port in the world by steamship lines. The Port has modern terminals for every need.

The Port of Baltimore is open all year and receives thousands of deep-draft vessels every year. The channel leading up Chesapeake Bay to the port is now 1,000 feet wide and fifty feet deep.

There are about seventy water ports in Maryland. Cambridge has docking facilities and a good channel. It can serve medium-draft vessels.

A busy Maryland waterway is the Chesapeake and Delaware Canal. This canal crosses the neck of the Delmarva Peninsula and saves thousands of ships many miles of travel as they travel north from the Bay.

Foreign trade and trade with domestic ports, too, has always been a major business in Maryland. Today the Port of Baltimore contributes billions of dollars each year to the economy of our state. One in every ten jobs in Maryland is involved in some way with the Port of Baltimore.[1]

Maryland Resources

Water is a most important natural resource, aside from its usefulness in floating ships. Agriculture needs water, forests need water and homes need water. Industry, too, needs a great deal of water. We consume about six per cent of Maryland's average annual rainfall, which exceeds seven billion gallons of water.

Speaking of water leads us to the subject of fish. Watermen bring in valuable catches each year. Oysters, clams and crabs produced in Maryland bring watermen five million dollars a year. The Chesapeake Bay is one of the largest oyster-growing areas in the world. A million dollars worth of fish is harvested from the Bay each year. Maryland seafood is prized across the nation. Scientists and watermen constantly work to preserve Maryland's waterways, its fish and shellfish. Our water resources help Maryland to live up to its nickname, "Land of Pleasant Living."

Courtesy Maryland Office of Tourism Development.

Baltimore City, Maryland.

About forty-four percent of Maryland's six million land acres is considered forest. Each year millions of board feet of lumber are cut from state-owned and commercial forests.

Important wood products are veneer woods, pulpwood, posts, pilings, poles, barrel staves, wood for fuel, wood for charcoal, forest greens and Christmas trees.

Mineral wealth in Maryland is considerable but not based, as one might think, on iron or coal. It is stone from quarries and clay. Each year millions of dollars worth of stone and clay are taken from Maryland land.

Sand and gravel are important money-makers with coal production following these. Natural gas is an important resource. Altogether, mineral products of Maryland's mines and quarries today total a value of nearly 300 million dollars a year.

Research and Development Activities

Research and development activities are an important a part of Maryland employment and business as is shown by the following partial listing of research centers. These research facilities are in addition to employment at large federal installations such as Andrews Air Force Base, the Naval Air Test Center at Patuxent Naval Air Station and several other large military reservations in Maryland.

Atomic Energy Commission
NASA, Goddard Space Flight Center
National Institute of Health
U.S. Army Biological Laboratories
National Bureau of Standards
Naval Ordnance Laboratory
Naval Research Laboratory
Naval Medical Research Institute
Walter Reed Army Institute of Research
David Taylor Model Basin
Metallurgy Research Center
U.S. Army Chemical Center

U.S. Army Aberdeen Proving Ground
National Science Foundation
Agricultural Research Center

These and hundreds of privately-owned firms do research and development work in Maryland.

Education Today

The first free school opened in Annapolis in 1696. Education progressed very slowly until the twentieth century. Yet today there are over a million students attending private and public schools in our state. [2] At the college level this number includes about 47,000 University of Maryland students; 10,000 students attending Johns Hopkins University; and 168,000 students in other Maryland universities and colleges.

Many of the students attending Maryland institutions of higher learning earn their own expenses, others are helped by their families, still others obtain student loans and scholarships that are available. Almost half of both boys and girls who graduate from Maryland high schools go on to college.

There are nearly 1,000 public elementary schools in Maryland, 315 public secondary schools, over 500 private schools, and forty-eight degree-awarding colleges. In recent years the counties have set up very active community college programs. For students with special needs there are many special schools. About one and a half billion dollars a year is spent by the state, and more than that amount is spent by local governments to pay for public education each year.

Recreation and Tourism

We have seen how important are the fields of manufacturing, transportation, research, and education. Now there is also the important field of tourism, which may be Maryland's third largest business. Many people from other states come to this state to enjoy water sports, to view historic sites, and to enjoy the beauties of nature. From the Cumberland National Road, the Chesapeake and Ohio Canal, and historic Hager House, in Hagerstown, to the Chesapeake Bay Maritime Museum in St. Michaels, and the beaches along the Atlantic, Maryland has hundreds of points of interest for the tourist.

Baltimore attracts many visitors. It is a city famed for its inner harbor, its Peale Museum, its Enoch Pratt Library, and its Walters Art Gallery as well as for the many monuments and other historical places. Each year there are many plays, concerts, tours and exhibitions to entertain residents and visitors alike. Then, too, there are big league sports in Baltimore's new stadium. At historic Pimlico Race Course and at Laurel, there is a full program of horse racing. Horse racing is popular in several Maryland counties and the state has long been famous for its fine horses.

Jousting: Unique to Maryland

Jousting, the official state sport, is something uniquely a part of Maryland. Fifty or more jousting tournaments are held here each year, and it is a sport not widely known elsewhere in the nation. Jousting was first tried in America about 1700 near Annapolis. The first tourney on record was held at All Hallows Church in southern Anne Arundel County, in 1692. At that time each "knight" aimed his long lance at a wooden knight astride a wooden horse. It was called "riding at the quintain."

Today, each knightly contestant rides his horse rapidly down a track, a seven-foot lance in one hand. Three arches hang over his path. On each is hung a small ring, suspended from a cord. He tries to spear the ring with the tip of his lance, a test of keen judgment and horsemanship. In the contest with three trips through the arches, a total score of nine rings is possible. Then smaller rings are put in place until finally a victor emerges. The winner now rides forward to claim his prize and to crown a selected lady his "Queen."

From jousting to water sports, from golf course to museums, from ski slopes to ocean beach, and with its numerous State Parks, Maryland offers the resident and the visitor a wealth of recreation. All of this activity is set against a variety of scenery from the mountains to the west, eastward to the beautiful Chesapeake Bay and the ocean beaches. All through Maryland are historic buildings and sites to see. The state possesses an unusual blending of historic past and space age future.

---

1 For information on the Port of Baltimore contact: The Maryland Port Administration, World Trade Center, Baltimore, MD 21202.

2 The Maryland public schools had an enrollment of 684,000 students (pre-kindergarten through grade twelve) in the fall of 1987. Non-public schools at that time (same grades) had a total enrollment of 134,000.

CHAPTER LXIX

YOUR VOTE

V OTING is such an important duty for every citizen that no story of Maryland would be complete without a brief outline of how one votes and a short history of the voting process.

Primary Elections

Before an official can be elected, he or she (usually) must win the support of their political party. Several people in one party may wish to run for the same office. These people make public appearances, talk to as many voters as they can and try to get voters registered with their party to support them in what is called the "primary" elections. When a person wins a primary election he or she has not won the office sought. It only means that he or she has become their party's choice of candidate to run for office. Now the candidate faces another round of appearances and meetings to try to get registered voters of all parties to vote for him or her in the "general election."

Voters are sometimes confused over the difference between primary and general elections. A voter may be annoyed, in primary elections, not to be allowed to vote for a particular candidate because that person is not a member of the voter's party. We can see that the primary election is simply to select candidates from within a political party. It is the general election that then decides which of the persons running, wins the office.

Registration

When a citizen wants to vote in an election, the first thing that he or she must do is find a registration place in the area, or go to the county or city court house to register. There voters' names are entered (registered) in books and/or computers.

To register one must be a resident of Maryland, and of the county in which one resides (lives). The voter must have been a county resident for a certain amount of time, too. To vote one must be at least eighteen years of age.

The Garrett County Court House is shown in this 1967 photograph.

Losing the Right to Vote

You may lose your right to vote if you have ever been convicted of certain serious crimes after becoming an adult. Also, a person whose mind is unsound may not vote. Elections laws, further, stop from voting those persons who have been found guilty of bribery in elections or of voting in an unfair manner (attempting to vote twice, for example).

Absentee Votes

Sometimes it is not possible for a citizen, even though properly registered, to be at their voting place on election day. In that event, the law provides ways that people can cast a vote by means of an "absentee ballot." People in the armed services do this, as do people who are for some reason away from home. If a person is not able to leave home because of illness, that voter may still vote by using an absentee ballot which bears a doctor's signature.

General Elections

There are several kinds of general elections. We vote to help elect our national officials:—the President and Vice-President of the United States' and members of the United States Congress. Congress is a name given to cover the two "houses," the House of Representatives, whose members are called Congressmen; and the Senate, whose members are called Senators.

Then, too, we vote to elect certain of our State officials:—the Governor, the Lieutenant-Governor, the Comptroller of the Treasury, and the Attorney General.

In addition to all of these, a voter in local elections votes for representatives serving in the Maryland legislature, the General Assembly. These may be elected to the Maryland House of Delegates, or may be running for the Maryland Senate. Usually, in the same election, the voter also picks those who govern the county and the town or city.

Public Opinion

Unfortunately, many citizens fail to register, and many registered voters fail to vote! It is a citizen's duty to study candidates and vote for those who appear to be able to do the best job. A voter should not make the mistake of believing the one vote is not important. The fact is that many elections have been decided by just a very few votes. Each of us, then, should take an interest in politics and try to vote intelligently at election time.

In the United States of America, we must never feel that "it's no use" to fight for what we believe is right. We have the power of free speech, the legal right to speak and vote, and the duty as citizens to see that capable, honest men and women are elected to office. It is a wonderful, a priceless heritage. Public opinion *is* important.

Even before coming to a voting age, young people should read newspapers and learn about their leaders in government. Then, when the time comes, they will be well prepared to speak out for their candidate and to cast a telling vote.

After reading this story of our state and our nation, we can have no doubt that our rights to rule ourselves and select our own leaders are important. Voting is a privilege that has been bought with the blood, tears, and years of devotion of our ancestors.

Your Maryland Heritage—Freedom

Americans are usually very jealous of their freedoms and rights. We engage in extended arguments over new laws, over taxation, over all manner of other public issues. In Maryland, we may have a right to be just a little extra proud of our freedoms. Here, many new ideas were first put into practice in the New World. Here there grew the belief that a person's individual life must be carefully safeguarded and his rights fully protected. The states bordering the Potomac River are known to historians as "the cradle of democracy." In Maryland and Virginia there were men, from the very first days of settlement, who believed in the sacredness of individual rights, dignity, and freedom—whatever the rank of the person or whatever amount of property he owned.

So used to the idea of each man having these rights are we, that it seems strange to discover that, when the colonies were first settled, the lower classes and poor people were thought of as inferior and possibly little more than slaves or serfs.

We have seen how much George Calvert, the First Lord Baltimore, believed in giving freedom of worship to all. His son Cecil, too, made sure that this freedom was given the settlers of Maryland.

Act of Religious Toleration

Complete freedom of worship was an idea that even Marylanders could not understand. Still, in 1649, they created a law that was far ahead of its time. It was actually written by Cecil Calvert, though the first part may have been taken from his father, George Calvert's work. The Maryland Assembly called the law an "Act Concerning Religion," and it has come to be known as the "Toleration Act."

The Act said that "no person or persons whatsoever within this province . . . professing to believe in Jesus Christ, shall from henceforth be in any way troubled, molested, or discountenanced for or in respect of his or her religion, nor in the free exercise thereof . . ." The passage of such an act was a new and unusual thing for the early 1600's.[1]

Church and State Are Separate

As soon as the colony was settled, the second Lord Baltimore made sure that the church and the civil governments were entirely separate and required that the church authorities in Maryland obey this rule. He gave all religious groups in the colony great encouragement at the same time.

Puritans Upset Toleration Act

True, toleration in Maryland, just five years after the Toleration Act was passed, was temporarily suspended by the Puritans. But, if the Puritans did away with freedom of worship for a time, still they could "not erase its spirit from the minds of men." So it was that in 1661, when Cromwell had died and the English throne had been restored to King Charles II, Marylanders put the Act of Toleration back into force.

The Act then stayed in effect for thirty-one more years. Then, William and Mary, rulers of England, overruled the Act and required all English citizens to pay taxes to support the Anglican Church of England.

Still, though freedom of religion had its ups and downs in Maryland, we see that Maryland was among the first governments in the world to lead the way toward giving the people it governed the right to worship God as they chose.

Ordinary Men

In addition to freedom of religion in Maryland, another freedom was becoming evident in the same period of history. Men were beginning to feel that they had a right to govern themselves. The English government was so far away, and the Proprietors were usually living in England. Some sort of government on the spot appeared to be necessary. In all the English colonies in America there were such practices of self-government as town meetings and assemblies begun and demanded as a logical right.

In Maryland, while the men of wealth and rank were perhaps the primary leaders in the government of the colony, the freemen of lesser importance found that they could have a voice, too. In all of this the right to vote and the acceptance of the decision of the majority were important steps in the colonists' learning to govern themselves.

Maryland Voting Laws Change

Under the Maryland Constitution of 1776, which became the law of the land in November of that year, every free man in Maryland over twenty-one years of age, who owned at least fifty acres of land in the county in which he planned to live and vote, or property valued at forty pounds, and who had resided for one year of his residence in the county, had the right to vote. The law said further that those eligible and wishing to vote must go to the seat of government in each county, to vote *by voice* for his candidate!

The 1776 voting requirements, then, required that certain property be owned; and in those days no women were allowed to vote, and there was no secret ballot. All of the counties, by 1799, were divided into voting, or election, districts.

Property requirements to vote were partially removed in 1802 when most of the free, white, male citizens were given the right to vote. Also, in the years 1809 and 1810, voting was changed so that instead of voting by voice, written ballots were to be used. And, as already noted, in 1825 people of the Hebrew faith were given the right to vote.

Black men in 1870 were enfranchised, that is, given the right to vote in Maryland elections. Fifty more years, however, were to pass before the women of Maryland would be allowed to vote (1920). There is an exception to this last statement, however, in the way in which the town of Still Pond was incorporated.[2] When the town was incorporated by an act of the General Assembly in 1908, an important section of this act provided that the legal residents, women included, who were twenty-one years of age or over, and who had lived in the corporate limits of the town for at least six months, and who paid taxes, were to have the opportunity to vote for three commissioners. On Saturday, May 2, 1908, at least fourteen women were eligible to vote and three women did cast ballots, and so, according to a 1908 newspaper account, "they became the first women in the State of Maryland to exercise the privilege of suffrage." However, with this exception, women in Maryland were not allowed to vote until 1920. Many other changes in voting procedures have been put into practice, such as voting by machine, two-party poll-watching practices, redistricting of the State in order to give places with more population more representation, and other changes. Voting practices are still being altered, as, for example, the recent change in the voting age from a minimum age of twenty-one to that of eighteen.

Governors of Maryland

It is interesting to review those who served as Governor of Maryland in the last half of this century. These men became a part of Maryland's history.

Theodore R. McKeldin was Governor of Maryland from January 1951 through December of 1959. He was born in Baltimore City, November 20, 1900, one of eleven children. As a young man he attended the University of Maryland and Johns Hopkins University. After his graduation in 1926, he began to practice law in Baltimore City. There he met and later married Miss Honolulu Manzer.

The young attorney soon turned to public life and became an active member of the Republican party in Maryland. He was elected Mayor of Baltimore for the 1943-1947 term of office. A few years later he was elected Governor of Maryland and served eight years. After this he returned to Baltimore and in 1963 again was elected Mayor of that city. McKeldin was known as a public speaker and was active in his church. He wrote several books and many articles. He liked to travel and visited many foreign lands.

J. Millard Tawes was Governor of Maryland for eight years (1959 - 1967). He was born, April 8, 1894, and raised in Crisfield, Somerset County, Maryland. It was in that county that he began his long years of public service. There, at the age of thirty-six, he was elected Clerk of the Court for the county.

Tawes was often asked to speak to local organizations. His reputation as a public speaker grew and he became a valuable member of the Democratic Party of Maryland. In 1939 he became Maryland's Comptroller of the Treasury and served in that office for eight years. He then served as State Bank Commissioner; and was made Comptroller of the Treasury again in 1950. In all, Tawes served Maryland as Comptroller for nearly seventeen years.

In 1958 he was elected Governor of Maryland and served two busy terms of office (1959-1967). The state was growing in business and population very fast. A great deal of construction was in progress, private homes, business buildings. Much building also had to be done to provide schools, highways, bridges, colleges, government buildings.

Tawes and his wife Helen Gibson Tawes raised a son and a daughter. Mrs. Tawes worked for the cause of those suffering from mental illnesses, while her husband was in public office. Both the Governor and his wife were active in their church.

When Tawes left office he said that he hoped that he had succeeded in leaving behind him a sound, stable and progressive State government. He left a surplus of money in the Treasury, which is not an easy thing to do.

In 1967 they returned to live in Crisfield, expecting to spend the rest of their days among old friends there. A tranquil retirement, however, was not to be, for in July 1969 Tawes was called upon to be Maryland's first Secretary of the Natural Resources Department, a post he held until September of 1971.

Retiring again, he was again called upon to fill an unexpired term as Treasurer from June 1 of 1973 until January of 1975. This post he left only to be asked to become a member of the Board of Trustees of Maryland State Colleges, again to fill an unexpired term. Upon completion of the term in June 1975, he was asked to take a new term that expired in 1984.

Spiro Theodore Agnew was Governor of Maryland for only twenty-four months before being selected as the Republican candidate for Vice-President of the United States. Yet, in those months Agnew accomplished enactment of fair housing legislation, started programs of air and water pollution control and began several prison reforms.

Agnew was born in Baltimore City on November 9, 1918. His father had come to Maryland from Greece and operated a successful restaurant business in Baltimore.

After three years of studying chemistry at Johns Hopkins University, Agnew decided that the study of law was more to his liking. He attended the University of Baltimore to work toward a law degree. In 1942 he married Elinor Judefind of Baltimore. His education was interrupted by World War II service in the Army. After the war, however, he earned his law degree in 1947. The Agnews had three daughters and a son.

By 1950 Agnew had become interested in politics and was becoming known in the Republican Party of Maryland. He served on the Baltimore County Board of Appeals and then was elected County Executive of Baltimore County in 1962. In 1966, when the strong Democratic party in the state was split into factions, voters elected Agnew the fifty-fifth Governor of Maryland. He took office in January of 1967. He resigned the office on January 7, 1969 to become the thirty-ninth Vice-President of the United States. He is the first Maryland man to serve in that office.

As Vice-President Agnew represented the United States at home and abroad on many missions. In 1973, however, he became the first Vice-President in United States history to give up his office because of criminal charges. Rather than engage in court battles he resigned, pleading *nolo contendere* (no contest) to a single charge of federal income-tax evasion in 1967 and denying all other charges. He was fined and placed on suspended, unsupervised probation for three years.

Marvin Mandel became the fifty-sixth Governor of Maryland when the Maryland General Assembly met, January 7, 1969, to pick a successor to Spiro T. Agnew (who had resigned to become Vice-President). It was not an election year, so by an unusual selection process which has been used only twice before in Maryland, a Governor was chosen by the General Assembly.

Mandel was born on April 19, 1920 in Baltimore City and lived most of his life there. He graduated from City College in 1937 and went on to further studies at the University of Maryland and then attended that university's school of law. He received his law degree in 1941. He married a Baltimore girl, Barbara Oberfeld and a son and daughter were born to them.

From 1942 until 1944 Mandel served in the Army. After World War II he was able to resume his interrupted law career. He became interested in public affairs in 1950 and soon after was a very active member of the Democratic Party of Maryland. In fact, he was elected a member of the Democratic State Central Committee in 1951 but left that post in 1952 when asked to fill a vacancy in the Maryland House of Delegates as a member representing Baltimore City. By 1963 he was a respected veteran in the House and was elected Speaker that year and every succeeding year.

When Agnew resigned to become Vice-President, as noted above, Marvin Mandel was selected by the General Assembly to fill the office of Governor and serve out Agnew's term. Then, Mandel was elected in the November 1970 elections to a full four-year term.

Governor Mandel and his first wife having been divorced, in August 1974 he married the former Jeanne Blackistone Dorsey. In the fall of 1974 he was elected to a second term as Governor. It was to be a very troubled term.

In November of 1975 Governor Mandel and five other men (owners of the Marlboro Race Track) were indicted by a federal grand jury for mail fraud and racketeering. Mandel was accused of accepting money and gifts to support Maryland legislation favorable to the Marlboro Race Track.

In the spring of 1977 Mandel's health failed and Lieutenant Governor Blair Lee, III took over the duties of Governor.

In August of 1977 the six defendants were found guilty. Judges then heard appeals but the convictions stayed in effect. Mandel was disbarred from practicing law in Maryland. In May of 1980 Mandel began serving a four-year sentence in federal prison. His five co-defendants were heavily fined and given prison sentences. One sentence was suspended but four others were served. These four were later released; as was Mandel in December, 1981 when he returned to Baltimore. In 1989 the criminal conviction was overturned on a technicality.

The trials and appeals were very complex. For more information one may study newspaper articles of the time and a book.[3] In any case, the next governor of Maryland was Harry R. Hughes.

On January 17, 1979, Harry R. Hughes was inaugurated as the fifty-seventh Governor of the State of Maryland. He was elected to a second term in the 1982 election.

He came to the office with sixteen years of experience as a legislator behind him. Also, he had served six years as a cabinet officer directing Maryland's Department of Transportation.

Governor Hughes was born in Easton, Maryland, on November 13, 1926. He lived in Denton, and attended public schools in Caroline County. As a young man he considered a career in professional baseball.

World War II intervened, however, and Hughes enlisted to serve with the U.S. Navy Air Corps.

After leaving the Navy he entered the University of Maryland and received a B.S. degree in 1949. He then attended law school, graduating in 1952 with his LL.B. degree. He was admitted to the bar and began to practice law in Denton that same year.

Hughes was elected to the Maryland House of Delegates in 1954 (serving 1955-1958). In 1958 he ran for the Maryland Senate and served 1959-1970. In 1971 Hughes was appointed by Governor Mandel to head the newly created Department of Transportation. Major projects were undertaken and completed during his term as Secretary of Transportation. In May 1977, however, he resigned his position over what he termed unethical and improper interference with his Department's procedures for awarding a contract to manage construction of the Baltimore subway system.

Hughes married Patricia Donoho. They have two daughters. After leaving State service he became a partner in a Baltimore law firm.

William Donald Schaefer was elected 58th governor of Maryland in the fall of 1986, inaugurated January 21, 1987.

Schaefer was born in West Baltimore on November 2, 1921. He went to Baltimore's public schools and graduated from Baltimore City College in 1939 and from the University of Baltimore's school of law in 1942.

World War II was beginning, so putting his legal career aside, Schaefer joined the Army. He became an officer and administered hospitals in Europe for the Army.

After the war Schaefer took up his practice of law, specializing in real estate law. He went on to earn a Master of Laws degree from the University of Baltimore. Then he formed a law firm with two attorneys to practice general law. He soon became interested in city planning in Baltimore which led him into politics. In 1955 Schaefer was seated on the Baltimore City Council.

Rather than seek a fourth term as Councilman, in 1967 Schaefer ran for Council President. After four years in that position, he successfully ran for Mayor of Baltimore City. Inaugurated as Mayor, December 7, 1971, he served four terms, a total of 15 years there, until elected governor of Maryland in the fall of 1986. Schaefer was elected for a second term in the fall of 1990 and began the term in January of 1991.

1 There were provisions in the Toleration Act for the severe punishment of the crime of blasphemy, that is, cursing or reviling God. Reading the Act today, too, you may wonder if perhaps Jewish people were treated badly. There were very few members of the Hebrew religion in the colony. Happily, the records show no persecution of Jewish families, though it was 1825 before they gained the right to vote.

2 This information was brought to the author's attention by Dr. William H. Wroten, Jr., Chairman of the Department of History and Political Science, of the Salisbury State College. The incorporation of Still Pond was accomplished via the introduction of House of Delegates Bill #21-1/2 by the Kent County delegates, on February 20, 1980. The Bill was accepted on March 20 of that same year. The Bill became law (Chapter 160, pages 893-901) with final approval as law on March 30, 1908.

3 For details of Marvin Mandel's trial: *Thimbleriggers* by Bradford Jacobs, Johns Hopkins University Press, Baltimore, 1984; article "Mandel Fraud Ruling Still Void," *Prince George's Journal*, June 20, 1989, p. A3 and editorial by Pesci, p. A7.

APPENDIX

Agle, Nan Hayden. *Princess Mary of Maryland*. Hatboro, PA: Tradition Press, 1967.

Alden, John R. *A History of the American Revolution*. New York: Alfred A. Knopf, 1969.

Andrews, Matthew Page. *History of Maryland: Province and State*. Facsimile reprint of the original 1929 edition. Hatboro, PA: Tradition Press, 1965.

Angell, Pauline K. *To the Top of the World*. Chicago: Rand McNally & Company, 1964.

Ballweber, Hettie. *The First People of Maryland*. Lanham, MD: Maryland Historical Press, 1987.

Bancroft, Frederic. *Slave Trading in the Old South*. New York: Frederick Ungar Publishing Company, 1931 and 1959.

Bard, Harry. *Maryland Today*. New York: Oxford Book Company, 1961.

Bendini, Silvio A. *The Life of Benjamin Banneker*. New York: Charles Scribner's Sons, 1972.

Bergman, Peter M. *The Chronological History of the Negro in America*. New York: Harper & Rowe, 1968.

Bodine, A. Aubrey. *Chesapeake Bay and Tidewater*. Baltimore: Hastings House, 1954.

Brewington, Marion V. *Chesapeake Bay: A Pictorial Maritime History*. Cambridge, MD: Cornell Maritime Press, 2d ed., 1956.

Buchholz, Heinrich Ewald. *Governors of Maryland from Revolution to 1908*. Baltimore: Williams and Wilkins Company, 1908.

Burchard, Peter. *One Gallant Rush*. New York: St. Martin's Press, 1965.

Burns, Vincent Godfrey. *Maryland's Revolutionary Hero: Colonel Tench Tilghman*. Washington: New World Books, 1963.

Byrd, Elbert M., Jr. *The Judicial Process in Maryland*. College Park, MD: Bureau of Governmental Research, College of Business and Public Administration, University of Maryland, 1961.

Byron, Gilbert. *Early Exploration of the Chesapeake Bay*. Baltimore: Maryland Historical Society, 1960.

——————. *The War of 1812 on the Chesapeake Bay*. Baltimore: Maryland Historical Society, 1964.

Callcott, George H. *A History of the University of Maryland*. Baltimore: Maryland Historical Society, 1966.

Callcott, Margaret Law. *The Negro in Maryland Politics, 1870 - 1912.* Baltimore: Johns Hopkins Press, 1969.

Chapelle, Howard Irving. *The Baltimore Clipper: Its Origins and Development.* Salem, MA: Marine Research Society, 1930.

Coles, Harry L. *The War of 1812.* Chicago: University of Chicago Press, 1965.

Conrad, Earl. *Harriet Tubman.* Washington: Associated Publishers, 1943.

Cunliffe, Marcus. *George Washington: Man and Monument.* New York: Alfred A. Knopf, 2d ed., 1966.

Current, Richard N. et al. *American History: A Survey.* New York: Alfred A. Knopf, 2d ed, 1966.

Dexter, Elisabeth Anthony. *Colonial Women of Affairs.* Boston: Houghton Mifflin Co., 1931.

Diehl, Harold S. *Tobacco and Your Health.* New York: McGraw Hill Book Company, 1969.

Dozer, Donald M. *Portrait of a Free State.* Cambridge, MD: Tidewater Publishers, 1976.

Dupuy, R. Ernest and Trevor N. Dupuy. *The Compact History of the Revolutionary War.* New York: Hawthorn Books, Inc., 1963.

Foner, Philip S. *Life and Writings of Frederick Douglass.* Volumes I, II, III and IV. New York: International Publishers, 1950.

Forman, H. Chandlee. *Tidewater Maryland Architecture and Gardens.* New York: Architectural Book Publishing Company, Inc., 1956.

Fredericks, Pierce G. *The Civil War as They Knew It.* New York: Bantam Books, 1961.

Furlong, Rear Admiral William Rea, and Commodore Byron McCandless, edited by Dr. Harold D. Langley. *So Proudly We Hail: The History of the United States Flag.* Washington: Smithsonian Institution Press, 1981.

Gambrill, John Montgomery. *Leading Events in Maryland History.* Baltimore: Cushing Company, 1903.

Giles, Ted. *Patty Cannon: Woman of Mystery.* Easton, MD: T. Giles, 1965.

Graham, Shirley. *Your Most Humble Servant.* New York: Julian Messner, 1949, 1967.

Green, Elmer. *The Making of Maryland.* Baltimore: E. and M. Green, 1934.

Greenbie, Sydney and Marjorie Barstow Greenbie. *Anna Ella Carroll and Abraham Lincoln: A Biography.* Tampa: University of Tampa Press with Falmouth Publishing House, Inc., 1952.

Gutheim, Frederick. *The Potomac*. New York: Rhinehart and Company, 1949.

Hall, Clayton Colman, editor. *Narratives of Early Maryland: 1633 - 1684*. New York: Charles Scribner's Sons, 1910. Barnes and Noble, 1946.

Hanson, Henry Harold. *Costumes and Styles*. New York: E. P. Dutton & Company, 1956.

Herbert, Wally. *The Noose of Laurels: Robert E. Peary and the Race to the North Pole*. New York: Atheneum, 1992.

Herring, Hubert with Helen B. Herring. *A History of Latin America*. Chapter 4 "The African Background." New York: Alfred A. Knopf, 3d ed., 1969.

Hoffman, Ronald. *A Spirit of Dissension: Economics, Politics and the Revolution in Maryland*. Baltimore: Johns Hopkins University Press, 1973.

Holland, Celia M. *Ellicott City, Maryland: Mill Town, USA*. College Park, MD: C. M. Holland, 1970.

Janvier, Meridith. *Baltimore in the '80s and '90s*. Baltimore: H. G. Roebuck and Company, 1933.

Johnson, Gerald W. *The Maryland Act of Religious Toleration: An Interpretation*. Annapolis: Maryland Department of Information, 1957.

Kaessmann, Beta. *My Maryland*. Baltimore: Maryland Historical Society, 1955.

Kenny, Hamill. *The Origins and Meaning of the Indian Place Names in Maryland*. Baltimore: Waverly Press, 1961.

Lang, Varley. *Follow the Water*. Winston-Salem, NC: John F. Blair, 1961.

Larrabee, Harold A. *Decision at the Chesapeake*. New York: Clarkson N. Potter, 1964.

Leonard, Lewis A. *Life of Charles Carroll of Carrollton*. New York: Moffat, Yard & Company, 1918.

Lester, Katherine Morris. *Historic Costume*. Peoria, IL: Charles A. Bennett Company, 4th ed. revised, 1956.

Lord, Walter. *The Dawn's Early Light*. New York: W. W. Norton & Company, 1972.

McMahon, John V. L. *An Historical View of the Government of Maryland*. Vol. I. Baltimore: Lucas, Cushington, Neal, 1831.

McPharlin, Paul. *Life and Fashion in America, 1600-1900*. New York: Hastings House, 1946.

McSherry, James, edited and continued by Bartlett B. James. *History of Maryland*. Baltimore: Baltimore Book Company, 1904.

Manakee, Harold R. *Indians of Early Maryland*. Baltimore: Maryland Historical Society, 1959.

——————. *Maryland in the Civil War*. Baltimore: Maryland Historical Society, 1961.

Manakee, Harold R., et. al. *Wheeler Leaflets on Maryland History*. Baltimore: Maryland Historical Society.

Medical and Chirurgical Faculty - 1830 - 1930. Centennial Publication. Baltimore: Waverly Press, 1931.

Melville, Annabelle M. *John Carroll of Baltimore*. New York: Charles Scribner's Sons, 1955.

Miller, Floyd. *Ahdoolo! A Biography of Matthew A. Henson*. New York: E. P. Dutton and Company, 1963.

Montgomery, Elizabeth Rider. *The Story Behind Great Inventions*. New York: Dodd, Meade and Company, 1944.

Morsbach, Mabel. *The Negro in American Life*. New York: Harcourt, Brace & World, 1967.

Muller, Charles G. *The Darkest Day: 1814*. Philadelphia: J. B. Lippincott Company, 1963.

Murphy, E. Jefferson. *Understanding Africa*. New York: Thomas Y. Crowell Company, 1969.

Norris, Walter B. *Annapolis: Its Colonial and Naval Story*. New York: Thomas Y. Crowell Company, 1925.

Oliver, Roland and J. D. Fage. *A Short History of Africa*. New York: New York University Press, 1963.

Owens, Hamilton. *Baltimore on the Chesapeake*. Garden City, NY: Doubleday, Doran and Company, 1941.

Parkes, Henry Bamford. *The United States of America: A History*. New York: Alfred Knopf, 1959.

Pogue, Robert E. T. *Yesterday in Old ~St. Mary's County*. New York: Hearthstone Press, 1968.

Quarles, Benjamin. *Frederick Douglass*. Washington: The Associated Publishers, 1948.

——————. *The Negro in the Making of America*. New York: McMillan Company, 1969.

Redding, Jay Saunders. *The Negro*. Washington: Potomac Books, 1967.

Richardson, Hester Dorsey. *Side-Lights on Maryland History*. Baltimore: (1913) Genealogical Publishing company, 1967.

Riley, Elihu Samuel. *The Ancient City: A History of Annapolis in Maryland 1649 - 1887*. Annapolis: Annapolis Record Printing, 1887.

Rollo, Vera Foster. *The American Flag*. Lanham, MD: Maryland Historical Press, 1989, 1991.

——————. *A Geography of Maryland*. Lanham, MD: Maryland Historical Press, 1985, 1993.

——————. *Henry Harford: Last Proprietor of Maryland*. Lanham, MD: Maryland Historical Press, 1976.

——————. *The Government of Maryland*. Lanham, MD: Maryland Historical Press, 1985.

——————. *The Proprietorship of Maryland: An Annotated Account*. Lanham, MD: Maryland Historical Press, 1988.

Ruskin, Thelma G. *Indians of the Tidewater Country of Maryland Virginia, North Carolina and Delaware*. Lanham, MD: Maryland Historical Press, 1986.

Scarborough, Katherine. *Homes of the Cavaliers*. New York: The MacMillan Company, 1930.

Scharf, J. Thomas. *History of Maryland*. Volumes I, II and III. Facsimile reprint of the 1879 edition with a foreword by Morris L. Radoff. Hatboro, PA: Tradition Press, 1967.

Searight, Thomas B. *The Old Pike: A History of the National Road*. Uniontown, PA: Thomas B. Searight, 1894.

Schaun, George and Virginia. *American Holidays and Special Days*. Lanham, MD: Maryland Historical Press, 1986.

——————. *Everyday Life in Colonial Maryland*. Lanham, MD: Maryland Historical Press, 2d ed. 1982.

——————. *The Greenberry Series on Maryland*. Annapolis: Greenberry Publications, 1968.

——————. *Maryland: Biographical Sketches*. Lanham, MD: Maryland Historical Press, 1984.

——————. *The Story of Early Maryland*. Annapolis: Greenberry Publications, 1968.

Semmes, Raphael. *Captains and Mariners of Early Maryland*. Baltimore: Johns Hopkins Press, 1937.

——————. *Crime and Punishment in Early Maryland*. Baltimore: Johns Hopkins Press, 1938.

Sheads, Scott. *The Rockets' Red Glare*. Centreville, MD: Tidewater Publishers, 1986.

Sparks, Francis E. *Causes of the Maryland Revolution of 1689*. Baltimore: Johns Hopkins Press, 1896.

Spencer, Jean E. *Contemporary Local Government in Maryland.* College Park, MD: Bureau of Governmental Research, College of Business and Public Administration, University of Maryland, 1965.

Stampp, Kenneth M. *The Peculiar Institution: Slavery in the Ante-Bellum South.* New York: Alfred A. Knopf, 1956.

Statistical Abstract of the United States: 1992. Washington: U. S. Department of the Census, Government Printing Office, 1992.

Stefansson, Vihjalmur and Olive Rathbun. *Great Adventures and Explorations.* New York: Dial Press, 1947, 1952.

Stevens, William Oliver. *Annapolis, Anne Arundel's Town.* New York: Dodd & Meade and Company, 1937.

Surgeon General of the United States' Advisory Committee. *Smoking and Health.* Washington: U. S. Department of Health, Education and Welfare, Public Health Service Publication No. 1103, 1964.

The Health Consequences of Smoking. Washington: U. S. Department of Health, Education and Welfare, Public Health Service Review Publication No. 1696, 1967.

Tobacco in the United States. Washington: U. S. Department of Agriculture, Argricultural Marketing Service, Misc. Publication No. 867, 1964.

Tocqueville, Alexis de. Edited by Richard D. Heffner. *Democracy in America.* (Observations made in 1831 and 1832.) New York: The New American Library, 1956.

Townsend, George A. ("Gath"). *The Entailed Hat.* Easton, MD: Tidewater Publishers, reprint 1955.

Tully, Andrew. *When They Burned the White House.* New York: Simon, Schuster & Company, 1961.

Van Doren, Carl. *Benjamin Franklin.* New York: Viking Press, 1938.

Verrill, A. Hyatt. *The Real Story of the Pirate.* New York: D. Appleton-Century Company, 1923.

Vokes, Harold E. *Geography and Geology of Maryland.* Baltimore: State of Maryland Board of Natural Resources, Department of Geology, Mines and Water Resources, Bulletin 19, 1957, 1961.

————————. *Miocene Fossils of Maryland.* Baltimore: Maryland Geological Survey, 1957, 1968.

Wagandt, Charles L. *The Mighty Revolution: Negro Emancipation in Maryland, 1862 - 1864.* Baltimore: Johns Hopkins Press, 1964.

Weems, John Edward. *Peary, the Explorer and the Man.* Boston: Houghton Mifflin Company, 1967.

White, William Chapman and Ruth White. *Tin Can on a Shingle: The Full Story of the Monitor and the Merrimac.* New York: E. P. Dutton & Company, 1957.

Willey, Gordon R. *An Introduction to American Archaeology.* Vol. I. (North and Middle America.) Englewood Cliffs, NJ: Prentice-Hall, 1966.

WPA Writers' Program compilation. *Maryland: A Guide to the Old Line State.* New York: Oxford University Press,1949.

County Name with 1970, 1980, 1990 Population Figures	Date Founded	County Seat	Origin of County Name
Allegany 84,044 80,413 74,946	1789	Cumberland	From Indian word meaning "Beautiful Stream."
Anne Arundel 297,539 369,914 427,239	1650	Annapolis	Named for the wife of Cecil Calvert, Second Lord Baltimore.
Baltimore 621,077 651,105 692,134	1659	Towson	Named for Calverts' Irish Barony.
Baltimore City 905,759 783,320 736,014	1729	Incorporated 1797	Named for Irish estates owned by Calvert family.
Calvert 20,682 34,308 51,372	1654	Prince Frederick	Known as Patuxent until renamed to honor the Calvert family.
Caroline 19,781 23,148 27,035	1773	Denton	Named for Lady Caroline sister to the Sixth Lord Baltimore.
Carroll 69,006 96,056 123,372	1836	Westminster	Named for "The Signer" Charles Carroll of Carrollton.
Cecil 53,291 60,113 71,347	1674	Elkton	Named for Cecil Calvert Second Lord Baltimore.
Charles 47,678 72,343 101,154	1658	La Plata	Named for Third Lord Baltimore, Charles Calvert.
Dorchester 29,405 30,549 30,236	1668	Cambridge	Named for the Earl of Dorset, a friend of the Calvert family.
Frederick 84,927 111,687 150,208	1748	Frederick	Probably named for the Sixth Lord Baltimore, Frederick Calvert.
Garrett 21,476 26,502 28,138	1872	Oakland	Named for John W. Garrett, a prominent banker.

County / Population	Founded	County Seat	Named For
Harford 115,378 145,592 182,132	1773	Bel Air	Named for Henry Harford the last Proprietor of Maryland (Sixth).
Howard 61,911 118,443 187,328	1851	Ellicott City	Named for Maryland patriot, John Eager Howard.
Kent 16,146 16,680 17,842	1642	Chestertown	After English county of the same name.
Montgomery 522,809 574,106 757,027	1776	Rockville	For General Richard Montgomery who served in the American Revolution.
Prince George's 660,567 657,707 729,268	1695	Upper Marlboro	Named for Prince George of Denmark, husband to Queen Anne of England.
Queen Anne's 18,422 25,520 33,953	1706	Centreville	Named for Queen Anne.
St. Mary's 47,388 59,799 75,974	1637	Leonardtown	Named to honor the Virgin Mary.
Somerset 18,924 19,041 23,440	1666	Princess Anne	For Mary Somerset, sister-in-law of Cecil Calvert, Second Lord Baltimore.
Talbot 23,682 25,496 30,549	1661	Easton	Named for Grace Talbot the sister of Cecil Calvert, Second Lord Baltimore.
Washington 103,829 112,764 121,393	1776	Hagerstown	Named for George Washington.
Wicomico 54,236 64,979 74,339	1867	Salisbury	Named for Indian words for house (wicko) and for building (mekee); also Wicomico River.
Worcester 24,442 30,303 35,028	1742	Snow Hill	Named for the Earl of Worcester.

THE TOTAL POPULATION OF MARYLAND IN 1970 WAS 3,922,399 PERSONS.
THE TOTAL POPULATION OF MARYLAND BY 1980 WAS 4,193,378 PERSONS.
THE TOTAL POPULATION OF MARYLAND BY 1990 WAS 4,781,468 PERSONS.

1633-1647	Leonard Calvert
1647-1649	Thomas Greene
1649-1652	William Stone
1652	Parliamentary Commissioners
1652-1654	William Stone
1654-1657	William Fuller and Council (Appointed by the Parliamentary Commissioners)
1657-1660	Josias Fendall (Appointed by Lord Baltimore)
1660-1661	Philip Calvert
1661-1676	Charles Calvert
1676	Cecilius Calvert Since Cecilius Calvert was a minor, the actual governing was done by first the Deputy Governor Jesse Wharton, and later, by Deputy Governor Thomas Notley.
1676-1679	Thomas Notley
1679-1684	Charles Calvert returned as Governor. He now was the Proprietor of Maryland and held the title of the Third Lord Baltimore.
1684-1688	Benedict Leonard Calvert. He was only a young child at the time and the actual governing was done for him by a Council of Deputy Governors.
1688-1689	William Joseph, President of the Council of Deputies
1689-1690	John Coode, Leader of Protestant Associators
1690-1692	Nehemiah Blackiston

In 1692 the English crown sent Royal Governors to Maryland. Charles Calvert, the Third Lord Baltimore, who was Proprietor at that time, lost the right to appoint Governors. He did retain the legal right to Maryland and certain benefits and profits from the Province.

ROYAL GOVERNORS

Sir Lionel Copley	1692-1693
Sir Thomas Lawrence	1693
Sir Edmund Andros	1693
Nicholas Greenberry President of Council	1693-1694
Sir Edmund Andros	1694
Sir Thomas Lawrence President of Council	1694

Francis Nicholson	1694-1699
Nathaniel Blackiston	1699-1702
Thomas Tench	
President of Council	1702-1704
John Seymour	1704-1709
Edward Lloyd	
President of Council	1709-1714
John Hart	1714-1715

PROPRIETARY GOVERNORS

(In 1715 the right to appoint Governors of Maryland was returned to the Calvert family, Proprietors of Maryland.)

1715-1720	John Hart
1720	Thomas Brooke, President of Council
1720-1727	Charles Calvert
1727-1731	Benedict Leonard Calvert
1731-1732	Samuel Ogle
1732-1733	Charles Calvert, Lord Propriotor
1733-1742	Samuel Ogle
1742-1747	Thomas Bladen
1747-1752	Samuel Ogle
1752-1753	Benjamin Tasker, President of Council
1753-1769	Horatio Sharpe
1769-1776	Robert Eden

GOVERNORS OF THE STATE OF MARYLAND

Elected Under the Constitution of 1776 by the Legislature for One Year:

Thomas Johnson	1777-1779
Thomas Sim Lee	1779-1782
William Paca	1782-1785
William Smallwood	1785-1788
John Eager Howard	1788-1791
George Plater[1]	1791-1792
John H. Stone	1794-1797
John Henry	1797-1798
Benjamin Ogle	1798-1801
John Francis Mercer	1801-1803
Robert Bowie	1803-1806
Robert Wright[2]	1806-1809
Edward Lloyd	1809-1811
Robert Bowie	1811-1812
Levin Winder	1812-1816

Charles Ridgely of Hampton	1816-1819
Charles Goldsborough	1819-
Samuel Sprigg	1819-1822
Samuel Stevens, Jr.	1822-1826
Joseph Kent	1826-1829
Daniel Martin[3]	1829-1831
Thomas King Carroll	1830-1831
George Howard	1831-1833
James Thomas	1833-1836
Thomas W. Veazey	1836-1839

Elected by the People for Three Years Under the Constitution of 1776 as amended in 1838:

William Grason	1839-1842
Francis Thomas	1842-1845

Thomas G. Pratt	1845-1848	John Lee Carroll	1876-1880
Philip Francis Thomas	1848-1851	William T. Hamilton	1880-1884
Enoch Louis Lowe	1851-1854	Robert M. McLane[6]	1884-1885
		Henry Lloyd	1885-1888

Elected Under the Constitution of 1851 by the People for Four Years:

Thomas Watkins Ligon	1854-1858	Elihu E. Jackson	1888-1892
Thomas Holliday Hicks	1858-1862	Frank Brown	1892-1896
Augustus W. Bradford	1862-1866	Lloyd Lowndes	1896-1900
		John Walter Smith	1900-1904

Elected Under the Constitution of 1864 by the People for Four Years:

Thomas Swann	1866-1869	Edwin Warfield	1904-1908
		Austin L. Crothers	1908-1912
		Phillips Lee Goldsborough	1912-1916

Elected Under the Constitution of 1867 by the People for Four Years:

		Emerson C. Harrington	1916-1920
		Albert C. Ritchie[7]	1920-1935
Oden Bowie[4]	1869-1872	Harry W. Nice	1935-1939
William Pinkney Whyte[5]	1872-1874	Herbert R. O'Conor[8]	1939-1947
James Black Groome	1874-1876	William Preston Lane, Jr.	1947-1951
		Theodore R. McKeldin	1951-1959
		J. Millard Tawes	1959-1967
		Spiro T. Agnew[9]	1967-1969
		Marvin Mandel[10]	1969-1979
		Harry R. Hughes	1979-1987
		William Donald Schaefer	1987-

1 James Brice of Annapolis, a member of the Governor's Council, became Acting Governor upon the death of Governor Plater on February 10, 1792. He served until April 2 of the same year when he was suceeded by Thomas Sim Lee.

2 Governor Wright resigned on May 6, 1809. James Butcher, a member of the Governor's Council, became Acting Governor and served for one month, or until June 5, 1809, when his successor, Edward Lloyd, qualified.

3 Governor Martin died in office on July 11, 1831. George Howard, a member of the Governor's Council, succeeded him. Governor Howard was subsequently elected by the Legislature for a one-year term in January, 1832.

4 Governor Bowie served three years by special provision of the Constitution.

5 Governor Whyte resigned on March 4, 1874. Governor Groome was elected and assumed office on the same day. Because of a family business disagreement, Governor Whyte changed the spelling of his surname to distinguish his branch of the family.

6 Governor McLane resigned on March 27, 1885. Henry Lloyd, as President of the Senate, succeeded him as Acting Governor until January, 1886, when the Legislature elected him to complete the remainder of Governor McLane's term which expired in January, 1888.

7 Because of a 1922 constitutional amendment which provided for quadrennial elections, the Governor elected in 1923 served for three years. Thereafter gubernatorial terms began in odd years.

8 Governor O'Conor resigned on January 3, 1947 to accept a seat in the United States Senate. William Preston Lane, Jr. was elected by the Legislature to fill the unexpired term. Governor Lane was inaugurated on January 3, 1947 for the remainder of Governor O'Conor's term and on January 8, 1947 for the full four-year term.

9 Governor Agnew, having been elected Vice President of the United States at the general election of November 5, 1968, resigned on January 7, 1969. Marvin Mandel, then the Speaker of the House of Delegates, was elected on the same day to fill the balance of Governor Agnew's unexpired term.

10 Governor Mandel was elected by the people in November of 1970 for a full four-year term. He was inaugurated for this term in January, 1971. Reelected, fall 1974.

THE GREAT SEAL OF MARYLAND

OBVERSE   REVERSE

In the middle 1600's Cecil Calvert, Second Lord Baltimore, sent out a new Great Seal to his colony to replace that lost to Ingle. Though new seals were adopted later, in 1876 the original seal sent by Lord Baltimore was selected as the official Great Seal of Maryland.

The obverse side of the seal shows Lord Baltimore on horseback in full armor, holding a sword. Around the edge the Latin words meaning "Cecilius, Absolute Lord of Maryland and Avalon, Baron of Baltimore" appear.

On the reverse side of the seal is a coat of arms, supported on one side by a fisherman, and on the other side by a plowman. It rests on a scroll bearing the motto, "Deeds males, words females" as literally translated from the Latin, or it might be translated in meaning as "Manly deeds, womanly words." The top half of this side of the seal shows a special cap with a ducal crown and a flowing mantle inscripted around with words that possibly refer to the good will of the English crown, "Thou hast crowned us with the shield of thy good will."

The fisherman shown on the seal probably refers to the fishing industry of the Avalon colony belonging to Lord Baltimore. This colony was founded in the early 1620's in Newfoundland and much of the prosperity of the settlement depended on fishing.

Maryland, Lord Baltimore's other colony, is represented by the figure of a farmer with a spade in one hand, since Maryland's wealth lay in her agriculture.

405

MARYLAND STATE FLAG

Maryland's flag bears the arms of the Calvert and Crossland families. Calvert was the family name of the Lords Baltimore who founded Maryland. Crossland was the family of the mother of the first Lord Baltimore. The escutcheon or shield in the Maryland Seal bears the same arms. This flag in its present form was first used about 1886. It was officially adopted in 1904.

MARYLAND STATE FLOWER

The Black-eyed Susan is the flower emblem of the State of Maryland.

MARYLAND STATE TREE

Photograph courtesy Dept. of Economic Development

The State Tree of Maryland is the White Oak, and the specimen chosen to represent the species officially is one of the largest in the world. It is the famous Wye Oak at Wye Mills on the Eastern Shore. It is 100 feet high, with a branch spread of 165 feet, and over 400 years old. The land surrounding it has been made into a State Park.

MARYLAND STATE DOG

The official State sport of Maryland is jousting.

Chesapeake Bay Retriever

407

INDEX

409

410

411

W

War of 1812: 175, 207, 209-228, 246, 356.

Washington County: 402.

Washington, D. C.: xiii, 88, 95, 105, 163, 168-169, 197; (1812), 218-221; railroad, 243, 253; Civil War, 268, 275, 277, 278, 285, 357; after 1865, 292, 293, 296, 298, 319; gen., 331, 338, 345, 351, 364; today, 373, 375.

Washington, General George, 86, 97-100; Am. Rev., 125-127, 129, 130, 132-141, 143, 144, 147, 149-153, 174; after Rev., 155, 157, 158, 163, 174, 188, 197, 206; (1812), 211, 227; 279, 317.

Weems, Philip, 352-354.

West Virginia: 28, 88, 89; (1861), 273.

Wheat: 104, 105, 126, 157, 179, 247.

White, Father Andrew, 16, 17, 20, 21, 34-36, 64, 65.

Wicomico County: 43, 44, 95, 402.

Wilkerson, Dr. James, 143.

Winder, Gen. William H., 218, 219.

Witchcraft: 74, 75, 204.

Women: 25, 45, 47, 52, 54, 56, 66, 79, 115, 144, 145, 231, 386; see M. Brent, A. E. Carroll, M. Seton, H. Tubman.

Worcester County: 95, 149, 402.

World War I: 318, 350, 353, 360.

World War II: 318, 351, 353, 360.

ABOUT THE AUTHOR

Vera Foster Rollo began writing about Maryland history in the early 1960s. She established the Maryland Historical Press in 1964 to provide books on Maryland for schools and libraries. Today the press publishes books by several noted authors and continues to serve Maryland with textbooks and books for supplemental reading.

Dr. Rollo was born in North Carolina in 1924 and grew up dreaming that one day she would be a writer, fly airplanes and be a wife and mother. She achieved these goals.

In 1943 in Florida she learned to fly and won her flight instructor certificate. (She taught flying until 1988 and accumulated over 4,000 hours in the air.) Married in 1949, she looked for ground employment and became a writer for an aviation magazine in Washington, D. C.

Later, living in Maryland, at the age of 40 she began work toward a degree at the University of Maryland, College Park, Maryland. This took some time. She earned her B.A. and a Master's degree in American History; then went on to earn her doctorate in Education Development, Policy and Administration, at that university.

Meanwhile the author continued to write and to operate the Maryland Historical Press. She was an Associate Professor of History and coordinator of the Aviation Program at Wilmington College, Delaware in 1977. After this she began to write college-level aviation textbooks and biography. Books on Americana followed.

Dr. Rollo followed up her work as a flight instructor with volunteer flying for the Civil Air Patrol, Maryland Wing. Several trips to Europe were made researching Maryland colonial history and the Calvert family. Dr. Rollo now lives in Maryland where she operates her publishing company; enjoys gardening, homemaking and various dogs. She very much enjoys visiting her daughter Sally Foster in Georgia; and her son, Michael Foster, his wife and their two children, in California.